W9-BIA-278

E. F. SCHUMACHER

E. F. SCHUMACHER

His Life and Thought

Barbara Wood

1817

HARPER & ROW, PUBLISHERS, New York

Cambridge, Philadelphia, San Francisco, London,
Mexico City, São Paulo, Singapore, Sydney

This work was originally published in England under the title *Alias Papa: A Life of Fritz Schumacher*.

E. F. SCHUMACHER: HIS LIFE AND THOUGHT. Copyright © 1984 by Barbara Wood. All rights reserved. Printed in the United States of America. No part of this book may be used or reproduced in any manner whatsoever without written permission except in the case of brief quotations embodied in critical articles and reviews. For information address Harper & Row, Publishers, Inc., 10 East 53rd Street, New York, N.Y. 10022.

FIRST U.S. EDITION

Library of Congress Cataloging in Publication Data

Wood, Barbara.
 E. F. Schumacher, his life and thought.

 Includes index.
 1. Schumacher, E. F. (Ernst Friedrich), 1911–1977.
 2. Economists—Great Britain—Biography. I. Title.
 HB103.S38W66 1984   330'.092'4 [B]   84–47612
 ISBN 0-06-015356-3

84 85 86 87 88 10 9 8 7 6 5 4 3 2 1

If you look at it this way, you find that if one could make visible the possibility of alternatives, viable alternatives, make a viable future already visible in the present, no matter on how small a scale ... then at least there is something, and if that something fits it will be taken ... If the little people can do their own thing again, then perhaps they can do something to defend themselves against the overbearing, big ones.

So I certainly never feel discouraged. I can't myself raise the winds that might blow us, or this ship, into a better world. But I can at least put up the sail so that when the wind comes, I can catch it.

E. F. SCHUMACHER
Good Work

This book is dedicated to all those who have the courage to put up their sails in the hope that the wind will come.

Only a person who can find a value in every sort of activity and devote himself to each one with full consciousness of duty, has the inward right to take as his object some extraordinary activity instead of that which falls naturally to his lot. Only a person who feels his preference to be a matter of course, not something out of the ordinary, and who has no thought of heroism, but just recognises a duty undertaken with sober enthusiasm, is capable of becoming a spiritual adventurer such as the world needs.

ALBERT SCHWEITZER
My Life and Thought

Contents

Contents

Illustrations

(Following page 204)

Acknowledgments

I am deeply indebted to my stepmother, Vreni Schumacher, for her confidence and encouragement in this undertaking and for the access she gave me to all books and papers in my father's archives.

Those I interviewed are too numerous to list here. There were almost a hundred. I thank all of them for the warmth of their reception, their hospitality and their help. Some are mentioned in the book, others will recognize their contributions in the text and will, I hope, accept that as my thanks. Those who do require special mention are David Astor, Werner von Simson and Walter Fliess, all of whom patiently read through the manuscript at an early stage and contributed considerably to its improvement.

I am grateful to David Astor for permission to use illustration no. 15, and to Gritta Weil for no. 17.

My thanks are also due to Xandra Hardie, my editor, who showed the utmost tact in directing the evolution of the manuscript into its present form, and to Christine Sacre and Cecilia Scanlon for typing the manuscript.

Most of all I thank my husband, Don, for putting up with domestic chaos while never ceasing to encourage me, and my six children for the occasional moment of peace.

BARBARA WOOD

Kew, Surrey
1983

Prologue

It took a long time before I realized that the man who died on September 4th, 1977 was my father. There was little room for a sense of personal loss when the obituaries mourned the passing of a 'prophet standing against the tide', or, 'A man who asks the right questions of his society and of all societies at a crucial time in their history,' or which claimed, 'To very few people is it given to begin to change, drastically and creatively, the direction of human thought. Dr Schumacher belongs to this intensely creative minority.' (Governor Jerry Brown, Senator Charles H. Percy, *The Times* respectively.) Such comments were followed by letters of condolence from heads of states as well as countless lesser-known people from all over the world whose contact with this man, Schumacher, had somehow affected their lives.

Even more unreal were those who called at the house asking for some memento. One asked for his hat, another for his typewriter. Had this man been some sort of saint, I wondered, whose relics were now being collected for posterity? Others came wanting to set up Schumacher centres and Schumacher societies.

Slowly it dawned upon me that this world figure, guru, prophet, was supposed to be my father – Pop. I had wanted to write Pop's biography ever since he had started telling us stories about his life one Christmas Eve. He was a superb story-teller and I was always riveted by his tales. But the character in those stories was flesh and blood, not some remote superman. As I reflected on those stories and on the man I had known as my father, on the changes he had undergone even in my lifetime, I began to feel that his story was much more important than the success he had achieved at the end of his life. Senator Percy said that he had asked the right questions of society; I knew he had also asked some far harder questions of himself. His story is the quest for the answers, a search which took him to many places both in a physical and a mental sense and led him to some disturbing conclusions about himself and his outlook on life.

There was no shortage of material to help me as I started in my task of piecing together my father's story. It soon became apparent why his study was such a sea of papers: he had never thrown anything away. There were also scores of people to whom I knew I must talk. Their different approaches turned out to be as revealing as the interviews themselves.

I began with the men in my father's life. Many of them I knew had opposed him fiercely, or at very least ridiculed him when he first came out with statements that later were regarded as prophecies. There was no sign of any antagonism in our friendly conversations. However hard I tried to play devil's advocate the picture I got was consistently one of harmony and good will. My father appeared too good to be true.

I then turned to the women. They were one of my father's weaknesses. His good looks and charm had captivated quite a few hearts. He needed women around him, to care for him and listen to him. The first to be a sounding-board for his ideas had been his sister Edith; later on Julia Porter, a friend whom he respected more than most of his male colleagues, was one of the most important. But despite the mutual admiration and affection, these female colleagues and friends were harder with their final verdicts than their male counterparts. Only by talking to the women did the weaknesses I already knew about, or had suspected, come to the fore and allow my father to take shape as a human being.

The third stage of my research took place in Germany. I had been conscious of a tension in my father when he was with his German friends and family. I thought of him as a German but I wondered what others thought and what he himself felt. An old English friend told me that he had heard my father say, 'Ich bin ein Vaterlandsloser Geselle' – I am a fellow without a Fatherland.

The question of national identity brought me face to face with a subject that my father had avoided talking about: his decision to leave Germany and the effect this had had on his life and relationships. It became clear that history had put up a barrier which had distanced him from some of his family and friends, which had made them very critical of him, at times even harsh in their judgments. In Germany a picture emerged of a self-centred and egotistical man, whose criticism of scientific progress and academic endeavour was attributed to his own lack of thorough academic training.

In the face of these extremes of adulation and hostility I have tried to avoid making any judgments in this book. I have told the story of my father's life as truthfully as possible. There were times when this was painful, more often it was fascinating and rewarding. My father and I were great friends, I understood him as a friend as well as a daughter, but I had no part to play in the forces that shaped his life. For this reason, and to avoid the temptation of making subjective judgments, I have kept out of the narrative as much as possible.

E. F. SCHUMACHER

1

Grown in German Soil

Fritz Schumacher was born on August 16th, 1911 in the German city of Bonn. He had been preceded by twins – a boy and a girl – who were just over a year old when he was born, but as he was a healthy, strapping baby he soon caught up with his more delicate brother and sister so that the three of them came to be known by all their acquaintances as the triplets.

Fritz was named after his father's brother; the twins after their parents, Hermann and Edith. The name Hermann carried with it the burden of generations of eldest sons. Since the fourteenth century they had served their country loyally, performing civic duties in the Hanseatic town of Bremen, where the first recorded Hermann Schumacher was elected mayor. Subsequent generations of Schumachers bore the office and in 1604 Bremen publicly acknowledged their service by adding the Schumacher coat of arms to those of other notable families in the town hall.

The traditional ties with Bremen town hall were broken by Fritz's grandfather. He wanted to play a wider role in the world and went abroad with his wife, two small sons and a baby daughter, first to be German Ambassador in Bogota, Colombia, and then to be German Consul in New York, where two more daughters were born. Their life in the wilds of the Andes and amongst the skyscrapers of New York was not always conventional. The two boys were more or less left to educate themselves. After a brief and unhappy period of formal schooling in a New York establishment their father was convinced that they would learn more left to their own devices; they were given a printing press and the young 'Schumacher Brothers: Printers' set themselves up in business. They learnt mathematics by keeping their accounts and literacy through typesetting, their father insisting only that they carried on their printing business with proper professionalism and dedication.

In 1882 Ambassador Schumacher was posted to Lima and the two boys were sent home to Bremen for a more formal education. They felt like orphans away from their parents and sisters. Bremen seemed to be full of critical aunts of all shapes and sizes who peered at 'the two German shoots grown on American soil' through curtained windows as they walked down the street on their way to school. Hermann, the elder, found it particularly difficult to settle down and recorded many years later in his memoirs that this episode in Bremen

> strengthened the north German tendency in my personality, but also tied me to my brother in an unusually close bond. From then on we lived – almost as orphans – in the house of my mother's older sister ... However friendly our reception was, it could never take the place of our parental home. As Fontane says, home 'exerts its influence from minute to minute in those formative years of the soul', where example is more important than teaching. That feeling of natural belonging which one takes for granted could only develop slowly and with more difficulty for the older (brother) than for the younger.[1]

The absence of continuous family bonds, exacerbated by the early death of his father, all helped to make Hermann single-mindedly wrapped up in his own life: dogmatic, authoritarian and dedicated to the pursuit of his career, breaking only to holiday with his brother whenever their busy lives allowed. His career progressed well. He studied first law and then economics. By the age of thirty-one, in 1899, he had already gained the distinction of being appointed to a chair of economics, at Kiel University, without having acquired the usual obligatory academic qualification of a doctorate. Once he was a professor, the world opened out, particularly after he had founded a

school of economics in Cologne in 1900, the first to have
university status in Germany. As Hermann's reputation spread
to the upper echelons of society he was appointed tutor to the
Crown Prince and his brothers. He travelled widely to the Far
East and China, collecting economic data, and twice to New
York, where on his second visit in 1906 he was the first 'Kaiser
Wilhelm Exchange Professor' at Columbia University, return-
ing after a year to the chair of economics at Bonn University.

Professor Schumacher was a dedicated teacher and a gifted
one. He took enormous trouble, not only with the material he
presented to his pupils, but also in his interest in their progress.
The 'Schumacher students' regarded themselves as a privileged
group and formed a society, the 'Schumacher Verein' in which
they honoured their teacher even after his death.

The Professor combined a personal interest in his students
with a firm belief in his own authority as their teacher. Just as
it would not occur to him to question the authority of a legally
elected government, even if he disagreed with its policies, so he
did not expect his pupils to question his position. His pupils
accepted this, for it was an attitude commonly held amongst
the Professor's contemporaries, and one which later was to
result in tragedy for Germany. But it was less easy for his
children to tolerate. Their father's interest in them often took
the form of unsolicited and dogmatic advice, and his authori-
tarianism, lacking the compensating qualities of sensitivity but
rather made worse by touchiness, oppressed them, particularly
in the way it affected their mother.

Professor Schumacher was over forty when he married,
while his wife was barely older than some of his students. His
approach to marriage was essentially practical. Finding there
was less pressure on him in Bonn, he decided it was time to
renounce his bachelor existence and find a suitable wife. A
highly respected colleague and professor of law, Professor
Ernst Zitelmann, had three striking daughters. Professor Schumacher first noticed them while on holiday with his brother
Fritz at the North Sea. He decided that any one of the girls
would suit him but was at a loss how to proceed with the
selection. He wrote in his memoirs:

The meeting on the North Sea beach was a short but im-

3

pressive prelude. Returning to Bonn the situation was simplified. Although the father guarded his daughters like a personal treasure, the middle and most energetic had the courage to get engaged and in fact, to marry, and the eldest went to Paris and Brussels to complete her artistic studies. So only the youngest was left. The elimination, which I could hardly have managed by myself, was decided upon by a sympathetic fate.

Edith was eighteen years younger than her future husband, but her beauty seems to have struck the Professor less than her shyness and modesty. He was amazed to discover, some time after their marriage, that she was also a talented mathematician who had managed to solve a problem that had been puzzling mathematics professors for some years.

Professor Schumacher courted Edith at archaeology lectures which she attended with her mother. Not surprisingly, given his inexperience and her shyness, it was hard going. Even his proposal was unromantic in the extreme. On his way to her house he stopped to buy flowers for the occasion: the flowers he grabbed absentmindedly were artificial.

Such insensitivities were wounds that Edith Zitelmann received on many occasions after her marriage, but her husband was generally oblivious to her sufferings. One washing day soon after the birth of their twins the Crown Prince called unexpectedly. He wanted the Professor to accompany him on a visit to the Far East. After some minutes of conversation the Professor invited the Prince to step into the garden. It did not occur to him that it would humiliate his wife to walk the Prince past the flapping lines of laundry.

Shortly after this incident the Professor departed for China, Japan and Indonesia leaving his wife with the twins and expecting a third child. The trip turned out to be a disaster. The Crown Prince abandoned it before the Professor had reached their rendezvous in Singapore. Professor Schumacher nevertheless pressed on alone, only to catch malaria so severely that the doctors attending him on his return marvelled that he had survived the journey.

With her husband to nurse and twins of just one year old to look after, Edith Schumacher gave birth to their third child.

He was christened Ernst Friedrich, Ernst after his grandfather, Ernst Zitelmann, and Friedrich after his uncle and godfather, Fritz. It was a happy choice, for the uncle and his nephew had more in common than just their names. They had a mutual respect and affection and they were to share a similar sense of humour and a liking for writing apt and pithy verse. Uncle Fritz was an authority on Goethe and a distinguished and influential professor of architecture and town planning, eventually to redesign and rebuild a considerable part of Hamburg and Cologne. He was somewhat less dogmatic and authoritarian than his older brother, possibly because his two sisters lived with him and kept him in order. These two spinsters were not favourites of their nephew Fritz. His childhood memories were of two formidable ladies whose affections were concentrated entirely on a little dog with digestive disorders which filled the house with an intolerable stench that seemed to escape their notice.

Fritz's first playmates were naturally his brother and sister, Hermann and Edith. Fritz was more extrovert than Hermann and his charm and intelligence succeeded in stealing the limelight from his older brother on many occasions, particularly when family friends and relations provided an audience. Edith was more like Fritz than her twin in this respect and the two of them formed a close bond. She was Fritz's companion and confidante and though she argued with him constantly and challenged everything he said, she believed early on that he possessed an extra dimension of perception. Later, when they were both adults, she saw him after a long separation and said to herself, 'He is like another Beethoven.'

Edith was artistic and imaginative. She was also determined to prove that such insights were not flights of fancy. She genuinely believed that her brother Fritz had superior abilities and understanding. There is an old nursery rhyme called 'Hänschen klein'. The words, roughly translated, go: 'Little Hans goes out into the world with nothing but his hat and stick for company. But mother weeps bitterly now that she has no more little Hans and the small child, realizing this, returns home quickly.' Edith, although she was already six, had not consciously heard the second part of this rhyme until she heard Fritz singing it to himself. She concluded that with his com-

5

passionate wisdom he had put himself into the shoes of little Hans's mother and made up a verse on her behalf. Edith's faith in Fritz was so strong that she refused to accept his assertion that the verse had existed long before he had.

Life in the Schumacher household was disciplined and regular, dictated by the Professor's needs. These were silence when he worked in his study and modesty and thrift in his wife's housekeeping. But outside events soon imposed a certain irregularity. In 1914 Europe was plunged into catastrophe. The children were probably more affected by the birth of another sister, Elisabeth, that year, than the outbreak of war but they would certainly have noticed the changes that suddenly took place around them. The colours of everyday life were transformed into a monotonous grey. The Professor wrote:

> The outbreak of the war made itself visible with almost uncanny speed in the appearance of the street. Its brightness suffered a sharp decline. As with one stroke all motor vehicles were painted grey and all the many colours that the uniforms had had up to now were displaced by the standard field grey. Life had taken on a more serious and monotonous appearance.

As young people went into the army, the number of the Professor's students dwindled, reducing his income. He began to write for local newspapers and give outside lectures. Soon the Prussian Minister for Trade, Von Sydow, summoned him to Berlin to discuss wartime economics and particularly the problem of war profits. Then the problem of food supplies became pressing. There was an element of black humour in Professor Schumacher's involvement in these discussions. The Germans, with their reputation for enjoying a good sausage, were faced with the dilemma that a vast population of pigs was competing with the population of humans for limited supplies of cereals. It was a question of bread today or sausages tomorrow. Professor Schumacher advised bread today and the resulting slaughter of pigs went down in history as the *Schweinemord* – the pig murder. It caused a controversy which rumbled on beyond the end of the war.

In 1917, just as Fritz was reaching school age, Professor Schumacher was appointed professor of economics at Berlin University and the family moved to the capital city. The Professor was delighted with the move. It meant more to him than just academic promotion. In Bonn the family had lived in the Zitelmann's old house. In Berlin, for the first time, he bought a house of his own. He wrote in his memoirs: 'Here a feeling of home could develop. The ownership of the house, even more than the new professorship, made me believe that I had reached the goal of my life.'

The new house was to be the family home until the early 1940s. It was a large and typical nineteenth-century German house with a high gabled roof and carved veranda. A conservatory led into the garden, well stocked with fruit bushes and shrubs - lavender, lilacs, roses and rhododendrons. Around it were other similar houses and gardens. Steglitz was a respectable, middle-class suburb of Berlin where many professional families had settled. Arno-Holtz Strasse, where the Schumachers bought their house, was half way up the Fichteberg, the highest point of the area from which one could look down over the whole of Berlin, and also led directly into a botanical garden where the Professor took a daily walk.

The Schumachers' move to Berlin coincided with the beginning of hard times in Germany. By 1917 food was getting scarce. It was no longer enough to live frugally; extra measures had to be taken to live respectably. The Schumachers tried unsuccessfully to grow vegetables and then turned the garden over to livestock. Chickens, rabbits and goats became part of family life and gave the children some of their happier memories during those difficult years. The goats, which at one time numbered ten, gave them the most pleasure. They were housed in the cellar but the kids were allowed into the drawing-room where the poor creatures tried to take their first shaky steps on the slippery parquet floor. Even the Professor was amused by the entertainment.

As food shortages bit harder it became more difficult to feed the goats. The children would go out daily, foraging for scraps in their neighbours' dustbins. They became a familiar sight running about on the Fichteberg in bare feet (for shoes had become a luxury) with their buckets in their hands. But the goats got thinner, their milk supply dried up and they were relegated to the stew pot. The children seem to have been very unsentimental about this, remembering only their interest in seeing the inside of the goats as they were cut up before going into the cooking pot.

It was not a time to be sentimental. In the last months of the war and in the years after the fighting had ended the children felt real hunger. It made a deep impression on Fritz. He never forgot the feeling of emptiness, the feeling of exhaustion which lack of food produced, and later recalled vividly how he would have to rest on his way up the Fichteberg when he carried his violin back from a music lesson. For a while the family felt real deprivation, so much so that when the Red Cross selected undernourished children to recover in their camps from the rigours of the war, the Schumacher children were amongst those chosen.

If hunger was a formative experience for Fritz, so was the bitterness felt by many patriotic Germans at their humiliation by the Treaty of Versailles, leaving them without any hope in their future. Professor Schumacher expressed the opinions of many when he wrote in his memoirs:

> That Germany was robbed of her ability to negotiate polit-ically by having to hand over her warships, by being forbid-den an airforce, by having to pull down her defences and by the utmost reduction of her strength at sea was understand-able. But that Germany was weakened as no other country before by having important lands in the east and west of the country taken away, as well as all colonies, that the remain-ing territory was torn apart by the Polish Corridor, that the most important part of her merchant navy was taken, that her foreign investments were liquidated and initial refusal given to most economic plans, as well as being burdened with war indemnity under the name of 'reparations' that would have exceeded even her unweakened economy, was hard to understand. All reconstruction that a modern four-year war demands was made impossible. Constant new un-rest was unavoidable.

The immediate effect of post-war unrest on the Schumacher

household was that ten young soldiers, part of the force sent to restore order in Berlin, were billeted on them. It marked the beginning of a new flow of visitors. To supplement his income the Professor decided that the family must take in paying guests. The first was a high-born Indian who was related to the writer Rabindranath Tagore. His contribution to family life was a passion for home-made wireless sets, and for classical music which he brought to the house on the still imperfect new medium of gramophone records. He was followed by countless others, most of them from England or the English colonies.

Apart from paying guests the family was also often supplemented by one or other of the Professor's students. As young soldiers returned to civilian life, the Professor noticed a different, more serious approach amongst the swelling ranks of his students. The more promising were brought home and made part of the family, among them the Hungarian economist Thomas Balogh (later Lord Balogh and adviser to the Labour government under Harold Wilson). Balogh recalled that such friendliness was very unusual among the professors in Berlin.

Professor Schumacher was not involved solely with his teaching. As the economy collapsed he was again called to discuss the problems with the government ministers in Berlin. As inflation reached the crisis levels of 1923 the secret talks grew more and more desperate. Many eminent economists were involved, including John Maynard Keynes and the Governor of the Bank of England, but the problems appeared insoluble. By the beginning of November 1923 the Minister of Finance, Hans Luther, believed that 'a dissolution of the social order was expected almost from hour to hour'. [2]

November 1923 in fact marked the turning point and the end of the economic chaos, and most authorities attribute the control of the inflation crisis to Hans Luther and the Reich's currency commissar, Dr Hjalmar Schacht, who later became Hitler's 'economic miracle worker'. Professor Schumacher has a slightly different story to tell.

At the end of October or beginning of November 1923 the newly appointed Finance Minister, Luther, called together another meeting at which five or six men were present, myself

included. It was soon obvious that the convenor of the meeting had not had the opportunity to acquaint himself thoroughly with the monetary problems. This was the first stroke of luck at this meeting: it was not necessary to overcome preconceived ideas. The second was that soon after the meeting began Luther was called away to a long telephone conversation. We therefore had the unusual opportunity of discussing the matter amongst ourselves. We discovered that we were all in agreement: the never-ending demands made on the Reichsbank by the treasury, with which it had been essential to comply because of the war, had to stop now that the wartime necessity had ended. With that the spiralling prices would stop. Then the value of paper money had to be put back to a sensible level. The Reich's finance minister was for a moment taken aback, then he recapitulated what had been said in a few words and declared decisively: 'That will be done gentlemen. Thank you.'
... On November 23rd, 1923 the German currency was stabilized, one billion old marks were replaced by one new Reichsmark and the inflation had been overcome.

Fritz, only a schoolboy when these important meetings were taking place, could not escape the reality of the problems under discussion. Inflation was a terrifying everyday experience in which the children were also involved. They were sent out to join the queues for food, their shopping bags bulging with paper money which took up more space than the few essentials which they hoped to buy. They were always afraid that prices would have been put up before their turn had come. Then they would have to return to their mother empty-handed. She too had been thrown into a panic when her fifth child, Ernst, was born in 1922. She heard that the fees in the nursing home had been put up to 3,000 million marks a day and would have discharged herself had not her husband managed to convince her that his salary had kept pace with these staggering figures.
 While these disturbing experiences taught Fritz modesty in material matters, his experience of school fostered in him an intellectual immodesty. He and his brother Hermann both attended the Arndt Gymnasium, a large and imposing school with high academic standards and well born pupils, not far

from their home. It was fortunate that he and Hermann, although in the same year, had different interests and were therefore in different parts of the school. Hermann's leanings were towards the sciences whereas Fritz preferred the humanities. Fritz generally assumed that he knew better than Hermann in most fields of knowledge so their separation enabled Hermann to prosper quietly without being constantly undermined by his precocious younger brother.

Fritz's sense of intellectual superiority grew with each term although it was by no means always justified by his results. His interests were wider than the school curriculum and his ability to ask searching questions tested his masters to their utmost. Aware of this and bored by the lack of challenges, Fritz directed much of his sharp wit into making fun of those teachers for whom he had the least respect, in particular the German literature teacher, Herr Alphonse Marx. Marx in return gave Fritz as low marks as he dared. When Fritz matriculated in the spring of 1929 he dealt the final blow to Marx's self respect by publishing a cutting poem in the school magazine. It began:

When he stands at the desk and teaches us verse,
The meaning distorted so that we all curse,
He glances at one piece then turns to the next
So the students all shout because they are vexed ...

Mathematics lessons bored Fritz most of all because he worked so quickly that he was rarely allowed to participate, the master dismissing him with: 'Not you, Schumacher, I know you know the answer.' The master knew too that most of the class copied their homework from Fritz. He set different work for each boy but Fritz still managed to get round all those who needed help. Fritz was rather proud of the way he finally hit back at the maths master. His eyes still lit up with glee as he related his triumph to his children many years later. He began to take books into class. The master soon bellowed: 'Schumacher! What are you doing?' 'Reading' came the reply. 'Bring me the book.' The next lesson the same thing happened. Another book was confiscated. Again and again the exchange was repeated until Fritz wore down the master by bringing so many books in at a time that the entire lesson would have been taken

11

up with confiscating Fritz's books if the master had not relented and allowed Fritz to read.

These antics which infuriated his masters amused most of his classmates, who liked Fritz for his sense of fun and respected his intelligence. A few who had been the targets of his stinging wit liked him less: class or status did not protect them. Fritz named one boy, a German aristocrat, '*der Punkt*' – the dot – following Euclid's definition of 'something with position but no substance'.

Frustrated in lessons, Fritz put more effort into non-academic activities. He was an enthusiastic member of the drama society as an actor and a playwright. On his seventeenth birthday he completed a long play about the struggle for German unity in the twelfth century. It was called *Heinrich der Löwe* and was successfully performed and well reviewed in local newspapers. The play still exists.

Eight months later, in the spring of 1929, he matriculated, glad to have finished with school. But he felt that something was eluding him. As an adult he expressed these early frustrations in *A Guide for the Perplexed*: 'All through school and university I had been given maps of life and knowledge on which there was hardly a trace of many of the things that I most cared about and that seemed to me to be of the greatest possible importance to the conduct of my life.'[3]

As a youth, he did not yet know what really was important to him but by the time he was sixteen he had come to regard the holidays as the only time in which he could try to delve deeper. He worked with such discipline that his mother began to fear for his health. She begged him to take a rest in his work, without success. 'As there are so few moments during term time that I can give to this world of books and ideas,' he explained, 'and as all sorts of desires to achieve something out of this world occur to me during this time, I often need part of the holidays to follow them just a little. And if I don't have this time I cannot find real peace and happiness in myself.'

Two years later, on April 5th, 1929, he wrote again of this feeling of restlessness, the lack of fulfilment he had first experienced at school. This time it was to his sister Edith:

That you are so completely happy despite the amount of

work – or rather, no, no doubt because of it – is an enviable condition. Not because of the work but altogether. Unfortunately I can never quite manage it. I have a strange and restless longing in me that cannot be fulfilled. Perhaps hopefully in the future but not yet. – Well, never mind. I am content and happy now when I find a tolerable level of inner harmony.

2

First Taste of England

In the spring of 1929, aged seventeen, Fritz matriculated into freedom. Unlike most people of his age it was intellectual freedom rather than freedom from the restrictions of family and childhood that he wanted. He had great hopes that he would learn things of importance at university. He left home in high spirits, returning to Bonn, the town of his earliest childhood memories, where his maternal grandparents still lived.

Fritz was determined to enjoy himself at university as well as to work. He wrote at once to his sister Edith:

> Tennis – you must admit is more important than anything else. I play about 2 hours a day but that can be increased. Otherwise I cultivate peace, read a little, learn a little shorthand and English, go for walks and contemplate the appalling effect of being too busy – Well you see I have fully grasped the seriousness of one's first term.

But he added that he had signed up for twenty-five hours of lectures a week as well.

He viewed his first term at university as an opportunity to look around at what was on offer academically and socially. Like his father he was drawn to law and to economics. Both subjects also had inspiring professors. He found the most exciting was Professor Joseph Schumpeter and wrote to his parents: 'a terrific fellow! I am already looking forward immensely to his next lecture on Monday. He doesn't parade a dry scholarliness but an incredibly lively knowledge. One feels the whole fellow behind each sentence.' Unfortunately Schumpeter left Bonn for a lecture tour before the term was over, but if one person was responsible for inspiring Fritz to take up economics that was the man. It would be over three years before he was taught again by a teacher of such stature.

The professor of law, Professor Dölle, also ranked high in Fritz's estimation. 'If the whole of Law was as it is with Dölle then it would be something for me,' he wrote home (in April), leaving unsaid that he found the other law lectures deadly dull and therefore soon abandoned the subject.

Fritz's first term was marred only by ill health which was to plague him throughout his student life. He had recurrent boils, often on his face which gave him debilitating headaches, eczema on his hands, often so severe that he would have to wear gloves, and asthma which struck at most inconvenient moments. These ailments, from which Uncle Fritz also suffered, seem to have been closely related to his state of tension. In his mid-twenties they gave way to mysterious stomach pains that remained with him intermittently until his fifties.

His parents wanted to be told every detail of his life: his health, the books he was reading, the other students and the societies he joined. Fritz wrote home dutifully and regularly, nearly always signing himself, 'in grateful love, Fritz'. His father always replied in detail, commenting on each piece of information Fritz had sent him, suggesting that this football club might be more suitable than that, one student society more advantageous in the long run than another. Fritz received all the unsolicited advice without protest, thanking his father for his concern with exemplary filial respect. He knew he was protected by the distance between them and that there was no point in alienating his parents in obvious defiance or argument. He generally did what he wanted anyway but never made an issue of it, even though some of his father's comments must have irritated him enormously. He could not even take a few days' holiday without detailed and critical comment from his father. For example, in July, on Fritz's return from a three-day jaunt by motorcycle, his father wrote:

Basically, I see in motorbikes a mode of transport that leads to superficial travelling. In this area particularly one should develop a depth of approach. A journey must be a voyage of discovery. One must be able to discover more in the beautiful and interesting than others ... Only then can one's life be enriched. Even if one does not remember every detail, the formative influences remain. I hope with my heart that you too will still be able to experience this. A few trips on a motorbike are nice. They practically belong to the life of a young person today, but one must be clear that something different and better exists. I would like to believe that you too are beginning to realize this deep down. The things of beauty that do not lie beside the main road are usually the best and the most worthwhile. One has to learn how to find them.

The fact that Fritz had had to cut his excursion short because of an asthma attack served only to strengthen the Professor's case. There was no doubt, he pointed out to Fritz, that this had been caused by the dusty ride on the motorbike. It must be remembered that Fritz's father belonged to a generation that still regarded holidays as essentially a time in which to walk. He and Uncle Fritz had on many occasions put on their walking boots and trekked off across the countryside together in true German *Wanderlust*. Perhaps Fritz, too, took this into account when he replied in defence of the motorbike: 'I can only agree with you about the superficiality of travelling by motorbike. It doesn't develop but rather misleads. And one does not need to let oneself be misled ... The motorbike is primarily a means to an end ... I believe we used our motorbike pretty correctly in our last trip, namely only to take us to the area that was of particular interest.'

Professor Schumacher showed less concern for Fritz's work than for his social life. Rather than pressing him to make a decision about which subject he intended to study, the Professor suggested that Fritz should first spend a few months abroad. Fritz agreed at once but was less enthusiastic when his father suggested France. 'I believe it is better – if (I am to go) at all – to wait till the attitude of the French towards us is better and the (German) Rhineland has been vacated (by the French),' he wrote to his parents in June 1929.

Fritz felt deeply with his fellow Germans that France had much to answer for in Germany's economic problems. He was convinced that the occupation of the Rhineland had been responsible for Germany's hyperinflation, and remained convinced of this throughout his life (although this view is refuted by economists such as J.K. Galbraith). Professor Schumacher obviously took France's position in German affairs less to heart than Fritz, otherwise he would not have suggested a visit, but his memoirs show that he was also affected by anti-French feeling. English visitors to the Schumachers at that time[1] and over the next ten years recollect that their politics seemed to be judged less by their attitude to Germany than their attitude to France.

It was decided that Fritz should visit England. He began at once to prepare himself by acquiring a rudimentary knowledge of the English language, attempting his first letter in English in August. It was to his sister Edith: 'We must learn, awful many things, but that's a graet plesure for anyone, who know that he learnt and who does it with joy. What I have done in the last quarter of year except the learning for the study and the later life.'

Had Fritz known that England would later be his home he would have been very dispirited by his first impressions that autumn. The English, he soon concluded, were not very civilized, particularly the doctor's family with whom he stayed in Tottenham. He could hardly believe his eyes when the boiled potatoes were served still in their skins. He began to appreciate the little comforts of his home that he had always taken for granted. He wrote to his father, in German:

> My housing here is not exactly ideal. But it does not matter ... The wallpaper hangs in tatters and the ceiling is falling down in places. But that doesn't matter. The only unpleasant things are the bad bed, but I have managed to make it bearable with all sorts of devices; and the lack of electric light. There is a gas light here. But it is very weak and flickers like a film which strains the eyes. Apart from that it always stinks of gas. Still, while there are still long hours of daylight it is not too bad.

As there was little to do but work, Fritz risked the eyestrain from the flickering gas light and set himself the daily task of learning a hundred new English words and reading *The Times*. Soon his vocabulary was extensive enough for him to read Bernard Shaw, and Adam Smith's *The Wealth of Nations*. It was the beginning of a life-long admiration for Shaw and a life-long involvement with economics, although he did not finish *The Wealth of Nations* on that occasion because, as he wrote to his parents in September, 'though I was interested Ad. Smith had a rather old language, which is not quite as useful for me as a more modern one. For that reason I am reading now with no less joy: *The Intelligent Woman's Guide to Socialism and Capitalism* by B. Shaw.'

Fritz's father was more interested in the progress of Fritz's English. After a month Fritz wrote to him in English and thereafter letters home in German became the exception. The English letters were not without mistakes but they were written with confidence and style. As Fritz never mastered any other modern language, but relied almost exclusively on his knowledge of Latin and his inventiveness to communicate in all other European languages, his speedy mastering of the English language must have been entirely the result of hard work. Fritz's struggles with English had their amusing moments. When describing the beauties of the Rhineland he told a shocked audience, 'It is of course, a region famous for its rapes.' Puzzled by the reaction he clarified his statement by adding that he preferred the rapes once they had been transformed into wine. He did not, he said, like his wine *'en pillule'*.

Fritz stayed with the family in Tottenham for less than a month before finding other lodgings in Chorley Wood. The move improved his surroundings but not his landlords who merely confirmed his opinion that the word *'gemütlich'* could not be adequately translated into English because the English had never experienced its meaning. Clearly Britons were a nation who specialized in uncomfortable beds and bad food. Even the famous English gentleman seemed to be non-existent. Disillusioned, he gave up family life and found a room in Student Movement House in London which, if not more comfortable, at least offered the possibility of more stimulating company.

In his new location Fritz promised himself great things. London was now much more accessible to him. He wanted to attend some lectures at the London School of Economics. But neither the L.S.E. nor London came up to his expectations. He wrote to his father in November:

At the School of Economics I heard ... a public lecture by Prof. Bonn, Berlin ... His lecture was simply scandalous ... The other lectures are not particularly interesting. The most attractive man at any rate is Prof. Laski. But his lectures are from beginning to end nothing but propaganda for his socialism. I think the School of E. is very disappointing ... London is becoming more and more dirty, ugly, misty, noisy – whatever you like or rather: you don't like nor I. The streets are covered with almost everything you need, and the wind is blowing it straight in your mouth, nose, eyes or wherever you don't like it. If you look for the sun, which can never be seen, you see a grey kindless heaven, as far as you can see it. All other is some dirt, houses of the most terrible architecture, streets, red busses making noise and smell, what is the advantage of the houses that they don't. You see at every corner begging men, who painted some silly pictures on the pavement and looks on you simply bursting with unhappiness. If you escaped and hope to see something more pleasant you find yourself surrounded by a crowd of the dirtiest children you ever saw, crying for a copper and following a long time.

Fritz's negative view of London may have been partly coloured by one feature which dismayed and upset him. He was struck by the respect the English had for their war memorials, particularly in Whitehall where not a bus passed without every male passenger raising his hat: 'A wonderful gesture,' he wrote home. 'If only we had such a Memorial and such a custom.' But the inscriptions hurt him: 'To Those Who Gave Their Lives For The Freedom Of The World.' His view of the war was quite different. He came to the conclusion that the English were as anti-German as ever, without any real idea of how Germany had suffered as a result of the war, still entertaining the heinous lie about Germany's so-called 'war guilt'. He wrote angrily to his mother, abandoning his customary English.

I read here an English description of the outbreak of war. It was not a good idea because it is so upsetting. Today we are fifteen years further on. But, nevertheless, it was incredibly instructive to see how England, by the slogan 'Right for Belgium', attacks a race to which it is related because it is frightened of German recovery, and how, because of its own fanatic bent for power and gold, builds up a picture of lies about Germany's 'lust for power over the world' so that in the midst of the storm the hearts of the people can be conquered.

But – that was fifteen years ago.

The highlight of Fritz's first visit to England came towards the end of November when he obtained an introduction to a man he already admired: John Maynard Keynes. He left for Cambridge at once. Despite his slight knowledge of economics, Fritz made such an impression on Keynes that he was invited to attend Keynes's highly selective seminars, a triumph which impressed even Professor Schumacher: 'That Keynes has actually invited a young person as yourself to his famous seminars exceeds even my wildest expectation,' he wrote to his son when he heard the news.

The encounter with Keynes and other Cambridge economists such as A.C. Pigou and D.H. Robertson removed any remaining uncertainty about which subject Fritz should study. His first English journey had begun with Adam Smith and ended with Keynes. Moreover, as England had unexpectedly provided this stimulation Fritz began to consider whether it might not also be the place to continue his studies. With this in mind he returned to Germany for Christmas, his whole future uncertain. Should he return to England? If so, how could his studies be financed? There were stringent currency regulations even if his father could find the money to assist him.

The answer came almost as soon as Fritz arrived home. He saw announced in the newspaper that the Rhodes Scholarships to Oxford, discontinued for Germans during the war, were to be resumed. On closer examination, Fritz saw that he had missed the closing date for application by six weeks but he applied anyway. He was summoned for an interview by return of post. But for Edith he might have missed it – and an opportunity which set the course of his life. It was a beautiful winter's day and Fritz planned to take an English visitor on a walk through the Grunewald. He loved the forest, with its paths through beeches and silver birches, oaks and ashes, an oasis of silence broken only by the songs of birds and the cackling of wild fowl. As the two young men were about to leave, Edith decided that she would join them and disappeared upstairs to dress for the cold. Time passed. Fritz grew impatient. He did not like to keep his visitor waiting. As he paced up and down there was a flurry of excitement at the door: a message had been delivered. Fritz Schumacher was to come at once to the Rhodes Scholarship Selection Board; the committee was waiting. Without stopping to change out of his knickerbockers into formal dress, Fritz left his friend to Edith and hurried to the Berliner Schloss where a dozen other candidates were already assembled.

The qualities for which the selection committee were looking had been laid down by Cecil Rhodes in his Will when he founded the scholarships in 1901. His vision had been 'to promote freedom, justice and peace throughout the whole world by awakening a desire for unselfish public service in a number of young men in every generation, selected from all parts of the English-speaking world and Germany'. They were to have 'the qualities of mind and character to enable them to see visions and devote their lives to realizing them in action',[2] in the hope that 'an understanding between the three strongest powers [Britain, Germany and America] will render war impossible, for educational ties make the strongest ties'. To fulfil these lofty aims candidates had to possess the qualities of truthfulness, courage and devotion to duty; sympathy for the protection of the weak; kindliness, unselfishness, fellowship; moral force and leadership. It was a demanding brief for the selection committee and a responsibility for the scholar to live up to such a picture of perfection.

After a day at the Berliner Schloss, which consisted of a lot of waiting about, an interview in English and a luncheon during which the candidates were on trial all together, the scholarships were announced. The selection board decided that the potential they required was evident in the young and handsome, if excessively thin candidate, whose sense of humour and intelligence had become quite obvious as the day proceeded. Their opinion was backed by the high praise of the warden of Student Movement House in London who had written to Dr Morsbach of the Akademischer Austauschdienst saying that he had been deeply impressed by Fritz's 'keen intellect and ripe judgment . . . I can vouch for his complete integrity, his strength of personality and his high moral character.' In the late afternoon Fritz and a candidate from Hamburg, Willi Koelle, were told that they had been selected to represent Germany at Oxford University the following autumn.

There were two terms to go before Fritz left for Oxford and New College, the college of his choice. He decided to spend them in Berlin, living at home and attending lectures at the university. There are no records of these eight months except for an event which gave Fritz one of the few memories he later recalled with a touch of bitterness, and which suggests that he continued to study economics. After some months of attending lectures he decided to write down some of the ideas he had had. It was his first attempt at an independent paper on economics, as opposed to a set essay by a university tutor. Proudly he gave it to his father to read. The Professor, so concerned with the welfare of his students, showed less than courtesy to his son. The paper remained unread on his desk. It was a bitter disappointment to Fritz.

At last in early October Fritz left Berlin for Oxford. His intellectual expectations were high. After his brief experience in Cambridge almost a year earlier, he had no reason to believe that Oxford economists would be less stimulating. It did not occur to him that he would find the Oxford academics as uninspiring as his schoolmasters had been. Otherwise he was much as other young men of his age. He was particularly fond of dancing, and he found girls an attractive addition to life's pleasures. He had already made one or two conquests, including an attractive Swedish girl who sustained him with affectionate letters. He enjoyed tennis and some winter sports, and he was always ready for a serious discussion, putting the world to rights over a glass of beer or wine. All this, he assumed, would be part of Oxford life as it had been part of student life in Bonn and Berlin. But he was to be disappointed.

3

Oxford

In October 1930 Fritz took up his place at New College,
Oxford. He found his rooms excessively cold and uncomfortable but not enough to dampen his sense of humour. He wrote
to his parents during his first week:

> Oxford is the most funny place I ever knew. At 7.30 the
> 'scout' comes into my room, opens the blind and says
> 'Twenty-eight past seven, Sir,' then he brings in order the
> washing stand and turns out. I have to hurry to get up if I
> want to take my bath before 'roll-call' otherwise I can sleep
> until the bell begins to peal. I put on my flannels and my
> sports coat and wind a shawl round my neck (to cover the
> nightshirt), I get on my slippers and – most important – the
> gown, and rush over to the Hall, where a 'Don' is crossing
> my name. That is 'Roll-call'. After that, if I haven't before,
> I take my bath. Then I go to the J.C.R. for breakfast.
> (Porridge, Ham and 2 eggs, bread, butter and tea.) The
> morning from 9 to 1 is fairly free. One 'does some work',
> 'sees his Tutor', goes to a lecture (which are mostly very
> bad) and reads some newspapers in the J.C.R. After lunch
> one usually goes to the Playground to have some sports. I
> do 'athletics' i.e. running and jumping. There is not much
> tennis during winter so that I shall scarcely get a chance of
> playing it.
>   After I had tea with some friends, I will try to do some-
> thing, but every half an hour somebody is knocking my door

– come in! – and wishes to see me. Mostly they try to persuade me for a Club, but I refused everything as far as that, except the Union Society. There are the most extraordinary Clubs in Oxford and it is one of the chief difficulties of a 'Fresher' to find out the right ones. 7.15 *pünktlich* Dinner. *Soweit ganz gut. Nachher*: 'social life'.

A fortnight later he was able to identify some strange habits among the students: one of these was '*talken*', which he described to his parents as: 'a very strange function of the speech organs, and is essentially concerned with staring into the open fire', and concluded: 'An odd lot these English, most of them stiff as pokers but on particular occasions they become completely mad.' The famous English sense of humour was quite beyond him. 'The active humour consists of messing up people's rooms. Passive humour, certainly extraordinary, consists in not taking offence – more or less a condition of one's purse. The "sense of humour" is an amazing Folklore that works so well that you can do anything to anybody. But when they do it to you it is generally anything but humorous.'

Bemused as he was by the English sense of humour, as this letter home shows, some of it amused him enough to join in. In his fifties he still chortled over the memory of a rope slung across the quadrangle with a student at either end sliding their chamber pots down to smash together. He was less amused by pranks played on him. One evening he returned home to his rooms to find a group of students sitting in a pile of shredded economics periodicals, laughing drunkenly. Thirty months of useful backnumbers now lay scattered around his room. As far as he could see, the English students' idea of fun was merely drunken stupidity.

Fritz did not find much consolation in the female students either. 'Oh yes, the college girls here. It is no laughing matter,' he wrote to his parents at the start of his second term. He could not even find a decent dancing partner. One evening he risked a blind date only to discover that his partner was 'not quite one metre high ... she might still grow. Apart from that she was also somewhat underendowed with brains, but I fear that is unalterable.' The next time she invited him to dance, Fritz developed a limp. This low opinion of English girls did not improve even in his second year at Oxford when he wrote home, 'In spite of my being a second-year man, there is absolutely nothing going here socially. It is because the old monk principles still hold good here ... Last year there was at least a dance club in which the male and female students were allowed to dance together (a symptom of the collapse of custom). This has, however, gone under because of the increasing mediocrity of the female student.'

Oxford struck Fritz at once as a very unhealthy place. He was ill with boils immediately he arrived and felt tired and listless for most of his first year, frequently referring to the debilitating effect the atmosphere had on him both physically and mentally. Yet he also realized that he was amongst a physically privileged group. He had noticed with astonishment on his arrival in England that he seemed to tower above most Englishmen. In London, too, he had come to assume that the English were a rather small race. In Oxford he suddenly noticed that he no longer stood out in a crowd. He realized that he was now amongst people who had not suffered generations of poverty or lack of nourishment.

Aware that he was in a privileged group and with high expectations of the intellectual stimulation he would receive at Oxford, it was hardly surprising that Fritz should feel somewhat let down when he discovered that no real thought had been given to the German Rhodes Scholars' academic position. An Oxford degree took three years and he and Koelle had only two years for which no formal course existed. Yet they were told that it was not permitted to study without a formal qualification in mind. After lengthy discussions with his tutor and the Warden of New College, H. A. L. Fisher, Fritz decided that his ultimate goal would be a B.Litt., to be submitted at the end of his second year. In order to qualify for this he would have to sit examinations for a diploma in Economics and Political Science at the end of his first year. He was dismayed by this news. Much of the work for the diploma seemed irrelevant to his longer-term aims and yet he was required to pass the examination with distinction. It was just like a continuation of school, he complained. He little thought that this would turn out to be the only paper qualification he was ever to acquire.

It was not merely the seemingly irrelevant study of subjects such as Latin and British Constitution that caused Fritz frustration in his first year at Oxford. The whole system of study, he found, prevented him from getting to grips with the real essentials of economics, a point which he put quite frankly to the German Rhodes Committee in his first report.

> The Tutor was something totally new for me, a system to which I am quite unaccustomed. On the whole I cannot complain ... but he has distracted me more in my studies than helped me in his suggestions. We have dealt with many different aspects of a great variety of big problems, but never with one complete problem. There is enough stimulation. The literature is not hard to find – but many small details do not amount to knowledge – and there is no time to go into it in depth. My tutor's programme is big. The list of books that I am supposed to read during the holidays (five weeks) amounts to thirty tomes. (I just ask myself, is this the English sense of humour?)[1]

His judgment did not change. He produced the work required of him and his essays were returned with praise. He sat his exams and passed his diploma with distinction, qualifying him to begin work on a B.Litt. But as his real interests became clearer to him the work he was forced to do became more irksome. He had been right: the first year at Oxford had been little better than school.

The frustration Fritz felt in the generalized studies of his first year was increased by his growing sense of the importance of the speciality he had chosen to study for his B.Litt. His brief introduction to international economics by Professor Schumpeter in Bonn had led him to think in wider terms than the discipline of economic theory. He began to analyse and understand the whole unhappy post-war history of Germany in economic terms and saw in the post-war economic distortions a grave threat to the peace of Europe.

Arriving in Oxford in October 1930, soon after the September elections in Germany had shown the startling swing to right, he found he had plenty of opportunity to develop and express his views.

Many students in Oxford wanted to know why six million

voters had supported Hitler's National Socialist party. Fritz welcomed the opportunity to explain what he saw as Germany's predicament. He took his role as representative of Germany as seriously as his duty as a Rhodes Scholar to promote peace and understanding. He felt that anti-German feeling was growing in England and that either through ignorance or deliberate malice the British press were misrepresenting the truth about Germany. Not only was the 'war guilt lie' still being perpetrated, but there was also no understanding of the disastrous effects of the treaties ending the war. Fritz believed that the English were ignorant of the suffering in Germany and were therefore unable to understand how Germany's economic ills could pose a grave threat to world peace. His message in a nutshell was: Ignore the problem and you will open the door to the kind of fanatical nationalism which is preached by Hitler. Giving a talk in Oxford on November 9th, 1930, Fritz spoke candidly and with feeling:

> When we speak on this day to you, sir, who consider this day as the cheerful day of victory, of the end of a terrible struggle, we do not want to open old wounds, but we do think we may try to give you an impression of our country, how it lives and starves and struggles for life.
>
> November 1930 is perhaps a turning point in our history. Germany makes – I assure you – the last desperate effort to bring in order her finance and to diminish unemployment. If the Brüning programme fails, the last barrier will fall for Hitler and his followers and either Hitler will, as his programme indicates, try the most dangerous experiments, or he will break down, because if Hitler does not want to risk anything and everything – he will have to disappoint his followers as deeply as any other party leader did before. If this last effort fails, it will be proved that it is not a matter of governmental leadership if things go better or worse, that the underlying cause is Germany's political situation: reparations, unequality, outlawry.

Again and again Fritz pointed out that Germany was being crippled by the debts imposed on her by the war settlements; she was being ruined by the unreasonable attitude of the Allies towards her efforts to pay reparations which they demanded in cash payments and would not accept in kind. When Germany attempted to put her own house in order by deflation she was severely criticized by the rest of her European trading partners because they were thus put into a trading disadvantage. How else was Germany to raise the cash? Fritz asked his audiences. Whatever Germany tried was condemned by the Allies. He tried to explain that many of Germany's economic problems were hidden and not immediately obvious to the casual observer or journalist. Border changes after the war had opened the doors to an influx of one and a quarter million refugees. The effect on the already overstrained housing stock and on the population was disastrous. Unemployment was increasing and the rate of inflation was again gathering speed.

Repeatedly Fritz pointed out that, as a result of the Treaty of Versailles and other post-war impositions, Hitler had, on the face of it, a valid and important contribution to make to German politics. Hitler confronted the German public on three sensitive issues: nationalism, anti-bolshevism and anti-semitism. These issues did not affect a country like Britain. In a debate in New College in his first term he expanded on these themes. The motion was 'This House believes that England needs a Hitler':

Nationalism has . . . nothing to do with militarism. Hitler's nationalism means: national self-consciousness, concentration of feeling people, and the will to defend German country and German people against the attacks of unscrupulous neighbours. This nationalism needs no propaganda in this country [England]. You have full liberty in your armaments . . . there is military training all over the country, at schools and universities, which fills the young people with the spirit of manlike self-consciousness and makes them ready to defend their country against any foreign attack.

You will not call that militarism. But that natural spirit is not allowed in a country which is ever so much more liable to foreign attack than England . . . You can't realize how great the necessity is for Germany to be able to defend herself . . . But you must realize that the helpless weakness of Germany is the greatest danger for peace in Europe. Six million voters felt that the present state of things is unbearable and disastrous. Hitler leads the way to a united and strong Germany which is necessary to keep up the balance of power in Europe. Hitler seeks to repair all the crimes committed against Germany since the war. He wants the rehabilitation of Germany as it concerns the war guilt lie. He wants to liberate Germany from her financial obligations, which put a cultured nation of 60 million people in economic slavery.

Fritz suggested that Hitler's anti-bolshevism was even less easy for the British to understand because they did not have the threat of communism on their doorstep as Germany did. Nor was there a Jewish problem in Britain. The British had to understand that there was a genuine problem in Germany, that many Germans believed that Jewish traders were threatening their commercial existence, and that Hitler had recognized these fears. Anti-semitism existed in Germany and it was not difficult for Hitler to whip it up into a potent force. Fritz concluded his comments: 'Hitler's party will become less extreme the more it grows. But there is no doubt that in this respect something has to be done.' In this same speech, in which Fritz had been asked to defend the motion: 'This House believes that England needs a Hitler', Fritz made some regrettable remarks which showed that some of the anti-semitic feeling that was rife in Germany had rubbed off on him. His main purpose was not, however, to defend Hitler (in his opening remarks he expressed quite clearly his reluctance to speak for a motion so much easier to oppose) but to point out once again that Germany's grievances were real and a danger to Europe. England, he argued, needed a Hitler, in order to show them that Germany's economic problems had to be taken seriously.

In all his talks on Germany that autumn of 1930 Fritz's argument was centred on Germany's economic problems. Politically he was a liberal, disliking extremism of any kind. He was not interested in day-to-day politics but in long-term policies. He was against Hitler from the very beginning, but not because of his methods, which were already visible in 1930 – in the street fighting between the S.A. and the communists, in the terrorizing tactics of the S.A., in the increasing public disorder and in Hitler's extraordinary rabble-rousing demagogy. Fritz barely mentions these facts although they were evident to all in Berlin. He was against Hitler because Hitler's solutions were in his view completely inappropriate to the real nature of the problem. Fritz was certain that the root cause of Germany's problems lay not in the Jews, nor in the communists, nor in the ailing Weimar Republic, but in the economic stranglehold which had been largely brought about by the policies of Britain and France.

> It is one of the difficulties of our day that the economic relations and fluctuations of our day are to a very large extent disturbed by political events. A natural balance of trade or payments is made impossible by political payments from one country to another ... If a durable peace can be established it is by economic means, by a thousandfold net of international co-operation in production, distribution and consumption of wealth. That, however, cannot be established as long as one of the leading industrial nations is tremendously handicapped, as long as political things – like reparations – bring the whole sensitive apparatus of international interrelationships into disorder and cause such severe economic world depressions as that from which we are suffering today.

The restoration of international order, in Fritz's opinion, had to begin with a 'sensible revision of the Young Plan and the Treaty of Versailles'. This, he pointed out, was, however, up to the allies. The German government was powerless to revise the Treaties and he warned that if a man like Hitler achieved power he would not be interested in economic solutions. Hitler had quite another way. As Alan Bullock put it many years later: 'To audiences weighed down with anxiety and a sense of helplessness Hitler cried: If the economic experts say this or that is impossible, to hell with economics. What counts is will.'[2] Fritz insisted that this kind of talk posed a grave threat to European peace. He believed that the prerequisite to peace was the free flow of trade and a smoothly working system of international financial relationships and it became clear to him that it was this aspect of international economics in which he wanted eventually to concentrate his studies.

Fritz decided to spend his first Christmas holidays in England – for the sake of his English. He accepted an invitation from an Oxford friend, Charles Gould, to stay at his home in Somerset. During this holiday an outspoken and passionate defence of Germany finally caused him trouble and he decided thereafter to keep a lower profile. He had been invited to address the Rotary Club of Yeovil on 'Young Germany and why a Nationalist Hothead like Hitler finds millions of followers'. It was an ideal opportunity and Fritz spoke frankly. He considered his audience uninformed and he pulled no punches. He ended with the rallying and provocative cry: 'It is now the turn of other countries ... to do something for peace: to disarm, to abolish the unbearable tension and friction in Central Europe by playing a fair game and revising the treaties.' There was uproar and one of the Rotarians wrote to Professor Schumacher, who also happened to be a Rotarian, about his son's address. 'It is true that he hurt us,' he wrote, 'but with that we are pleased, for such wounds harden the skin of friendship.'

Fritz was furious when his father wrote asking him to explain what had happened. He replied:

S——is a completely ignorant man, who designs gardens and writes articles about jam ... I am intrigued to know what he will make of your German letter because, firstly he won't be able to read it and secondly, it will fill him with embarrassment when he has it translated.

S—— also came to Mrs Gould and told her the rubbish about the skin of friendship and the wounds ... I hope you won't waste any more time on the gardener. I would send him some skin cream!

The Yeovil Rotary Club is a typical sentimental society. All they want to hear is how much one loves England and loves humanity and how one wants to avoid war by treading the path 'of promoting better understanding between peoples'. My God, these sentimentalists are the worst enemies of world peace.

Professor Schumacher wholeheartedly supported Fritz over this incident: 'There is no disputing that things are not easy for many of the English; but their fate and ours is not comparable,' he wrote. He added, however, in his next letter, that Fritz should take more care and withdraw a little from political discussions.

From now on you must talk about the German situation only, in Oxford or elsewhere, when it would be impolite towards the English not to do so. Otherwise you cannot discount a reaction. The average Englishman is very sensitive, even if he doesn't let it show immediately. It is all the more essential to be careful as I have heard, to my great regret, from reliable sources that there has been a swing against Germany in London's city ...

It was natural that you should be first and foremost a German in your first term at Oxford and you have done this excellently and no doubt benefited the Fatherland. In your second term I would try very consciously to appear first and foremost as a student in the best sense of the word. You will be able to help your Fatherland most in this way and it will be good for you if you unburden yourself a little from the responsibilities that you have had to carry in the last months. Then the valuable sides of English life will reveal themselves to you.

The rest of his stay confirmed all Fritz's worst prejudices about England. 'Christmas itself was perfectly bloody,' he wrote home despondently.

It really does consist only of Christmas cards and a great gorging for lunch on the 25th in this pathetic country. It deserves our sympathy. Those people who have finished their shopping on Christmas Eve go to the cinema in boredom. The 25th is the most deadly day of the year and everyone is glad when it is over. There is no distribution of presents. If anyone gives a present to anyone at all it is pressed into the recipient's hand at any time. The servants get their presents in envelopes in the kitchen.
Most people can't stand (or digest) the black, heavy

Christmas pudding. But it has to be eaten. Luckily my stomach managed to cope with it.

It was a stark contrast to the warmth and festivity which he was used to at home. The Schumacher family, in true German tradition, celebrated on Christmas Eve with candles and carols. The presents were ceremoniously opened together. It was a time of delicious food, delicious wine, companionship and joy.

After Christmas things improved. For a start it was the season of dances and balls and not many days passed without an invitation. After his stay with Charles Gould in Somerset Fritz moved on to two other families who had connections with the Rhodes Trust. First to Torquay, to stay with a widow and her two very devout daughters who disapproved of smoking, drinking and much more besides. The other Rhodes scholar guest, Bob, soon discovered this when he casually asked whether parrots laid eggs. It was made clear that such things did not interest the girls. Nevertheless, the week in Torquay passed pleasantly enough with three balls at which other 'very nice girls' made the evenings a success.

Fritz's final stay was with the Portal family in Hampshire whose wealth came from a monopoly on the paper on which bank notes were printed. This stay was the highlight of his holiday for he discovered on his arrival that four of the five children were daughters, three of whom were young, at home and unmarried. One of them particularly attracted Fritz and he tried hard to arrange an exchange with his sister for the Easter holidays so that he could resume his friendship in Berlin. It never came to anything and Fritz was left with the feeling that his suggestion had somehow overstepped the boundaries of etiquette. In general, however, the holiday served to confirm his low opinion of the English. At the end of January he wrote to his father: 'These English, whatever clan they are from, are, according to our conceptions, incredible ignoramuses. I have met heaps of Lords and Ladies who haven't got the faintest idea about anything . . . Most people are "frightfully nice" and that's about it.'

A year later he had still not changed his opinion, complaining to his sister Edith, 'Unfortunately there are very few people here with whom one can have a really good discussion . . . That is quite different in Germany. Of course, it is very good if one does not always talk shop or politics, and I have learnt a lot in this respect, but still there is nothing better than a really stimulating discussion with really committed people.'

Fritz could not help being a committed person himself. He found it hard to pass the time in frivolous pursuits. It was not that he did not enjoy dancing, or driving in the Oxfordshire countryside with friends who had cars, or dabbling in sport varying from squash to fencing, but his real interest remained Germany, which even his leisure activities reflected. In early 1931 he accepted first the post of secretary and then of President of the university German club. He was determined to put the club on the map, and widen its membership in the cause of Anglo-German understanding. To the French too he held out a reconciling hand, arranging a joint evening with the French club. His efforts and those of Willi Koelle, who later succeeded him as president, were very successful and the club grew from a handful of members to a regular attendance of about a hundred. The highlight of his presidency was to be the annual dinner to which Albert Einstein was invited, but unfortunately he was prevented from attending at the last minute. He came to Oxford shortly afterwards and Fritz had the honour of sitting next to him at high table.

Fritz's involvement with the German club ended less than happily in an incident which reflected the realities of German politics. Towards the end of the Christmas term of 1931 a group of Nazi sympathizers, both English and German, tried to take over the club. There was an unpleasant row during which Fritz showed a rare display of anger, an emotion which he usually kept very much under control. Although the Nazis were ousted, the very fact that it was suggested that their opinions should be represented in the club in order to reflect opinion in Germany dampened Fritz's enthusiasm for the club and he was relieved when he was able to hand over the presidency to Willi Koelle at the end of term.

The dissatisfaction Fritz felt with the events at the German club were equalled by the dissatisfaction he felt with his work in the beginning of his second year at Oxford. He had returned enormously stimulated and full of optimism after a successful summer holiday which he had spent in the Hamburg banking house of M.M. Warburg. He had been fortunate to get the job through his father's contacts because the economy in Germany was again on a down-turn and a number of people had recently been made redundant at the bank. Then, shortly after he began work, the bank was thrown into confusion by the collapse of the Donat Bank, followed by the collapse of the Credit Anstalt in Austria. It was the beginning of a new financial crisis for Germany and a most instructive opportunity for Fritz to discover at first hand what happened when the whole system of international finance was thrown into disorder. This knowledge was essential before he could begin to think out how to correct the faults in the system.

The summer of 1931 in Hamburg passed fruitfully. After the immediate effects of the crisis had passed Fritz worked his way through each department at the bank with varying degrees of interest. His one aim was to get to the managerial floor, to gain experience of the level where the decisions were taken. After he had at last spent a week there and the summer came to a close he wrote with satisfaction to his father in September: 'Such a practical intermezzo is unbelievably instructive – not only in relation to one's subject ... It makes subsequent study much easier (apart from anything else, one learns how to work) and, besides pointing out alternative views, also gives one colossal encouragement.'

It was a lesson which held one of the keys to the rest of Fritz's life. He discovered that there is no substitute for practical experience. Gradually this unshakeable opinion hardened into a degree of contempt for academics. Fritz believed that academic training without practical experience was generally valueless. To him 'knowledge' incorporated experience of the real world.

He returned to Oxford in October 1931 more certain than ever that he should make a detailed study of the whole mechanism of international finance the subject of his B.Litt., but his enthusiasm to get down to work received a blow when another administrative mix-up meant that he would no longer be able to submit his thesis the following summer. This delay turned out to have unexpected advantages. First of all Fritz had the greatest difficulty in narrowing his subject to manageable proportions. It took him until the beginning of 1932 to establish the limits of his study, to be called 'The Development of the London Gold Market'. Even then he wanted to place it into a broader context of other international money markets, a task for which he would need more time. The only way he could do this was to request a year's extension to both his Rhodes Scholarship and his B.Litt. In his application he added that he wished to spend the additional year at Columbia University in New York so that he could acquaint himself with the workings of the New York money market, an essential part of his studies. To his delight his plan was accepted.

By this time he was almost at the end of his fifth term at Oxford with only the summer term ahead. While working hard to acquire as much information as possible about the London Gold Market he also became more involved in another Oxford society, the prestigious and highly select Bryce Club, of which he was elected president in the spring of 1932. The club's purpose was to discuss international affairs, and eminent speakers were invited to address the members. In this club Fritz found more stimulation of the kind he had expected from his fellow students and a wider outlook to the international questions with which he was so preoccupied. He ended his term of office with a speech at the club's fifth annual dinner which summed up his own outlook on world affairs:

> I am afraid when we go down from Oxford ... we shall see how very much harder it is to practise an international spirit in real life than to study it here ... World opinion is slowly beginning to realize that while nationalism and inter-- nationalism are incompatible, a true patriotism and inter- nationalism are almost identical ... Blind nationalism has in many quarters superseded that type of healthy and highly admirable patriotism ... But on the other hand *a certain type of sentimental* internationalism has grown up, equally much superseding patriotism, which can never do any good, just because it is lacking that sound basis of that very feeling which we call patriotism.

Soon after this event term ended and Fritz left Oxford with little regret that his student days there had come to an end. He could not see much to recommend future scholars to the place.

The university had not been throbbing with intellectual activity and profound understanding of important world issues as he had hoped. Nevertheless he left with a number of good friends to give him at least some pleasant memories. Some were to last a lifetime, among them David Astor, Emmanuel 'Sonny' Wax (a lawyer), the two German Rhodes Scholars who came up in Fritz's second year, Adam von Trott and Adolf Schlepegrell, and even a female student, Stella Tucker. It was perhaps fortunate that they did not altogether understand or even realize Fritz's distaste for Oxford life, although Schlepegrell was aware that Fritz's inability to identify fully with student life was partly due to his 'aversion to students'. To his friends Fritz had immense charm, a sense of fun, was ridiculously young-looking with a physique so thin and delicate that David Astor thought it would break when he first saw him on a football field. They also recognized that he had an unusually serious attitude towards world affairs so that his work seemed to be the result of more mature reflection than their own. Some, such as a fellow Bryce Club member, Clunie Dale, went so far as to say that Fritz was slightly apart from and above the normal student but that that did not make him any the less likable or loyal a friend.

Oxford seems for Fritz to have been very much a man's world. He attracted many women when he reached America and he had had girlfriends before he went to Oxford, yet his only serious relationship during his Oxford days was with a German girl, Ingrid Warburg, a daughter of the banking Warburgs in Hamburg. Meeting Ingrid, a dark and beautiful Jewess, had been one of the successful ingredients of his holiday in Hamburg. They had kept in touch throughout his second year at Oxford, meeting in the holidays, their relationship reaching a climax the following summer of 1932 in Hamburg where Fritz spent the last few days before leaving for America. Perhaps this was one of the reasons why England failed to appeal to him at this time.

Reflecting on his two years at Oxford once he had reached America only hardened his negative impressions, which seemed still to debilitate him. In November 1932 he wrote:

I am fighting a great battle against the negative legacy of

Oxford. I am making an effort to utilize the positive aspects – in order to prove that the much-coveted years in Oxford as a Rhodes Scholar do not have the same bad influence on a German as they do on an American Scholar. Here the definition holds that 'a Rhodes Scholar is a man with a great future behind him.' They are 'clever', 'brilliant' but no use for anything. That really is one of the main factors in my life at the moment: to get away from the atmosphere of Oxford – perhaps one can still extract oneself from this lethargy. Thank goodness that I never fell in love with Oxford life: on no account would I return! ... Perhaps you will find this aversion strange – but it is not only negative, it means that I have set my aims higher and am fighting a battle that most of those who were in Oxford as foreigners could no longer take on.

He wrote even more strongly a month later: 'Oxford has much of beauty and interest to recommend it but I fear that it damned easily leads one to intellectual enervation.' And, 'I could not recommend anyone to go to Oxford with a good conscience. I am beginning to despise this nest.'

Five years later, more experienced and an émigré in England, he was able to look back on his Oxford days with more positive judgment.

Oxford, as in fact everything English, is such a strange affair that I always find it difficult when I try to express something definite about it ...

The course my studies took was anything but orthodox. In fact I reproached myself for not getting the best out of it 'academically'. Nevertheless, I would not know which other way to take if I had to make the choice again ...

Apart from the things that Oxford offers that are fine and useful, there are certain dangers for the young German. If one stays in Oxford for three years ... one gets used to a way of life and develops an attitude to life that can only be harmful, particularly as a German. This constitutes such a danger that I believe that this consideration should override the consideration of attaining the best examination results ...

I always regret it when those few Rhodes scholars that we (Germans) have use their time in Oxford to pursue a particular specialization, when it is the strength and purpose of the Oxford system to provide an education for citizenship. This education, which means a really general education, is best provided by Modern Greats. This is the most characteristic course that England can offer as well as being the most beneficial for a German ... as far as I am concerned, there is nothing that can show a young person what constitutes England's strength better: the citizens' feeling of responsibility. That seems to me to be the key to the English person. And I don't think one need worry about learning things that one won't be able to 'use' later. One might quickly forget many details; understanding, empathy and overall view remain ... I see that England's great strength lies in the availability of people for the highest positions who, apart from hard work in their careers, have a really comprehensive education – who have the courage in their youth not to specialize for three years but to concern themselves with the most general problems of human existence and society.[3]

4

In New York One Walks on Air

'People say about me – "he seems to enjoy just everything; – one of those jolly Germans" – whereas before I always had to hear: "You don't seem to enjoy life, what's the matter with you?" ... Something must have been the matter; but it seems unfair to blame Oxford for all of it,' Fritz wrote, in a series of letters to his parents in which he gave a detailed account of his impressions of America. Though Fritz had not been able to enjoy Oxford, he could not do otherwise than enjoy New York. He came to the New World and appropriately a new life began for him. He sailed from Southampton on September 2nd, 1932 in a Canadian Pacific steamship, *The Duchess of Richmond*, armed with two books with which he hoped to prepare himself for the new life ahead: not books on America or economics but books which he hoped would nourish his spirit: Albert Schweitzer's *Life and Thought* and Ortega y Gasset's *Rise of the Masses*. Both books stimulated him enormously and were a foretaste of the way his own thinking was to develop. But in 1932 he had few of the convictions which were later to become an integral part of his thinking, both about the developing countries and the West.

The voyage itself was symbolic of the change in Fritz's life. It began in England in 'typical English weather'. Dull and dreary, visibility nil and company, in his opinion, awful. He survived as an amused observer. 'If the public travelling First

Class are hardly attractive, they do offer something for the eyes of the humorist. One could make a film that would make René Clair pale into insignificance. There are primarily elderly people on board, whose ugliness would be hard to beat. One would have to search for a long time to find such a collection again.' His other amusement was an elderly lady theosophist who tried to convert him to her views over tea each afternoon. He made fun of her constantly but she remained, as far as he could make out, unaware of his sport.

Suddenly, as the ship passed the point of no return and the end of the journey was in sight, everything changed. The weather brightened, Fritz's spirits rose and, as if from nowhere, there appeared a group of young American girls with whom Fritz was able to dance the remaining nights away. It seemed a good omen and he disembarked in Canada in high spirits.

Fritz had chosen to travel to New York via Canada not only to see as much of the world as possible but also because he was aware of the enormous contrast between America and Europe, between the hectic life of New York and the stifling atmosphere he had found at Oxford. Canada seemed a gentle introduction to the possible shocks that awaited him. But he also wished to begin his studies at once and so he was not entirely sorry when, due to the sudden illness of his host and friend from Oxford, Clunie Dale, their sightseeing tour had to be cancelled and Fritz unexpectedly found himself with time on his hands. He used it to visit all the banking contacts he could muster and within a few days he had formed a useful picture of the Canadian banking system. He was exhilarated and impressed by the courtesy with which he was received by men whom he believed had 'the best monetary brains in Canada'. The chance to throw himself into independent work was like an injection of adrenalin. By the time he reached New York on September 23rd, he was prepared for the euphoria he was to feel in the next few weeks declaring: 'In New York one walks on air.'

I find New York glorious, comfortable, wonderful, interesting, stimulating – everything! The people are most obliging, most of them particularly charming ... Healthwise I seem to be on the road to the best recovery ... In fact I haven't felt in such good form for the whole two years at Oxford. I intend to do great things ...

New York appeals to me enormously. The climate is so wonderful that one always feels refreshed. The food is good ... So everything is provided for bodily needs. And there is masses of stimulation. The university life particularly appeals to me. Oxford really suffers in comparison. Never mind, it was useful to me in other ways. (For example, bringing me over here!)

One can, of course, write volumes about fascinating, impossible, mad New York. The Empty (sic) State Building (that actually is empty) is a dream of marble, glitter, light, lifts and technical daring. In fact the architecture of most of the skyscrapers is of unqualified barbarity; but the idea is so outrageous, so fantastic, that one cannot stop gaping. The Grand Central, the most astonishing station in the world, and the Washington Memorial Bridge: fantastic! The greatest beauty attainable in engineering. Like a Fata Morgana! Hovering over the river ... although it is the longest, most expensive, widest (etc. etc.) suspension bridge in the world, there is nothing of that crass, crazy desire to break records, of that childlike and naive desire of the masses for superlatives, but the greatest triumph of technical elegance, the conquering of space, the most convincing example of beauty of the appropriate. However, now they do want to bungle a lot of it: there is to be a restaurant on one of the bridge's pillars and with that the whole thing will become stupid.

Within days of his arrival Fritz was registered as an independent research student, had been welcomed by his professors and staff and had begun to attend the lectures of Professor Parker Willis, the professor of banking. 'What a contrast to Oxford', he wrote home in relief to his parents. 'Prof. Willis alone makes the course at Columbia University extremely worthwhile.' 'An unbelievably clear thinker and of such wide experience that one can only listen open-mouthed.' At last Fritz had found a teacher from whom he could really learn.

43

Parker Willis immediately recognized Fritz's ability too and admitted him to his 'inner study group', a group of about twelve students from his banking seminar. This group was set the task of studying the American banking crisis of 1929–32, each member given a related topic to prepare for eventual publication. Thus Fritz, without even a degree, suddenly found himself in intensive research work on 'the Gold position of the U.S. 1929–32'. Not only was this useful for his B.Litt. but more important to Fritz, he was at last free to immerse himself in his work in his own way.

Fritz soon discovered that Parker Willis was more than just an inspiring teacher. He was a controversial figure in the world of banking and in the inner sanctum of Wall Street. Within a few weeks Fritz gained the confidence and co-operation of several important banking houses – the International Acceptance Bank, one of the major dealers in gold on the New York financial market, and the Federal reserve bank, both of which allowed him free access to their statistics and papers for his research. His position required tact and diplomacy. Parker Willis was strongly disliked, indeed, 'stood on an absolute war footing' with Wall Street. The outspoken professor had dared to criticize the handling of the American banking crisis by the banks; he considered the crisis extremely serious and was regarded as a prophet of doom. The mere mention of his name elicited a contemptuous reaction. Mr Sproul, the deputy governor of the F.R. Bank, who took Fritz under his wing, begged him: 'All right if he is a stimulating teacher, but for Christ's sake don't let him convince you of his ideas.' Mr Sproul did what he could to ensure that Fritz was in complete possession of all the facts against Parker Willis's idea, and Fritz, sufficiently confident to judge for himself, kept quiet and revelled in the battle for his intellectual assent. It was the ideal learning situation from which he could only benefit, although, as far as he could see, those whom he thought really knew what they were talking about were not amongst Parker Willis's enemies.

While backing Wall Street's prophet of doom, Fritz also shared Parker Willis's diagnosis of the American economic crisis. He was thoroughly pessimistic about Roosevelt's 'New Deal', a view very much out of step with many other Americans in academic life, government and industry who viewed Roosevelt's policies optimistically and with excitement. In March 1933 Fritz feared that Roosevelt's economic policy would cause inflation of German proportions; the only difference between Roosevelt and Hoover was that Roosevelt had a more positive approach but

> everyone knows that there is virtually no difference between the economic programme of the Republicans and the Democrats ... The Northerners say: he [Roosevelt] is the greatest president since Lincoln; the Southerners say he is the greatest president since Jefferson, and the economists say he is the greatest president since Hoover ...

As the crisis deepened, banks closed and the government gave increasingly huge loans through the Bank of Reconstruction and Development. Fritz saw bribery and corruption to an extent unheard of in Europe. After reading about one particular scandal where a prominent senator of Louisiana had managed to poll a total of 3,000 votes in an area with a population of just under 2,000 Fritz could only sadly conclude: 'One sees a great deal here, but only a very small part seems worth copying.' He could not help comparing the economic problems with those he had experienced in England and Germany. He wrote home: 'My experience of the crisis in England and Germany has come in very useful. But the chaotic situation here did not occur in either of these two countries.'

His own life reflected the extremes of living produced by the chaos. A depreciation of sterling (in which his scholarship was paid) against the dollar had reduced his income by almost a third. He had to take drastic economy measures. For some time he lived in digs where the squalor was such that he was able to negotiate a reduction in his weekly rent based on the number of bed bugs he had caught. He spent as little as possible on food, living almost exclusively on grapenuts and pigs' brains which he would eat late at night after he had finished his work. Not surprisingly he was unable to withstand the rigours of the New York winter and succumbed to a severe bout of influenza which he got over only through the kindness of a friend who took him into his own flat and nursed him.

Yet throughout this period of poverty Fritz was conducting a social life of breathtaking pace in prominent and wealthy circles. He had come to New York armed with letters of introduction from his father to former colleagues who received Fritz warmly. The disadvantage was that his father wanted reports of all these friends and Fritz found it hard to find time to look them all up as well as meeting the demands of his own contacts in the banking world and the Rhodes Scholarship circle. Within the first few weeks of arriving in New York he managed to dine with Mrs Rockefeller, be taken by the vice-president of the Chase National Bank, Mr Shephard Morgan, to hear Leopold Stokowski conduct *Tristan and Isolde* (to which Fritz commented that 'Wagner would have turned in his grave') and get himself invited to the country for the weekend by President Aydelotte of the Rhodes Foundation. From then on it was a string of parties, dinners, concerts and weekend invitations. Fritz was in constant demand. In January 1933 he wrote home ruefully: 'If one is not extremely impolite one gets socially harassed to death. Tonight I was very strict in that I refused a dinner invitation to the Woodbridges, an invitation to a ball, a dinner invitation to the Burns's, another very enticing invitation to a dance and an after-dinner invitation to some friends. So I shall stay at home.'

He wrote very little to his parents about the girls he met. They too compared favourably with the girls he had met in Oxford. Many of the invitations were from affectionate match-making mothers who adored the handsome German who charmed and amused them. Of the many girls Fritz met, two stood out: Virginia and Joan. For Joan, a fellow student, he risked his neck climbing up to her room at night. They remained in contact long after both had settled down to marriage. Virginia lived on in his memory well into middle age, until he named his second daughter after her. His eyes always lit up with a twinkle when he mentioned her name, leaving his family to imagine what they had been up to. Fritz was glad that his social life took him away from student life. He found it no more attractive in America than he had in Oxford. Nor was he prepared for the multi-racial aspect of American student life he found when he first lived at the universities' International House. He wrote home: 'For my taste there are rather too many coloured people, but that is very bad and, for God's sake, I am not allowed to say that here (that brotherhood may prevail) ... there are all sorts of different types of people here whom you mainly get to know under the shower in their original state of nakedness.'

In view of his aversion to students it was fortunate that Fritz did not remain among their ranks for long. In April 1933, barely seven months after he had arrived in New York, Parker Willis made him a surprising offer: would Fritz consider giving a course of lectures and seminars the following autumn term? Fritz was both amused and flattered by this unexpected suggestion. To be invited to take a place on the academic staff of a prestigious institution like Columbia University without even having a degree appealed to his sense of humour. But it was also a welcome gesture of recognition for Fritz had been feeling low in health and spirits ever since his bout of flu earlier in the year. He had been very depressed by the lack of news since Hitler had come to power in January 1933. American newspapers were more concerned with America's internal economic problems than events in Germany and only gave ill-informed snippets of news which Fritz did not want to believe but which worried him so much that he could not work. Parker Willis's offer gave him new zest. Within one week he had advanced his thesis by thirty pages. But the German situation still preoccupied him and he wondered whether he should return home at the end of the academic year. For once his father came up with advice which he warmly welcomed. Professor Schumacher had been overwhelmed by Parker Willis's offer to his son and in May wrote Fritz a rare letter of unqualified praise:

Your last letter gave us huge surprise, which filled us equally with pride and joy. I congratulate you on your great distinction. Even in Germany it would have been difficult if not impossible for you to achieve the post of assistant lecturer at your young age. That you have achieved it in a foreign country, particularly as the post of assistant includes even wider duties than is the case here, is a great achievement.

Professor Schumacher added that it was a relief to him that both his grown-up sons were out of Berlin during this period of political uncertainty and that Fritz would be well advised to accept Parker Willis's offer without any feeling of obligation towards Germany.

With these doubts removed Fritz accepted the offer and prepared himself for another year's stay in New York. Ahead of him was the long summer vacation and rather than accept one of the holiday jobs that had been offered him he decided to celebrate his transition from student to semi-academic by an ambitious trip across the United States. It was a risky venture for someone not of the strongest build, with an aversion to students. He was to travel with three other students, two of whom he did not know at all, in two old Fords, and only one tent.

Ulli Solmssen, Heinz Lessing and Werner Brückmann soon discovered that Fritz's idea of a holiday was not quite the same as most. He was unable to relax and did not attempt to put aside the work that had been occupying his mind for the past months. Not only did he talk about it to the others, but he also insisted on visiting every conceivable factory, industrial concern, mine and bank until he felt that he had genuinely gained an impression of the diversity and complexity of American life to qualify him for his new role as teacher at Columbia University. His companions generally found these excursions interesting but they were less taken with Fritz's air of assumed superiority. He made sure that they were aware that he, the youngest of the group, had also reached the highest distinction by his appointment at Columbia University.

The trip, lasting fifty days, was remarkably harmonious although there were moments of tension. Werner Brückmann kept an extensive diary of the trip and Fritz later had to read how his sharp tongue sometimes stung his friends who grew to dread the evenings around the camp fire if Fritz was in a mood to show off. Brückmann saw it as a power struggle for leadership:

Fritz remained the victor in that our scale of values were subordinated to his either in so far as we were naturally able to agree with the demands of his values or by an effort demanded by our travels. This was possible because Fritz had the strongest conviction of the validity of his values and because his demands were in fact those of the day . . . Now what were Fritz's scale of values? They were Western, modern, of world and life-affirmation – but after all, we all agreed with world-and-life affirmation. But he represented the extreme of this world view, he rejected every kind of reflection, basically his nature was not contemplative. His scale of values was based on speed and efficiency, and Fritz not only possessed both but was also unlovable, a quality which he regarded highly. He presumably considered the sharp wits which he possessed to be the highest of intellectual qualities. He was the youngest of us ... and the most successful ... From time to time he made suggestions about the problems of life, about the really serious questions; and he usually did this when things were moving a little slowly for him, when nothing much seemed to be happening. Activity was his religion; on the whole he regarded the trip, at least in part, as a waste of time ... His intellect did not find enough nourishment on the way so he occupied it by making fun of us in the evenings, which got on our nerves more and more. For those who could not master this technique, and none of the rest of us could, it was as good as impossible to defend ourselves ... Actually he didn't really intend harm. One could see this when one was alone with him. Then he was the most pleasant and companionable person. He only became sarcastic when he had an audience, and one need hardly say that he needed one. Perhaps he really was the best man of us all, but he had to show us every evening that he was the best, the cleverest and most amusing. His jokes were biting, but hilarious ... He, who was the most dangerous, sharpest and least merciful critic was also, if it came to it, the most loyal and best friend.[1]

The journey from New York to California took Fritz through every state except Florida. The four young men met in Chicago on June 9th, 1933 at the World's Fair (its theme was 'A Century of Progress': Fritz called it 'A Century of Madness'), and finally they reached the Pacific Ocean on July 29th. A short step further through the Californian Redwoods brought them to Berkeley, the end of their journey. They had travelled 10,000 miles in fifty days. Fritz summed up the trip for his parents:

We saw how big America is, we experienced the variety of nature and tasted the charm of a new, unfamiliar way of life. We were so involved that we often failed to notice the most impossible situations in which we found ourselves. But we hope to return better people. We discovered what it means when only 500,000 live in the rich state of Montana which is as big as Germany; when there are still areas where, if they bother to make the effort, people can obtain land from the government free of charge – fruitful land, and animals and equipment thrown in.

But Fritz was glad that it was all over and that he could return to work. While his friends continued their holiday in California he took up with his older and dearer friends, Keynes, Schumpeter, Robertson and Beckhart, whose books, treaties and articles awaited him at Berkeley, until he was able to find a new travelling companion for the journey back east. Then he bought Werner Brückmann's Ford and drove flat out, non-stop back to New York.

In New York Fritz had a new status. He was no longer a Rhodes Scholar in receipt of funds to finance his thesis but an inadequately paid part-timer. He was faced with the prospect of earning a supplementary living with very little time in which to do it. With time at a premium it was clear to him that an additional job had to do more than enlarge his income; it had to complement his academic work.

This was more difficult to arrange than he expected, both because of his lack of formal qualifications and because the serious banking crisis was forcing unemployment on to the banking world, where he wished to work. He turned to his contacts, pulling what strings he could until eventually he was offered not one job but two. Fortunately the second offer was one he could postpone, ensuring that he had work until well into the new year.

His first job was to prepare a series of briefing papers for Congress on various aspects of the New York stock market. It was an enormous task to be completed in only six weeks under the supervision of two professors living several hundred miles away in opposite directions. Fritz plunged into the new project, blossoming under the pressure and the stimulation of a new subject. The inaccessibility of his supervisors did not bother him at all. He was quite confident on his own, making this clear by pointing out a series of errors in one of the professor's calculations. They had little alternative but to let him get on with it.

The job of lecturer at the School of Banking at Columbia University was another milestone in Fritz's own education. After his first lecture, when some of his students had joined him for coffee, he learnt that he had failed completely in getting the ideas of Keynes, which were so clear to him, across to them. He began again over coffee and felt later that his real teaching had taken place then. Thereafter it became a regular feature of his course to meet informally afterwards, but he took greater care to make simplicity and clarity one of the hallmarks of his lectures.

Part of the clarity of Fritz's own understanding was due to the visual element in his mind. For example, he saw numbers in a specific pattern curving out into space and it was with astonishment that he learnt much later that his was not everyone's experience. His visual image was so clear that he could literally read off the answers to mathematical problems as on a graph in his mind. His mental picture of economics was similarly clear. There was a precise moment when, sitting in the library at Columbia University, all the pieces of information dropped into place and he suddenly realized that economics was simple, and, as he liked to express it, could be written on the back of an envelope. He made little use of calculators once they became available, relying always on his slide rule which he kept in his breast pocket.

Unexpectedly, he also had some teaching duties in his second supplementary job which he began in the new year as rotator at the Chase Bank. He worked through the bank's departments much in the same way as he had done at M.M. Warburg's two years earlier, using the opportunity to learn as much as he could about American banking. Then one morning he was sought out by a member of the personnel department. The bank was running a special training course for young employees and their lecturer had suddenly been taken ill. Could Fritz step in?

'Gladly,' Fritz replied.

'Could you talk about the German Banking system?' he was asked.

'Well, of course,' Fritz said, 'but it's a difficult subject. At what time?' It was then 10.15 a.m.

'At 11.00' came the answer.

By the time he had gathered his wits, Fritz had only twenty minutes left to put together the framework of a talk. He was very pleased with the result. Not only did he feel that his lecture and the discussion that followed had been a success, but he had discovered that his English was good enough to enable him to speak more or less off the cuff for a good one and a quarter hours. Modestly, for once, he wrote home that it must have been the fact that English lent itself so much better than German to public speaking.

Although necessity had forced Fritz to combine his theoretical work with a practical job in his second year in New York, his practical experience had an unexpected effect on his thinking. He came to believe that economics could in fact only progress through a rigorous application of pure theory. He thought the School of Banking lacked the courage and energy to do this and was determined not to make the same mistake himself. In early 1934 Parker Willis asked him to contribute a chapter to a book he was compiling with his banking seminar students on inflation. It turned out to be the most theoretical piece of work Fritz ever produced, so much so that Fritz was worried that Parker Willis would find it unacceptable. He admitted that his dry work might be 'complicated to the point of unintelligibility to the untrained' but did not think that this should constitute an argument against it because all his conclusions were based on his observation of reality. There is little in this work of the man who was later to declare that 'an ounce of practice is worth a ton of theory'. Nor does the summary of his approach to economics which appears in one of the drafts of this paper give any indication of how his thinking was to develop:

The dismal science of Economics has driven many a good man into despair. At times people have thrown up their hands and declared that there is no mind great enough to understand its complexities; they have given up pure theory and have taken to collecting facts – data – statistics . . .

The empirical approach has broken down – not because it could not collect a sufficient number of facts, but because facts have to be interpreted and understood – and in their effort to interpret our economists have allowed themselves to be guided by theories they themselves were not fully conscious of, and some of these theories turned out to be fallacious ...

But today, it seems, that economists realize that it is better to go about our measurements with a theoretical background which we have worked out logically and consistently, rather than be guided by unconscious theories.

Just as the engineer who was called upon to design the Washington Bridge, did not have to decide whether the bridge would be desirable on economic grounds, or whether it was good to establish another connection between New York and New Jersey, or whether it was at all proper to spoil the beauty of nature with a construction of that kind (which does not mean that all these considerations would not have to be taken into account) – in the same way the economist should not be bothered with politics and psychology or such hybrid and pseudo-science as sociology – which of course does not mean that there are not other considerations to be made than economic ones.[2]

5

Hitler

Bei allen Schmerzen
Bereit zu Scherzen (E.F.S.)
[Be prepared to joke at every pain]

While in America Fritz felt happier than ever before in his life. His feeling of 'walking on air' in New York was not just a physical feeling of well-being given by the air he breathed for he soon tired of skyscrapers and longed for trees and expanses of sky. But in New York he felt free: free intellectually and free from the weight of Europe. There was no doubt about his own Europeanness, about his Germanness, but he was far away from the preoccupations that had cast a shadow over much of his student life: the problem of Germany.

Much of Fritz's negative reaction while a student in England, had been connected with events in Germany and the reactions he encountered in England; amongst students, the British press and British politicians. Without the intellectual stimulation to keep up his spirits he had been unable to resist the emotional drain of the fact of his Germanness. 'England', he wrote in 1933 to the Warden of New College, G. K. Allen, 'was of incalculable value to me because – besides acquainting me with England – it helped me to understand Germany.'

England made him into a patriotic German, gave him 'that sound basis of that very feeling we call patriotism. We cannot live without that feeling! It is – born of gratitude – an active acknowledgement of that debt we owe our Fatherland ... We

54

must never forget the soil upon which we have grown, and the organism of which we are part.'[1]

It was a feeling that had its increasingly painful side. Germany, as Fritz saw it, was being maligned, misunderstood and attacked, and he in his role as ambassador and executor of Cecil Rhodes's ideals of peace and understanding between nations, had spent much time and energy in its defence. He was not blind to the dangers inherent in National Socialism and its principal exponent, Hitler, but he could understand and tried to explain why political life in Germany could find room for such extremism. This was before January 1933.

By the autumn of 1932 Fritz was in America, far from the turmoil of European politics. The United States was having its own problems and was in one of its isolationist and inward turning phases. Fritz, as an economist, mixing with economists and bankers, was as informed and involved as any foreign student could be about the American economic crisis which he and his colleagues discussed and analysed. For a time the dark cloud on the horizon of Europe receded, and Fritz, stimulated and fully engaged on his work, was happy.

But it was only a temporary respite. The very isolationism of America had its negative aspect. The U.S. press, concerned with its own problems, provided only tantalizing snippets of German news. This irritated Fritz. He did not want to lose touch with affairs in Europe and believed that the columns devoted to Germany in American newspapers were not factual accounts but what he called 'English propaganda'. He was back in his role as defender of the German people. 'There is a fundamental lack of understanding here for European problems', he wrote to his father, hoping for consolation from home. But his parents' letters were not more helpful. Although living in the heart of the political arena, in Berlin, Professor Schumacher no longer had access to politicians as when he was advising the government before and during the First World War, and he was as confused as the next man. In the winter of 1932 he had replied to Fritz's plea for facts, 'The situation is extraordinarily difficult in every way and no real insight is possible although if one examines the circumstances calmly and more closely there appear to be dubious developments. I hope that the National Socialists and the Centre Party succeed in being included in the Cabinet. They would balance each other and then we could at least halt this radicalization of our people.'

The Professor's letters did not become more informative. On January 7th, 1933, three weeks before Hitler became Chancellor, Professor Schumacher was reassuring Fritz, 'Thank goodness quiet has entered politics here. This is undoubtedly also having a beneficial effect on the economy. Only it is progressing much more slowly than most people hoped or wished. I hope that the clever and sensible man to whom Germany's fate is now entrusted will succeed in holding on to this new path with a strong grip. It won't be easy.' In view of the speed of developments in German politics, Fritz cannot have had much confidence in his father as a source of accurate political reporting. However, it must be said in Professor Schumacher's defence that he was not alone in his lack of political foresight.

As late as January 15th the Chancellor of Germany himself was similarly falsely optimistic in a conversation with the Austrian Minister of Justice. The Minister reported, 'General von Schleicher showed himself to be exceptionally optimistic with regard to the state of affairs in the Reich ... particularly as regards its economic and political prospects ... Herr Hitler was no longer a problem, his movement had ceased to be a political danger, and the whole problem had been solved, it was a thing of the past.'[2] Most informed opinion in Berlin was not so blind. It was widely known that Hitler and Von Papen had had a secret meeting on January 4th and that deals were being made.

A week later these rumours had reached the Schumacher household and Professor Schumacher was sufficiently worried to repeat the warnings he had given Fritz over the past few years not to stick his neck out and take sides. In the tense atmosphere in Germany he knew that those who backed what turned out to be the wrong side would be marked men. The Professor was glad that both his elder sons were away from Berlin and the political upheavals. But such warnings were not what Fritz wanted. He wanted information and his father's letters were as infuriatingly vague as the press. Fritz wanted to know what was going on in Germany and what the actors in the drama were really like. Hitler's accession to power was the first piece of solid information he had received. But what did it mean? Fritz cried out desperately to his parents for proper information and reassurance:

> For Heaven's sake, what is going on in Germany? ... we are all in a state of tension here, even the professed Nazis ... According to the press reports here, which incidently have a calm and factual tone, Germany has finally and completely succumbed to barbarity. Practices are being described which one only expects from countries like Rumania and Cuba. But I will not believe these press fellows on principle.

As rumours and counter-rumours flew around Fritz was greatly in demand for speaking engagements. He was well respected and his opinion, as a German, valued. But he now began to avoid public discussion. What could he say? He knew no more than anyone else. His one aim was to keep the peace and try to be positive, try and keep alive the hope that the new leadership had something worthwhile to contribute to the solution of Germany's grave economic and political problems. He consented to speak at the Society for the Friends of the New Germany explaining the Nazis' economic policy. But this was an exception for which the generous fee may have been partly responsible. He was distressed at how the German people were making a spectacle of themselves with their flag-waving hysterical response to Hitler's demagogy. This type of political agitation was, he saw, rapidly ruining Germany's standing in the world.

While warning Fritz to keep a low profile because Nazi blacklists were being drawn up, Professor Schumacher tried to bolster Fritz's attempt at optimism. He too wanted to believe in the good of the Nazi movement and in March 1933 was still trying to convince Fritz that the excesses of the new régime were because 'we are in the middle of a new revolution, one must not conceal this from oneself. But there is consolation in this. The revolution must end soon and only then is the way clear for sensible and constructive activity.' This reply is illuminating and typical of many non-Nazis who did not at first recognize that there was no positive side to the revolution. They clung on to the hope that eventually Hitler would control the undesirable forces and bring about a new Germany.

Professor Schumacher admitted that it was hard for the positive qualities of the National Socialists to come to the fore. The men at the top were of poor quality and the speed at which things were happening left everyone confused. Fritz was not convinced. It was becoming increasingly difficult to ignore the evidence. Within a month the opposition to Hitler was being crushed. What was Hitler playing at? he asked his parents. 'Yesterday's news about the banning of the Centre Party by the Nazis once again makes one's hair stand on end. So now by far the majority of Germans are (supposed to be) great scoundrels and in fact, not proper Germans!'

What a bitter twist this statement had, made in irony in early 1933; two or three years later Fritz really came to believe that under Hitler it was impossible to be a proper, patriotic German. At this stage he still felt passionately and patriotically German. He found it a less and less easy role, although his conciliatory attitude saved him from suffering much socially. 'One really only discovers what patriotism is when one lives as a single German abroad,' he wrote to his parents. 'At home one only has to join in the shouting. Out here one has to swim against a tremendous tide of hostile opinions on one's own ... As a decent person one is ... treated decently; as a German ... pitied.' It was a sad statement, and he had to admit to his parents, to whom he rarely admitted negative feelings until well after the event, that worry about Germany was in fact affecting his work and ability to write.

The shocking news continued to reach Fritz. While its source was the media he was able to modify the unbelievable reports by assuming they contained an anti-German bias and sensationalism, but events such as the public book-burning were difficult to rationalize away, as was the news of prominent and well respected citizens, academics, musicians, scientists being boycotted, dismissed from their posts and forced to leave Germany merely because they were Jews. It was when the first refugees reached New York and gave reports of what was going on that Fritz realized that he was trying to defend the indefensible. It was the turning point for him. He wrote sadly of his new position to his father: 'I have talked to and visited a large number of people here and have tried to explain and appease, but there is nothing more to be done. We now no longer have right on our side.' This was March 30th, 1933.

Fritz made one last attempt to defend Germany and look for the positive qualities in Hitler's policies. It was at a large gathering in New Jersey one day in May when Hitler had given an important address in Germany which had been broadcast around the world. Fritz had listened carefully to the speech and 'for the sake of a better understanding and in order to establish a common basis for co-operation between the two countries,' agreed to explain it to his American public. He was pleased with his address. After an emphatic rejection of anti-semitism he proceeded to explain what he thought could be useful, favourable and hopeful in Hitler's programme. It was not appreciated by a group of Jews in the audience who protested loudly 'that anyone should say anything in favour of Hitler at all'. Fritz had not yet reached the stage of complete rejection because to him it would involve rejecting Germany as well. He was irritated by the heckling and finally retorted, 'I can assure you that *so far* I have not been anti-semitic.' This statement, which Fritz thought rather clever, silenced the hecklers, but when he left the hall he was confronted by a furious shouting mob and had to be escorted away by the police. The incident showed that Fritz still suffered from some prejudice: he contemptuously dismissed it as typical of the hysterical reaction of the Jews against all Germans. But it was his last public appearance on the subject of Germany.

Fritz's parents shared the same view as many other middle-class, intellectual Germans. They believed that the success of the revolution Germany was experiencing was dependent on the involvement and commitment of Germany's youth. They did not reject the concept of a Führer, rather they welcomed a strong leadership after the weak government of the immediate post-war years. They acknowledged the excesses and negative aspects of the new régime but they did not believe that they were necessarily characteristics. They attributed them to the weak men who surrounded the Führer, but assumed that enthusiastic and committed support of the good aspects of Hitler's policies would eventually remove the weaknesses. In May 1933 Professor Schumacher summed up his views to his eldest son, Hermann, who was also experiencing difficulties in adjusting to the social aspects of the new régime:

1. One must accept historical facts. First of all one has no choice. Secondly the Fatherland demands that we.wholeheartedly support the good forces that are at work and that are, to a certain extent, personified in Hitler. If we do not succeed in obtaining a positive national renewal there will be nothing left but chaos.

2. Nothing is regarded as worse by those currently in power than standing on the sidelines and *Eigenbrödelei* (introspection, concern with self). They rate comradeship much higher than friendship, and there is undoubtedly something in this from the State's point of view.

A copy of this letter was also sent to Fritz. He was emphatic in his rejection and told his father that nothing would induce him to join any political organization, Youth Group or branch of the S.A.

Professor Schumacher, sixty-five years old, out of the mainstream of public life and, in 1933, retiring from teaching at the university, was bound to have a different view of things from Fritz whose decisions at the age of twenty-two could have a profound effect on the rest of his life. Fritz recognized this and tried to explain it to his parents who were worried by his constant anxiety about German affairs. 'Forgive me if I write to you about these matters, but they happen to take up a great deal of my thoughts and feelings. And, after all, they are of vital importance for later life.'

Professor Schumacher, although anxious himself, could only repeat his hope: wait and things will get better. He belonged to a generation brought up to accept authority. Hitler's party had not assumed power illegally, and the Professor believed that a legal government's authority had to be accepted. Dogmatic and autocratic himself, he did not expect his opinions to be accepted only by those who happened to like them. Preference had nothing to do with authority. He clearly did not like everything about the new government and spoke out critically on several occasions; to his students and to his rotary club. He refused to sign a protest against Lord Halifax, the Chancellor of Oxford University who had made a critical speech on a visit to Berlin. But he soon came to the conclusion that the Nazi régime was a storm that had to be weathered, that criticism however slight would only have unpleasant repercussions on his family and that the best thing he could do for his children was to encourage them to take a positive and active part in the New Germany. Ernst, like many other young Germans, became an active member of a Youth Group. Marching, uniforms and patriotism became an integral part of his life. Hitler had given youth an opportunity to flower again. The family never dreamt that it would have to pay a severe price for this compromise.

Fritz consistently refused to have anything to do with Hitler Youth groups, or the S.A. Just two months before he was due home Professor Schumacher wrote to him again that it was imperative for him to join the S.A. He had even gone to the trouble of selecting a group he thought Fritz would find congenial. Fritz was still trying to keep his mind as open as possible about Germany and still intended to return home to complete his studies, but such exhortations increased his apprehension. So did the ever-growing Jewish community in New York swelled by German refugees of all kinds each with an appalling tale to tell. Then came a letter from his erstwhile travelling companion, Ulli Solmssen, who had returned to Germany in the autumn of 1933 to complete his studies. The letter was from Switzerland. Ulli wrote that it was no longer possible to study in Germany without compromising oneself with the régime.

The news made Fritz's decision to return home all the more difficult. America had proved to be a land of opportunity. He knew that if he stayed he was likely to have a successful academic career before him; he had already achieved more than most by his lecturing appointment and Parker Willis had assured him that there would always be a place for him at Columbia University. He knew too that he could live reasonably happily in America despite the tension over Germany; he had learnt to live by tact and diplomacy and prided himself on managing to keep on good terms with most of the German community. There was no reason why a long vacation should not suffice to satisfy his desire to find out for himself about the changes that had occurred in Germany during the five years of his absence and to see his family again. He was particularly curious to see his little brother Ernst, whom he had last known as a child and who was now almost a teenager and an active and enthusiastic member of a Nazi Youth group.

Yet he decided to turn his back on his future and return to Germany. At that point he put his career to one side in order to find out for himself what the truth about Germany really was. He was too much a German to accept the condemnation of his country from the mouths of others. The cause of Germany had been close to him for five years and he could not abandon it without trying to live there first and seeing for himself whether it was too late for change. It was with a heavy heart that Fritz left New York on April 1st, 1934. His voyage home was as symbolic as the voyage to America had been two years earlier. For a start, it was April Fools' Day! And then he fell ill with rheumatic fever and spent most of the journey below deck in his cabin, full of self-pity. He was returning to a sick society where many of the ill deeds were below deck, hidden from public view. His depression and the debilitating effect of his illness stayed with him for many months after his return to Germany. He found it was very hard to adjust to the changed circumstances in which he found himself and it was not until the autumn that his health began to pick up.

Depressed in health and spirits, Fritz was not tempted to be more positive about the situation he found in Germany than the facts warranted. When he had left Germany it had been a free country despite the ailing, weak governments of the Weimar Republic. Now he saw that the rumours and reports he had been loath to believe while abroad had not only been true; they had been followed by far worse. He only had to look at his father, who five years earlier had been a pillar of the community and well respected by all his students. Now he was retired and glad to be so. Teaching had become an intolerable and at times humiliating experience. The Professor told Fritz of how he had been heckled by students he believed had been planted in his lectures because he did not hold political views acceptable to the régime. He told Fritz how it was no longer possible to advance an academic career without supporting the

Nazi line; appointments and promotions were dependent on it. But it did not make the Professor urge Fritz to look elsewhere for a career. On the contrary, he again urged Fritz to join an appropriate Nazi society; his future depended on it.

Fritz found his father's line unacceptable. He could not consider such a course of action because he saw the issue as far bigger than one of freedom of choice or the opportunity to further a career. It was not that the Nazis said, 'We don't like you so you can't have a job,' to which he objected, but that they said, 'We don't like you therefore everything you say, whatever its merits, is automatically wrong and untrue.' It was interference in the pursuit of truth that Fritz found intolerable, evil and not to be countenanced. Yet the truth of the matter, as far as he could see, was that the academics did countenance it. There was no wholesale uproar when men like Einstein were hounded out of the country and their works declared untrue and banned. On the contrary, in the case of Einstein, for example, only a few like Werner Heisenberg, Nobel prize-winning physicist and soon to marry Fritz's sister Elisabeth, had the courage to defend him and uphold the truth of his theories. It was a courageous act which cost Heisenberg his job at the time and prompted vicious personal attacks on him in scientific publications. But Fritz seemed to disregard the fact that heroism was needed for such acts. In his view, eminent scientists, economists, philosophers, writers and musicians who allowed their colleagues' work to be attacked and reviled on political and racial grounds without protest, without upholding intellectual honesty and scientific truth, were not doing their duty and were not worthy of the privilege of intellectual learning and the pursuit of truth. He believed purity, courage and honesty were essential and indispensable qualifications for such a privilege. In failing to live up to these qualities academics and intellectuals in Germany laid themselves open to the responsibility of the catastrophe that had befallen their country. Why the intelligentsia of Germany should have failed in their vocation in this way was a question which Fritz did not attempt to answer until much later when he saw the meaning of 'truth' in a wider context than the scientific facts which at that time he held to be the cornerstone of progress. But his analysis remained the same. It was the abandonment of truth that lay at the centre of his opposition to the Nazi régime and its effect on German life. All the other evils of the régime stemmed from this root.

He did not have to look far for the evils that had already sprung up and were growing rapidly. His father told him of the street violence that had accompanied Hitler's assumption of power; the clashes between the Nazis and the Communists: two vicious and extreme parties fighting over the dying body of the Weimar Republic. Professor Schumacher himself had narrowly escaped injury as stray bullets had once come through his study windows at the university. He had not realized that Hitler then occupied the room above his own.

By the time Fritz had returned to Germany, the Communists had been banned along with other political opposition and the Nazis held absolute power. But the violence continued, not as a result of fighting between warring factions, but instigated by the Nazis themselves. In the final weekend of June 1934 any last lingering doubts were finally removed as Fritz decided to visit his brother Hermann who was studying in Göttingen. When he knocked at the door of Hermann's lodgings, the landlady appeared terrified as she opened the door. No, she had no knowledge of a Hermann Schumacher, she insisted, never heard of him. Fritz persisted. 'He is my brother,' he assured her. Only then did she let him in, explaining that one couldn't be too careful, she had been afraid that Fritz might have been the Nazi police. It shook Fritz to experience the extent to which the population had been affected by fear but it was nothing to the horror he felt when he learnt that that weekend there had indeed been reason for such fear. The S.A. had been purged. It had been carried out in the style that was to become so familiar: the knock on the door at night, disappearance, execution.

There were some well-known names among the victims who lost their lives that weekend: General von Schleicher and General von Bredow among them. But there were also numerous others, many with no connections with the S.A. but who just happened to have fallen foul of the régime, others who happened to be Jews. After the weekend's raids and executions there was uncertainty and apprehension everywhere but the government made no attempt at a statement or explanation.

Rumours abounded, horror expressed only in fearful whispers. Fritz wrote to his friend Franz Curtius with whom he had shared a flat in America, expressing his disgust and concern. He had shared a great deal with Franz and was very fond of him. Franz's reply was unexpected and shocking. He wrote that although he was not happy about the events of the weekend in question, he was far more concerned that the government had failed to give adequate information about who had been shot. A few weeks later, early in August, he wrote again to Fritz, asking him if he was 'still listening to sensationalism and spreading rumours whose truth was really questionable'. Unfortunately there is no copy of Fritz's letter and his so-called unsubstantiated rumours. Nor is the truth of what really happened that weekend in June known to this day - except that over a hundred people lost their lives by summary execution.

In the months that followed the chief questions that Fritz had to answer were: in what direction should his career, which he still assumed would take some academic form, progress, and how far would it be possible to continue in academic life within the confines that political life in Germany now presented? The question underlying everything was: could one lead a moral life within an immoral system without compromise?

It seemed that most people believed that they could. Fritz saw that men like his father, men in eminent positions at the university, in government administration and in the professions in general, with whom he tried to discuss the evil nature of the régime, and who he felt had a responsibility to speak out, demurred, calling him a hothead or dismissing him with that wave of the hand that expressed the amused tolerance of an older generation to the indignant outpourings of angry young men. They clung to the belief that the excesses of National Socialism would pass, that they were a necessary evil to be tolerated while the good in the movement gained strength. Time and again Fritz heard the phrase: 'Where there is planing there must be shavings'. Fritz rejected this justification completely. There was no beautiful carving emerging from the wood of National Socialism but an obscene and evil monstrosity. Each time, he was shocked and saddened to see that men deserving of respect should be so utterly lacking in the courage to see things as they really were, to recognize the intrinsic philosophical evil which the rejection of truth meant.

In a lighter-hearted vein he once commented at a party that the impact of the régime could be seen in half the faces of Berlin; almost every man in the street wore a ridiculous Hitler moustache. As an embarrassed silence fell he saw, too late, that even in that room full of respectable, liberal-thinking Germans, Hitler's mark was to be seen on the majority of the men's faces.

Living at home again with his parents in Steglitz, it was inevitable that Fritz should find politics a subject which caused tension. Fritz's father maintained that Fritz's questioning and murmuring would not do him or his family any good. The government had been legally elected and it was the duty of every patriotic German to support the good while avoiding the bad. Ernst was encouraged in his Hitler Youth activities. It seemed to the Professor that nothing but good could come out of the patriotic fervour and enthusiasm which Germany's youth now felt and which was injecting new life and hope into a despairing society. He wished only that Fritz would take a similar positive attitude.

Fritz, with his dislike of conflict and his desire to uphold the truth, found himself in a difficult and unhappy position. It was less easy to be diplomatic face to face than it had been by letter. The tension between himself and his father was not helped by his lack of a proper occupation, or even an idea of what he was going to do next. At first, after returning from America he had struggled to finish his theoretical paper on 'Inflation and the Structure of Production'. Ill health and depression slowed down his progress and it was already well into the summer before he was ready to send the work to Professor Parker Willis. To Fritz's relief it was well received and published in due course. The next step was to qualify for his B.Litt. Unfortunately his inflation paper was not suitable and by the end of the summer it became clear that he could not possibly have another thesis ready in time. The academic gates seemed to be closing. Brief inquiries soon revealed that he would have to abandon his B.Litt. altogether. Another extension to his time would not be allowed.

All the time his father was pressing him about his future. What was he intending to do? To whom was he writing? What efforts was he making to find a job? Professor Schumacher was quite prepared to take an active role in organizing Fritz's future and obtained funds from the Rockefeller Foundation for him to do a study on 'the world market for iron and steel'. Perhaps this would serve as material for a doctor's thesis in Germany? The catch in the arrangement was that Professor Schumacher was to be Fritz's supervisor. Such an arrangement was bound to fail. The tensions between father and son spanned more areas than just politics. Their different approaches to economics effectively ruled out any satisfactory co-operation.

Fritz was too independent-minded to accept his father's dogmatic guidance but he was also a different type of economist. His father had spent a lifetime in academic work. Apart from his advice during the war and the 1923 inflation, his forays into practical application were strictly limited to descriptive analysis. The 'iron and steel' project was along the lines of his fact-finding missions to the Far East about world raw materials and resources. It was not Fritz's approach. He had made that clear when he had written the words already quoted in his inflation paper: 'The dismal science of economics has driven many a good man into despair. At times people have thrown up their hands and declared that there is no mind great enough to understand its complexities; they have given up pure theory and have taken to collecting facts – data statistics.'[3] He saw this as one difference between himself and his father which accounted for their fundamental incompatibility in their common interests of economics. The 'iron and steel' paper was doomed to failure.

It is hard to imagine how Fritz would have survived those difficult months had it not been for his sister Edith, who again took up her childhood role of friend and confidante. Many evenings she listened to him in his room where he lay draped over the bed. He talked and talked, full of ideas which he needed to try out on a sympathetic soul. He tossed them at Edith relentlessly until she would cry out, confused, 'I don't understand.' But he pushed her protests aside. '*Doch, doch,*' – Yes you do, yes you do. On other occasions they would drive out in his car – 'the wild coal-scuttle', as the little black box was affectionately known. Edith found these excursions with her brother delightful. Their father was less approving. The car was yet another example of Fritz's irresponsibility.

Pondering and discussing Germany's situation, seeing how his predictions were indeed coming to pass, Fritz began to try and think more positively about Germany. As he had told his Oxford audiences, it was the people's despair that brought Hitler his followers. In 1934 there was still economic despair. The six million unemployed had not yet been absorbed by Hitler's economic miracle. Without a job and without work that really interested him, although the iron and steel paper was supposed to be his main occupation, Fritz's mind began to wrestle with the tremendously debilitating problem of unemployment. Gradually the question of how, in the face of mechanization and general economic depression, the tendency to reduce the labour force could be reversed, took him over completely. He worked with dedication and with enthusiasm so that the plan he eventually conceived earned the name 'Fritz's World Improvement Plan'. He could talk of little else and it crept even into his letters to his former girlfriends in America.

The plan was basically an incentive scheme to manufacturers to employ labour rather than machinery. Fritz proposed that all workers in the manufacturing process should be paid a guaranteed minimum wage by the government which the employer would then top up. The government wage would be paid for by a tax on turnover. In this way successful firms would pay for those companies prepared to use labour rather than machinery.

Fritz was utterly convinced of the brilliance of his scheme and charmed by its simple ingenuity. Early in 1935, while on holiday, he sent it to his father and to his uncle Fritz for their comments. Their response was shattering: that of his father cruel in its brevity. He wrote that he was surprised that Fritz should want to produce such a plan at all and dismissed its value in a few sentences, ending his letter, 'Anyway, there is no shortage of plans to fight unemployment. The Ministry of Work passed the 25,000 mark two years ago in its famous collection of plans.' It was as crushing as the first time Fritz had presented his father with his work when still a student in Berlin, and his father had not bothered to read it.

It was Uncle Fritz's criticism that persuaded Fritz to abandon the plan he had hoped would solve Germany's unemployment problems. Uncle Fritz at least treated the scheme seriously and sent Fritz a detailed critique. But the pages of notes Fritz received showed him that he had failed to put over the philosophical basis to his argument. Against this weakness, the failure of certain nuts and bolts was hardly significant. In fact, his father's and Uncle Fritz's opposition was more than a failure to understand the principles from which he was working: there were ideological differences that prevented their agreement. The elderly brothers were both liberals and they disliked the interference of the state essential to Fritz's plan. Fritz had approached the problem from a different angle. He had begun with the need and the right of men to work. As the free market had failed to cope with the problems, he had had to consider the role of the state in bringing about a solution. It was the beginning of a new direction in his political thinking, and the beginning of an approach to economics that was to occupy him for many years: how to devise a system which allowed for both freedom and control. In this 1935 plan for employment he had achieved this balance to his satisfaction by giving the manufacturers the right to choose whether or not they would take advantage of the government's minimum wage guarantee and increase their labour force, or whether they would go for machinery for which they would have to bear the entire cost. There was no force involved, merely the 'hidden hand' of encouragement. For this reason alone it is unlikely that Fritz's plan would have appealed to a régime whose method was enforcement and not encouragement. There was no free will involved in the methods by which Hitler's ministers achieved the 'economic miracle' and the full employment of the next two years and which led the German people to believe that, after years of uncertainty, their economic troubles were at last over.

Fritz did not share the optimism that Hitler's 'good years' generated because he based his critique of National Socialism not on its achievements or its evil manifestations, but on the fundamental fault he had seen when he returned to Germany in 1934, namely the abandonment of truth. This was a remarkable achievement. To quote Sebastian Haffner writing forty years later in *The Meaning of Hitler*:

> At that time ... it required quite exceptional perception and far-sightedness to recognize in Hitler's achievements and successes the hidden seeds of future disaster, and it required quite exceptional strength of character to resist the effect of those achievements and successes. His speeches, with their barking and foaming at the mouth, which nowadays cause revulsion or laughter when listened to again, were delivered at the time against a background of facts which deprived the listener of the strength to contradict, even internally.[4]

Between 1935 and 1937 the excesses of the régime seemed to fade away, there was comparatively little violence, the German people felt more secure, they were in the hands of strong leadership at last, and most remarkable of all they witnessed a spectacular economic recovery: full employment without inflation, unheard of since the war. Germany was going up in the world again, Germans could hold their heads high in Europe, they were regaining their position and even rearming without significant protests from their former enemies. It appeared that those who had predicted and hoped for the victory of the 'good' over the negative aspects that had been associated with the initial revolution of the National Socialist Party had been right after all. If there were incidents that might have cast doubt on this hope then many would murmur to themselves: 'Ah if the Führer knew about it, it would not have happened.'

Fritz found this acceptance of Hitler utterly depressing. For someone who a few years earlier had pleaded for the necessity of holding fast to patriotic feeling, the spectacle of the German people abandoning everything that they had held sacred by failing to uphold the truth was a painful if not agonizing experience. This was no longer Germany, the place of his roots, where his heart had been all these years.

At the end of March 1935, on the first anniversary of his return to Germany, he wrote sadly to the girl he was eventually to marry:

It has just occurred to me that today – now, at this moment, it is a year since I boarded the boat in New York. 'Sailing shortly after midnight on April 1st.' And what a year! If I had known what it was to be like I would have lost courage. It is good that we cannot look into the future. We would go mad one way or the other. I was right to be depressed even though I was going home. But what does it mean – home – for political beings like us? The trusted surroundings where one spent one's childhood? Yes, that is sufficient for a day but what then? Now one searches and searches and realizes that of one's homeland, which is not just a landscape, there is not much left. 'It's always best at home' and 'Ubi bene, ubi patria' – both of these: so my Fatherland is the place of my birth. But what else is there to the nationalism of our upright citizens? Yes, one does not want to be here merely for one's own benefit. The world that one does not know – humanity – is too large. There remains: one's own people. Again, rather simple and rather primitive. So today we are in fact without a home. I have been for a year now. Strange, what there is to a year. The earth has revolved once around the sun – and now we contemplate what happened when we last passed this spot. It is rather limited if one thinks about it but it happens to be an old sentiment ... We just happen to be rather poverty-stricken earth-dwellers.

6

Muschi

Not long after his return to Berlin in April 1934, Fritz was invited to a party by Ulli Solmssen and his sister Lilli. He accepted the invitation although he had resolved that he would take life more seriously in Germany than he had in America, where his social life had sometimes threatened to get out of control. Arriving at the Solmssen's party, Fritz found the house teeming with young people and as he stood watching the guests he was captivated by an attractive girl walking down the stairs, a young man on each arm. Fritz said that his heart sank when he saw her. He knew at once that all his resolutions for singleminded work would come to naught. He saw, as he later told her, that the girl was 'unique, the only woman I know to whom I can "pray", as I have known since the spring of 1934.'

Despite this instant recognition no particular friendship developed, although it is likely that he encountered the girl again in the following months, for they had more acquaintances in common than just the Solmssens. It was not until the beginning of the new year – 1935 – that he began to know her better. The girl was Anna Maria Petersen. She was to provide more than a distraction to Fritz's serious nature. She could hardly have been more different from him. She was short, reaching only to his shoulder, her blue eyes were deep and full of feeling. She was utterly unintellectual. Her warmth and spontaneity made people who knew her say that to be with her was like warming your hands on a fire. She responded to every situation with her emotions, unpredictably radiating unqualified delight or horror. Her mother, who adored her, sometimes despaired about her inability to stick to her enthusiasms for more than a second, particularly when she took up and cast aside her boyfriends. She had trained as a kindergarten teacher but, devoted as she was to children, her love of distractions and the fact that the Petersens were not short of money enabled her to take delightful interludes at her family home in Reinbek, a village outside Hamburg, as well as several trips abroad, so that her career never took off. She was undoubtedly spoilt, and loved pleasure, parties and beautiful clothes, but she was compassionate and had a serious desire to seek after more worthy things. As Fritz got to know her better he realized that she had human qualities which did not come naturally to him and which he lacked.

People responded to her because she was a lovable person, not because of her brains or her ability to amuse them. She radiated something which attracted all those who met her and which, as David Astor put it many years later, 'made you feel that you were a nice person after all'. Fritz realized that she was someone from whom he had a lot to learn.

Muschi, as Anna Maria was known to all her friends, came into Fritz's life at a moment when he most needed support and love, when, feeling that all around him the good and the worthwhile was disintegrating, he longed for someone to believe in him and his values. Not that Muschi simplified his life. Her spontaneous and unsystematic approach was totally alien to him and sometimes bewildered him. One minute she would be inviting him to join her on a skiing holiday and the next she would leave him in agony and torment because she had not written to him for a month. Although he had been brought up in a strict and conventional code of manners, Muschi forced him to abandon his natural reserve, and he found himself chastizing her for neglecting him after he had only known her better two or three months, 'Dearest best Muschi, don't be angry with me if I write like this. The normal rules of politeness are really stupid if they cause us to play hide and seek in an area which is difficult enough at the best of times to find one's way through.'

He need not have apologized. Muschi wanted him to be open and demanded that he should be so in a way that was quite new to him. She was not interested in his mind, which overawed her and made her feel inadequate, but in his person, in his inner life, in the realm of feelings which he kept hidden as much as possible. She wanted a relationship in which there was a real meeting of hearts and souls, and unless Fritz was prepared to admit her into his inner sanctum she was not interested in furthering greater intimacy. This was made quite clear to Fritz from the very beginning of their friendship. He was then very much taken up with his world improvement plan on employment and could talk of little else. 'Iron and steel' was also on his mind because it was a task he had not yet managed to complete. Muschi thought a skiing holiday much more entertaining and, urging Fritz to join her, told him to 'throw your iron and steel into your desk, keep your world improvement plans in your head – or better still out of your head – so that you can give yourself without restraint to the beauty of nature and the enjoyment of sport.'

Fritz's friendship with Muschi was interrupted from time to time by her absences in Hamburg. Their correspondence suggests that although he was drawn to her in a powerful way he did not feel able to cope with the kind of intimacy she demanded. He would retreat into the realms of the mind for which he would be severely reprimanded. Nor was he in the position to consider anything more serious or permanent without any prospects of work on the horizon. A proper occupation was still his first priority. Since he had come to realize that an academic career in Germany would not be possible he had toyed with finding academic work abroad, he had thought of taking a job in journalism and had even considered writing a book, but nothing had come to fruition.

In the autumn of 1934 the possibility had arisen to go into business with some young acquaintances, Muschi's twin brother Gustav among them, but no immediate job had materialized. Professor Schumacher's daily questions about his career plans also increased the pressure on Fritz. He had no proper answers to satisfy his father or himself. Once again his health suffered and his only consolation was that this gave him the excuse to escape from time to time on short holidays where he could at least be alone with his thoughts. By the summer of 1935 little seemed to have improved. Towards the end of July he went on holiday by the North Sea. Walking along the beach before lunch he was suddenly aware of cries for help and saw a man quite far out thrashing about in a rough sea. Without a thought Fritz went to his aid, although he was not himself a strong swimmer. The drowning man turned out to be very large and by the time Fritz reached him he was already face down in the water, but somehow Fritz managed to drag him towards the beach where help was soon on hand and the man was brought round. Fritz collapsed with exhaustion and was ill for some time with pneumonia, but his act did not go unnoticed. The man he had saved turned out to be an eminent Nazi and Fritz was thanked by the Führer himself, who awarded him Germany's highest medal for bravery. Fritz wore the medal on one occasion only. He was at a formal reception in Berlin where decorations were to be worn. As he stood with his one medal on his breast a man covered in decorations bore down upon him. He fingered Fritz's little ribbon, sneering, 'What is this little thing for?' Fritz was furious. 'My medal is for saving life,' he retorted, 'yours, presumably, are for taking it.'

After recovering from the pneumonia brought on by his act of heroism, Fritz's fortunes began to change. First he was asked by the Ministry of Justice to act as an interpreter at an international conference on prisons. It was only for a week but it turned out to be of immense importance to Fritz some five years later. He was attached to the English delegation amongst whom were Harold Scott and Alexander Paterson, both eminent men in the field of justice and penal institutions. In their week travelling around Germany together the delegates and their interpreter became firm friends and when they parted Fritz knew that he had allies in England should he ever need them.

Then at last the job with which Muschi's brother Gustav was associated and which had first appeared on the horizon in the autumn of 1934, showed signs of becoming a reality. Edith had an admirer, a young lawyer named Werner von Simson. They had met at a party in the diplomatic circles of Berlin while Fritz was still in America, and Werner had been struck at once by her extraordinary beauty and her vivacity. Edith was an artist, excited by every new experience, pressing it into the consciousness of every available listener. Her enthusiasm has never dimmed: even at the age of sixty-five she could hold forth on such subjects as the virtues of compost for five solid hours without losing her audience. In fact, in some ways she was very like her brother Fritz. Both were utterly convinced of the rightness of their own thinking and unable to comprehend any opposition. The truth to them was crystal-clear, so that they could only conclude that those who failed to see it their way must have some gap in their intellectual make-up.

At this time Werner von Simson tolerated Edith's dogmatism because it served to heighten her colour and increase her beauty. He became a frequent visitor to the Schumacher household and knew the whole family well, apart from Fritz. Werner acted as a kind of substitute big brother to Elisabeth who was still a rather awkward young lady in her teens, very prone to blushing at the slightest provocation. He made quite a sport of her embarrassment: 'Are you wearing your Sunday dress?' he would ask if she appeared in a particularly old dress, knowing that Elisabeth would colour to the roots of her hair.

Werner was working for a group calling themselves the *Syndikat zur Schaffung Zusätzlicher Ausfuhr*, which organized trading arrangements on a barter basis. This had become necessary because Germany's trade had come to a virtual standstill under the guiding hand of Hitler's economic miracle worker, Hjalmar Schacht. Schacht had made a unilateral decision to stop paying Germany's reparation payments and in so doing had also frozen foreign bank accounts held in Germany and put severe restrictions on currency movements. The penalties for illegal currency movements were very harsh, including incarceration in what were to become concentration camps. Thus without the money to pay for goods, trade was made almost impossible.

The *Syndikat zur Schaffung Zusätzlicher Ausfuhr* sought to get over this problem legally by organizing a syndicate of the major industrial firms and export houses in Germany, for whom it set up barter trading arrangements, as a means of releasing their frozen assets in Germany.[1]

Four young men ran the Syndicate, travelling around Europe and beyond arranging bilateral deals in which, for example, German coal was exchanged for Brazilian coffee,

German ships for Norwegian whale oil and German coal for Polish pork. The deals represented big money and the Syndicate earned 1 per cent of every successful transaction. In one year they had already earned enough to finance their annual overheads by the end of the first week in January.

The group interested Fritz very much. It represented an ideal opportunity to study the problems of trade from the inside. Since Oxford he had considered the disruptive effect of reparations payments on Germany's trade a major danger to peace in Europe. It was a subject that drew him more than any other.

Werner von Simson was not initially particularly impressed by Fritz. He thought him rather too full of himself and rather too theoretical. Nevertheless he took him along to the elegant offices in the Pariser Platz, overlooking the Brandenburg Gate, to introduce him to his colleagues. There Fritz met the brain behind the whole scheme, Ludwig Rosenthal, a Jew who was leaving the country because pressure was building up against him, Erwin Schüller, another founder member whose family contacts in the banking world made him a central figure, but whose Jewish background also made him think of leaving, and Gustav Petersen, Muschi's twin brother, who had joined the group via his father who owned the important import/export firm of R. Petersen and Co. The negotiations between Fritz and the *Syndikat* took almost a year before he was finally admitted into their ranks. By that time Rosenthal had left the country and Erwin Schüller was about to leave for a job in London with Lazard Brothers.

Fritz was appalled to witness the growing anti-semitic atmosphere in even the highest circles in Berlin, many of whom were Jewish. He and his friends belonged to a highly sought-after club and there came the day when he witnessed some of its members talking in undertones about the undesirables in their ranks. It became clear that they were talking about Erwin Schüller and that their objections to him were purely racial. Fritz was disgusted at this lack of loyalty to friends and walked out of the club for ever. Shortly afterwards the club announced that its doors were closed to all non-Aryans.

Fritz finally joined the Pariser Platz office in August 1935, with another new recruit, Rüdiger von der Goltz. Fritz was very enthusiastic about his work. He knew that he could learn a

great deal and the busy travelling schedules of the members
meant that he was often left alone in the office. He rejoiced at
the opportunity that this gave him: 'It is marvellous what this
teaches me,' he wrote to his mother, 'I just happen to be lucky
to be able to work completely independently.' He also enjoyed
the opportunities he had to travel, mainly to Eastern Europe
where he successfully concluded the deal to exchange German
coal for Polish pork.

Getting to know Muschi Petersen the Christmas before joining the Syndicate had given Fritz another route into the group
whose business partnership was firmly cemented by strong
friendship. Muschi and Gustav shared a flat in Berlin. Erwin
Schüller had been a long-standing friend of the Petersen family
and a very close friend of Muschie and Gustav's; Werner von
Simson, knew her family well too and was a particular
favourite of Muschi's mother. Rüdiger von der Goltz was marrying into a Hamburg family and Muschi's father, Rudolf
Petersen, owned one of the key firms in the group, R. Petersen
and Company. The group could hardly have been more inti-
mately knit together. They shared many leisure activities, fre-
quented the same parties and spent a considerable amount of
time in each other's company. Fritz soon found himself part
of the team. When Rüdiger von der Goltz got married in Hamburg, Fritz made one of the speeches and took a major part in
writing the script of the entertainment. The office seemed to
run the whole show: 'As Simson played the organ and Schüller,
of course, organized everything, it became apparent to everyone that an unusual amount of teamwork exists in the Syndicate,' he told his mother. It was a recipe for life-long friendship.

The success of the Syndicate and consequent financial benefits it bestowed on Fritz gave him new freedom. Not only was
he earning at last but he was making more money than he was
to make ever again while in employment. He could now think
seriously about his relationship with Muschi. They made an
attractive couple, elegant on the dance floor and off it, both
well dressed, particularly since Muschi made sure that Fritz's
clothes were of the same high quality as her own. Muschi
enjoyed life and Fritz's sense of humour added to their fun and
popularity. But Muschi loved his seriousness too and spent
hours listening to him, although his constant intellectual tur-

moil took her into realms of thought far beyond her ability to follow or understand.

He thought about the problems of the world in a way that was quite unfamiliar to her. He was irreligious, mocking conventional beliefs, yet he was extraordinarily moral and concerned about the ethical collapse which he saw in German society. His mind, never at rest, probed and theorized, developed plans which put the world to rights at a breathtaking rate. Muschi listened as best she could, understood that he was brilliant, that she was not, and came, in a way, to worship him.

Muschi's impact on Fritz was at first total confusion. Her spontaneous and warm nature was very different from the more formal relationships of his own family, who although devoted to each other, retained a degree of reserve. They were all intellectuals who made contact through the medium of ideas and Fritz was perhaps the most extreme user of this means of communication. Muschi's family lived very differently. On both sides her ancestors came from old patriarchal families of Hamburg. Her father's family had been traders and businessmen, as he now was. They were solid, unintellectual people whose informal lifestyle and friendliness made their Reinbek home a haven for all who came. Muschi's mother was never more happy than when the house was teeming with young people. She had had eight children, six sons and two daughters, of whom Muschi was the elder, and all their friends were welcomed with open arms at all times. Fritz's sister Edith once described her as 'beautiful and radiant like the Queen Mother. One is submerged in the warmth of her look.' When Fritz first went to Reinbek he could not fail to be overwhelmed by the warmth of his reception. But he did not feel entirely at ease. He could not identify with the Petersens' unintellectual approach to life, and their emotional responses. At first he was bewildered. On Christmas Day 1935 he wrote: 'Dearest, best little Muschi, you have always given nobly, and I cannot do more than sometimes tell a few stories – about the office, always about the office. It is only occasionally a holiday with me, as it is when I am with you, but even then work breaks in somewhere ...' but a few weeks later he had more insight: 'To be separated from you is really hard for me. It seems extraordinary to me but there it is. I could absorb myself in my work, with my friends and heaven knows what. But somehow I am not complete.'

He sensed that with Muschi's qualities to complement his own, his personality would benefit: 'For me you are like a saint, that will make me into a better person. I believe in that.'

In the May of 1936 Fritz finally took the plunge and asked Muschi to marry him. They were walking arm in arm down the wide avenue which led from the Brandenburg Gate into what is now East Berlin. It is called Unter den Linden. Fritz was, as usual, talking earnestly about some plan or other, some theory with which his mind was grappling. Muschi's concentration began to wander until she became aware that he was looking at her expectantly. She was at a loss for words, not having listened to the drift of his conversation, and Fritz had to repeat, 'Will you marry me?'

They kept their engagement a secret because Muschi had already planned to visit England for three months that summer. Life seemed to lose its point for Fritz when she left at the end of May and her irregular letters compounded his agony, especially as she was obviously enjoying herself. He wrote almost daily, cursing England for removing her from him, until at last she returned, early, at the beginning of August, when their engagement was officially announced.

The announcement produced an avalanche of congratulatory letters from their many friends and relations. Tea parties were arranged so that the two families could meet each other. Muschi's parents were invited to Berlin to take afternoon tea and supper with the Schumacher parents. Muschi was not present so Fritz wrote to her afterwards describing the meeting:

Now things are not as informal with us as they are with you, preparations are made, wines selected, new tablecloths and napkins laid. In short, from 6 o'clock onwards the whole family was upside down and Papa was pacing up and down like a lion saying that he could not understand what was going on. It was a situation that needed a Mark Twain to describe it ... When the doorbell finally rang at 9 o'clock and Papa and Mama [Petersen] came in beaming, there was an atmosphere of catastrophe. You can imagine what it was like. In spite of all the affectionate friendliness of the newly arrived, there was an icy silence and stern expressions. I acted as intermediary between their Majesties, looking at one soothingly, the other encouragingly. After the meal, which had collapsed from overcooking, had been resurrected and appreciated after all, the atmosphere improved and after half an hour had dissolved into the most beautiful harmony. The storm in the tea cup was over. Their Majesties came closer to each other.

The wedding was to be a larger affair than Fritz's more modest taste would have wished and therefore the earliest date that could be agreed upon was October 10th. Fritz did not want to wait so long, not least because there were tax advantages in marrying by 1st September and eventually, despite Muschi's objections to the lack of romance in the suggestion, a compromise was reached. They were married civilly before the end of August, some six weeks before their 'real' wedding. Muschi's father, Rudolf Petersen, supported Fritz over this decision. He appreciated anyone who was careful with money.　·

The wedding celebrations, which began on October 8th with a grand Polterabend, lasted three days. A local hotel was taken over for the guests, but the party took place in the Petersens' home which, transformed by masses of flowers, accommodated the hundred guests for dinner and dancing. The high point of the Polterabend came when the sketches depicting past events in the couple's life and then a vision of the future were performed by Fritz and Muschi's friends and relations. Muschi was seen coming in in her dressing-gown, barefoot. The kettle was boiling, the bath running and the doorbell ringing. She was oblivious to everything except her pearl necklace which she retrieved from the soap dish. Then Fritz was seen coming in. He was given a towel by Muschi and left to wait. He examined his nails until she returned dressed, put on her shoes which lay untidily in a corner and sat down opposite him. Then Fritz proceeded to give Muschi a learned lecture on the Absolute and the Relative until suddenly from all sides of the stage heads appeared singing, 'Muschi do you understand it, Muschi are you enjoying it?' It was an accurate prediction!

The next day, October 9th, the company assembled again to collect Werner von Simson off the *Cap Arcona* which had just sailed in from Brazil, where Werner had been doing business. The young people breakfasted on board – consommé, rolls and port – were shown around by the captain and then spent the rest of the day sightseeing around the harbour.

Then it was October 10th, the day of the wedding. It dawned bright and clear, a beautiful autumn day. By 10 o'clock the guests had assembled on the lawn in front of the Reinbek house. A brass band was playing. Below the garden the Reinbek lake stretched into the distance absolutely calm and like a mirror, reflecting the trees around it. Fritz and Muschi stood together arm in arm on the terrace above the lawn, both in black, Muschi with golden jewellery, watching, occasionally exchanging a few words. The village children played under the huge beech trees that framed the lawn, eating the piles of cakes brought to them by Muschi's sister Olga. Suddenly the musicians broke into dance melodies and the atmosphere changed into a village fair, couples dancing on the lawn until midday. The church wedding was not until 5 o'clock so Papa Petersen went to the office for a few hours while the last-minute finishing touches were made to the church and Fritz and Muschi finished their packing.

As they drove to the church it began to drizzle. Muschi, in a long white veil which twirled upward as she walked up the aisle over the underfloor heating, was accompanied by four bridesmaids, Fritz's sisters Edith and Elisabeth, her sister Olga and closest friend Lilli Solmssen. The Minister, Pastor Schroeder, a devout man, knew the couple well and was able to deliver a homily which even Fritz, despite his ridicule of religious matters, could appreciate. He and Muschi had chosen the text together: 'Peace I leave with you, my peace I give you: not as the world giveth give I unto you. Let not your heart be troubled, neither let it be afraid' (John xiv, 27).

Back in Reinbek the wedding feast was being prepared on long tables covered with roses. Fritz and Muschi were radiant. Even Fritz looked without a care, which was so unusual that his sister Edith made a note of it. Champagne flowed, Hamburg specialities were served and then the speeches began. First Papa Petersen, warm, speaking directly to Muschi, giving her his blessing. Then Papa Schumacher, at first nervous till he warmed to his subject, speaking about the two families, what they had in common, about Fritz and how he had at first been disappointed when Fritz had given up his academic career but how he was now reconciled to the idea of Fritz as a business man, especially since he had clinched the deal by marrying into a family so successful and well respected in the business world. Then Fritz stood up. With head bowed, speaking very seriously, quietly, and with great dignity ('as Socrates might have spoken at his defence', commented Edith), he thanked his parents-in-law for their daughter. Then the dancing began again. The ladies took roses for their hair and couple after couple led the dancing, the village children watching, faces pressed to the window till at last at 11 o'clock the newly-weds got up to lead the final dance, before leaving for their honeymoon hotel under a shower of rice.

Generally it is appropriate to pass over the next few hours of a married couple's life. Fritz was no ordinary young man and even his honeymoon night was unusual. He and Muschi slept in separate beds. This was not due to a lack of feeling on either side but it showed very clearly how Fritz's mind rather than his heart and his emotions ruled his life. He had observed that in many families the eldest child seemed to have the most difficult character. In some cases he thought it amounted almost to a handicap in life. He concluded that the reason must be that these children were generally conceived when the couple were too excited and inebriated, as they inevitably were on the night of their wedding. It was not a risk he wished to take.

The next morning they rang down for breakfast. They expected something very luxurious. But there were no luscious fruits, eggs or warm crusty rolls that morning. In order to save national resources, Hitler had decreed that certain days should be *Eintopf* days. *Eintopf* is an economical stew made only from leftovers. October 11th was such a day.

On Capri, where they spent their honeymoon, Fritz and Muschi were removed from German politics and its effects on everyday life, but it was less easy to escape their filial obligations. Fritz, relaxing these duties for a brief spell, let a few days pass before writing to his parents. His father could not imagine that the joys of newly married life could provide such a distraction and wrote a typically worried letter asking whether

Fritz's silence was due to any mishap: 'I always have to think of my own honeymoon which belongs to the most ghastly experiences of my life ...' The letter ended, 'I could hardly get any sleep and felt very unwell. For this reason we left Italy and went to Switzerland to consult a doctor who soon discovered that I had a fever and confined me to bed for nine days. My wife nursed me very well ...'

After three weeks Fritz and Muschi returned home to begin their married life in a little house in Berlin, which their mothers had prepared for them in their absence. Fritz, who had been happy and relaxed on his honeymoon, immediately lapsed back into the tension produced by the situation in Germany. Although he enjoyed the work of the Syndicate, its very success posed for him a dilemma. It was true that many of their clients were Jews who wanted to leave Germany and much of their work had the effect of releasing resources for their emigration, but nevertheless, the work they were doing was also helping to implement Schacht's economic policy. By its success, the Syndicate was making a contribution to the economic success of the Nazi régime. In working hard for themselves they were working hard for a detestable dictatorship. All four colleagues were united in their disgust of the Nazis and all four had at times discussed the possibility of leaving Germany. They had seen Ludwig Rosenthal leave, then Erwin Schüller. Soon after Fritz joined them, Gustav Petersen left to work abroad, a departure that was also to become permanent.

For some time before his marriage, Fritz had been putting out feelers for jobs abroad. The desolation which he had expressed to Muschi in his letter on the anniversary of his departure from New York was still with him. Although the upturn in the German economy and the comparative quiet in politics had reassured many Germans that Hitler was after all a boon to their country, Fritz remained unconvinced. The general approval confirmed his conclusion that the Germany to which he belonged no longer existed. To be a patriotic German under Hitler was a contradiction in terms. Yet he was a German, felt German and loved Germany. Some of those opposing Hitler argued that it was wrong to leave Germany, that one should stand firm for one's country and fight the evils that had taken over. It was a question which Fritz was to turn over many times with his friends in the next few years. In his own mind the issue was becoming increasingly clear. The Nazi régime was so well entrenched, so generally accepted and supported that internal opposition was no longer a real possibility. His motto was 'occupy yourself with the things that can be changed.' Change was impossible under the Nazis.

In a memo he wrote a year later (to R. H. Brand) he summed up his view:

> It is true that there is a great deal of criticism in Germany. This criticism, however, refers to very different things for each section of the population, and there is, so far, hardly one single topic on which several sections concentrate their criticism. On the other hand there are a large number of things which meet with the general approval of all sections of the population ... With criticism divided and approval concentrated the régime can at present always count on having the majority behind them on each special issue, and there is no reason to believe that this should change quickly.

He began to conclude that the only possible course of action was to leave the country. The prime responsibility of decent Germans was to survive, to be around when the Nazis' nightmare came to an end so that Germany could be morally rebuilt. To stay in Germany would be to risk either compromise or concentration camp. Yet he did not want to cut off all links with Germany, business or personal. He wanted to continue working for the Syndicate, manning an office abroad, possibly London. He believed that joining the Syndicate had been 'one of the great bits of good fortune' that had happened to him in his life and he did not want to throw it aside lightly.

As so often happens, the opportunity, when it came, was quite unexpected. Fritz and Muschi returned from their honeymoon to a heap of letters bearing international postmarks. Since their engagement not a day had passed without congratulations from somewhere in the world. Fritz went to his post at once. Amongst the good wishes was a letter that began in a different way: 'Lieber Fritz, Pass auf!' Dear Fritz, pay attention, it began. The general director of Unilever, George

Schicht, a member of a wealthy and prominent family in the business and financial circles of Europe, wanted a financial wizard to look after his investments. He had heard of Fritz because the Syndicate had arranged trading deals for Unilever, and wanted to see him. Fritz left for London immediately and within a week informed Muschi that he had decided to take the job. They were to move to London early in the New Year. Muschi was shattered. She was under no illusion that life with Fritz would be quiet and tranquil: a mind like his, forever challenging conventionally accepted ideas was a turmoil in itself. She was content to accept his ideas and to discard her own if he told her to, assuming always that he must know better than she did, but behind her was always the security of her family. When they had discussed their future in terms of the future of Germany before their marriage, she knew that Fritz was seriously considering leaving Germany, so much so that while she was in London she had written to him specifically about living in England: 'I would find it very nice but I fear that you would fit into England too well for my liking. I am very little like the English although I like the customs very much.' She also knew that it would be difficult when the time came to make the decision, but she was completely unprepared for it to be so soon. There would be no time to put down roots in Berlin and draw Fritz closer into her family circle in Reinbek. It was like the shattering of a dream.

The news of their imminent departure was no less of a bombshell to both sets of parents. Muschi's father was furious. He too had his dreams about his partnership with his gifted son-in-law and was not going to let go of them so quickly. The atmosphere between them immediately darkened. Muschi's mother was more concerned with Muschi's own happiness. Fritz's parents took similar positions, the Professor distraught at yet another change in his son's career when he had only just come to terms with the last change and Fritz's mother sad to lose her son abroad again and to witness the intensification of the tension between father and son. Neither set of parents understood the real issue: that Fritz felt he had to leave Germany because of the evil presence of Hitler. Fritz was already certain that Hitler's policies would inevitably lead to war. In the next year both parents came to believe this too, but it did not occur to them that Fritz would not fight for Germany in such a war. For them it would become a question of the defence of the Fatherland, irrespective of Hitler. They could not understand that for Fritz the Fatherland no longer existed; and that he believed it could not exist again until the blight of Hitler had been removed, that to him fighting for the Fatherland would mean fighting against the Germany defiled by Hitler. Muschi too was sometimes to find this paradox hard to understand and Fritz had to remind her even days before the war did indeed break out:

Political theories, lessons, methods, successes or failures do not interest us do they? Instead we are interested solely and exclusively in moral obligations, unfettered by boundaries, whether national, racial, occupational, religious or anything else. The development of a person towards good consists largely in a continuous broadening of the boundaries of his moral responsibility, that he conquers the moral indifference by which prejudice limits his boundaries until he realizes what appears to be a higher purpose in his living and thinking, namely that he regards all men 'as equal before God'. Whoever imposes a moral 'charter' on other nations, races, groups, or individuals will find their inner life eroded and will go to the dogs.

He was reminding Muschi that their stand was based on an obligation to the truth and to freedom. She was torn between the pressure from her parents to stay in Germany and the high ideals of her husband. Her heart drew her to Germany but it also told her to stand by Fritz, that he was on the side of right even if it was a side that would cause her great pain to support.

In early 1937 when she joined Fritz in London all these emotions and split loyalties already gnawed at her happiness. She was stepping into the unknown, into a hostile country where she had no home, where she would be alone while her husband was at work. She had already remarked on his greater affinity with England than her own, an opinion echoing an earlier comment by Werner Brückmann who had recorded in his American diary: 'Fritz was a Berliner, but in his way he was also an Englishman. One could describe his manner and appearance as Prusso-English. A tall thin figure with a Berliner's face but an English posture.'[2]

7

London

Christmas 1936, the first of their married life, was memorable for its mishaps. Muschi was depressed. The prospect of leaving Germany a few weeks later hung over her. She was pregnant and her natural instinct was to stay put, close to her family. She had tried to prepare a traditional Christmas but on Christmas Eve a candle fell off the Christmas tree and set the curtains alight. The fire was not serious but Muschi was very shocked and the Christmas room spoilt.

Fritz's mind was on winding up his affairs. A month later he was ready to leave, first for Amsterdam to acquaint himself with the Schicht empire and then to London. Muschi went to Reinbek where, in the familiar security of her family, the future without them seemed bleaker than ever. Fritz, in trying to reassure her, had to put his own difficulties to one side. Despite another unpleasant attack of boils which had incapacitated him during his first week away, he wrote, 'Nothing *can* happen, as long as you are well; and even if I keep thinking what a shame it is that we did not set foot on this island together yesterday, "in order to conquer her", it means nothing and I *never* feel sorry *for myself.*'

Muschi joined Fritz towards the end of February, ending his bachelor existence in the Cumberland Hotel in Marble Arch. They found rooms in Virginia Water and began to search for a house. She was cheered by the beautiful countryside and by the knowledge that there were still plenty of opportunities to visit Germany. She had arrived in England knowing that she

89

would be returning home at least twice in the next few months for the weddings of Fritz's brother Hermann and his sister Elisabeth.

In London they already had some friends from Germany Erwin Schüller among them, as well as numerous others who passed through so that hardly a weekend was spent without friends visiting Virginia Water. It was a lovely spring and summer and the scenery grew more beautiful with each day. Muschi, despite her swelling figure, played tennis with Fritz and they often walked in Windsor Great Park. Before the summer was far advanced they found a large house set in an attractive garden on St George's Hill in Weybridge. It was called Highclere and both knew at once that it was just what they wanted. Fritz described his feelings to his parents: 'No – to have it so good! We are just trying to earn it so that we can really enjoy it and at the same time live as simply and as modestly as possible in our big framework. I don't like great pretensions – and we won't assume any here. But one should enjoy what one has.'

Muschi had plenty of scope for entertaining, space for a maid and for the new baby. Peter Christian was born on August 27th, 1937, just eleven days after Fritz's twenty-sixth birthday. Fritz was overjoyed. No father could have been more full of wonder and admiration. 'A son is something wonderful,' he wrote ecstatically to his parents, 'the most civilized baby I have ever seen.' 'Compared to the other babies on the balcony he seems by far the most civilized.'

Muschi's delight was tinged with anxiety. Christian had a minor physical defect which required an immediate operation. Fritz spent no time in deliberating what he could afford but immediately engaged the top surgeon for the job, although it meant approaching Muschi's family for financial assistance. Towards Muschi he maintained an attitude of unshakeable delight and optimism. A week after her confinement he wrote to her, 'My dearest, as it is the first (week's) birthday of *our* son today, I am writing in red ink. I am incredibly pleased. This morning in bed it became quite clear to me that the chap can't help but become a magnificent fellow.'

Such optimism and positive attitude towards all mishaps never left Fritz throughout the trials that were to come his way during his life. He was more aware of the evil and dangerous influences about in the world than most of his contemporaries and he considered that most people were less well equipped to combat them than he was, but he was still an idealist and believed that practical action, however small, was significant. His attempts to change the world through his world improvement plans did not rule out his own small gestures of compassion. His memory of hunger as a child made him respond at once to an article in the *Evening Standard* about a poverty-stricken family and send ten shillings, or, on a larger scale, take on the financial responsibility for a Jewish refugee. There was work for everyone, he wrote in a letter to the *Spectator*:

Man will never achieve the kingdom of God on this earth, but if he stops working for it and is satisfied with being shocked and blaming it on his predecessors for their failure to bring it about, if he sits back waiting for leadership from somebody else, then he will lose all possessions of culture and humaneness which he professes to treasure so highly.

Where are our ideals? ... Where are the men in this generation who are prepared to work as our fathers did and still do, who will keep on fighting for everything that is good and healthy and beautiful, no matter whether they succeed or not? Our generation will achieve Utopia no more than any previous generation did – but there is a tremendous (not an *appalling*!) amount of work to be done in small and in large ways ...

There is plenty of scope for all of us. It begins in our own heart and soul. Why are we here? What is expected of us? What are our responsibilities? What do we want? If Christianity does not offer us a solution, there are great philosophers, artists and statesmen we can consult and from whose sufferings and services we can learn. This is serious and not to be treated lightly. If we stop working and searching we are lost. Life is but a short spell and we shall have to account for what we have done with it. If 'orthodox religion has failed in its appeal to youth' has the example of Christ himself also failed in its appeal? *He did* give up his life for something greater. We shall not get out of all this so-called mess until we are prepared to give our life to *something*, unless we live for something more than ourselves. We shall not find an answer to the most important problems of our life. There is no ready made solution – that is what may make us worthy of the culture, civilisation and humaneness which we have inherited. If we are lamenting that time is getting lost we are throwing it away ourselves ... If we cannot feel that we can bring about the kingdom of God, we can still defend the Kingdom of Man we have inherited, but we want men who are not too lazy to grasp what it is all about, and women who do not have 'fears that burn up half their energies'.

This is not the time for lamenting but for becoming active ... Let never the height of an ideal or the magnitude of a task be a deterrent to anybody to do his share of it, be it small or large. There is plenty of work for all of us, work on ourselves and work for others. There is need for help everywhere. We can make life worth living for the unfortunate, sometimes by very little things but these little things need all our heart and all the human understanding we are capable of. And when we can tell the good from the bad, let us work for the good wherever we can find it. Let us develop it, treasure it and fight an evil force with all our determination. A long and difficult path leads up to the ideals which shall give direction to our life; nobody will reach the top, but no man will refuse to walk upon it because of that.[1]

This letter, responding to a pessimistic article in the *Spectator*, reflected the serious view Fritz had of life. He was searching for direction, trying to live out ideals expressed in hard and painstaking work, doing his duty however small. He was not a Christian, despite the Christian references, but he was a believer in the high ideals that had brought about Western culture and civilization. Christianity, he frequently told Muschi, could not stand up to rigorous investigation or logic. His inspiration came from philosophers like Schopenhauer and Nietzsche and writers like Goethe. Fritz's admiration of Nietzsche was open to considerable criticism and misunderstanding by many in England who saw Nazism as a logical development of Nietzsche's philosophy but Fritz vigorously denied this. He saw Nietzsche as a man who wanted peace through persuasion, a man who had been grossly misunderstood, particularly over the idea of a new European race which according to Fritz 'sprang from innumerable intermarriages between the various peoples of Europe and the Jews,'[2] and not from the Nazi perversion of the Aryan superman.

Philosophy was child's play compared to the more troublesome details of everyday life. During one of his sister Edith's visits the car inexplicably refused to start. Fortunately Erwin Schüller was there and was able to tow it to the garage. The garage was unable to locate the fault and eventually it was Fritz who discovered the cause of the problem. Edith had backed the car into a pile of sand thereby blocking the exhaust pipe. A poke with a stick cleared it and the car started immediately. Some days later the garage sent Fritz a bill. He was most indignant and disputed it, pointing out that the actual problem had been solved by himself at no cost to the garage. A long correspondence developed in which Fritz at times resorted to veiled abuse and sarcasm until some nine months later a compromise was reached and he paid a much reduced sum.

On another occasion he corresponded with a young lady who had presented him with a bill after an accident to her bicycle. She claimed damages for inconvenience while her bicycle was being repaired. Fritz told her that this was quite unjustified as the accident had been her fault, but in the end he sent her ten shillings to show good will.

All these little administrative tasks were part of Fritz's new role as husband, father and householder. He avoided changing nappies but he liked to play with the baby in the evenings. He found new pleasure in the garden too and was delighted when a business acquaintance sent him a scythe to cut the long grass. But these were just distractions from the real issues that occupied his mind: Germany and his work.

His work at first filled him with the usual positive enthusiasm. He worked in an office in the City at 4, Winchester Street and advised George Schicht on his stocks and shares. He had a great deal of responsibility and studied the movements in the economy with care. He was very pleased with himself when he predicted the 'gold scare' of spring 1937 and hoped that such evidence of his skills would win his employer's confidence and trust. But he continued to view his main aim as one of learning as much as possible and wrote hopefully to a friend in business in Germany, Harry Renkl, 'I consider it very fortunate that I have the opportunity of working in London at a time when the world economy is passing through all sorts of highly interesting changes of which very little is known at home.'

Unfortunately he was not able to sustain his enthusiasm. By May 1938 he was ready to admit his disappointment over his job to his parents 'which is increasingly appearing to me to be rather unnatural and pointless. I no longer have the feeling that I am adding enough to my knowledge and that is all that counts in these years.'

The frustration he felt at the seeming pointlessness of his work was increased by the unsatisfactory relationship he had with his employer. George Schicht found Fritz to be less of a financial whiz kid than he had hoped. Fritz did make him some gains but they were generally offset by his losses. Schicht cared more about an increasing bank balance than Fritz's understanding of the world economy, and Fritz was more interested in finding productive investments than in playing the stock market. He came up with one scheme after another for the use of Schicht's money, from the manufacture of dry-ice machines to that of vegetable-canning equipment. But most suggestions fell on stony ground. Despite this lack of encouragement and a steady deterioration in their relations, Fritz remained loyal to his task, eventually advising Schicht in March 1939 to take his money out of Europe altogether because he foresaw that a European war was imminent. In a long, carefully thought-out memo he suggested that Schicht should safeguard it in a country unlikely to be drawn into the coming conflict such as Argentina. Schicht's reply was brief: 'It is kind of you to bother your head but I don't think your suggestion is of any interest.'

Towards the end of his first year with Schicht Fritz began to look around for another job. He was still uncertain where his future really lay. Perhaps production, he thought. He wrote to Muschi, who was on a trip to Reinbek in the spring of 1938, 'I am longing to be directly concerned with the actual basis of the economy, namely production.' He toyed with the idea of suggesting to Harry Renkl, who had a small factory in Germany, that they should join forces. His disappointment with work in England tempted him for a moment to put his career before his political and moral convictions. Oddly more trouble at work eventually restored his determination to stay in England.

After a few days with Muschi in Germany in the spring of 1938, he returned to find that a colleague had tried to stage a coup by telling George Schicht that Fritz was disloyal and was pursuing his own interests at Schicht's expense. Fritz was stunned and furious. Suddenly his future in England seemed utterly bleak. He wrote to Muschi asking her to make inquiries at once with his contacts at M. M. Warburg to see whether there would be any openings for him at the bank. The Warburgs were friends of the Petersens too. But he retained some caution: 'Tell them,' he instructed Muschi, 'that although things are going very well for us over here, I do wish one day to return to Hamburg because we belong there and I have the feeling that it will only really be possible to build up something solid and permanent in Germany.' For Muschi's ears only he added: 'However, this does not mean that I have made up my mind to break camp. On the contrary, my aim will be to stay here at all costs. But the wise man prepares the way ahead.'

After a few days the row blew over and the allegations were withdrawn. But Fritz became more wary. He told Muschi that mud always stuck somewhere when it was thrown and that as the colleague had not been discredited by his actions but was as firmly in favour as before, his own position was obviously less secure. Nevertheless he took Schicht's assurances of renewed confidence at their face value and resolved to work harder than ever to prove his worth and to stay in England. He knew now that that was what he really wanted and when six months later a tempting offer of a job came from Germany he had no hesitation in turning it down.

During this period of uncertainty Fritz took comfort from his friends in London who all believed, as he did, that to leave Germany was the only possible course of action. There was Erwin Schüller from the Syndicate who now worked at Lazard Brothers, highly intelligent, but with whom Fritz did not always see eye to eye in the approach to problems; Adolf Schlepegrell, a fellow Rhodes scholar who was set for Canada; a couple called the Hammelmanns; a journalist called Johannes

Uhlig; there were English friends such as David Astor and Sonny Wax from his Oxford days, and new acquaintances such as Ivor Worsfold, a colleague who was becoming a close friend. There were others who, passing through London, would join the group and voice very different views. They argued against what they saw as an abandonment of the Fatherland in its hour of need. This point was most strongly made by Adam von Trott, whom Fritz had got to know in Oxford and who was a close friend of David Astor. Von Trott believed that Hitler had to be fought from the inside. He planned to work his way up in the German government, get to know the strengths and weaknesses of the régime and those who ran it and, when the time was right, to strike a fatal blow.

Fritz disagreed fundamentally with von Trott. He had long come to the conclusion that the effect of the Nazis was far more pernicious than the atrocities that signified the nature of the régime. Germany, he said later, was like a glass of water with a sediment of dirt, the Nazis had stirred up the mud and the whole glass had become cloudy. It would take more than the removal of the leadership to effect a cleansing process. He tried hard to get this point across to von Trott and dissuade him from his plan, which he did not consider heroic but foolhardy. Von Trott was trying to do more than any man could be expected to do. Not only was his plan dangerous, but it would not succeed in saving Germany. He would be risking his neck for a useless cause. Fritz failed to convince von Trott, whose commitment to his chosen path was almost fanatical. He was prepared to die for his cause and tragically did so when he was gruesomely executed for his part in the ill-fated plot to assassinate Hitler on July 20th, 1944.

Fritz's brother-in-law Werner Heisenberg, who was married to Elisabeth, was another patriot of the staying variety. He could not bring himself to leave Germany despite pressure from his colleagues, particularly in America. The attack by the Nazi press to which he had been subjected because of his support of Einstein made Heisenberg's decision to stay heroic too, though it was quite a different kind of heroism from von Trott's. Inevitably the Nazis would want to exploit his knowledge and abilities in their war efforts. He was a leading atomic physicist. For such a man to lie low and remain uninvolved was extremely difficult. Heisenberg did not risk his life in the same way as von Trott, but he risked life-long stigma and suspicion that he had in fact been a Nazi supporter.

When Fritz first met Heisenberg in 1937 he had written to Muschi: 'He is a fine chap and seems also to be a good person, at any rate a man who embodies much of the best of Germany.' He did not alter his view of this brother-in-law but they had differences of opinion, which no amount of argument could settle. Men like Fritz believed that Germany no longer existed because it had in essence been destroyed by the Nazis; they believed that true patriotism was to disassociate oneself completely from the régime, and they left everything behind to begin again in surroundings that became increasingly hostile towards them, because they were German. The other view was that true patriotism meant staying in Germany, either underground as Adam von Trott or trying to live a clean, uncompromising life as Werner Heisenberg.

Both stands were in their way heroic and left their marks. Fritz said later, when discussing the question of German leadership in the years after the Second World War, that the problem for Germany was that all those who might have been suitable material for leadership had either been out of the country during the war, thus making themselves unacceptable to the German people, or had in some way been compromised by the Nazi régime. Another contemporary who had left at a similar time to Fritz was more extreme. He said that those who had left Germany were regarded by the Germans as either cowards or traitors. They were sentiments which were buried deeply, perhaps even unconscious, but which nevertheless existed and had their effect on post-war relationships. Many families were split down the middle and Fritz's and Muschi's were no exceptions.

While discussions with his friends reassured Fritz of the rightness of his course of action, particularly during the row with Schicht in May 1938, they did not remove the fact that his working arrangements were unsatisfactory. He wanted to get out of the stock exchange into production and saw his chance in a new scheme which Schicht had been asked to finance. It was a plan to produce and promote battery-driven electric delivery vehicles. The foundations of the idea had already been laid by two men, Ivor Worsfold and Cecil Kny, and to Fritz's delight Schicht agreed to put some money into the company provided that Fritz was part of the management. Fritz threw himself into his new job heart and soul. It had many advantages, not least being that he no longer worked in the city but in a pleasant little office in Dean's Yard, just by Westminster Abbey. But it was the ideals behind the idea that inspired Fritz and renewed his motivation for hard work. Here was something real at last.

Battery-driven vehicles were a cause for which it was worth fighting. They were cheap to run and maintain, simple to construct, quiet, clean and most important of all in an unstable Europe, not dependent on the import of foreign fuel. Fritz and his colleagues conceived a broad plan. Besides manufacturing the cars they planned to set up a network of battery hiring, charging and vehicle service stations throughout England and various other parts of the world. Fritz had kept in touch with the Syndicate and he intended to make use of his contacts. Outlets were planned in North and South America. Fritz was absolutely confident of success and wrote airily to Harry Renkl: 'Running a business is somewhat like running a new car. As long as you have no experience it looks a very difficult thing. Once you sit at the steering wheel you move almost automatically.'

His confidence proved misplaced. Battery Traction Ltd, as it was called, did not run automatically: it never ran at all. Apart from obtaining a licence to manufacture, sell and service vehicles in the U.K. and Empire from a German manufacturer, Bleichert Transport Anlagen GmbH, a great deal of hard work on the part of Ivor Worsfold and Fritz produced little but paper. Unfortunately it was not just the ultimate failure of B.T.L. that made this an unhappy time for Fritz. Tension in international affairs was growing as German actions became more and more aggressive. As a German in England, Fritz had to face increasing hostility. After the invasion of Czechoslovakia in the autumn of 1938, he wrote to Rüdiger von der Goltz: 'The anti-German atmosphere has worsened here in the last few months, so that every one of us gets to feel it personally. However, one cannot praise the behaviour of the English highly enough. They know how to make distinctions.'

It was a struggle to prevent the tension and potential conflict from depressing him. A few months later he had to admit that life did have its hardships for him. He wrote to his parents:

The mood here, although not as depressed as last September, is all the more bitter. As I have been building up my life on the possibility of an Anglo-German friendship and co-operation, I have to submit to certain attacks which make me lose courage. But what is not possible in general can still be achieved in the particular.

The 'certain attacks' to which he referred were within the office. For the second time while working for Schicht he found himself facing a hostile colleague. Fortunately Fritz had a loyal friend in Ivor Worsfold who was also devoted to Muschi, and often spent the weekend with them at Highclere.

Throughout the beginning of 1939 the pressure built up. Fritz and his friends, now certain that war was imminent, spent many evenings discussing the political situation and the problem of Germany. Inevitably the discussion turned towards the future. How would such a situation be prevented from happening again and again in Europe? What had caused the present situation? All the Germans around the table agreed that a root cause was the settlement after the First World War. It had been imposed on Germany without any consideration for the German mentality or Germany's needs and wishes. Post-war German history amply demonstrated this folly and Fritz and his friends believed that it was essential that any future settlement after the war that now seemed inevitable must ensure that Germany had a say in planning her own destiny. It was too late to prevent war but they could not begin too early in planning for a longer-term future in a peaceful Europe.

Fritz had his own ideas about the basis for peace. He had argued all along that the basis for peace must be economic and this was a train of thought which he was to develop further in the next few years. Erwin Schüller had other ideas and wrote papers to leading politicians and men of influence urging them to think ahead. Schüller wanted to form discussion groups of experts – economic, political, social, military and all other relevant subjects – to consider what kind of settlement should follow the war that was coming. He believed that if young Germans such as those who belonged to his group of friends, all with expertise and with a deep love for their country, but without any taint of Hitler and Nazism on their characters, could get together with international experts then the mistakes of the First World War could be avoided. These discussion groups, Erwin Schüller believed, should be part of the International Institute at Chatham House. He won the support of Thomas Jones (then assistant secretary to the Cabinet) through whom he hoped to get to Members of Parliament, and he had several discussions with Lord Astor, whose backing would have been invaluable.

Politically, however, the plan was ill conceived. For eminent British experts to be seen discussing the future of Germany with Germans as war was about to break out would have been unacceptable to both Parliament and people. Fritz felt very uneasy about the whole idea although he agreed in principle. He also had his own ideas so that when Erwin approached him formally to lend support, much to Erwin's aggrieved bewilderment, he declined.

In the summer of 1939 Fritz had quite enough to occupy him without trying at the same time to solve Europe's political and economic problems. Muschi and Christian went to Reinbek on holiday. Fritz viewed these trips with mixed feelings. He hated to be alone and missed Muschi and Christian dreadfully, but he enjoyed the days of quiet where he could do exactly as he wanted. This time he hoped to concentrate on his own studies and anticipated the pleasures of a bed to himself where he could stretch his long legs out fully and give himself up to the philosophy of Nietzsche and Schopenhauer without disturbance. But he was too tense to indulge himself as he had hoped. His nerves were jarred and his anxiety about the political tension crowded in upon him at night depriving him of rest. The days were marred further by the antagonistic atmosphere at the office. Then uncertainty reached unbearable proportions when his labour permit expired. With that his residence permit also expired and the threat of being forced to leave England became a nightmare. Men were being called up in Germany. To return at this juncture would be the cruellest blow. He knew that Schicht was indifferent to his fate: relations were not ideal between the two, and Schicht indeed quibbled about applying for another permit for Fritz. Fritz responded by writing the letter to the Home Office for Schicht: all that was required was his employer's signature. In the end Schicht agreed but before the new permit was issued Fritz found himself in an even worse predicament. In the middle of July during a night of fitful sleep he suddenly awoke to a searing pain. In his restlessness he had turned and inexplicably broken his right shoulder. The pain was excruciating but worse still was the numbing effect of the painkillers on the functioning of his brain. Pathetically he wrote to Muschi with his left hand in the script of a small child. Apart from the numbing effect of the painkillers, he assured Muschi, he was all right. He could manage without her. But his handwriting alone was enough to convince her that she must return to nurse him. Leaving Christian with her mother in Reinbek she returned to Weybridge. It was the end of July.

Then it was August. Hitler was negotiating with Stalin, then with the Italians. He was planning to move into Poland at the end of the month but he was keeping very quiet about it; no one quite knew what he was up to. All Fritz knew was that Europe was on the brink of war and that the family was divided; Christian in Germany and he and Muschi in England. It was too risky for him to leave England now. Germany needed all the manpower there was and he could not rely on his broken shoulder to save him from call-up indefinitely. Muschi would have to make the journey to fetch Christian alone, and at once.

The trip to Germany, her last for seven years, was a nightmare. It was a journey full of pain and anxiety. Muschi knew it would be the last occasion to see her parents for some time and that the separation would be real. She had survived the last three years in England because she knew that there would be a frequent exchange of letters, telephone calls and even visits to sustain and maintain her closeness to her parents. Now, as she travelled to Germany she was faced with the consequence of her choice of a life with Fritz. Fritz had chosen England in 1936 and had turned his back on Germany. She had accepted his decision without questioning his wisdom, but it was not without a heavy heart. His decision had been and was still based on moral issues and with those she could not argue. Yet as she was called upon to face the final justification and confrontation with her parents she must have felt torn in half. Fritz had questioned Germany as his home in 1935 when he had written to her asking, 'what is one's homeland?' She knew the answer as she sat in Reinbek with the people she loved: her parents, her brothers and sister. There was never any doubt in Muschi's mind where her home really was and would always be. It was there in that spot, in Reinbek. Yet she could not protest and submit to her feelings for she believed that Fritz was right in his stand. Instead of leaving with memories of fond farewells she had to leave with memories of anger and grief. In his last attempts to make Muschi see what he believed was sense, her father had been very angry and forceful and she knew she was leaving without his blessing.

As she came to the German border to cross for the last time, before the outbreak of war closed it, Muschi could only feel numbed with fear and sorrow. She was afraid, for she knew that the border police would want to know why she was returning to England. Sure enough the angry questions came: 'Why are you leaving? Where is your husband? When are you coming back?' She knew it was essential not to give the impression that she was fleeing the country. Through the haze of anxiety and distress she heard the border guard's unfriendly voice: 'If you don't return with your husband, your family will know of it.'

Muschi was panic-stricken. Her family endangered by her action! It was essential that no undue attention should be thrown upon them for they were vulnerable too. Her paternal grandmother had been a Jewess. She bluffed her way through as best she could and, emotionally and physically exhausted, arrived in Weybridge to put the problem before Fritz.

Fritz suspected that the threat had been a bluff on the part of the border guard but he knew that there was a risk that retribution could be carried out on the Petersen family. He had to do something. Throughout his stay in England since 1937 he had been careful not to give the impression in the letters he had written to his parents that his move to England was a rejection of Germany. His parents always believed that in the

event of war he would return to fight for Germany. The Petersens had been given to believe the same. He therefore knew
that his sincerity would not necessarily be doubted if he seemed
to be making efforts to return to Germany. Banking on the
fact that with war so close the German embassy in London
would be in complete confusion, he sent a messenger to the
embassy urgently requesting that a new passport be issued.
The messenger was instructed to get a receipt for the letter of
request. With this evidence of his apparently genuine attempt
to obtain a passport for his return home, Fritz dispatched the
letter of receipt to the authorities in Germany complaining
that he was trying to return, as the enclosed receipt showed,
but that the embassy was proving very tardy in providing him
with the necessary documentation. It was a calculated risk.

A few days later, on September 3rd, 1939, war broke out,
frontiers were closed and all communication ceased with Germany. There was no way of telling whether their actions had
endangered Muschi's family or whether Fritz's ruse had been
effective. It was to be more than five years before they were
able to communicate directly with their families again.

Now began a tension in Fritz's life that was never quite to
leave him. He was confident that he was on the side of right.
He was relieved and thankful that no sudden quirk of fate had
removed him from his chosen path of leaving Germany per-
manently. He could not, would not return until Hitler had
been removed and all traces of his régime destroyed. Yet now
that war had been declared and only a total victory over Hitler
could achieve the removal of his influence, Fritz and Muschi
were in the impossible and heartrending position of having
their beloved families as enemies. Throughout the war they
would have to suffer the agony of hearing the rejoicing of their
friends in England as yet another bombing raid had successfully devastated a German city that they knew, and that perhaps contained members of their own family. They could not
rejoice under such circumstances. Yet how else could Germany
be defeated and the Germans released from the tyranny of
Nazism?

At least, it was assumed, the war would be short. Fritz and
Muschi hoped that eventually the German people would themselves come to see that the cause they were fighting was that of

the devil. That surely would sap the strength of their ferocity. The fact that this turned out not to be the case made their dilemma all the more painful. It became clear as the war progressed that it was a war to the death. It was difficult to distinguish German from Nazi and required an effort to do so. Hitler could not achieve his astonishing successes without the passionate support of his people, people whose strength stemmed from a belief in their cause.

8

A Change in Lifestyles

It was not easy for Fritz to escape the pain that Germany's fate caused him. Quoting Goethe he noted down, 'My heart is full of affection for Germany. I have often felt bitter grief at the thought that the German people so estimable individually should be so despicable in the mass.'[1] But he had little time to reflect on his grief. His own life was taking a critical turn. He had only one cause to rejoice: the outbreak of war in September 1939 finally resolved the anxiety of whether or not he would be forced to return to Germany. With closed borders his only option was to stay in England.

In England he and Muschi were now in a new situation. They were no longer merely subject to the varying intensity of anti-German feeling; they had become enemy aliens. As such they had no idea what might be in store for them. They could not but feel very insecure, Muschi again living through anxiety during her second pregnancy and afraid that the emotions she was experiencing might adversely affect her baby.

More shocks were in store. Fritz, facing one disappointment after another as potential investors withdrew, finally decided to take action over the discord in the office. He did not trust one of his senior colleagues, whose position at B.T.L. was such that it was impossible to work properly without his loyal and reliable support. Fritz believed it was his duty to inform Schicht of his doubts. It was a mistake; Fritz had overestimated Schicht's loyalty to himself. A new row exploded over him. With accusations of slander flying through the air, Fritz, angry and upset, offered Schicht his resignation, which was accepted.

Fritz's resignation had serious implications. Not only did it mean that he was without an income but also that he was threatened with homelessness. The tenancy of Highclere was part of his terms of employment with Schicht. Fortunately Schicht proved generous on this point and allowed the tenancy to be extended six months to enable Muschi to have her baby while Fritz was looking for alternative accommodation.

Through all this, despite the anger and disappointment he felt about the unhappy events at work, Fritz managed to maintain an optimistic view of life sustained by his belief in the integrity and fairness of the English. He wrote to an acquaintance of his, Mrs Ollemeier:

> Meanwhile our friends are holding on to us in a wonderful way. The true humanity which I find practised so thoroughly in the personal sphere gives me hope that out of the present turmoil there must be created something better than we had before. So we shall pull through all right.
>
> Our troubles such as they are, are exclusively in the spiritual field and we have reason to be grateful for good health and, let it be said, comparative economic security.

Of the 'spiritual troubles' more will be said later. Meanwhile 1939 came to an end. Fritz and Ivor Worsfold tried to salvage the B.T.L. idea but without success. War had obliged what potential investors they had to look elsewhere, and Ivor was soon called up to join His Majesty's Forces. Fritz tried to earn a little by writing articles. His care with money now proved useful, he had some savings to tide them over, though not enough to pay for Muschi's confinement when another son, John, was born on January 16th, 1940. He was forced to approach the doctor in charge and ask for a reduction in fees. The doctor generously agreed to halve the bill.

Early in the New Year a new threat appeared. Weybridge was suddenly declared an enemy protected area. That meant that Fritz had to leave the house within twenty-four hours to avoid arrest. He moved in with friends in London. He was very uneasy in hiding, particularly as his friend, a highly placed civil servant, would be in serious trouble if it was discovered that he was sheltering an enemy alien.

Such loyal signs of friendship increased his confidence that he was on the side of right and that all would be well. It was not misplaced, for soon David Astor came to his rescue as the tenancy of Highclere came to an end and Muschi and the boys had to prepare to leave. Astor realized that Fritz would probably have to be content with a menial if not manual job for some time but that this would be an intolerable hardship for Fritz if he was devoid of any intellectual stimulation. His uncle, Robert Brand (later Lord Brand), had a beautiful estate in Eydon, Northamptonshire, which was a working farm, both arable and dairy. He needed farm hands and could offer them a tied cottage. This seemed to Astor the ideal solution. He was sure his uncle and Fritz would get on well, they had similar minds which thought on a grand scale and Brand had the sort of contacts which Fritz would find invaluable. He suggested a meeting.

Fritz had come across Brand before and had been impressed. It was in New York in November 1932, when Brand had given a lecture which Fritz had admired as much for its contents as for its delivery. He wrote to his parents afterwards that Brand had one of the best kinds of English brains. Meeting Brand face to face he felt that his first impression had not been wrong and it gave him added satisfaction that the admiration was mutual. David Astor had been right in his judgment and wrote to Fritz early in 1940:

Dear Fritz,
I want to compliment you *in writing*! on having such a long and successful talk with Old Brand. I regard him as the litmus paper for intelligence tests. You may not be given a medal for developing your mind, but I consider an afternoon's talk with Brand in office hours when you are less than thirty is an achievement in itself.
Yours respectfully,

David

Soon after this David Astor began to call Fritz 'professor'.
By June 1940 the job and Eydon Hall cottage were Fritz's.

It was something of a comedown after life at Highclere. The labourer's cottage was without gas or electricity, had only one tap inside, an outside lavatory and was very small. The bath tub in the kitchen had a wooden cover so that it could also be used as a table. There was no place for silver and crystal here. On forty-five shillings a week the Schumachers would have to learn a new way of life. They had an added burden of two extra mouths to feed. Two Jewish refugee girls had joined them, Caroline and Gina Ehrenzweig. Caroline, the older of the two, a capable and intelligent girl in her twenties, had studied at the same Froebel institute in Hamburg as Muschi.

Somehow the six of them crammed into the tiny cottage. Gina and Caroline were meant to help Muschi in return for their keep. Caroline, however, was not strong and before many days had passed was forced to take to her bed for what turned out to be almost a year. Fritz was also soon exhausted by the unaccustomed farm work. On his first day he was shocked at the leisurely pace of the other farm hands. They did not seem to have the first idea what hard work meant. Fritz thought he would show them and worked at twice the pace. After three days he collapsed exhausted. Physical work, he had discovered, could only be sustained at a steady, rhythmic pace. After that he learnt the pace from the other workers.

He did not have long to accustom himself to his new way of life. The fifth column activity which had led to Holland's collapse under Hitler's invasion in May 1940 had thrown the British authorities into panic. To prevent similar activities in Britain all Germans, whether Jew, communist, anti-Nazi or otherwise, were under suspicion and rounded up. Soon after arriving in Eydon Fritz too received an ominous rap on the door and was ordered to accompany the waiting officers. He was taken to a hurriedly erected internment camp on Prees Heath near Whitchurch on the borders of Shropshire and Wales, where he found himself with 1,400 other prisoners.

The first few weeks were terrible. It rained most of the time and the overcrowded tents were surrounded by mud. Fritz, whose health was never robust, succumbed immediately to the deprivations, the cold and the damp, and became extremely ill. The captain in charge of the camp was unfriendly and unsympathetic. 'The cemetery here is very beautiful,' he sneered as he refused to transfer Fritz to the hospital tents for special treatment. Fritz had to fight against the feeling of depression that now took hold of him. He had three desperate worries: his health, Muschi's stamina, and his future in England. Past experience had told him that he could not rely on his health to stand up to the strain of his new conditions. The physical hardship and the emotional and mental anxiety that the camp imposed on its inmates were greater than anything he had gone through before; his health had let him down under less.

As for Muschi: he had left her with little money, cramped conditions, responsible for two refugees, one of them sick, as well as the two children, in an unfamiliar part of England without friends or acquaintances, and he could offer her no hope or consolation as to the length of their separation. He was not even sure whether he could hope for Brand to hold open his job and allow her to remain in the cottage to wait for his release. Soon he discovered Muschi's burden was even greater than he had imagined. Caroline's illness had taken a dangerous turn; she needed urgent medical help and nursing.

Yet these worries paled into insignificance when he thought about the greatest horror he might now face, that of deportation. Prees Heath was only a temporary camp; men were being sent away all over the world and to find himself on a boat to Australia or Canada was an unthinkable nightmare. Towards the end of July, when the immediate threat seemed to have passed and he was allowed to write to Muschi, he shared his fears with her.

> The worst thing at this time has been the news of internees deported overseas. To leave England now would break my heart ... The danger is over ... We will be together again. No one will tear asunder the threads of my hope. Let us hold to England whatever happens to us. My motto: I will not leave you, then you will bless me. Will England understand me? ... I can see my tasks more clearly than ever: Europe, a new Europe: Coming from England.

The nightmare of the first few weeks soon passed. As his health began to improve and news of Muschi reached him, with the reassurance that she would be allowed to stay at Eydon Hall cottage, his old optimism returned and he began to look on this new experience as something positive. He discovered within himself strong inner resources which lifted him above the daily problem of living.

Dearest little wife,
Today at last, on the birthday of the great Goethe, who was never interned, the sun is shining again after a long period of bad weather. The sun is everything. The night was evil and cold, but the sun dispels much. I am sorry that I had to miss yesterday (Christian's birthday). Let us continue to be patient. The children will grow, the course of the war will improve even if I am sitting behind barbed wire. As long as you do not lose courage and maintain your confidence. One day the nightmare will have dreamed itself out. For most of that small minority of highly strung people to which I belong, internment means unbelievable and unimaginable hardship. But I have established with satisfaction that I, on the other hand, have reserves of strength to which others do not have access. My inner holding is such that most people assume that I am completely untouched by everything, so far as it concerns me. This is good. You would be amazed to see what a marvellous reputation I enjoy here in the camp. As the old and the ill recently left for the Isle of Man, many of them told me of their sincere high esteem. You see, even if you live like a dog, nevertheless you still don't live like a dog. This time will be useful to us later on. What does not kill us makes us stronger ... Apart from this I am trying to uphold peace and unity in the camp. I think I am succeeding well which represents quite a service to the community. I have the reputation here of having the motto: I have never met a man I didn't like.
But I *love* you.

Fritz

Fritz's 'motto', which he had seen on the gravestone of the famous American cowboy, William Rogers, on his trip across America, at first elicited nothing but ridicule from his fellow internees. 'How can you say that you like that man over there?' someone jeered, pointing at an internee who had made himself particularly obnoxious. Fritz went over to the man in question and after a few minutes' conversation discovered that the burden of grief the man was carrying over a lost son was such that Fritz could find nothing but sympathy for him. 'Once you discover a man is human, however outwardly disgusting,' he explained later, 'then, of course, you like him.'

It was not always easy to recognize the human element in the internees or their captors. In the degrading squalor of the camp many men sank to less than human behaviour. The internees were an unbelievably mixed bag, not only professionally and socially but also in their attitude to England and the war. The internment policy had picked up prisoners indiscriminately, regardless of whether they were anti-Nazi like Fritz, Jews and communists fleeing persecution, or fervent Nazis. There could be no unity amongst the prisoners with such differing attitudes.

Amongst such a diverse group Fritz had a tremendous stroke of luck. He found himself in a tent with a man named Kurt Naumann. Naumann was a large and energetic man who had been an active communist and anti-Nazi worker in Germany until he had found himself on one of the Nazi blacklists of wanted men and had escaped into Czechoslovakia. In Czechoslovakia he had left the Communist Party, disillusioned by a lack of humaneness about it and had joined the New Beginning branch of the Socialists. When the Germans invaded Czechoslovakia and he found his enemies again on his heels, he and his wife Hanna fled, eventually finding refuge in England.

Naumann and Fritz were united in their disgust at camp conditions and together set about organizing camp life in a more tolerable and humane way. On his birthday, August 16th (for which Muschi sent him the inappropriately worded telegram 'Many Happy Returns'), Fritz was elected camp leader with Naumann as his deputy. They began their reforms at the most basic and essential level, organizing the men into sanitary squads and forbidding indiscriminate urination around the camp. The cooking was reorganized so that the daily diet of herrings was served in more imaginative ways. Fritz entered into negotiations with the captain to prevent the pilfering of the men's food parcels by his staff and clothes were obtained for those in need. There were a hundred and one tasks to be seen to. Fritz had never been so absorbed in non-intellectual

111

tasks in his life and it was an eye-opening experience. He wrote
to Muschi at the beginning of September:

> I am keeping quite well. My position, without any rights and
> with plenty of duties, is very difficult, but good training. My
> method of 'ruling' which is based on human kindness and
> persuasion, seems somewhat strange to the 'military mind'.
> But with so much misery about I am convinced it is the only
> method. I wonder how long they will deny us any rights
> whatsoever. About my release ... I beg you to be very
> patient, like me. A few days don't matter, a few weeks won't
> matter, and even months shall not matter. At present *we* are
> quite unimportant. It is only the big fight that matters. If we
> are the forgotten men, it won't be for long. And when we
> shall emerge again we shall be stronger and better, we shall
> be more convincing for what we have stood through, for our
> faith, our ideals which are beyond the might of men to
> corrupt. Then there is peace in my mind. There is all the
> hope and confidence in the world. Whatever the British are
> doing to us now, as long as they win I shall be satisfied.

Several days later he added: 'I am learning a great deal: how to
deal with many different types of men, how to smooth over
difficulties arising between them, how to be just, impartial,
generous and patient. It is a hard school but a good one, and
I am making some progress.'

Fritz's hard work was not without its rewards for not only
did he win the respect of the men but also eventually that of
the captain. It brought him together too with other like-minded
men in the camp, particularly refugees who had been working
in Oxford before their arrest, among them a respected economist called Frank Burchardt, who worked at the Oxford Institute of Statistics. There were opportunities for lively and
stimulating conversations after all, although none as illuminating as those he held with Naumann.

By profession Naumann was a communicator, a journalist
and writer, well able to put across his passionately held left-
wing convictions. Fritz was immediately captivated. At Oxford, when so many of his fellow students had been left-wing,
Fritz had stuck to the liberal traditions of his middle-class

German background. Naumann was the first full-blooded Marxist he had listened to seriously, and he found the experience a profound eye-opener. It was as though the scales fell from his eyes and his education had at last begun.

The Concise Oxford Dictionary defines 'university' as: 'Educational Institution designed for instruction or examination or both of students in all or many of the more important branches of learning.' Fritz had had little sense of being instructed in the more important branches of learning while at university. But there at Prees Heath he felt that he was at last being educated. This was his real university. Instead of feeling hopeless and powerless in the situation in which he found himself, he rose with new strength. Marx made sense of it all. Marx explained the political and the social upheavals in terms of economic status and economic activity. Here were ideas that needed to be studied in depth. Suddenly Fritz could see how he had failed to take proper account of the political dimension of the economic issues which had concerned him. Poverty and plenty, oppression and justice were put into a new perspective by Marx's penetrating analysis.

As Fritz learnt from Naumann, Marxist analysis came to life around him. Prees Heath was a microcosm of the ideas Marx had put forward: the oppression and exploitation of the masses of prisoners by a few captors. Fritz's intellectual and academic mind was exposed to the realities of life. He had always been an elitist, mixing by virtue of his birth and intelligence with the intellectual aristocracy; and he saw as he mixed with the men that although he was a prisoner without rights or status, he was still privileged and that others had far harder deprivations. He was conscious of his experience and was grateful for all that he was learning. When he was released from Prees Heath, he came out not as a man emerging from the hard conditions and pressures that go with the deprivation of liberty, but as though he was returning from a stimulating seminar, on fire with new ideas and new visions. He left Prees Heath invigorated, released from a torpor which had gripped him in the years leading up to the war when the plight of his country descending ever deeper into madness had robbed him of real creativity.

The main frustration Fritz had to face while still in the camp was being able to do little to speed up his release. He had to leave that in Muschi's hands. The wheels of bureaucracy moved slowly and only the cases of men urgently needed for the war effort were given priority. Fritz saw that the reasons for release could be bizarre. A small Japanese prisoner was released very quickly. The camp had buzzed with excitement: 'What was so special about him?' He turned out to be an expert on sexing day-old chicks, apparently an indispensable part of war-time agriculture.

Fritz wanted his own release to be on grounds of his expertise. Much as he wished to be a free man he dreaded being released on health grounds. He had to gain freedom on his merits not his weaknesses. Muschi kept him informed about her efforts on his behalf. She had rapidly contacted all their friends and acquaintances after Fritz's arrest and they soon set the ball rolling towards his release. Among the first were Harold Scott and Alexander Paterson for whom Fritz had acted as interpreter in 1935 at the Prison Governors' conference. Both proved loyal friends. Paterson visited Fritz as soon as he was able. His report to Muschi renewed her courage.

> I visited his camp on Saturday afternoon, and he and his colleagues gave me an excellent cup of coffee, and we sat outside the tent and had a good talk. Thanks to the fresh air and the excellent weather we have had in the past weeks, he looks very much better, having more colour in his face than I have ever seen before. You know his spirit, and so it is hardly necessary for me to tell you that he is as brave and cheerful about it as any man could be in the circumstances.

Paterson, himself a prison governor and one of the most significant penal reformers of his time, willingly added his voice to those pressing for Fritz's release, which included Lord and Lady Astor and Harold Scott. Scott's support was crucial. He was shortly to be knighted for his services as Deputy Secretary at the Ministry of Home Security and his influence hastened the consideration of Fritz's case. Also vital was Brand's assurance to the authorities that as an agricultural worker Fritz was urgently required for the war effort. All hands were needed for the harvest.

It took just over three months before Fritz was released from internment. Back in Eydon he was a free man but if he wanted to visit London or anywhere else beyond the boundaries of Banbury, permission had to be obtained from the police. He was still an enemy alien. The villagers greeted him as such. Most of Eydon had not seen Fritz before his arrest and had built up a picture in their minds of a strong, blond, Nordic type of German. They were unprepared for a tall, dark and thin man who still looked like a boy, and the rumour quickly spread that Fritz was a spy who was being hidden at Eydon Hall cottage. Even when this rumour was laid to rest, feeling against the Schumacher family ran high. As they walked down the high street to do their shopping, doors closed and notices appeared – 'no Germans'. Only one shopkeeper, Mr Tyrell, had the courage to serve them. Not even the presence of Caroline and Gina reassured the angry villagers that Fritz and Muschi were not enemies. One night there was a noisy commotion outside the cottage; then stones pelted the windows and villagers armed with pitchforks and other offensive weapons began to shout outside. Fritz, after the patient and long-suffering stand he had taken at Prees Heath, was enraged. He tore open his front door and bellowed into the darkness, swearing and using every term of abuse that he could think of, both colloquial and Shakespearean. The villagers retreated but the hostility continued. The 'battle of Eydon', as Fritz called it, had not yet been won. It was only when Brand called a public meeting that the fears of the local people were finally allayed and Fritz and Muschi at last began to enjoy their country life. Christian found friends in the village, Muschi found help, and it came to be the happiest time of their lives. Muschi's warmth elicited a response in many people, and where Fritz was admired for his brains, she was loved for her personality.

Eydon was also ideal for children. Christian was, in Fritz's words, 'a human dynamo'. He was always bursting with energy, roaring about the place, noisy, wild and demanding, followed about by John whose agility combined with Christian's force to make them like a couple of little monkeys, never out of mischief. Fritz's greatest pleasure was to observe the development of their minds. He wrote them little verses, invented games which always had plenty of intellectual content but he also rejoiced in their uninhibited and lively ways. He had no intention of submitting his children to the formality of his own childhood and wanted them to have as much freedom as possible. Later the boys became quite unruly and Muschi found that she was unable to handle them at all. Unable to impose discipline herself, she found little help from Fritz, who defended the children to anyone who complained and then retired into his study away from the battlefield. But at Eydon their freedom was complete and both parents delighted in it.

Despite the initial antagonism in Eydon, Fritz soon made his way amicably with his work mates. Soon after his arrival a farm girl asked him his name. 'Fritz,' he replied. 'Ooh, we can't call you that,' she tittered, 'we'd better call you James.' So James he became, working alongside the others gathering in harvest, seeing to the cows, making silage, building and repairing walls and fences, and learning all the time. The fresh air and the physical labour soon had its effect and the improvement in his health at Prees Heath was consolidated and it at last took a turn for the better. The delicate youth was turning into a reasonably robust man. But he still looked ridiculously young and once, when Muschi opened the door to a villager and he asked for her son, it took her a few moments to realize that the caller must mean her husband. Only his prematurely lined brow hinted that the boyish looks belonged to a husband and father.

Fritz spent eighteen months at Eydon Hall farm. Unexpectedly, as Prees Heath had done, it turned out to be a break for him – an important formative experience. He remarked on this in a letter to Werner von Simson when the time came for him to leave Eydon, wondering whether he was taking a step in the right direction.

I am sorry to leave Eydon. I should much rather be a farmer than an economist. The trouble is that I am not a farmer (and have no farm) but an economist. I have the reputation of being unorthodox and even a bit of a crank, which I hope, will enable me to combine the life of a farmer with the work of an economist. At any rate, it seems that Eydon will turn out as having been not merely an episode but a turning point.

Fritz had too active a mind to be able to toil away at his tasks without thinking and his spell at Eydon also turned out to be one of the most productive periods of his life. He worked late into the night on economic ideas, studied Marxism and corresponded extensively with his friends, particularly David Astor, Werner von Simson, and, to a lesser extent, Ivor Worsfold. On the farm he was unable to undertake a task without subjecting it to rigorous thought and sometimes rigorous reorganization. He was glad when Brand asked him for his comments on the way the farm was being run and confidently gave his opinions, criticizing farm policy freely. Brand was receptive to Fritz's ideas, but the other farm hands were less impressed by the intellectual in their midst. They dug their heels in firmly when Fritz came around asking awkward questions and making suggestions. As winter came he noticed that the appalling stench of the silage repulsed even the hungry cows. When he compared the Ministry of Agriculture instructions to the methods used by the men on the farm he found that they did not correspond.

'Why don't you do it the way they say in these pamphlets?' he asked. 'We have always done it like this,' came the reply. Such answers explained a great deal. There were other similar experiences. 'For the last few weeks', he wrote to Brand, 'I have been rebuilding walls that the frost brought down ... I couldn't help wondering why the walls here should keep falling down, as I have seen walls in Italy, for example, which had outlasted two thousand years.' By asking a few more questions he soon discovered that the men did not mix enough cement into the mortar. Their reason was that cement cost too much and that anyway it was far more laborious to rebuild walls built with better cement. Fritz wrung his hands at this logic. Why worry about rebuilding walls in two thousand years' time? he asked.

Observations such as these led him to some inescapable conclusions about the future of British agriculture. He believed that the secret of success lay not in the solution of technical problems such as soil fertility, the price of labour, capital availability and other such criteria. The key factor lay in the quality of the farmers themselves. He wrote to Brand:

> For generations there has been going on a process of 'negative selection'. The best have left the land and the dullest stayed behind. The rural population of today strikes me as less enterprising, less adaptable, less efficient, less methodical than the town population. But farming needs people who are enterprising, adaptable, efficient and methodical.

His general suggestions on how to improve farming were in line with an acceptable economic approach and reflected his newly acquired left-wing ideas. He believed that agriculture was being impoverished because it required too much capital to farm properly. What future could a young, intelligent person hope for in farming when he needed at least two to three thousand pounds in order to set himself up? Without such capital his prospects were dim: life-long poverty as an agricultural labourer.

Twenty years later, reflecting on the same theme, albeit capital shortage of a far more extreme nature in places like India, his diagnosis of the flight from the land and the impoverishment of rural life remained fundamentally the same, but the solutions he offered were very different. Then he was to recommend scaling down agricultural equipment to make it accessible to the ordinary man. In 1941 he discarded any suggestion of establishing a system of smallholdings because the cost needed to equip even a small farm would be beyond the ordinary man. His solution was almost exactly the opposite. Politically he found it unacceptable that large areas of land should be concentrated in a few hands passed down through generations of rich landowners; economically direct redistribution did not make sense. The answer lay in the intervention of the state, as he wrote to Brand.

> If the state were to become the owner of a substantial part of the land, (say one third), it could create a substantial number of senior positions of foreman, state bailiff, local organiser, area supervisor, etc. The most humble labourer on the land would know that he could apply for a rise into

118

such a position. There would be something *to go for* ...
Many excellent arguments have been adduced for some
measure of land nationalisation. They all point to the improvements which could be realised by a more centralised
control. But the decisive argument – to my mind – is the
human argument. The state and only the state, could make
agriculture into a career.

The 'flight from the land' is a problem that is agitating
many governments. The first inclination of the legislator is
to put obstacles in the way of those who desire to leave or to
bribe them into staying ... But I should think rather than
tying the rural population to the land, governments should
aim at bringing townspeople into the country. Agriculture
needs fresh blood.

9

World Improvement Plans

Fritz's recommendations for improving British agriculture never reached the stage of any great plan. They were written as part of the conscientious execution of his duties as Brand's employee, part of his daytime persona – that of James. The real interests of Fritz, husband, father and economist and world citizen, lay elsewhere, so that farm labour completed, he would return home to Muschi, the boys, and above all to his world of ideas. Then he became a man with a mission, a man who believed that he had the ability to make a major contribution to making the world a better and safer place.

His ideas absorbed him late into the night when he would sit hammering at his typewriter, working out his ideas and reading, reading, reading. With an income of forty-five shillings a week there was not much left over for books and he felt very guilty when he went to Blackwell's bookshop in Oxford and spent half of his week's wages. Sometimes he tried to hide his new books by putting old covers on them so that Muschi would not guess at his extravagance. Fortunately his friends were very good to him. Ivor Worsfold gave him the complete works of Lenin and David Astor sent him new books from time to time.

Reading and studying hard every night, Fritz felt exhilarated and stimulated but also lonely. He threw his ideas at Muschi but she could not be the intellectual sparring partner that he needed. He would look forward to Brand's visits to the estate when he would be invited up to the house for a talk. But Brand was not at Eydon very often and shortly after Fritz and Muschi arrived he left for America, where he worked for the British Food Mission.

The isolation would have been unbearable had it not been for the existence of Mr A.P. McDougall, who managed Brand's affairs and to whom Brand took care to introduce Fritz before he left. McDougall was a man of much experience whose career spanned academic as well as practical farm work. He wrote on agriculture as well as advising Lord Astor on his Scottish farms and this combination of practical expertise and intellectual endeavour made him a man with whom Fritz could have a useful exchange. He had other uses to Fritz too. He was the local estate agent and a pillar of the community of nearby Banbury. He introduced Fritz to Rotary clubs, W.E.A. (Workers' Education Association) classes and other groups who required speakers, so that Fritz could try out his ideas on a wider public. The two men got on very well personally, the older McDougall generously admiring his young friend to whom he once wrote, 'I greatly enjoyed the time I had with you yesterday. Your mind is like a Rembrandt painting or a Beethoven Symphony.'

Fritz's mind was certainly working on a large canvas at that time. Not surprisingly his thinking revolved around the most fundamental question of the day: how could a real peace be achieved? He was not concerned with the short term question of how to win the war, but with questions that were much more basic. What caused wars to recur? Were there any removable causes of war? How could things be arranged so that a lasting peace could be achieved? What was needed in a post-war world? What could be done about Germany to remove not only the effects of the present war but also the more fundamental tendencies that might lead to war again in the future?

This last question absorbed him both as a German and as a citizen of the world. The problem of Germany he now saw was greater than the repercussions of the First World War, which he had blamed for so long. Now that he used a much wider range of tools for his analyses, his more advanced economic thought, his newly discovered political understanding, and a rigorous application of scientific thinking which ruthlessly

121

rooted out all emotional reaction and moral judgments, he could put the problem into a wider context.

The starting point for his ideas was that first most fundamental question of all. What causes war? Fritz knew that it would be the height of folly to believe that he could find the conclusive answer to this question and above all he wanted to make a practical contribution. He knew it could serve no purpose if he were to analyse the causes of war if nothing could then be done about them. Only removable causes were of interest. He suggested 'that to look upon war as an accident writ large is a useful way of looking at it - useful because it makes you see all sorts of things. Dangerous corners; slippery surfaces; level crossings; not *only* drunken drivers and reckless speeders ... There is no one single, simple solution.'[1] In his analogy to accidents, Fritz pointed out that it was the aim of traffic experts to make roads safe, not to fix the blame for accidents. He saw his task as making the hazardous road of international relations a little safer, so that when the next driver drunk with lust for power should lurch and swerve along its path there would be less risk of the rest of the world being drawn into another ghastly conflagration.

Fritz had already formed some ideas on the dangers to peace prior to the outbreak of war before he had been touched by the transforming brush of Marxism. His new political thinking did not alter the fundamental principles of his economic analysis which remained the cornerstone of his work during the war years. He believed that he had hit upon something fundamental although he kept stressing: 'I am *not* claiming that the economic causes of war are the sole and exclusive causes. I *am* claiming that they are *important* - important because we can do something about them ... Let us remove all removable causes of war and not waste time searching for "sole" causes, "fundamental" causes.'[1]

Within the framework of economic causes, Fritz had isolated one problem which in his view required urgent attention in the interests of future world peace. This was the unsatisfactory system of international trade and exchange. It was the area of economics which had interested him most ever since he had embarked on his studies. All his experience, his academic studies in Oxford and New York, his practical work in the banks in Hamburg and New York, his study of the history of the gold standard, led him to the conclusion that there were serious malfunctions in the system of international exchange that not only failed to cope with the economic needs of a twentieth-century world but which, in transmitting depressions from one corner of the world to another, had in its malfunctioning the seeds of war. It was a thought that had struck Fritz well before the outbreak of war and no doubt contributed to his certainty that war would be inevitable, in the second half of the 1930s. It was not merely Hitler's will and actions that would in the end be fatal, war was endemic in the economic system.

As Fritz's study of Marxist economics deepened, his analysis also took in more factors in the internal economies of individual nations, particularly the powerlessness of the masses to escape the economic oppression of a powerful minority and rise above their poverty. When he had worked on the problem of unemployment several years earlier he had been motivated by a belief that it was the fundamental right of every man to work and earn a living. Without realizing it, he had been arguing for socialist principles. He had put forward that the successful should subsidize the less fortunate, for the good of the people. One should act because it was man's right to have the necessities of life and not because the poor and hungry might constitute a danger to society. In any case, Fritz believed that those who could be largely satisfied by material things such as food, work and homes, did not tend to become dangerous when they had to do without; they were more likely to become apathetic. He believed that the danger lay in what he called the 'dynamic minority', those creative, extraordinary individuals who were not satisfied by material things alone. Their need was the opportunity to fulfil their creative potential. This dynamic minority, even if prosperous, was likely to cause war if it could not fulfil its potential peacefully. In the past, the pioneering days of geographical expansion, it had been comparatively easy for the dynamic minority to fulfil its creative urges, but 'The great problem facing the western world is that this age of primitive expansion has come to an end and that outlets for creative ability have now to be found not so much in extensive, but in intensive cultivation.'[2]

This argument was not new but Fritz added his own ideas to it. The message he wanted to preach was that the malfunctioning of the economic system prevented the creative minority from operating successfully within the system. They saw the possibilities but were frustrated because they could not realize them. 'The outstanding fact of our age – to my mind – is the staggering discrepancy between our economic possibilities and our actual achievements during times of peace ... It seems quite plain to me that no moral, political, or social structure that we might build up after the war can last for long, unless the economic problem – this problem of discrepancy – is solved.'[3]

Fritz did not dispute the necessity to correct some of the more obvious discrepancies in the economy by such measures as the redistribution of income. He was also particularly interested in the structure of industry which he believed had become top heavy because too much investment had gone into capital goods and not enough attention had been given to consumer needs. He was very much a Keynesian in all these matters. But he was too realistic to suggest that such solutions could be applied world wide.

Thus he returned again and again to the idea that to preserve the possibility of peace without tampering with the internal freedom of individual countries, something had to be done about the framework of international economics. The question of transferring economic ills across national borders had to be tackled, as well as the tendency within the system which made it almost impossible for any country to shift out of their difficulties because of international pressures.

We cannot have a peaceful international economic system as long as one or several countries have a permanent excess of exports (in the widest sense) over imports, because they will always get the rest of the world into unpayable debt ... This therefore is the strategic point of control where international action – international co-operation – should set in. Let every country (including Germany) pursue any such internal policies as it sees fit, let it distribute its national income according to its own principles or lack of principles, let it pursue any employment policy it likes – *insist* only that every country should keep its foreign trade in balance, that it should currently spend on foreign goods and services as much as it earns by providing goods and services to other countries.[4]

A method for achieving greater international co-operation had already occurred to Fritz while he was still in New York in 1934 but it had not been until he was unemployed in the autumn of 1939 that he had begun to work seriously on a scheme. The aims of his system were twofold: to produce a long-term tendency towards balance in international trade and to remove the evil effects of short-term imbalance. He saw that conventional thinking on trade balances had to be turned upside down. It was considered a virtue to achieve and sustain a surplus in the balance of payments, but Fritz realized that it was the surplus countries that were the danger to economic peace not the deficit countries. He pointed out that it was easier to spend a surplus than it was to reduce imports without disturbing the international freedom of trade. If the attitude in the world towards trading balances could be reversed then a new sort of moral pressure would be put on trading nations. The obligation to change things would be put on to the strong instead of the weak. International pressure would not be on deficit countries to find ways of financing their deficits but on surplus countries to get rid of their surpluses by spending more abroad. In February 1940 he wrote to Werner von Simson: 'The principle of "Balance" is the only one which is compatible with international economic peace, and ... any nation which achieves a surplus ... is endangering the economic security of some other nation or nations – unless, indeed, we manage to devise a system, whereunder the surplus is the thing that hurts and the deficit is shorn of its terrors.' In a later paper Fritz explained:

It is considered prudent policy to achieve a surplus, to spend less than is earned. Yet, since one nation's spending is another nation's earning, if all nations strive to earn more than they spend, they want the moon. If they set their mind to it with determination, they must get into conflict with one another.

No wonder that international trading which should be a

peaceful exchange of 'specialities' has become anything but peaceful. It has become a mad struggle for surpluses, super-charged with political tension; every nation trying to 'steal' every other nation's trade and protecting itself with all the modern armoury of bilateral clearing, quotas, exchange control, etc.... Well you may consider me a utopian, but I believe that politics and economics march together, and that once order has superseded chaos in the economic relations between nations, the day will not be far off when mankind will rid itself of the scourge of war.[5]

Fritz considered himself anything but utopian. His aim was to further world peace by action. He had understood that war had underlying economic causes which were partly due to faulty thinking – praising the rich and powerful surplus countries and condemning the weak deficit countries – and which were institutionalized by the way the international economic system worked. His task was to devise a new system which encouraged a different attitude to trade whereby surplus countries had to spend what they earned in the long term while financing the deficits of the economically weaker countries with their surpluses in the short term. In order to achieve this, Fritz believed it was essential that world trade be organized on a multilateral rather than bilateral basis, and that order would be maintained by a central banking and clearing system which would keep tabs on all the to-ings and fro-ings of world trade, making sure that all short-term imbalances tended towards long-term balance.

Fritz worked on the technical details of the multilateral clearing office late each night after he had finished a hard day's labour on the farm. He believed that he had tumbled upon another idea to save the world and his one desire was to get his world improvement plan to the light of day, to the attention of people of influence who would take action. With the interruptions of moves, internment camp and harvest to contend with, it took him almost a year before the thoughts which at the beginning of 1940 he had described to Werner von Simson as 'a favourite idea of mine for a long time' had been welded into a memorandum which he felt could be circulated more widely.

One of the first to receive a copy was David Astor. He was one of the few friends still around whose opinion Fritz respected. Most of Fritz's German friends had not been as lucky as Fritz and were still in various different internment camps, Werner von Simson being hit hardest in the group. He and his English wife Kathleen had left Germany only weeks before the outbreak of war and he was therefore under much greater suspicion than others who had already shown their colours several years earlier. Fritz put in a great deal of effort in trying to procure his friend's release, using all the contacts which had helped his own, but it was well over a year before Werner was allowed to rejoin his wife and family.

Once Werner von Simson was free he was to become an important sounding-post for Fritz's ideas but until then it was largely the Astor family and their contacts to whom Fritz turned. The first reaction came via Lord Astor, who had sent Fritz's paper to Geoffrey Crowther of *The Economist* and Professor Fisher for comment. Their remarks, coming early in the new year, were not encouraging. Crowther concluded that Fritz's views were 'rather too highly coloured by German experience and ... (took) ... too little account of the circumstances and experience of other countries.' It was an opinion that enraged and hurt Fritz. He was not afraid of criticism but such an accusation of partiality he found unjust and totally unfounded. He made his point very clear to Lord Astor:

> Considering that since 1929 when I left school, I have spent hardly three years in Germany and nine years in England, the United States and Canada, that moreover, I have never studied economics in Germany at all, but have spent nearly five years over it at English and American universities, I should understand if someone suggested that my views were too Keynesian – I consider Mr Keynes to be easily the greatest living economist – or too American, but too highly coloured by German experience? In any case, it is my ambition that they should be highly coloured by *experience*, whatever extraction or nationality.

The reference to Keynes gave away the standards by which Fritz wished to be measured and against which he would find criticism acceptable and useful. His admiration for Keynes had grown steadily from the first encounter with him in Cambridge in 1929. Since then he had explained Keynes in America, and studied the 'General Theory' as well as other works, until he genuinely considered Keynes to be one of the great men of the world to whom due praise should be given. He wrote to Keynes in 1940:

> I should like to tell you that there are very few books which have given me as much joy as yours and if this were not ... immodest, I should like to say that a certain familiarity with your thought is among the greatest gains I can show for the last ten years. Please forgive me when I say that it is joy which I derive from your books. This is a very un-academic reaction on my part. But something in me responds directly to the utter earnestness and sincerity of your writing and I cannot read your works without a feeling of gratitude and delight.

Such a display of emotion did not lessen Fritz's critical facilities as he read Keynes's books and when Keynes thanked him for his letter by sending a copy of his latest book, *How to Pay for the War*, Fritz did not hesitate to send Keynes a list of corrections to the calculations in the book, some of which Keynes acknowledged as faulty.

By mid-1941 Fritz was getting impatient that his memorandum on International Clearing was not reaching the right ears. Brand was due to visit Eydon in September and when a dinner invitation came from the Hall, Fritz made up his mind to discuss it with his landlord. He was astonished and delighted to discover that David Astor had already got the wheels in motion for him. Unbeknown to Fritz, he had sent a copy of the memo which Fritz had called 'Free Access to Trade' to his uncle and Fritz found that Brand was not only eager to discuss the scheme, but that he had actually sent it to Keynes himself for comment. Fritz wrote at once to thank David adding, 'That the great J.M.K. has now got it in front of him ... I consider very satisfactory indeed.'

Eventually, in mid-October the anxiously awaited letter arrived at the cottage. Keynes's reaction was positive and encouraging. He wrote:

Mr Brand showed me a note of yours on post-war international currency arrangements. Indeed I have myself been thinking along closely similar lines and have been putting up proposals which go perhaps rather further than yours, but bear a strong family resemblance to them. If you are giving further thoughts to these matters and writing out any notes, I should be very glad indeed if you would let me have the advantage of seeing them.

This was praise indeed; that Fritz's scheme should bear a close family resemblance to the work of the great J.M.K. Fritz was spurred on. Two weeks later a further memo was dispatched. But Fritz was impatient. Was it not time, he asked Keynes, to publish? Keynes's reply, while again encouraging about Fritz's work, was reticent about the prospect of publishing the papers. He wanted his own ideas to be protected. One November 5th he wrote:

Dear Mr Schumacher,
Thank you for sending me your further note. I find this as I found the previous one, excellent and, as I said, in line with what appears to me to be the right sort of constructive ideas.

But I am a little embarrassed what to do with it. I am working at some proposals of my own, which are more detailed and go rather further, but these are of a confidential description. Meanwhile would it or would it not be helpful for you to proceed to publication? Generally speaking, I am in sympathy with the feeling that there is a great deal to be said for bringing proposals to the bar of general opinion. But at this stage I am not sure how far this is true.

This is perhaps because I think that my own plan goes rather further than yours. I cannot disclose that yet, and it would be a pity to get discussion and criticism moving along different lines.

I must leave the matter to you. But what would help me most is that you should simply let me see your ideas on this matter and have a talk next time you are in London, but put off actual publication for the time being.

Yours very truly,

J.M. Keynes

Fritz did not press his wish to publish his article. In December a tea party with Keynes was arranged. Fritz was amazed at the untidy house, where even the stairwell was lined with books piled high on every side, but which also had a touch of the exotic provided by Keynes's wife, a ballerina. The afternoon, which he described a few days later in a letter to Kurt Naumann, was a great success and left Fritz feeling exhilarated.

I was with Keynes for several hours – a strange impression. A man of great kindness, even charm; but he was much more the Cambridge Don than I had expected. I had expected to find a mixture between a doer and thinker, but the first impression is overwhelmingly, if not almost exclusively that of a thinker. I don't know how far his practical influence goes these days but some tell me that it is extraordinarily significant.

The conversation was completely different from what I had expected. I was prepared to sit at his feet and listen to the words of the master. Instead an extraordinarily lively discussion arose, a very battle between heavy artillery – and all this despite the fact that from the beginning we were 99% in agreement. Somehow something got me and I contradicted him without the least shyness when my views differed from his. We threw all sorts of things at each other's heads (to the astonishment of a third present) and parted – I am sure – good friends. Anyway, this is certain: The fundamental ideas of my plan Keynes considers to be the only possible basis for the future. Technically there are still gaps. He himself, has gone rather further into the technical details, but, it seems clear to me at any rate, he is still rather behind in his fundamental thinking. He is still rather hooked on bilateralism. And I hope that the consistency of the multilateralism of my suggestions will have influenced him, or will still influence him in the future.

The meeting with Keynes was the high point of Fritz's double life at Eydon. His fellow farm hands had probably not even heard of Keynes and wondered what all the fuss was about when Fritz asked permission of the farm manager, a more knowledgeable man, to have the day off to go to London.

'What do you want to go to London for?' he asked Fritz. 'To take tea with John Maynard Keynes,' came the unexpected reply. Fritz described the look he received as 'the loony look'. The farm manager clearly thought Fritz had gone off his head.

He received the same look from the police sergeant at Banbury police station who had to issue him with papers to get out of the zone. What did a farm labourer want to go to London for? Fritz felt that it was perhaps time for him to look for a job which could help him devote himself more fully to the cause of economic peace.

Again an encounter arranged by fate settled the matter. Several of Fritz's fellow inmates at Prees Heath had been employed at the Oxford Institute of Statistics. Fritz had remained in touch with them and at the beginning of 1942 Burchardt, fondly known by his colleagues as Bu, told Fritz that there was a job going at the Institute for which Fritz would be considered an outstanding candidate; his interview would be a mere formality. Fritz applied for the job assuming that it was already his, but his optimism turned out to be misplaced. Suddenly he was informed that in fact there were five other candidates, one of whom was considered hot favourite. Fritz reacted angrily. The recognition of his ability by Keynes had increased his self-esteem, in which intellectual arrogance was apparent. But his feeling of insecurity as an enemy alien in Britain, without power or status, made him feel both vulnerable and unjustly treated. He knew that he could be turned away from the job purely on grounds of his nationality or a malicious word from an unknown enemy. He wrote at once to Harold Scott complaining of his treatment and asking Scott to put in a good word on his behalf. The irrational hostility at Eydon village had made him unusually touchy and suspicious.

His fears also turned out to be misplaced; he was formally offered the job and in March 1942 Fritz left Eydon for Oxford. He went alone, leaving Muschi and the children in Eydon. The plan was that he should live in a room at New College until such time as he could find suitable accommodation.

The main purpose in leaving the farm and becoming a professional economist once more was that Fritz would have

131

more time to devote to his scheme for international clearing arrangements. He was not sure that the move had many other advantages as he wrote to David Astor in March.

> I am not quite certain yet whether I have made a change for the better or worse by exchanging the status of a proletarian plain and simple for that of a '*stehkragen-proletarier*'. It has one advantage that I can push my 'Free Access to Trade' scheme a bit harder than I could before. And I can do about 10% more studying during the whole day than I previously did during off hours.

With his new status as an economist among economists, instead of an isolated intellectual farm hand, Fritz was certainly in a better position to further his scheme. Not only could he discuss it with his colleagues, but he was also freer to travel to London. His meeting with Keynes had provided him with a hopeful opening: R.N. Rosenstein Rodan, who ran the Royal Institute of International Affairs at Chatham House in London, had been the third person at the tea party with Keynes. He invited Fritz to circulate his paper to the Institute's members and throughout 1942, as part of his job at the Oxford Institute, Fritz travelled regularly to London to participate in discussion groups at Chatham House.

All publicity was useful and eventually in May Fritz's paper made its way into Government circles and the Treasury. It reached the desk of Sir Stafford Cripps, the then Chancellor of the Exchequer, to whom Fritz was summoned, as well as Sir Hubert Henderson, who held detailed discussions with Fritz. Fritz wrote to Muschi from London in high spirits: 'The Schumacher scheme is being discussed right and left. There are many supporters for it: Memos are being written, some for it, some against. But I haven't come across one single argument yet which forced me to think anew.'

In the February of 1943 Sir Wilfred Eady saw Fritz at the Treasury for further discussion. After the meeting he wrote to Fritz to clarify one or two points and added that he had sent a copy to Keynes who had once again described the paper as 'lucid and interesting'. The time had definitely come, Fritz decided, to publish in the May edition of the economists' periodical *Economica*. It was a month too late. In April Keynes published his scheme. It was called 'Proposals for an International Clearing Union', and it was prefaced with the following words: 'The particular proposals set forth below lay no claim to originality. They are an attempt to reduce to practical shape certain general ideas belonging to the contemporary climate of economic opinion, which have been given publicity in recent months by writers of several different nationalities.'[6]

One of those writers was clearly Fritz, but precisely how much influence Fritz had on the shaping of Keynes's ideas cannot be known. From Fritz's letters at the time it seems clear that he believed he and Keynes were thinking along the same lines and that in some ways he had gone further than Keynes while in other points Keynes had worked out the scheme in more detail. At no point does he either accuse Keynes of plagiarism or even insinuate that Keynes was using his work without acknowledging its proper origin. Nor do his colleagues recall that he expressed such sentiments at the time. Yet later Fritz always referred to the Keynes plan as his own plan, giving the impression that Keynes derived his ideas from Fritz's papers, ideas which are now enshrined in history books as the 'Keynes Plan' put forward at the historic Bretton Woods conference.

This is not quite consistent with his view at the time, for Fritz was critical of Keynes's final version of the plan for not being sufficiently multilateral (although not as critical as he was of the American 'White Plan' which was adopted by the conference and which led to the International Monetary Fund and its accompanying structure). Less than three years later in 1947 he went even further, criticizing his own ideas by saying, 'I used to think that we might be able to *cheat* our way out of the necessity of working out the New Law of Mechanics [of international trade] simply by matching the growth of units with the growth of reserves.'[7] Elsewhere he added, 'Experience shows this is "too simple". Nations won't lend to an anonymous debtor.'

The question remains why Fritz should later have given the impression that he believed that Keynes had used his ideas when he did not do so to his colleagues at the time. It is possible that he only came to the conclusion that he had had a significant influence on Keynes when he came to realize that Keynes was known to use other people's ideas without necessarily acknowledging their source, a fact which he may not have known at a time when he regarded Keynes with such admiration.

It is more likely that in the reality of war he was less concerned with the origins of the ideas than with their implementation. His commitment to his 'world improvement plan' was absolute. He believed that it could make a major and significant contribution to the preservation of world peace, a cause which he regarded higher than any other. Everyone who knew him knew of this commitment, knew of his plan and knew of his contact with Keynes. He had no need to make any claims to originality or brilliance. In a letter in August 1941 to David Astor he had already made his position very clear when he wrote (my italics):

> The measures I propose take full notice of existing conditions, they would throw nothing out of gear, but they supply a gearbox for something that has been out of gear for the last twenty years. Well I have praised my own child too much, forgive me ... I don't care who takes it up, *as long as somebody pays attention to the ideas and, if he approves of them propagates them.*

Later, his trips to London, his tea party with Keynes, his discussions with Government ministers made a very good story when they were set in the context of an enemy alien farm labourer leading a double life. It made a dramatic punchline to add that the famous 'Keynes Plan' was in fact the 'Schumacher Plan'. It did not mean so much that Keynes had stolen his glory than that his plan had been the same as Keynes's. Certainly that seems nearer the truth. Fritz and Keynes were working along the same lines, a fact remarkable enough in itself. It is quite possible too that Fritz's ideas contributed to the final shaping of Keynes's own paper just as discussions with Keynes probably helped Fritz finalize his version.

Fritz's association with Keynes did not end with his discussions over the multilateral clearing plan. He continued to regard him as one of the greatest economists the world had known and, as a known admirer, though not an uncritical one, he was asked by *The Times* newspaper to prepare an obituary of Keynes. It is the paper's policy to prepare obituaries in advance and Fritz felt like a murderer as he sat typing his final judgment on a man he knew to be still very much alive.

Shortly before his death Keynes pronounced his own judgment of Fritz. Sir Wilfred Eady of the Treasury was visiting him and Keynes told Sir Wilfred: 'If my mantle is to fall on anyone, it could only be Otto Clarke or Fritz Schumacher. Otto Clarke can do anything with figures, but Schumacher can make them sing.'[8]

10

Marx v. God

While devoting himself to his multilateral clearing plan with missionary zeal, Fritz also found time in Eydon to develop his political thinking. The seeds sown by Kurt Naumann at Prees Heath grew rapidly and Fritz nurtured them carefully. A year after his internment he had written to David Astor from his Eydon cottage.

> My intense interest in socialism is, as you know, a new departure ... For years I have been studying economics without paying much attention to politics. Now I realize two things: (1) that economics without politics is almost meaningless, because certain tacit assumptions regarding the social and political structure are always present, and (2) that most of my economic results, independently arrived at, appear to be more easily compatible with socialism than with any other political 'ism'. I say 'appear to be' because I am as yet far from having formed a final opinion. What my final opinion will be I don't know, but I am pretty sure that my nature does not allow me to embrace wholeheartedly as 'final' any political creed or system, any 'ism' or any panacea.

It was the second point that excited him so much about his 'discovery' of socialism: a discovery he had made through the logic of his purely economic thinking. He felt as exhilarated as an explorer discovering new continents, a feeling he described early in 1942 to Sir Richard Acland, a socialist writer of the day:

> I don't know if my case is a normal one or an unusual one. I am an economist, thoroughbred, so to say, in the tradition of liberal or classical economics. But in spite of this theoretical breeding I have seen a good deal of the practical working of our economic system on the Continent, in Britain, Canada and the United States. These experiences have led to a development of my economic views, so that a short while ago, without ever having read a single book of Socialist (or Common Ownership) literature, I had arrived at views which I now find compatible with and exceedingly close to those held by the progressives of the 'left'. They may smile at me for having discovered America for myself after so many had already successfully made the journey. But, at least I have got there on my own little ship, under the steam of my own efforts, and I now know the way there perhaps better than those who got across on one of those luxury liners of ossified doctrine.

Having 'discovered America', Fritz set about immersing himself in socialist literature. He read what he could on and by Marx, Lenin and Trotsky. Lenin he found 'more exciting and illuminating than anything I know'. He joined the socialist book club, he even enrolled Werner von Simson although some months later he coldly asked Werner to terminate his membership because he had not shown the same enthusiasm for Marx as Fritz himself felt. Fritz was scathing about von Simson's caution. In his eyes no serious student of world affairs could afford to disregard Marx: Marx was of supreme importance, as important as Keynes in an understanding of contemporary society, economics and politics. In a series of letters to von Simson at the beginning of 1942 he put his cards on the table:

> Of course, I am impressed by his (Marx's) arguments ... But it does not mean that I agree with all he says or with anything he says. Amongst other things I am impressed by the fact that so many people are impressed. But there is a difference between being impressed and being convinced. In fact, if you

want to know, I am also convinced – at the moment – that a great deal of Marxism is true.

Marx has looked the facts in the face. That is why I have studied him, learned from him and have even recommended him to others. His conclusions and generalizations have in some cases proved wrong and in surprisingly many cases proved right. He has left an indelible mark upon the thoughts of the world and, therefore should not be ignored by present day students.

Fritz's new political interests crystallized his aims as an economist. Economics he now saw as a means to an end. The end was generally given from outside the sphere of economics by political, philosophical or religious considerations, or by plain common sense. The economist was the specialist to procure the means. Nevertheless, he had his responsibilities too:

Specialists are experts on *means*. Every specialist should also be able to step outside his special field and consider the end ... The end and purpose of economics for me is the physical and spiritual well-being of men, women and children ...

Theoretically – I am interested in anybody and everybody's well-being.

Practically – I have to limit my aspirations to what is possible – What *is* possible?

The answer he suggested was to ensure a level of optimum consumption necessary for physical and spiritual well-being. The rich were above this optimum level, the poor below it, which led him to conclude, 'I am, therefore, interested only in the poor.'[1]

'... man *en masse* is determined by material factors of his environment. Do not wait for the spiritual revolution. Change the environment.'[2]

His position was summed up perfectly by words he often quoted from Bertold Brecht, a phrase extremely popular in the Germany of Fritz's youth: '*Erst kommt das Fressen, dann kommt die Moral.*' (First comes the belly, and only then morality.)

Having discovered that he was a socialist, Fritz did not try to hide the fact from his audiences. His message was often clearly identifiable with the 'left'. In a set of lecture notes he spelt out his whole world view:

As a socialist	– not in love with capitalism
As a businessman	– impressed by the achievements of large scale industry – 'semi-monopolies'
	– impressed by the waste and inefficiency in highly competitive small scale enterprise
	– impressed by the value of 'planning' and by the (short term) blindness of the unorganized market.
As an economist	– interested in economists not making fools of themselves with the 'practical man'. They have a lot to contribute.
As a student of politics	– interested in left wing intellectuals and Trade Unionists understanding one another.[3]

He came down firmly on the side of state planning, large-scale state monopolies, mass production and standardization. The size of state monopolies, he believed, ensured that money could be raised for research and technical progress; they would not be hampered by the profit motive of the private sector, and there would be less risk that employees would be exploited under the watchful eye of the public.

There were chinks in this socialist armoury however. Russia, as far as he was concerned, was not a land flowing with milk and honey as many European Marxists believed. Fritz saw that Marx was the kind of giant thinker after whose presence the world could never be quite the same and from whom there was a great deal to be learnt, but he was too much of an independent thinker himself to accept everything Marx said without question. He was aware that inherent in Marxism was a certain loss of personal freedom and he had not left the restrictions of Germany to embrace them in another form.

Marxist economics posed a challenging question however, one in which he was already intensely interested: how could freedom and planning be combined? His papers on international trading arrangements had this thought at their core as the title 'Free Access to Trade' implied. The freedom of nations to trade with whom they wished had to be safeguarded in a free world and yet he saw that the freedom of strong nations to do so jeopardized the freedom of weaker nations. The element of planning which controlled the anarchy of total freedom lay in the central clearing 'bank' which he had proposed. When it came to internal economic policy Fritz was in favour of greater intervention than the clearing idea implied in international trade. His analysis of the German economy was that a top-heavy capital goods industry had concentrated power in the hands of a few capitalists who had not acted in the interests of the consumer. In a paper of the early 1940s on 'The Need for Planning', he wrote: 'Industry exists, in theory, to meet the needs of consumers, but in practice public policy treats consumers as existing in order to provide profit for industry.' Only state planning, Fritz maintained, could correct this imbalance.

Immersed in socialist literature, Fritz was given great hope that Marxism would provide the answer to the German catastrophe. He wrote to Werner von Simson in February 1942:

> I think we are entering a period of very great social changes on the Continent. Those of us who contemplate a return to Germany after the war should study these changes with the greatest of attention. The drift on the Continent, in my opinion, is towards socialism, or to be more precise, towards a social structure in which the material and spiritual needs of those classes which have not themselves hitherto occupied ruling classes will assert themselves.
>
> These needs have been very clearly formulated in the writings of Marx, Engels, Lenin, and other writers of the 'left'. They should be studied. The breakdown of the Nazi régime will let loose violent revolutionary forces in Germany. The strongest political force - internally - will, in my opinion, be represented by German and foreign factory workers. Whether their attempt to overthrow not only the Nazis but the whole of the present day ruling class in Germany will be successful or not will depend largely on Russia

and the Allies. In my opinion it is necessary that the revolution should be complete. It is my intention to offer my services to the revolutionary workers as soon as the opportunity serves, because I believe that they will need in their great task, and be appreciative of the loyal co-operation of members of the intelligentsia. In fact I believe that the ultimate outcome of the revolution and the shape of the new Germany will very largely depend upon whether or not such support will be forthcoming in sufficient strength.

The creed of revolutionary socialism is, as far as I can see, compatible with the interests of the outside world. It is anti-imperialistic and anti-chauvinist; it aims at the full utilization of science and its further development; its preoccupation is with the welfare of the masses. Its creed (unless I deceive myself) had been my creed before I ever touched upon socialist literature. The question of whether it is right or wrong to work for a revolution has lost its significance for German socialism. The revolution will come almost automatically as a result of defeat. There can no longer be a question of reformism, etc. The task will be to make a completely new start. The risks are grave and the opportunity tremendous. I, for one shall not be a passive spectator.

Fritz's hope of a Marxist revolution cleansing Germany did not last long. Gradually it became clear that although a new Germany would be raised from the ashes of the old it would not be from ashes created by an internal workers' movement to topple the Nazis. It would take the combined forces of the Allies to remove the scourge of the Nazis and it would be their responsibility to mould the new society in Germany. This became a fresh avenue of thought and hope for Fritz. The Allies would have the chance to create something new, something better, just as he had hoped when he had written to Muschi out of Prees Heath: 'Europe, a new Europe coming from England.'

He saw the future in Germany combining everything he held dear: a combination of Western politics and Eastern economics. From the West, particularly England, came the noble political ideals of liberty, freedom of speech, human rights and a decent government which respected the individual. From the

East, by which he meant Russia, Germany could learn to plan in order to prevent the chaos which economic freedom had brought in the past.

Western politics and Eastern economics meant democratic freedom within a planned economy to ensure that the consumer was not treated as the source of profit for a controlling elite. It was a different kind of revolution from the one Fritz had envisaged at first but it was a revolution and one in which Fritz still wished to participate.

As Fritz wrestled with these important world issues he had no doubt in his own ability to make a useful contribution to their solution. As far as he could see there were very few people around who really had this ability to look at the problems correctly and draw the conclusions necessary to overcome them. Throughout his education and self-education he had been handed answers that experience in the world showed him just did not work. He believed that his knowledge and his experience, combined with his powerful intellect, enabled him to discern what was useful in the different systems offered, such as that of Marx and that of Keynes, and devise his own.

This extraordinary belief in himself, combined with the dissatisfaction he felt at the inability of others to recognize the chaos around them, let alone make sense of it, drove him on relentlessly. It had kept him going despite the frustrations of his work for Schicht and the failure of B.T.L. It kept him up late at night at Eydon where he often felt lonely and isolated. He believed that he possessed resources necessary to find the key to mastering the problems that he saw. He was unemotional and refused to moralize. The powerful ray of intellectual truth had to penetrate each problem to its core, discarding irrelevancies and irrational beliefs and putting in their place only logic and facts.

This scientific approach had its problems in his personal life. Muschi was the antithesis of his ideal of a clear thinker. She did not so much think as feel. She could not understand most of what Fritz told her but she knew that it was brilliant. Had he told her that black was white and white was black she would have had no option but to accept. She had no basis on which to question him. She only had her instincts to go by, she could only follow the dictates of her heart and as her heart belonged to him, he possessed her whole personality. Yet her feelings of intellectual inadequacy made her feel generally inadequate at times and doubt her worth as his wife. As he bombarded her with ideas and challenged the structure of her own beliefs she had a struggle to keep a grip on her own identity. Her role appeared to her to be that of a provider of comfort and support to Fritz so that he could carry out his great work with as little hindrance as possible, and she did it with as much devotion and commitment as she gave to securing the happiness of her children. It was her reason for living.

In Eydon she found her reward in a new opportunity to talk about the things that interested Fritz. Their relative isolation from the outside world meant that he talked a great deal to Muschi about his world of ideas and she felt that she shared his life in a new way, was more fully a partner to him. She was very happy despite the hardships that they encountered. She wrote in a letter eventually destined for her parents (probably via Eric Petersen in Brazil):

> Our life here often seems quite unreal. It encompasses so much that is wonderful. Fritz is a real farm labourer during the day and his work embraces everything one can think of. He has really got into the job and I have rarely seen him so fulfilled by a job as this one. He has never been so healthy. Apart from the occasional Sunday, we live in complete isolation and can pursue our interest fully. Fritz has always wanted it this way and I never had any idea how much the insight and knowledge of his books and ideas that I have gained by our close life together would enrich me and fill me with joy.

The joy of intellectual discovery through Fritz was derived primarily through the closeness of their relationship at this time. Thrust together in a hostile world Muschi felt more secure in their relationship than at any other time. Although many of the ideas on which Fritz was working were disturbing to her, she could maintain her inner equilibrium by her complete absorption in him and his life. Some aspects of his work were, of course, a delight to her. His work for peace in the sphere of economics, his growing interest in the plight of the underprivileged and in justice and equality which his study of Marx had shown him, were all causes which she could understand with her heart even if her mind did not completely grasp all the ins and outs of the matter. But the other side of his newly found political convictions were not so easy for her to digest or accept. His Marxist apprenticeship had driven him to another extreme, that of a passionate atheist. He had never shared her conventional but real enough Christian beliefs. He had poked fun at religion and made irreverent jokes, but he had not tried to destroy her faith. He had after all read Albert Schweitzer with more than a passing interest, although he preferred to read philosophers such as Nietzsche and Schopenhauer. But with the outbreak of war and all that followed, his position changed. The irreverent and even sneering atheist turned into a non-believer of passionate convictions. Religion to Fritz became more than just mumbo jumbo, it was a body of belief that a man of his intellect could not possibly accept. There was, he wrote to Werner von Simson, 'overwhelming evidence that there are more intelligent and knowledgable people amongst non-Christians (of the last fifty or a hundred years) than among strict believers.' Intelligence and Christianity were clearly incompatible.

As the starting point for his complete rejection of religion was the scientific and logical thought which had flowered in the last hundred years. He did not have to look far for evidence which showed him that the rigorous application of logic and science left Christianity trailing in the mud. He did not spare Muschi in trying to convince her of the foolishness of her beliefs. She wrote of it sadly to her uncle, Gustav Sieveking: 'Sometimes it is not easy to follow his long explanations, and sometimes I am very depressed when I have to revise my old familiar opinions.'

Unfortunately Fritz, with his brilliant, questioning intellect, had failed to investigate with his usual thoroughness the source of those qualities in Muschi which he had described as saintly or even angelic. He had failed to grasp that the strength and loving nature he had come to admire had its roots in the 'old familiar opinions' which he was trying to destroy. He did not see that because they had become so close in Eydon, he had become her strength and her inner life more than ever; it was no longer her own strength that sustained her but his optimism and his conviction that the war against Hitler was right and that their place was in England. He saw only that religion, and in particular Christianity, was full of statements that could never be scientifically proved. Only facts could ascertain truth, not speculation. He believed that he was truly seeking the truth and what was accepted as truth in religion was merely sentiment, morality, faith or some vague assertions of good and evil. Such beliefs, in his opinion, could not belong to a serious search for truth; he could not accept the existence of any absolutes. There could not be absolute good or absolute evil but only an answer to the question, good for whom, evil for whom?

His vehement rejection of religion, particularly established Western Christian religion, was two-sided. First of all, he believed, it could not stand up to any scientific examination. 'Science is the organized attempt of mankind to discover how things work as a causal system,' he quoted to Werner von Simson, adding:

> Since everything has a cause, the realm of science is everything ... I further hold that it is unworthy of thinking men to succumb to their *horror vacui* in the field of knowledge and understanding and to give answers to unsolved problems 'by act of faith' merely because they should like to have an answer. The smallest item of observational knowledge appeals more to my aesthetic, yes, also to my moral sense than the most glorious superstructure built by statements unsupported by or in contradiction with facts.

Fritz believed that morality was an historical product which, as any other human law, could be altered if it became inconvenient or no longer appropriate for the society in which it had evolved. He further held that as man was the product of his inherited character and environment he could not be held responsible for his behaviour and one could not hate him for what he did. Religion, with its concepts of heavenly reward or the punishment of hell, was therefore irrelevant as a motivating force.

Although Fritz rejected any concept of absolute morality he

also rejected Christianity because of what he believed to be its failure to provide a sound moral lead. He considered Christian morality not only to be ambiguous and full of contradictions, but to be anti-life, encouraging brutal revenge, war and a concern for the individual at the expense of society as a whole. He did not mince his words when expounding his objections to Werner von Simson, who was vainly trying to persuade Fritz that without some kind of moral code society could not rise above the mess it was in. Fritz wrote:

> My criticism of Christianity...is not merely that its doctrines include the most terrible and savage superstitions of a barbarous age, (the whole doctrine of Atonement, the slaying of a God, the eating of a God ...), but that as a moral code, it is totally insufficient, self-contradictory, and out of date ... You can read anything out of the Bible and into it. And that, in my opinion, condemns it as a moral code.

Nor could he see how his own work fitted into a Christian concept of what was worth doing. As far as he could see the Christian was supposed to be concerned with his own world and that of his neighbour. He, Fritz, had a far wider term of reference: his work was for the good of society as a whole. Again he wrote to Werner von Simson:

> Now I am a person who tries to establish harmony within himself, so that my right hand knows what my left is doing. My own religion (or lack of religion), has a place for my endeavours to improve the well-being of the world. When I am bothering my head about questions of international exchange, or the trade cycle, or unemployment, or about the relation between the birth rate and poverty, my philosophy tells me that I am doing right. Can you give me any saying of Jesus, or any explicit statement in the whole of the New Testament which would encourage me to go on with my work ... 'Render unto Caesar what is Caesar's' ... Yes ... but what I am rendering to mankind is more than that, it is my very best. Why should I do that, rather than go out and help my neighbour if I were a Christian, ... Give me rather one or two quotations which would encourage me to go on caring for the troubles of mankind. I left Christianity

because I could not find them, and I could not believe that it would be for the higher glory of God, if economics, politics, justice, if our whole social structure fell to pieces, because those who could have helped to hold it together found it more important to save their own souls.

Christianity, Fritz maintained, urged one to 'Help the poor and the sick.' But something quite different was needed: namely, to 'Fight disease and poverty.' This Fritz argued in a letter to David Astor was 'the morals of the future', not an outworn creed which left the 'field of religion making free to the Hitlers, Mussolinis, Mr Eddys, Buchmans, astrologers, spiritualists, and a host of other cranks.'

Fritz's vehemence against 'morals and sentiment' was partly fanned by his attitude to Nazi Germany and the war. Many people considered the war to be a kind of twentieth-century crusade – the fight of good over evil, Christianity and morality against Nazism. Fritz completely rejected this view. He discussed it with David Astor who suggested that 'only an individually held moral code makes people proof against Nazism and other forms of political gangsterism.' This Fritz accepted but he added:

I cannot possibly agree with the implied identification of Christianity and morality . . . In fact, wherever I look I seem to find that the men who combine high morality with constructive and progressive ideas, men of thought and men of action . . . are almost invariably 'free thinkers' . . . Christianity is a spent force . . . take Julian Huxley, Bertrand Russell, Shaw, Wells, Lord Moseley, Sir J.G. Frazer – to name only a few Englishmen; take practically every leading scientist, Einstein, Heisenberg, Levy, even Jeans or Eddington – everywhere you find the same picture. Nietzsche is merely the greatest synthesis of it all . . .

Christianity, in the minds of all the majority of people in all important countries, stands for 'vested interests', for the 'old order' and 'against the new order' or the 'free order'. Those who call this war a Christian crusade are not only voicing a minority opinion of proved falsehood; they are committing a political blunder. This war is more than just another Christian crusade. We are aiming higher in our peace aims than just the re-establishment of the Christian concept of man.

What Fritz was advocating was not an amoral society, or even a society without religion, but a society which had a new set of beliefs based on scientific rationalism, humanitarian behaviour, justice, and compassion. The fundamental question to be asked when framing a new morality was, 'Where does one want mankind to be led?' Fritz thought he knew. In his correspondence with von Simson he said, 'My own answer is derived from a perusal of the facts ascertained about human evolution. Man has raised himself above the level of the Ape, he can raise himself further to a level as yet beyond our imagination. That is my "Faith".'

Fritz's 'faith' was basically faith in himself, faith in his own intellect, faith in his own ability to raise himself above the ape and beyond. His beliefs, he thought, should benefit the thinking section of mankind although he admitted that the rest of mankind might need something a little more precise. He wrote:

> I personally, should feel that the 'religion of humanity' can give these non-thinkers far more valuable and truthful assurances, viz. that every good man considers it his sacred duty to fight poverty and disease wherever he can, relentlessly, determinedly, without the thought of personal gain; that he will devote his best energies to improving the social and political system, to render justice more complete, security of life and limb more perfect.

Fritz referred to himself as the 'anti-metaphysician par excellence' adding in parenthesis, '(at least in aspiration)'. Clarity of mind and close adherence to facts was, he felt, the only way forward to reform and enlightenment. His friends and acquaintances were left in no doubt about his stand. Whilst Fritz was at Eydon, David Astor and Werner von Simson were the principal recipients of his dissertations on his personal and political philosophy, largely by letter. Once in Oxford he lectured his colleagues and friends there. For a while he shared a flat with a colleague, Kurt Mandelbaum, with whom he discussed philosophical questions late into the night. Fritz's views were very much in line with the current Oxford philosophy: scientific, rationalistic, atheistic. Mandelbaum dared suggest that such a view was not entirely satisfactory; people concerned with metaphysics, raised some very interesting questions. Fritz dismissed the suggestion. 'Kurt, you are an obscurantist,' he said.

While he argued with his friends, the force of his views had penetrated Muschi and, as he rooted out what Christianity she had, a vacuum was left which was filled with himself. While they were together this did not affect their happiness, but as soon as they were apart Muschi was left without inner resources to strengthen her. The winter of 1941-2 heralded such an unhappy change in their lives. The new phase began with news that they had been dreading since the outbreak of war. On December 9th, 1941 a letter reached them saying that Ernst, Fritz's younger brother, had been killed in action on the Russian front, shortly before his eighteenth birthday. It was a bitter blow. Ernst, so greatly loved, so talented, so full of promise, had sacrificed his life fighting for a terrible cause. The blow was all the more bitter because Ernst had volunteered for the army, full of patriotic fervour. Fritz's grief was deep and long-lived.

'We had always hoped that fate would spare this young person, so full of hope,' Muschi wrote to her Uncle Gustav, 'and now it appears that he is the first to go. Fritz tries to bear it quietly. The most beloved young person has been taken away from him and those who knew him know how deeply those who loved him will mourn.'

Then early in the new year came the second blow – although this was for Muschi alone. Fritz was offered the job at the Oxford Institute of Statistics. Muschi, glad for him, was herself faced with the prospect of being alone in Eydon while he led a bachelor existence in Oxford. As he left in March 1942 she discovered that her life-support system had been taken away.

11

Oxford Again

During the war the Oxford University Institute of Statistics, housed in Nuffield College, was largely manned by an interesting collection of foreign economists and statisticians. The few Britons among them had generally not yet achieved the distinctions of their foreign colleagues and one of them, David Worswick, said that his job was 'simply to turn them all into Englishmen'.

The Institute had been founded in 1936 in order to introduce a little more scientific method into economics and get away from the rather literary approach of the nineteenth century. At first it was mainly a place where young post-graduate students could do their research under the guidance of the director, Jacob Marshak, and several other dons who supported the Institute such as R.F. Harrod and E.H. Phelps-Brown. Very soon, however, the upheavals in Germany began to have their effect and refugees arrived in Oxford, some already eminent in their own countries and others up-and-coming scholars at the institutes and universities they had been forced to leave. It became difficult to know what to do with this potential arriving in such quantity. Many of them spoke too little English to be able to contribute usefully to college life and security reasons barred them from any kind of government service.

The Oxford Institute of Statistics provided the answer. As war broke out and the Institute's English research staff were summoned to Whitehall to help with the war effort, or entered the forces, their vacant posts were quickly filled by the refugee economists, many of them able, several of them with engaging or interesting characters.

Most important amongst the new staff was a Polish economist named Michal Kalecki. Many regarded him as the equal of Keynes and he became a focal point at the Institute. As well as his intellectual stature Kalecki had an engaging personality, quite genuine, without affectations, party manners or small talk, and a remarkable dedication to his subject which excluded any preoccupation with his own advancement.

Between 1933 and 1935 Kalecki had written a number of articles which contained some revolutionary ideas. In order to develop these ideas fully he obtained a year's leave from his institute to work in Sweden. Shortly after his arrival in 1936 he was handed a copy of a newly published work that was causing a great stir in Western economic circles. It was Keynes's 'General Theory'. It was the very work which Kalecki himself was writing. When he realized that Keynes had got there first he said, 'For three minutes I was ill. And then I thought, well, Keynes is much more known than I am and these ideas will catch on much more quickly with him. And then he can get on with the important thing which is their application to policy and so on.' And without another word Kalecki turned his attention elsewhere and did not mention this near-miss again. It was not until after his death that this astonishing story, which had its similarities with Fritz's experience, became more widely known, through the posthumous publication of a collection of Kalecki's articles prefaced by a description of his early ideas.

Frank Burchardt, or Bu, as he was called, later the Director of the Institute, was less brilliant than Kalecki but was also highly respected in Oxford as a person and as an economist. His reputation was equally high in Germany, which he had left, so that when he returned in the 1950s to participate in a conference of professors and trade union leaders, he had the unusual honour of receiving a standing ovation as he slipped into the back of the lecture theatre after the beginning of the conference.

Amongst the most colourful characters to be seen at the Institute was the Hungarian, Tommy Balogh. He was already known to Fritz, having been one of Professor Schumacher's favoured pupils in Berlin. Fritz was aware that Balogh still resented the fact that Professor Schumacher had suddenly dropped him for another favourite and for a while there was a certain coolness between the two young men at Oxford, until one day Balogh strode across the road towards Fritz and shaking him by the hand said, 'I have wronged you.' He said he had read an article by Fritz and was sufficiently impressed to forgive Fritz for the wrongs of his father.

Balogh had been in England longer than the others. He was attached to Balliol College and was more part of the mainstream of academic life than his colleagues at the Institute. He was reputed to know everything about everyone that mattered and would casually drop into conversations that he had just been with the Prime Minister or some other important person. Keynes is said to have observed that in a new place he would rather spend half an hour with Tommy Balogh than with anyone else to find out what was going on!

The Institute's main work was to monitor the war economy, but Fritz worked with the International Committee, a group of economists loosely connected to Chatham House and concerned more with international questions of post-war reconstruction. These were the very matters on which Fritz had been working for the past few years, and it should have been an ideal situation for him. His colleagues were intelligent men who wanted to make a positive contribution to a better world. After months of isolation, here at last were people to whom he could talk, who were interested and able to understand what he was saying. Yet Fritz did not really appreciate his new company. He was entering one of the least attractive periods of his life and one of the more unhappy.

His self-made philosophy, his lonely pioneering road at Eydon, his insecurity and the absence of Muschi who was his anchor to human feeling, combined to complete his retreat into his intellect. A friend of David Astor's meeting Fritz at this time commented, 'I don't believe that man was born. I think he came out of a bottle.' Completely ruled by his head, he looked down on all his colleagues with arrogant contempt. In March 1942 after one week at the Institute he wrote to Muschi:

With the 'joint committee' meeting just passed here I have, I think (and hope), reached an all-time low period in my intellectual career. Give me farm labourers, or factory work-men – even shop assistants – I am certain they will talk more intelligently and more to the point than some of this scum of the earth, called Oxford post-war Reconstruction Plan-ners.

I have had a week of suffering from the fatuousness and stupidity of my contemporaries. Not a very nice thing to say I know. But there it is ... I have ... written a devastating criticism on a memo produced by one of my so-called col-leagues here and treated – in despair – two further memos as complete jokes, fit for immediate publication in *Punch*.

I have come to the point where I don't care two hoots whether people like me or not, but I shall force them to realize that I am made of somewhat different stuff. Sterner stuff, I am sure.

Fritz did not make such an instant and devastating impression. Or if he did it did not seem to affect his colleagues. Another month passed and he was as disappointed as ever. Again he wrote to Muschi:

I am bored with life, perhaps I shall go to a show tonight. Everything is terribly slack here. Some people are always very busy – but that is only to keep the machine going. Press cuttings, internal arrangements, etc. etc. But ideas? – none.

If they would only take up my ideas, and deal with them seriously; dismiss them, perhaps, but at any rate deal with the *problems* they were designed to solve. They are the big-gest economic problems of the lot. If they can't be solved, then all the talkie talkie is in vain. But no. They prefer the little problems – study the button industry, or the distribu-tion of sausages – they are scared of anything that may have practical consequences. It's a desert.

Harsh words. Was Fritz really close to despair? Had his arrog-ance really reached such a level of self-adulation and isolation? Where was the humour and charm that had carried him through life this far? Had his intellect eclipsed even that? A postscript to the letter gives one hope: '(PS: Don't take anything I say too seriously, because things change – sometimes quickly).'

The optimist was still alive in him after all, and according to most of his colleagues, so was the charm, the elegance that attracted so many to him. The key to finding Fritz charming and not in the least arrogant was either to be regarded by him as an equal or to acknowledge that one was not. Fritz did not suffer fools gladly, and his definition of fools broadly covered anyone who dared to question him, regarding themselves as his equal or even superior. If they were not accepted as such by Fritz, they were worthy of contempt. The most humble and ignorant secretary was treated with consideration and respect, the most eminent economist disregarded at kindest as a bad joke. Not even the honour of being asked to advise His Majesty's Government humbled him. After one such meeting almost a year later he wrote to Muschi:

> Well, this has been a very strange experience – and in a way depressing. There was such an extreme absence of understanding of modern economics that all our time was taken up by teaching fundamentals. We never got to the more concrete problems of post war Germany, etc. H.M. [Herbert Morrison] simply does not know how the Soviet system works – and why – how the fascist system works, how the war economy works, and why the peace economy fails to work. He swims in a sea of vague notions and orthodox prejudices. I am absolutely staggered. Ignorance and optimistic complacency are dancing on top of a volcano. None of Keynes or Marx has really got across and sunk in. The Left is as stupid as the Right. No line, no philosophy, no comprehension – only party politics. Little children playing with dynamite.

This conviction of his superior understanding never left Fritz although, as he grew older, the arrogance was softened by a kindly pity.

Fritz's situation at Oxford, leading a bachelor life during the week and returning to family life at Eydon at the weekend, did not help in keeping these isolating characteristics at bay. Nor did the quite evident decline in Muschi's spirits. The strong brave wife of internment days was less in evidence on this second period of separation. It was not only her weakened inner state that caused this. When Fritz had suddenly been interned, the drama of the situation had brought their friends rallying round. Fritz had written heroic letters full of hope and courage. Muschi could not but remain strong under those circumstances, despite the uncertainty. Fritz's departure for Oxford was a different matter altogether. He was going to a job that would fulfil him, would bring him into contact with people nearer his intellect than she could ever be.

He would be living a new and separate life from her. She would be left alone, existing only for her children, waiting for the weekends in which they would resume their married life for a brief moment. Her letters to Fritz reflect the inadequacy and uncertainty that she felt. Did he really need her? Perhaps he would find that he was better off without her. She was very much alone, a stranger in a foreign land. Even Fritz's letters were less comforting than before. For a start he no longer wrote in German. Much later she was to confide in her mother that words of love were not the same to her in a foreign tongue. The man she had married had wooed her in German, now said he loved her in English. It was not the same and remained a hardship.

Fritz's arrogance, boredom and loneliness further weakened her self-confidence. While she was generous enough to be glad at the opportunity he now had to go to the theatre, meet people and generally benefit from a return to town life it also made her feel restless and discontented in her own situation. She was even less happy when he began to write to her of a woman who sometimes accompanied him. It was clear that his companion meant more to him than just a friend and yet he seemed so absorbed in himself that he was blind to the anguish he was causing Muschi, alone and insecure in Eydon. He was confident that his relationship with Muschi was so secure that she would see that his affair in Oxford was quite insignificant and irrelevant to their life together, taking place at the periphery of his life and not disturbing the central fact of their love for each other.

Muschi accepted his reprimands with humility and unhappiness. Her faith in his wisdom made her assume that she must be at fault to have these disturbing doubts, that she must be unreasonably possessive. He told her that a proper marriage meant not possession but a close inner centre of unity which enabled each of them to be fully independent growing individuals. Muschi, who for the last six years had been more and more taken over by Fritz, was not only confused but sometimes desperate. 'This morning when I got up I had the conviction that I have to regain my independence ... What I shall have to try and avoid is to make *you* the whole contents of my life ... Your philosophy has slowly undermined my prejudices and moral codes but I am not yet standing on altogether firm ground.'

It was a long and sad letter, written in September 1942, groping towards some sort of understanding of the new challenges Fritz had put before her. The will was there to try not to fail him, to live up to the ideals he seemed to be setting up for them, but she was not convinced that she had the strength to carry them out. She could not understand his reasoning when he told her that his Oxford friend needed him but that she, his wife, should be more independent. Her letter ended sadly: 'Can you see how difficult it is for a mother and wife who loves her family to be independent? ... Often there is independence but not often coupled with burning love.'

Fritz did not appear to be willing to acknowledge that his actions were a legitimate cause for distress for Muschi. He would not even recognize that for Muschi at least it had caused a crisis in their marriage. He wrote to Muschi:

This is no crisis, neither in the ordinary sense of a turning point, because it is inconceivable that anything of importance should change; nor in the Chinese sense, because there is no danger in it, none whatever, neither for you or for me. Perhaps there is opportunity in it: that we should learn to trust one another completely; that we realize that the bonds between us are strong enough to hold without any kind of compulsion. Do you understand what I mean to say? I think that the best marriages are based on freedom, not on law or convention. Only if they can have freedom are they worth having ...

He did not hold this view for long. It was more of a rationalization of his behaviour than a deeply held conviction. When he felt disturbing suspicions himself because of Muschi's infrequent letters to him during another period apart after the war, he acknowledged the importance of faithfulness in marriage and saw his failure as a weakness which had to be overcome. He was not entirely successful in overcoming it but it developed in him a strong devotion towards St Augustine and compassion towards others who failed. In 1942, however, the problem could only be resolved by ending the separation and it was not a moment too soon for either of them when Fritz found lodgings at the end of the year where the whole family could be reunited.

Together again with Muschi and the children, Fritz became happier and more productive. He was very short of money, earning less at the Institute in his first year than at the farm and he began writing articles for newspapers and magazines to boost his income. He enjoyed writing and wrote with ease, rarely needing to alter his first draft at all. His articles covered wide-ranging subjects from road safety to international finance, although always keeping an economic angle, and appeared in equally varied publications.

Fritz's journalistic career began with the *Observer*, where, contributing as a freelance journalist rather than as a member of the *Observer*'s permanent staff, he found himself on the fringes of an extraordinary collection of journalists, many of them refugees, who had been engaged by David Astor. Donald Tyerman, political editor (simultaneously holding the deputy editorship of *The Economist*), referred to them as 'David's foreigners' and had the unenviable job of welding them into a team. They were all very different and very independent, and several of them brilliant men, later to become important political historians, such as Sebastian Haffner, a rather old-fashioned German conservative, later author of a book on Hitler; Isaac Deutscher, one-time member of the Polish Communist party, and best known for his biography of Stalin; Ruggero Orlando, an Italian who also broadcast for the Italian section of the B.B.C., and Jon Kimche, a Swiss. Even in this group (where he was regarded as a social democrat) Fritz did not consider himself to be amongst remarkable men.

It was not long before other papers approached Fritz. He wrote leaders for *The Times*; articles for *Peace News*; the *Architects' Journal* and many other publications, including a Fabian pamphlet. Occasionally he used a pseudonym, such as Ivor Moresby, when he wrote for the *Tribune*, or Ernest F. Sutor (derived from the Latin) for other periodicals which he thought might be sensitive to his nationality. Very occasionally he called himself Ernst, and some still called him James. But the name Schumacher was becoming known and Fritz's success was reflected in his growing post-bag of letters from readers, and more invitations to address conferences and meetings than his diary could accommodate. It seemed possible that he might be on the threshold of another career: that of journalism.

Donald Tyerman certainly thought it would be a good idea and wanted Fritz for the *Observer*. When David Astor took over the editorship from Ivor Brown at the end of the war, Tyerman wrote to him recommending Fritz:

The other essential piece in the new pattern is Schumacher. There on your books you have the man who, more than any other man I know, is capable of expounding and interpreting, with understanding and integrity, the social and economic policies of this Government, with all their implications, in simple and intelligible terms. Other economists will either (in the great majority of cases) survey these policies with a jaundiced carping and reluctant eye or else simply show quite expert enthusiasm.

But Fritz did not appear to consider journalism even as a serious option. His ambition lay elsewhere: it was not fame but action. In journalism he saw that something influential could be written that might lead to action but the effect of his words was not the journalist's responsibility. Fritz told David Astor bluntly, 'I could not bear the semi-responsibility of journalism.' And so once again a potential career became a sideline.

The publicity that writing gave Fritz, however, opened other doors. At last people began to take notice of him and people, moreover, who mattered. Members of Parliament asked for his advice, invited him to address their meetings and to brief them. By 1944, Lord Faringdon, the vice-chairman of the Fabian International Bureau, was offering to act as Fritz's mouthpiece in the House of Lords.

The names on his files grew – Jennie Lee, Michael Foot, Hugh Dalton, Tom Driberg, Clement Davies, Stafford Cripps. It was an extraordinary turn of events that the obscure farm labourer of a few years before should suddenly be called upon by so many public figures. As a vulnerable enemy alien, he might have been expected to lie low in a period of crisis such as the one Europe was undergoing, but Fritz had the wrong temperament and instead of keeping a low profile, allowed himself to be drawn more and more into public circles, where he would quite often be deliberately provocative and controversial. He was not afraid to speak out and he knew his views were radical and to some even shocking.

In 1944, for example, he was invited to speak at a Fabian Conference on the question of German reparations after the war. It was widely believed that it was now only a matter of time before the war would be won, and preparations were being made for the immediate post-war period.

Fritz followed another German speaker, Walter Fliess, who had been asked to speak on the history of German reparations after the First World War. Fliess, a Jewish refugee, was a convinced socialist, a member of the Internationale Sozialistischekampfbund, a strict anti-Marxist organization, founded by Professor Leonard Nelson. I.S.K. members were expected to have the highest standards of morality and ethics. They were all teetotal and vegetarian. Fliess and his wife Jenny, also an I.S.K. member, had opened a vegetarian restaurant, the 'Vega', in Leicester Square in London. It had become a central meeting place for a wide range of socialist groups. Fritz was to eat there often.

After a fairly straightforward, factual talk by Fliess it was Fritz's turn to address the Fabian conference on how reparations should be introduced to avoid the mistakes of the past. After some introductory remarks Fritz smiled at his audience with great charm. 'Well,' he remarked, 'if it goes according to the socialist principle of "to each according to his need and from each according to his capacity" then, as Germany is

E. F. Schumacher

ruined, and America is so rich, the Americans should pay reparations to the Germans.'[1]

The audience was outraged. They had not come to hear this sort of thing. Most of them at that time felt nothing but hatred for the Germans after such a long war. But Fritz was serious. He suggested that even if this advice was not taken for socialist reasons, nevertheless it might be implemented in order to build Germany up as a bulwark against Communism. Four years later in 1948, the Marshall Plan ensured precisely the flow of funds that Fritz had suggested to such a roar of outrage.

Later on, after their talks, Fritz and Fliess found that they were sharing a room. Fritz questioned Fliess about the I.S.K. When Fliess told him that socialism should be built on the ethical principle of non-exploitation, even of animals, Fritz retorted, 'There is no such thing as an ethical principle. It does not exist. Everyone has a different view.' They talked late into the night, Fliess trying to persuade Fritz that there were absolute and eternal truths that could be deduced from logic and experience, for example that one should treat others as one wanted to be treated oneself. As night wore on Fritz's ridicule and sarcasm grew. 'There is no eternal truth in this world or any other,' he firmly insisted. 'How about $2+2=4$?' asked Fliess, 'is that true or not?' 'It's only an approximation,' countered Fritz. By this time dawn was breaking. As they undressed for bed Fritz poked his finger at Fliess's plump figure and burst into a song from Brecht's *Threepenny Opera*:

> *Ihr die ihr euren Wanst und unsre Bravheit liebt,*
> *Das eine wisset ein für allemal:*
> *Wie ihr es immer dreht und wie ihr's immer schiebt,*
> *Erst kommt das Fressen, dann kommt die Moral.*

(Those of you who love your belly and our virtue, however you may try and wriggle out of the truth, I'll tell you once and for all: first comes the belly and only then morality.)

Despite his ridicule that night, Fritz developed a high regard and a lasting affection for Fliess. He frequently ate at the Vega restaurant until it closed in 1969 and said of Fliess, 'One thing

160

is certain. If we ever get to heaven we shall find Walter Fliess there.'

Central to the problem of the post-war economy was the question of employment. The war had wiped out the horror of unemployment that had cursed the Western world in the 1930s. War production and mobilization had mopped up every last pair of able hands. But as thoughts turned to a post-war world, the question of unemployment again loomed large. How could full employment be achieved in peace time, particularly as thousands of men and women returned to civilian life; and once achieved, how could it be maintained to avoid the cyclical slumps and depressions that had cursed the pre-war years?

It was a problem that began to receive widespread attention and in 1944 several publications appeared on employment. Fritz had a hand in two of them. The first was a study published by the Oxford Institute of Statistics. Entitled *Economics of Full Employment*, it consisted of six essays written by Burchardt, Kalecki, G.D.N. Worswick, Balogh, Mandelbaum and Fritz. In this study Fritz was concerned not with international economics but with public finance.

At the same time Fritz was involved in another study on full employment which was of more importance, both in itself and in its impact on Fritz's personal development. Once again the opportunity had come through David Astor. Astor had lunched with Frank Pakenham (later Lord Longford), who was at that time secretary to Sir William Beveridge. Pakenham told Astor that Beveridge was planning to follow his famous report on the Social Services with another on full employment, but that he had little idea of economics and needed someone to explain the basics to him. Astor said at once. 'I've just the man. You need Schumacher.'

Without first asking Beveridge, Pakenham employed Fritz who at once sat down and drafted a lengthy report. Beveridge was one of the last great Victorians. He was an autocrat, paternalistic, and arrogant, but had a deeply compassionate heart and a zeal for action. He gave himself to his causes entirely in order to see them put into action, and had taken up politics specifically to get his report on the Social Services, on which the modern Welfare State was to be built, through Parliament.

Employment policy was not an entirely new subject to Beveridge. He had written a book on the subject before the war and had strongly held views which were diametrically opposed to those put forward by Fritz in his draft report. Pakenham knew he was in for an interesting spectacle as Fritz and Beveridge, whom he told Astor must be 'the two most arrogant men in England', faced each other across the table with Fritz's report between them. Point by point Beveridge challenged Fritz and point by point Fritz argued and explained until Beveridge was won over to his way of thinking and accepted Fritz's draft as the basis of his report.

Other economists then added their contributions. Nicholas Kaldor compiled the appendices and Joan Robinson helped knock the final book into shape, but the basis was Fritz's. Unfortunately Beveridge's report *Full Employment in a Free Society* did not have the success of the report on the Social Services, which is now known as *The Beveridge Report*. The government was producing its own White Paper on employment at the same time and refused to co-operate with Beveridge over his. Civil Servants were forbidden to speak to him and he was not allowed any access to papers which might have been useful for his work. Nevertheless, there was plenty of publicity when the report was published.

As its main author, Fritz expected to be in the limelight; he alone could explain the report and properly answer the questions that were bound to come. To his chagrin, when the time came for open debate, Beveridge took the chair himself. Fritz was furious. 'He doesn't know anything about it,' he fumed. 'He is going to make an absolute fool of himself.' To his surprise Beveridge did no such thing. He had the ability, as Fritz himself had, to get straight to the point of a new subject and grasp its essentials with astonishing speed. He had actually accepted Fritz's ideas because he had understood them and been convinced that Fritz was right and he had been wrong – an act in itself showing he was a great man. Fritz generously acknowledged Beveridge's success.

As a result the audience had the impression that Beveridge had not only mastered the terminology and ideas in *Full Employment in a Free Society* but that he had invented them. Fritz was amazed at his performance. He did not mind losing the opportunity of being the spokesman for the report if Beveridge was able to give his ideas the force they needed to get across to the public.

Fritz was not after public recognition for himself. He wanted recognition for his ideas, so that they would lead to action. He did not mind taking a back seat, as long as someone was promoting his proposals.

Shortly after the publication of *Full Employment in a Free Society*, B.B.C. producer Christopher Salmon interviewed Beveridge and other eminent names in the employment debate with a view to making a radio programme. He also met Fritz to discuss the possibility of a more popular approach. Between them they cooked up the idea of writing a series of plays in which the issues would be raised. The 'actors' would be real – joiners, bank clerks, teachers and trade unionists – but they would have scripts. It was like a return to Fritz's childhood. He had always enjoyed writing plays and a play with a purpose appealed to him even more.

Of the eight broadcasts, three were written entirely by himself. David Worswick, from the Institute of Statistics, put together the other five by piecing together the dialogue which emerged from hours of planning meetings, recorded word for word by two stenographers, and then gave them to Fritz for editing. The result was a very successful series on the Home Service. Each programme was broadcast live and the script was always careully adhered to, although there was sometimes some disagreement over it by the Communists in the cast.

There were other problems too. During one interval an 'actor' had too much to drink and it was with great difficulty that he was prevented from extemporizing. The finale of the series ended in dramatic and carefully orchestrated chaos, when David Worswick, presenter and leader of the discussion, 'lost' control and the programme ended in an apparent brawl of squabbling participants, with Worswick hammering on the table to restore order. Much time was spent before the final broadcast discussing what would be the best object with which to hammer the table – it was in the days before the B.B.C. had a sound effects department – in the end a broom handle was chosen. There was a dramatic fade-out as Worswick's broom handle hammered out over the rising cries of anger around him.

Fritz's rekindled interest in unemployment and his subsequent work with Beveridge was of more importance than the report itself, or the immense pleasure that he got out of the B.B.C. programmes. Until he met Beveridge, Fritz's approach to employment was from an orthodox economic point of view. The report itself consisted largely of a critique of Keynesian economics and its implications for policy, and how to maintain an even flow of spending to ensure an even level of employment. Many interesting questions were raised in his analysis on how to achieve these aims. For example to what extent should the economy be controlled by government intervention? How far could private enterprise be allowed a free hand given its tendencies to severe swings between slump and boom and how should the priority of spending needs be determined and who should determine these priorities?

Beveridge approached the problem from a completely different angle from Fritz. He was not interested in a proper functioning of the economic system as an end in itself nor in arguments about what society could afford. He was a champion of the poor and in his fight against what he called the five 'giants' – of poverty, ignorance, squalor, idleness and disease – he insisted society had to afford certain social services if it was to be caring and humane. The same compassion motivated his interest in employment. He had no time for arguments put forward in some quarters that full employment was undesirable in a proper functioning economic system because it upset the balance of power or deprived society of a buffer of an 'industrial reserve army'. The unemployed were flesh and blood and not mere units in an equation. Moreover, while the five giants ran their oppressive régime, no man could be free; democracy could not flourish in an oppressed society. Only the right social, educational, employment, housing and health policies could achieve true freedom.

Although Fritz won all the economic arguments in his tussle to get Beveridge to accept his draft, the force of Beveridge's compassion, the ability he had to feel for the plight of the poor, had a profound effect on Fritz's own thoughts. His newly acquired socialism became the foundation for a more humane way of thinking, an attempt to put himself into the position of the poor and the deprived. He realized that if full employment affected the industrial strength and bargaining power of the workers then some thought must be given to secure their respect and understanding for what the Government was trying to achieve. At all costs, crude tampering with economic freedom had to be avoided; subtlety was necessary.

Fritz's earliest teachers came back to mind: Adam Smith and his 'hidden hand'. This surely was the most desirable method by which the economy could be controlled: the 'hidden hand' could achieve results without removing the feeling of freedom. It was the perfect combination of freedom and planning. He advocated the use of incentives and disincentives for industry, as well as some measure of public control, and suggested that works councils and production committees, for example, 'may succeed in giving the worker the feeling that he is more than a cog in a big machine controlled by others'. He went on to say that to gain the co-operation of the workers it was necessary to persuade them that there was some equity in income distribution.

His loyal support can be obtained only if he can feel that a more moral principle governs distribution than the principle of ownership.

The temptation is great to avoid the issue of income distribution altogether. Most proposals for a 'full employment' policy prefer to by-pass this central issue, so as to avoid raising controversial issues. Thus they dwell mainly on such matters as industrial efficiency or the type of control which would assure a better co-ordination of economic enterprise throughout society. These questions, while important, fail to go to the root of the matter. They give the appearance as if the problem of our society were a mere technical problem to be solved by experts. Unfortunately, it is much more than that: it is a moral problem. How are the material benefits which our system is capable of producing to be distributed amongst the various members of the community?

I do not know whether it is good or bad policy to leave this central problem in the background. Since any full employment policy involves the adoption of a great number of novel techniques and controls, I have the feeling that the necessary measures will be adopted only if justified by reference to more than temporary expediency: if justified by reference to a moral principle.[2]

Here was a change indeed. In trying to think his way into the minds of people, Fritz had had to admit to the necessity of morality – whatever that might mean. The admission of morality took Fritz out of the realm of economics. Morality implied concepts Fritz had rejected such as 'good' and 'bad'. He found that thinking about employment without such concepts did not take him far enough. Indeed, if work was a right and a need for man then Beveridge had not gone far enough in wanting full employment. Consideration should also be given to the type of work people did. 'Factory workers can justly be called "factory hands", and farm workers "farm hands", because it is only their hands which are utilized in the process while their brains, their hearts, their higher aspirations, their whole human personality is sentenced to frustration.'[3]

A new door had opened. Fritz was glimpsing through into a new landscape where the tools of economics had to be used 'as if people mattered'.

Beveridge's report was published late in 1944. At the beginning of February the following year the Liberal Party (for which Beveridge was an M.P.) held its assembly in Kingsway Hall, in London. One of the items on the agenda was Beveridge's report. Beveridge had anticipated a certain degree of opposition because of the emphasis on the need for state intervention to maintain full employment, but he did not anticipate what actually happened. Not only was he accused of betraying the Liberal cause by making suggestions more closely allied to socialism, but some maintained that the report was tantamount to advocating a totalitarian National Socialism. It was nothing less than a personal attack on Fritz whose involvement in the report had reached the ears of certain Liberal delegates. The attack was led by a Commander Geoffrey Bowles whose distorted view would have been laughable had it not had such potentially dangerous consequences for Fritz. Angrily Bowles shouted at the assembly: 'Herr Schumacher is a Prussian who came over here in 1934 and the National Socialism he left behind in Germany he is now advocating here in England. The Beveridge state slavery plan would require Englishmen to ask officials for a licence to live, and turn free Englishmen into Schumacher sheep to be herded about by officials. It is German state slavery.'[4]

Fritz was shaken. When interviewed by the press he dismissed the accusation light-heartedly saying that 'the suggestion that Sir William Beveridge has fallen under my influence is too much flattery.'[5] But he felt far from light-hearted. The attack was unjustified and contrary to all he had believed England to be about. He turned to his old Oxford friend Sonny Wax, who was working near Oxford during the war on a top secret government mission, and with whom he frequently put the world to rights over lunch. Wax was a lawyer and Fritz asked his advice. What should he do to defend his good name? Wax advised him to do nothing. 'Tomorrow the headlines will be different,' he said, 'by the end of the week it will be forgotten.' Fritz was reluctant to take his advice at first but by the end of the week he saw that Wax had been right. Moreover, by then, his friends had rallied round and restored his confidence. Tom Driberg, M.P., wrote a splendid profile of Fritz in the periodical the *Leader*, entitled 'One Good German', and while it elicited some bitter and critical letters, Driberg's post-bag contained more letters of praise.

One in particular, from Glyn Thomas, understood Fritz's position perfectly and leads the way into the next phase of Fritz's life: 'The fact that such folk as E. F. Schumacher, Burmeister and company are free in this and other allied countries, is one of the few hopeful factors which one can find these days towards the rehabilitation and re-education of the Nazi Germans. We should be glad they are here and thank friend Driberg for focusing our attention on them.'[6]

12

———∞∞∞———

Seeds of Change

In the spring of 1945, as the war was at last drawing to a close, the 'rehabilitation and re-education of the Nazi Germans' was very much in Fritz's mind. The rebuilding of Germany was not just a question of economic recovery but also the 'de-contamination', as Fritz put it, and re-education of the German mind, tainted by Nazism and years of false and pernicious propaganda. Earlier in the war he and Kurt Naumann had thought up a publishing venture to flood Germany with a series of well produced and lucid books containing information about all the important issues on which Germans had been deliberately misinformed. The scheme, which they called 'Star Publications', never got beyond the conceptual stage and by the end of the war Fritz knew he was destined for something much bigger. The first step came before the war ended. He and Kurt Mandelbaum were roped in to the American Bombing Survey of Germany. It was led by J. K. Galbraith. Fritz was issued with an American army uniform, given the rank of Colonel, and dispatched to Germany.

The Bombing Survey aimed to discover why the bombing of German industrial targets had been so ineffective in destroying Germany's military strength, but it soon widened into a general survey of the history of the German war economy. For Fritz, as for other Germans on the staff, it was an opportunity to join the millions wandering around Germany trying to trace their relatives and friends amongst the smoking ruins. After nearly six years he had little idea of the fate of his or Muschi's families, whether they all still lived or how much they had suffered and lost.

The impact of Germany on Fritz was profound and the reunion with his family brought him face to face with the lasting legacy of Hitler and the divisions which had torn many families apart. It needed all his humanity, all the inner resources he could muster to survive these encounters without succumbing to self-destructive bitterness, and in his suffering he turned to Muschi, writing her long accounts of his disturbing impressions.

The letters tell their own story. They are reproduced in full except where news of friends and relatives is of no interest to the reader.

June 12th, 1945   *Bad Nauheim*

Dearest Muschi,

This is a place where something is going on all the time, and the day passes like lightning. The impressions are so manifold that it is impossible to write about them. I hope that Lt Dennis kept his promise and rang you up to say that I had arrived safely. We got started without a hitch and had a wonderfully safe and comfortable flight. In Essen – somewhere on the outskirts, there was not much to see – excellent food. Then in another hour (or less) to Frankfurt. Germany, from the air, is very very beautiful. If one could forget about the towns (and a lot of other things) it would be heavenly. Here in Bad Nauheim, life goes on normally – or rather: most abnormally, since most of the shops are completely and utterly empty; there is practically no transport and no economic activity of any kind. It looks like Sunday every day: people walking about in bright coloured dresses – rather an English kind of Sunday. I've seen a lot of interesting documents and interviewed some interesting people. We live in the past – the present seems not to exist – and try to think about the future without knowing where to start. It is like trying to count your fingers when you have forgotten numbers one to five.

Soon I might be able to write more concretely, but not

169

yet. There is something uncanny about all I have seen so far – as if you saw a person walking about who you knew was dead. He speaks and moves and even laughs – and then you notice that he does not breathe. He does not seem to see you and you pretend not to see him.

We are short of nothing except news from England. Please send me *The Economist* and, if possible, the *Daily Herald* – at least occasionally. The fact that not an atom of English news ever seems to get here intensifies the strange sensation of living in ghost land.

With luck, I might see the Geheimrat [Professor Schumacher] this weekend – if I can find him.

The children over here don't look any different from Christian and John. When I see them my heart aches. When I think of you, it leaps with joy.

All love – F.

[No. 2]   *Bad Nauhèim*

Darling Mu,

I just saw Dr Alfred Petersen [Muschi's uncle] who was quite speechless when he recognized me.

Driving through Frankfurt I could say nothing but 'My God'. But one seems to get used to it: the town is still beautiful with wonderful rows of trees everywhere. In many houses the ground floors and cellars are still habitable. You see many shops in houses the three upper storeys of which are totally destroyed. Somehow the people seem to find shelter. But enormous numbers of them are still on the roads, moving about with their belongings. Everybody you see is carrying something. I saw one train yesterday which was so overcrowded that there was no room for another mouse. People are living on stocks; there is no production or transport worth speaking of. They fear two things: Russia and starvation.

Don't forget me.

Love F.

Dearest Mu,

Well, I just completed my first week, and I am beginning to find my way about. Yet it is still impossible to give even a preliminary summing up of impressions. I had another interview with Dr Petersen, at which his sister Clara was present. It gave me a great shock to listen to her general opinions – so narrow, so selfish, so unteachable. I should like to think that she is not representative of anything but herself. More about her and the whole meeting later. I may have to go and see the newly appointed mayor of Hamburg [Rudolf Petersen, Muschi's father] on Thursday. I hope to pass through Luneburg to find out where my parents are. Someone is going to Bavaria tomorrow to look out for Elisabeth [Fritz's sister]. I was out in the field yesterday going through Marburg, Giessen, to Fritzlar. Giessen is dreadfully knocked about. But Marburg and Fritzlar are still lovely – so is the whole countryside, indescribably lovely. The woods are so beautiful it almost makes me weep. The fields are large and generous, without silly little hedges everywhere. My present role, of being one of the 'upper dogs' doesn't suit my character well. I've been an 'underdog' for too long and developed an almost instinctive sympathy with the under-dog. Luckily the people around here still look wonderfully healthy, excellently dressed, and, in a way, happy.

I am writing this in the midst of crowds, noise, and distraction. I've not heard from you yet and am longing for you.

Kiss the boys.

Love F.

Dearest Mu,

From my last letter you will be expecting news from Hamburg. But I didn't get there. I couldn't get away. They have made me the boss of one of the 'units', which involves supervising a number of people who are inclined to be very unproductive – from inability or from laziness. This was the dilemma: to be irresponsible like the rest and to get a lot of travelling, or to do a decent job of work and become indispensable. So I haven't got out of this place yet, except for two short afternoon excursions. On the whole I am working from 9 am to 10.30 pm. This makes the time fly. Since there are no newspapers, and there is no radio, we are living outside world history. Friends of mine report that they have seen Rudolf Petersen 'who looks wonderful and is an excellent man'.

I had a long letter from Liesel [Elisabeth] today. Her parents [i.e. Fritz's parents] and Edith are in Überlingen/Lake Constance. Erich [Kuby, Edith's husband] is a P.O.W. since the fall of Brest. Five months after the capitulation of Brest Edith received a Red Cross message that he is well. Nothing since then. Hermann [Fritz's older brother] was in Norway till the end. Werner [Heisenberg, Elisabeth's husband] is presumably in Heidelberg (since May 2nd) where I shall make enquiries tomorrow.

(Note: My ink has given out. It is late at night. I can only find red ink.)

My mind is a chaos of thoughts and emotions, and I cannot describe what I feel. I need time to digest it all. There is also so much to digest of the stuff I am learning here. What a bunch of gangsters these Nazis were! I am now looking into their most secret stuff. And what an immeasurable tragedy – this régime and those shortsighted stupid people – owning the most beautiful country in the world, living in the most beautiful houses – and falling for the idiocies of power and glory.

I can't get cross with individual human beings, but I get very cross with those groups and classes which have caused all this misery. The individuals, as I have seen them so far, are mostly nice-looking people, the girls and children charmingly dressed – no signs of starvation yet – although (it seems) they have very little to eat. Yes, I curse the Nazis every day – even more passionately than I have done for fifteen years – as I see their traces in the countryside and in the minds of the people.

You cannot imagine how beautiful is this country of Germany. I had forgotten it myself. Ma [Kurt Mandelbaum] came back from Bavaria quite overawed by it. I look around and say nothing but, 'Why, why, why not be happy here? What is it that makes human beings so inhuman as a nation when they are (as you know, and as everyone can see here) so human as individuals?'

(I am surprised my ink does not turn into red, which would be appropriate as my heart seems to be bleeding over all these riddles of human existence – over this paradox of human folly!)

All these disjointed sentences really sum up to this: As Burke once said 'I know of no way in which an indictment can be drawn up against a whole nation.' Let us always value individuals for what they are in themselves. Let us not put nation over human being.

I had two wonderful letters from you – the second one today. Two days ago, the letter from Christian which made me feel extremely pleased. Many, many thanks. I am thinking of you, and the children, and myself as almost incredibly fortunate. Yes – what ought to be just 'normal' is now almost incredible.

I shall be very sleepy tomorrow if I go on much longer. It is 1.30 am. Start tomorrow at 8.30. So good night. I shall be missing you until I fall to sleep. Then this queer, puzzling, timeless existence will get hold of me again – when I wake up – and carry me through the day, without much direct thought of you, but leaving a background of intimate feeling for you which is always there and always gives me happiness.

Yours Fritz.

PS. Just call me 'Mr' on your envelopes. Love F.

June 29th, 1945   *Bad Nauheim*

Dearest Mu,

... I should like to write to you more frequently – knowing how anxiously I am always looking out for your letters. But this is a bad place for settling down quietly. It's a time wasting place. And new methods to waste time are being discovered every day. Well, I've been to Heidelberg hoping to find Professor Heisenberg but couldn't locate him. Heidelberg is lovely. After passing through Darmstadt and many other places even the ugliest house that is not blown to bits looks like paradise. I travelled back via Mannheim – Ludwigshafen, Worms, Mainz – crossing the Rhine twice on temporary bridges – to see all the bridges that have been wantonly destroyed makes one terribly furious. How lightly men take the important things of life. The Germans blew the bridges over the Neckar (at Heidelberg) when the Allies were advancing on both sides of the river. I hope other Germans will never forgive them.

If plans are not suddenly changed I shall go to the Bodensee tomorrow. Just had your two letters of June 22nd and 23rd. Many many thanks.

This letter was interrupted by a meeting – and by the news that I can go south tomorrow. I shall be back in two days. I am very excited.

All my love – F.

Forward HQ USSBS
Overall Effects Division
APO 413, U.S. Army

July 2nd, 1945

My dearest Fraule,
My assignment for the weekend, as I wrote in my Friday letter, was to go down to Überlingen to interrogate Professor Schumacher and also to look into some documents located nearby. I was naturally most grateful to the management for giving me this particular job.

We started out at 10.30 in the morning, got to Heidelberg just in time for lunch at 12.30 and arrived at Überlingen at 7.15 pm. It was a lovely sunny day and the countryside – well let me not attempt to describe its beauty, for there are no words to do it justice. We drove up in front of Rehmenhalde No. 5, as I said, at 7.15, and a crowd of little children immediately surrounded our jeep. The Rehmenhalde is the most outward part of the little town, up in the hills. The road is rough, winding through fields, and the houses lie hidden in the back of gardens with large trees. A little boy – the sweetest little boy you've ever seen – stepped up to me and asked: '*Hast du Schokolade?*' and I asked him his name. 'Thomas Kuby,' he said. So I looked at him and asked him where his mummy was. '*O, die Mutti ist oben und macht das Abendessen.*' [Mummy is upstairs making supper.] He was just as keen as John and Christian are to get into the jeep, to play about with the steering wheel and to blow the horn. He asked me if I would give him a lift, '*bis zur schiefen Ecke*'. 'Where are your grandparents?' was my next question, but he was much too pre-occupied with the jeep to answer for some time, and I was pre-occupied with looking at him. He then said, after several repetitions of the question: '*Die Grosseltern, meinst Du? Ja die sind weggegangen Kirschen kaufen.*' [My grandparents, you mean? They have gone to buy cherries.] At that moment Erich Kuby stepped out of the front gate and his surprise was as great as mine.

He went at once to fetch Edith, who exclaimed: 'I knew it would happen just like this. A few days ago Erich, and now you.' We went into their little two room 'Mansarde' where I unpacked some chocolate for Thomas and tried to clean myself a bit after the long ride in the open jeep. The door opened, and my mother came in with a basket full of cherries. She, like Edith, looked just the same as when I saw them last, and they said I looked just the same, only stronger.

Mama insisted that we should immediately go over to Papa, but I wanted her to quieten down first and then to prepare Papa so that he should not get too much of a shock. I made her go ahead of me but she could not keep more than five yards ahead, urging me to come as fast as I could. She rushed upstairs (in the house next door, where they had moved two days previously) – just one short flight of stairs. I was waiting at the bottom and urged her to keep her calm. She opened the door straight ahead and cried:

'*Hermann, der Fritz ist da!*' I saw a very old man sitting at a table and could not recognize him. He slowly got up, looked around and said: '*Was soll das bedeuten?*' [What does this mean?] Then he saw me standing at the bottom of the stairs, and I rushed into his arms. He, too, said that I had not changed a bit, and I did not tell him how difficult I found it to recognize him. He said he had not thought that he would see me again, '*denn meine Tage gehen zu Ende*'. [For my days are coming to an end.]

I insisted that they should go to bed early – at their usual time, as I would see them again the next day. All this happened on Saturday the 30th of June. I came back on Sunday and found that they all had had a very restless night.

There followed many long conversations which, inevitably, were not confined to economics or strategic bombing. I found myself talking most of the time of Christian and John, with Thomas sitting on my lap until Edith complained that I was a very bad husband, forgetting my wife over my children. I said that the boys presented me every day with difficult and often insoluble problems, while you did not. I felt it more strongly than ever before how good you are and how we have grown together into a harmonious unity.

In front of me, on the wall, I noticed the picture of a strikingly beautiful noble young man in uniform whom, I thought, I had never seen before. There was so much freedom in this face, so much honesty and intelligence, that I looked at it for a long time. It never occurred to me that it was Ernst. [Fritz's younger brother.] They then told me a lot about him, and what I heard tore up a wound which time had only incompletely healed. I went through some of his letters which reveal a personality so complete, so full of promise, so beautiful that I know of no one to compare him to – considering his age. They also show – is it a consolation or an additional cause of grief? – that he was abundantly happy till the last day, believing firmly that he was fulfilling a noble duty.

These letters are terrible to read. My father has written a biography of Ernst, about a hundred pages, which tells the whole story. They wanted me to take it along with me (the only copy), but I looked at it and decided to read it there and then. I spent the better part of a night over it, taking it back in the morning, just before leaving.

I could not take it along. I want to forget it. The day – that one precious day – at Überlingen was no time for bitterness. But I was very bitter during the night. Why did they corrupt the mind of Ernst with nationalist poison? There were Edith, Kuby, Liesel, Werner, and my own shadow to save his soul and perhaps even his life, but we could not prevail against the influences of an older generation which had learned nothing and worshipped evil gods. My parents find consolation in the thought that Ernst had sacrificed himself for the noblest of all causes. It is terrible to think that he has been sacrificed for the worst of all causes. I want to forget it, because if I go on thinking about it I shall become bitter against my father, who is a good and lovable man – and bitterness is no good.

It is more difficult for Edith, who has known Ernst better than I did, who lives with our parents, and whose husband has taken a strong opposite line in these matters. He was in the army from the start; he stayed a private; he always expressed his disapproval of the war and refused to do any real fighting. He was several times court-martialled and sentenced to one year and nine months imprisonment for being politically dangerous. He was arrested many times and lived in continuous dangers all the time. He never budged and somehow pulled through. Edith stands by him (and so do I): the smallest thing she says for Erich is taken by her parents as a direct attack on Ernst or on themselves. I feel very sorry for her, and also for the old people who just cannot understand. I feel very happy about Kuby.

So there was this bitter-sweet mixture in everything during those two days. The crisis of our time, the crisis of Germany, goes right through my family. These issues are so vital that they cannot be covered up by complete silence for long, although I pleaded with Edith to practise the utmost restraint and to let our old, unfortunate parents think what they like.

It is very hard for her; she has to swallow something all the time, and too much swallowing is bad for anyone's digestion. All I could do was to state our common view with so much '*Selbstverständlichkeit*' and vital optimism that Edith felt strengthened and the parents, without feeling hurt, became a bit more tolerant towards her and Kuby.

There they live in two rooms, without more than a couple of suitcases of their own. Papa is getting weaker every day and has no wish any more to stay alive much longer. Luckily, their landlords are extremely charming to them and do them little acts of kindness every day. They take their meals with Edith next door. Their present rooms are not heatable and they have to find something else for the winter. Edith and Kuby, however, have many friends in the neighbourhood and are confident that they can get them properly fixed up. The old people are courageous in their own way; their suffering is mental rather than physical. The young ones have a different sort of courage; they take all material difficulties into their stride and mean to fight for something radically better. They all love you for the memory they have of you and for what they could see you had done to me. Being with them, I loved you and the boys more deeply than ever. Little Thomas appeared to me like an angel. I could not turn my eyes away from him. But I thought with pride of our two little gangsters.

More news when there is time.

Yours completely, F.

July 9th, 1945   *Bad Nauheim*

My dearest,

I am sorry that a whole week has passed since I wrote you last. I would be quite wrong to say that I have too much to do to find the time for writing. What I *have* to do does not amount to very much, and what, in fact, I get done amounts to very little.

But I am living in a big crowd of men, and there is simply no limit to the number of opportunities of wasting time without achieving anything in particular. Perhaps, I shouldn't say 'wasting' time – although it feels like it. These innumerable haphazard conversations are perhaps necessary for the process of digestion – there is so much to digest. And this process is necessarily a subconscious one. All sorts of facts and impressions pile up before one's mind: the conscious effort of thinking about them cannot do much to sort them out – but meanwhile some sort of a picture, some sort of judgment, assembles itself in the subconscious mind

... So that I feel that I am at present learning more and developing faster than perhaps at any other time in my life.

Strange to say, I often find myself coming back to many of the old fundamental slogans which are (at present) believed to be the essence of Christianity – such as – love your neighbour as you love yourself. I am experiencing the greatness of this saying and the smallness of human nature. I don't like the doctrine of original sin – but the fact of human shortcoming is painfully apparent. '*Das ist der Fluch der bösen Tat, dass sie fortzeugend Böses muss gebären.*' [That is the curse of the evil deed, that it has to bring forth more evil.] So it goes on and on in a vicious circle. The upperdog embitters the underdog, and when the underdog becomes upperdog, the process continues as before, with roles exchanged. That two bad acts don't make a good one, seems to be too difficult for human beings to understand.

Of course details change. There are different degrees of decency and indecency. There are some things which the Nazis did and we shall never do. But there are others which the Nazis did; which we resented when done by them; and which we now cheerfully do ourselves. Few people seem to have understood that this is the time for human greatness; too many are afraid of their own virtues. So the vicious circle continues to drive us into unhappiness.

In England we are fighting for a system of Government and economic administration that is based on the notion that every human being *matters*. We are fighting against that callousness towards the ordinary man which has been the hallmark of capitalism. But we shall not succeed if, at the same time, we behave as if the ordinary man of German nationality matters nothing at all. The right hand must know what the left hand is doing. Our present attitudes are those of a split personality. We went to great lengths to fight Hitler because he had no conception of the dignity of man. Have we got the right conception ourselves?

My mind is revolving around these and similar questions. It *must* be possible to make use of the chance now offered to the upperdog – the chance of breaking the vicious circle of human smallness, greed, pettiness, callousness. I've learned the virtue of patience and I shall go on practising it. I know

179

that the breath of world history is slower than my own. Nothing has been decided yet – but the time for decision is approaching. England, I hope, will not lose her soul now that she is powerful. *Hochmut kommt vor dem Fall!* [Pride comes before a fall!]

Yesterday – to change the subject (otherwise I shall never get to bed) – I was sent out to interrogate Dr Harry Renkl. You can imagine his delight and surprise. He has lived up to all my expectations and is undoubtedly one of the best Germans – one of the best men in general – I have ever met – of the same class as Kurt Naumann or Waldmar Holt. He refused all war work, never joined the army, got into great difficulties with the Gestapo – but pulled through.

I've also had another very interesting talk with Dr Alfred Petersen, who seems to be doing a pretty good job in Frankfurt. He is one of those rare people who are quite indomitable – very much like your father. His energy and vitality are as astonishing as his – what shall I say? ... magnanimity – he has patience, understanding, optimism, in short, the things needed today and most lacking amongst the many small people on both sides. I hope that Christian and John have a strong Petersen strain in them.

Well, sweetheart Mule, I often wish you were here. There is so much that is beautiful and would still be more beautiful if we were together. I am exploring a little scheme whereunder you (or you and the kids) might come over for a short visit. But I rather doubt its possibility. I am living like a monk (which is less upsetting than I thought it might be) and find that life without the feminine element tends to be rather shallow – with two dimensions only instead of three. I find that other women mean nothing to me except to the extent that they resemble you. There are some American women attached to the survey who strike me as exceptionally dull.

The men here are of varying quality – good, bad and indifferent, as one would expect. Ma (with whom I am sharing a room) is one of the best. Kaldor has many pointless personal quarrels which somehow overshadow his abilities. I am I think, on good terms with everyone, often with people who hate one another like poison. I am often reminded of my experience in the camp. Will Rogers' slogan 'I have never met a man I didn't like' still seems to me the essence of successful living.

Your letters – No 5 of June 28th and No 6 of July 1st, after Boddington – are always eagerly awaited and make a red letter day when they come. The *Eastern Economist*, two numbers of the London *Economist* and a bundle of daily papers have arrived so far. Drop me a little love letter whenever you can. I've given away all my photos and am badly in need of a picture of you and the boys. Tell them I am trying to buy them some presents, but that I don't want to take anything here of which the Germans are even shorter than we are in England.

I am having three excellent meals a day [supplied by the Americans and not the starving Germans], and my work does not involve me in the kind of constant nervous tension which my Oxford/London work brought about. All the time there is the most glorious weather – brilliant sunshine (did you see the partial eclipse of the sun today, at around 4 pm?) and an even warm temperature. I couldn't have a more perfect holiday – except for your absence.

The mild kind of work I am doing here is in fact much better for me than no work at all. (I think I am putting on weight.)

People in London and Oxford must be wondering what has happened to me. I cannot bring myself to writing articles now – in any case I don't know whether the articles would get through. If anyone asks just say that I have too much to do.

I may be coming over for a weekend – in a fortnight or so. Perhaps, perhaps not. Don't count on it. The show here certainly will not last longer than say August 15th.

Oh, if I could have you here for just 24 hours.

Yours F.

July 30th, 1945   *Bad Nauheim*

Dearest Fraule,
I am working here almost every night till 12 o'clock on this

wretched Report, which I am trying to get done as quickly as possible so that there will be some time left for my journeys to Hamburg and the Walchensee.

Well, now, what do you say about the Great Victory? [The Labour victory at the general election.] I am enormously excited about it, as you can imagine. The British people – one cannot deny it – are a sensible lot. What does Christian say *now*? I think it is absolutely wonderful – the best thing that has happened since the Battle of Britain. Of course I have practically given up the idea of joining Group C.C. [Control Commission]. I am longing to get back to England.

Last Tuesday, I went to see Herbert M. [Morrison], Sir Wilfred Eady and Professor Blackett (with whom I stayed the night). They were all exceedingly nice and encouraging. Blackett knew nothing about Werner H. I think he must by now be back with Liesel.

Eady said he absolutely *wanted* me to go to Germany for the British Group C.C. but he would allow me to go to the U.S. Group if Sir Percy Mills was unable to have me. Mills meanwhile has asked the Americans to engage me and to lend me out to him. (But all this is now practically out-of-date, except as a stand-by.) Herbert M. didn't have much time, but was most charming. He said he wanted me for economic work and also said that, although he was against being easy with naturalizations, 'a man like you ought to be naturalized at once, if I can I shall do it'.

Of course, I know, everything takes a hell of a time with these people, and I may be coming back only to wait about 'while nothing ever happens'. But still I think this time it may be different. What a chance for Britain and for Europe! If they cannot make up their mind to use me there during the next six months, I shall go to Group C.C. (the one or the other) all the same. *On verra*.

Darling Mulekind, I hope there will be a letter from you in the post tomorrow. I want to know everything – but particularly about No 3 (or No 5). I love both of you very much.

I thought Christian and John were absolutely marvellous during the days I had with them. People here aren't half enough interested in children. But most of them either have none of their own or rather dull ones – if compared to these two.

Ever yours. Fritz.

August 6th, 1945   *Bad Nauheim*

Dearest Mu,

I had just settled down to write to you when your letter arrived. It was so good to hear from you – that all is well, that the boys are happy, and that – you feel as you do.

There is so much to tell you. I am working like a slave, making myself somewhat unpopular with some of the authors, but less so, I think, than others would do if they did the same job.

As so many papers are rotten from beginning to end, my 'editing' them means writing a completely new story. Yesterday (Sunday!), I wrote a twenty page paper to replace one of a hundred pages, but saved, I think, every single argument that was worth stating.

In the afternoon, I simply had to get out of this place, for a change, and drove to Kronberg, via Wetzlar and Limburg, to visit Chris and Peter [Bielenberg]. They told me many very interesting stories about Hamburg. The oldest and youngest of the family [Petersen], took a strong nationalist (even semi-Nazi) line till the end. It seems to be the same everywhere with the older generation – and with the youngsters whom they could influence most easily. Peter had enormous rows with his father all the time. But among the younger generation, on the whole, there is still a lot of good stuff.

I simply must get to Hamburg to have a look at it all, it doesn't sound too good. Of course a lot has changed since V-day, and the old grievances seem now to be forgotten. The personal side of it does not worry me a bit – neither for me nor for you, but the political implications are serious.

Mule, sweetheart, I shall try and describe to you how I think of you and the children. I move about feeling just a little bit lost (sometimes more, sometimes less), with something like starvation in my heart and mind; every now and then, I realize that what I am missing is you. When I meet a person like Chris, the feeling of starvation abates, because she serves as temporary '*ersatz*'; but, then, she reminds me of you so much that I consciously begin to miss you.

When my thoughts are wandering they reach you more often via the children than directly. Something reminds me of Christian or John – a child's shout in the street – and I become exceedingly pleased – with you. I pity the great majority of husbands who haven't got a wife that makes their children really delightful. Frankly, I am then also moderately pleased with myself, because I feel that we have taken this job seriously, distributed functions intelligently, and that we strengthen each other in the effort to do justice to the new generation.

My plans as I wrote in my last letter (and as you anticipated in yours), are now a bit uncertain. The schedule says that I shall be leaving Bad Nauheim on August 19th with the last party. I am still trying to work in two trips – one to Hamburg and one to the Walchensee – if necessary and if at all possible, after August 19th. I expect to be back around the 23rd. Then I shall want to reconnoitre the marvellously transformed scene of ancient Britain, to see what it may mean for me in the immediate future.

See you in just over a fortnight. I shall then make sure that you will not disappoint the boys and me (and perhaps yourself?) again.

Love, F.

13

An Englishman in Germany

Should our great bid for power fail, let us at least leave behind, for those who succeed us, an inheritance which will destroy them too. The catastrophe must be of such monstrous proportions that the despair of the masses, their cries of agony and distress, will be directed, not against us, no matter how patently guilty, but against those who feel themselves called upon to build up a new Germany out of this chaos. And that is my final judgment.

This quotation from Goebbels's diary was another reminder to Fritz that the evil legacy of the Nazis was more than physical or economic destruction. His return to Germany in July 1945 showed him more clearly than ever that his task was to help in the rebuilding of a civilized society there. It was on the proper accomplishment of this task that future peace and prosperity now depended. Exactly how he was to contribute to this immense work was as yet uncertain. First there had to be another period of unsettled waiting before he knew whether he would be able to work for one of the Control Commissions. Fritz tried to follow the path experience had taught him: to carry on as if he was not waiting for a change. He knew that the unfulfilled expectation of change was more debilitating than the certain knowledge that his hopes had been dashed.

He and Muschi had already decided to move to London and they bought a house in Aylestone Avenue in Brondesbury (Kilburn), where Fritz wrote articles to earn a small income.

His great hope was that Herbert Morrison would keep his word and hurry along Fritz's naturalization so that he would be eligible to work for the British Control Commission that had been established in Germany. Fritz had debated the question of becoming a British citizen before the war. It had been suggested to him during the war, when he was called upon to discuss economic matters in Whitehall, that an application to be naturalized would help him in his work and make him more accessible and useful. But Fritz had not thought it appropriate at that time. He did not know in what capacity he would return to Germany. In 1945 he decided that he could contribute most usefully with the British and was therefore anxious to change his nationality to make this possible.

It took ten months before Fritz's future was settled and the waiting had its effect. He was dogged by ill health constantly. It was an emotionally upsetting time. News only began filtering back from Germany slowly. It seemed ages before messages via visitors to Germany were replaced by letters. Fritz knew that he would soon be able to pick up the threads again himself and he had, after all, been to Germany to see some of his family. For Muschi the piecemeal news made the agony of separation all the greater. Everything was upside down for her. She was trying to settle down in a house of their own at last while at the same time Fritz was talking about returning to Germany. She did not want to put down roots in London when Fritz would soon be leaving her for Germany, separating them indefinitely. She longed to return to Reinbek and yet was terrified of what she would find and the effect it would have on the children. She devoted herself to them more than ever and to preparing the home for a new baby due in May 1946.

Christian and John were now of school age and Fritz took an active part in deciding on their schooling. His own stifling education and the unruly nature of his sons, especially Christian, made him look for an unconventional school and the boys were sent to an avant garde establishment in Hampstead called Burgess Hill School. The children were encouraged to express themselves freely and to evaluate their own progress. Christian's self-assessment revealed the exuberance of the boy, but little of his actual achievement: in his report he assessed himself in each subject as 'Supa'.

On April 3rd, 1946 the letter for which Fritz had been waiting came at last. He was a subject of His Majesty George VI and could now work for the British Control Commission in Germany. Without waiting for Muschi's imminent confinement, he prepared himself for his departure, and on May 8th, aged thirty-four, dressed in a battle dress far too big for him, he left for Berlin to take up the post of Economic Adviser to the Economic Sub-Commission of the British Control Commission.

This time Fritz knew what he was coming to in Germany and yet he was not prepared for the destruction he encountered in Berlin. Initially he avoided visiting the most badly bombed areas. His first port of call was to the Arno-Holtz Strasse in Steglitz to see his old family house. He was relieved to find it still there. And lucky. In the Steglitz borough of Berlin almost fifty per cent of the housing stock had been destroyed or rendered uninhabitable. Many of the remaining houses had been partially damaged – in terms of rooms left available, about one quarter were useless. But the rest of his old haunts took him longer to look up. It was a month before he could face the horrors of the place where he and Muschi had got engaged. He wrote to her in June:

Ten years ago – good lord, how things have changed. Two days ago I went to the Tiergarten – Pariser Platz – Wilhelmstrasse – Reichskanzlei. You *cannot* believe it. No person can imagine such a thing. It is impossible to believe it even when you see it. I couldn't sleep afterwards and had a headache all the next day. Dante couldn't describe what you see there. A desert. Walking along Budapesterstrasse – complete stillness – ruins, ruins, ruins, and not a living soul. Lützow Ufer – incredible. And then the Reichskanzlei!

Nothing was left.

Fritz, with his economist's view over the whole of Germany, was driven into unceasing activity by the knowledge that the real devastation was even greater than the visible effects of the war. He had already seen, flying over the country in the summer of 1945, that much of Germany appeared untouched by bombing and destruction. Then Fritz had estimated that about eighty per cent of the housing stock was still intact and seventy-five per cent of the industrial plant. Hard work could make good those losses, given time.

But the devastation of Germany was more than bricks and mortar. The entire economy had ceased to function and it was hard to know where to begin the reconstruction. There was no transport, no postal service, no economic activity of any kind. More serious was the fact that the entire top strata of society had to be replaced. One of the foremost tasks of the Allies was de-Nazification. It is in the nature of a tyrannical régime that all those with high positions, all those who prosper, all those who are well placed are able to be so because they are in favour with, and in some way connected to or compromised by, their association with the régime. Thus the Allies, in their task of rebuilding Germany, had first to dismantle it more by removing all those tainted by Nazism. It would take time for new men and women to be found who were both able and could be proved to be 'clean'.

Further, there was the question of reparations after the war. While the right hand of the Allies was concerned with the rebuilding of Germany, the left was briefed to dismantle what remained of the industrial sector. Factories, machines and equipment were taken to bits and shipped to Allied countries. The Americans produced a scheme to 'pasturalize' Germany. They believed that the only way to prevent Germany from again becoming a powerful force in Europe and a danger to peace was to return to the rural state of previous centuries. The use of the word 'pasturalize' alone indicates the kind of Germany the Americans had in mind: all Tirolean hats and *Lederhosen*. The dismantling process was also designed to act as reparations for the Allies: at least one lesson had been learnt from the First World War and Germany was not expected to pay in cash. The Russians lost no time in taking everything they could lay their hands on, both in their sector and the twenty-five per cent of the Western sector allocated to them. They were so thorough that they even dug six-foot-deep trenches to remove power cables: the savage invasion of the Soviet Union by the German army in 1941 called for retribution. The other Allies were less systematic; some things were removed, others simply blown up, but there was a feeling that perhaps the whole policy should be thought out more carefully.

For the German masses, who had got through the war without too much deprivation, the problem of staving off hunger, cold and the elements was becoming acute. The winter of 1946-7 was to be one of the coldest for many a year and the provision of the barest essentials for the population was becoming increasingly difficult. The housing shortage was exacerbated by the vast army of Allied personnel which commandeered all suitable housing and, more serious, by twelve to thirteen million refugees expelled from Eastern Europe. Food and other essentials in short supply were difficult to get hold of because of the collapse of the market economy. Money no longer acted as the means of exchange: by and large cigarettes had taken its place. It was not tramps who scoured the gutters for cigarette ends looking for a smoke, it was the ordinary person scraping together what he could to provide for the essential needs for his family. It was not unknown for quite senior German officials visiting British personnel in C.C.G.B. Headquarters to apologetically empty the contents of the ashtrays into their pockets.

Apart from this 'currency' the economy rested on barter. All over the country people would trudge carrying possessions on their backs with which they were prepared to part in exchange for the necessities of life. Workers in small factories were paid in kind by the goods they were producing and at the end of the week would be seen leaving the factory like a band of tinkers.

Such financial chaos did not only affect the day-to-day living of the people. It affected the whole of the Allies' reconstruction programme. How could they, forbidden to participate in the cigarette economy, get men to work who refused to be paid in cash? There were occasions when the powers of the military governments had to be enforced to draft labour into work which the men were willing to do but only if they were paid with something other than money.

Within days of arrival in Berlin Fritz was submerged by the enormous problems. Their solution was further complicated by the administrative machine which the Allies had imposed on occupied Germany. This had not been able to develop organically but had been a hurriedly constructed cobweb of officials and bureaucrats with the odd 'expert' among them. Although the Potsdam agreement, reached between Churchill, Stalin and Truman on August 2nd, 1945, had declared that Germany should be administered as one economic unit, in fact the division of Germany into four military zones had effectively divided the country, including the economy in all respects. The problems of the future were visible from the beginning. The four Allies had different aims and interests in Germany, which were reflected in their policies. It was not possible for Britain, France, the United States and Russia to reach a common view on anything. The administration of Germany was fraught with conflicts at all levels, and delays were inevitable. Every decision had to pass through committees galore before reaching the 'big shots', at the quadripartite talks.

Berlin was a microcosm of the whole of Germany. Surrounded by the Russian Zone and itself cut into four, it immediately mirrored the tensions of the rest of the country. Yet the Berliners themselves remained cheerful and energetic. Fritz was moved by their courage and took them to his heart, referring to them as 'his' Berliners. He felt that their fate was his personal responsibility, even more strongly than his commitment to the rest of Germany.

Fritz's position in Berlin was not at first clear-cut. He was supposed to have the rank of a colonel and therefore be eligible for certain privileges but he felt the suffering of the German people so acutely that he thought it unworthy of his position to spend valuable time on his own comforts. He was content to live in a miserable little room where the only luxury was hot water once a week, and in this way he felt he was sharing the hardships of the people he had come to serve. But his task was to work hard and he was therefore very concerned about the inadequate tools available for his trade. He wrote to Muschi:

It is nearly a week now that I left, nearly a week since I started work here, but I haven't settled down at all. What a collection of fifth-rate people with no idea how to tackle a job such as this. Here we are, trying to plan the entire economy for twenty-three million people, and do not possess even the beginnings of a properly organized library ...

Oh! What difficulties! I have no typewriter, no car, no decent room to work in. I shall get all I want – in time; but every day lost brings irreparable damage to Europe.

The belief that 'every day lost brings irreparable damage to Europe' gave Fritz an incredible sense of urgency and energy. He had the feeling that he was involved in a period where history was being made, but that the people who were supposed to be making it were quite unequal to the task they found before them. A few weeks later, he vented his frustrations on Muschi:

The man who poses as my boss has the brain of a sparrow, the character of a mouse and the imagination of a stone. Luckily he thinks the world of me and doesn't know what I think of him ...

I am not afraid of anyone here and it often amuses me to watch myself in conversation with the big shots. I am completely free with them – you would like it if you saw it. I feel just a little bit like a desperado ...

What a strange thing it is to be 'making history'. When one sees it from the inside one is not surprised that the outcome is lamentable. History, it seems to me, is always made in a terrific hurry, in the 'last minute' – with no time for quiet and detailed consideration. Territories may be shifted backwards and forwards, and no one has time even to ascertain how many people are involved. The 'great' men who finally take the decisions (which may or may not cause future *wars*) normally have no time to think and never seem to be able to do more than apply a little bit of common sense to all the bogus arguments that are floating about; a *little* bit of common sense, but not enough to kill the bogus arguments.

It took a few months for Fritz's position to be clarified in the Berlin headquarters. The British forces were led by General Sir Brian Robertson and under his leadership came the various sections that made up the Control Commission which controlled every aspect of German life from reparations to radio programmes. The following report in the *Daily Herald* of May 25th, 1945 may serve to illustrate the extent of control:

> Allied plans for controlling the newspapers, radio, books, films, theatres and music of Germany were disclosed here today . . . it may be necessary to ban some of Wagner's music because it is so closely linked with Nazi Mythology. Mendelssohn, long banned because he was a Jew, may now be played again.

(The link with Nazi mythology destroyed any appreciation Fritz had had for Wagner before the Nazis came to power. He never voluntarily listened to any of Wagner's music again.)

The Economic Sub-Commission to which Fritz was attached was headed at first by Sir Percy Mills, an autocrat, feared by many though liked and respected by Fritz, but followed soon after Fritz's arrival by Sir Cecil Weir. Sir Cecil Weir at once recognized Fritz's ability and by the end of June a reorganization had taken place so that Fritz was in a more independent position in the administrative structure. But as economic adviser his role was one entirely without power. He could not implement his own ideas and much of his time had to be spent lobbying and selling the advice for which he had been asked – or felt moved to give. He wrote of the dangers of his position to Muschi:

> As 'Economic Adviser' I claim that I am entitled to give economic advice on any subject I choose. But it is always somewhat risky to give advice without being asked for it. The people actually doing the job resent it. They don't know how little they know of the bigger connections and interdependencies. On the other hand, I know my limitations and I know also that I can see *Zusammenhänge* better than the 'practical man'. So I just have to *assert* myself.

He tried to get his own way by subtle methods and by his tenacious will. His lack of power taught him that there had to be other ways than force and bullying. His method was to use convincing argument and to hold on until others were weary. He wrote to Muschi in October:

I am quite confident there is no one here who is quite as single-minded about this work as I am, and therefore I shall win. There is no one here who has lived almost all his adult life in opposition or as an almost completely powerless minority, as I have done since 1929. I therefore know the technique of getting my way without power. Another six months, and Sanity will have won or I am out of here.

These outbursts are for nobody's ears but yours. I am not conceited, but I am in the mood of a desperado. For me, this is 'total mobilization' – and to hell with all the careful, timid, twopenny-halfpenny nincompoops!

Another asset he had was the ability to work hard, and enjoy it. In the same month he wrote:

It's no use denying that I like being really 'in demand'. I have now gained a fair idea of what all the 'big shots' around here are really worth, and my self-confidence stands pretty high. I can say it to you – though to no one else – that I know I have just done a good deal more thinking in my life than most of the others and have a clearer and more precise mind than anyone I've met out here ...

I've always wanted to measure myself against the great men, so-called, of this world. The result is quite satisfactory, as far as it goes. But, my God, against the problems of this world we are all as a bunch of children!

His appearance also helped to boost his ego. At thirty-five he looked twenty-five years old and yet he believed he had the experience of a 45-year-old. Those who first disregarded him because of his apparent youth were always startled by his knowledge and good sense and then took him all the more seriously. And Fritz was convinced that the purity of his intentions also helped him in his task. To his parents he wrote:

As I don't want anything for myself, that which I might have wanted is given to me. As I, without much thought for my future, give all I can wherever it is needed, the future looks after itself ... I have lost the fear of the future through the shocks of the past few years. The strain of this period has not taken away my strength but has made me tough. After long acquaintance with the hopeless situation of a small minority, I can no longer be disappointed by anything. I always expect the worst and am prepared for the best. Then generally the worst does not happen and that is a happy surprise.

It was not always easy to keep up such an optimistic outlook. His advice was sometimes resented, and other departments (particularly the financial department) often felt he was over-stepping his brief. When people seemed receptive Fritz was elated, at other times he felt that the odds against sense and sanity were tremendous. Again he wrote to his parents, 'My highest hopes depend on a reorientation of the way people think so that sense can slowly begin to grow.'

And with Muschi he shared his sense of responsibility and his growing awareness of man's weakness and ineffectuality:

I often think of a verse by Goethe – I think from *Wilhelm Meister*:

> '*Ihr treibt ins Unglück sie hinein;*[1]
> *Ihr lasst den Armen schuldig werden.*
> *Dann überlasst ihr ihn der Pein;*
> *Denn alle Schuld rächt sich auf Erden.*'

Have a look at it if you feel like it. These lines are terribly true. They apply not only to the Germans, but also to us here. One day posterity will point its finger at us and say: These men have been blind, stupid, incredibly short-sighted, lacking in vision, lacking in generosity, purpose, and sympathy. It may even add, if we experience another world disaster: They are only getting what is coming to them; they ought to have known better. And yet we are not really bad, not wicked, nor exceptionally stupid. '*Männer machen die Geschichte, aber sie machen sie nicht aus freien Stücken.*' *Und* '*dann überlasst ihr sie der Pein, denn alle Schuld rächt sich auf Erden.*' ['Men make history, but not out of independent pieces.' And 'then you leave them the agony, for all guilt is revenged upon the earth.']

I believe the main trouble is lack of willpower. Many

people start out with the best intentions; then they get a bit frustrated and tired; then they allow themselves to be eaten up by the day to day routine work; finally events take charge of them, instead of them determining the events. – Against this, I am determined to fight to the last. I shall never surrender. I am prepared to upset everybody; I am prepared to lose my job tomorrow, – to go home in disgrace ...

The first task he set himself was certainly controversial. Four years earlier he had written to Werner von Simson: 'The task will be to make a completely new start. The risks are grave and the opportunities tremendous. I, for one, shall not be a passive spectator.'

He had been referring to building a socialist Germany and almost as though those words were still echoing in his mind, the very first question with which he occupied himself was that of the ownership of German industry. With everything in possession of the Allies and many former industrialists gone or removed by de-Nazification, it was possible to make a completely fresh start in the ownership and organization of industry. Fritz had long believed that the structure of German industry had not a little to do with the aggressive and militaristic past of the German people.

In this first piece of work as economic adviser he made his position and approach to Germany's problems perfectly clear. He did not disguise his recommendations in economic jargon, and he took care to bring out all the non-economic issues involved:

At certain moments in history change becomes desirable for its own sake. Germany has arrived at such a moment. So terrible have been the happenings of the last thirteen years that a continuation of the old social relations – as if nothing had happened – becomes almost offensive. It throws the masses into apathetic depression and teaches them to feel that 'THEY' will always do well for themselves while the little man has to suffer for 'THEIR' mistakes. The energies that are needed for a reconstruction of the British Zone will not be forthcoming unless the masses can feel that the defeat of Nazi Germany means also the defeat of those social forces

195

that have been militaristic and aggressive long before Hitler was ever heard of.[2]

The thought behind this paper appears to be the ground work to some of his later thinking on industry and ownership. He was thinking about industry in terms of size, appropriate ownership and organizational structure. Germany's own structure had traditionally been on many levels: national, regional, local, each level having a large degree of autonomy. Fritz suggested that only a few vital industries need be nationalized, such as coal, steel and transport, although even here the regional centres of production should be given a certain degree of autonomy. All other industry should be dealt with according to what would be *appropriate*. The needs and functions of the business, as well as its size, would determine where, on the spectrum of state ownership to local group co-operatives, changes should be made. Fritz suggested that all businesses upwards of about twenty-five people *could* be suitable for socialization but that all businesses with more than two hundred employees *should* be socialized in some form, which should be decided according to the appropriate needs and functions of the business. The important thing was that the private ownership of any concern likely to affect many people should be abolished.

The reception of his paper encouraged Fritz. His next task was to lobby in the appropriate quarters, a far longer-term job. Six months later he was still at it, writing to Muschi in January 1947 from Düsseldorf where he had just been engaged in strenuous discussions:

The purpose of my visit here is to sound [out] German political leaders on 'socialization' and to induce them to bring in a resolution in the Landtag of North Rhine Westphalia asking Military Government to socialize Coal and Iron and Steel. It is a *very secret* mission. So far, it has gone well. The SPD is automatically in favour. But the CDU has the majority here, and they may be sticky. We (Allan Flanders and myself) obtained very definite promises and assurances from three prominent CDU leaders, – but yesterday, when we went to see Adenauer in Cologne, progress was more difficult. I had a two hour intellectual struggle with Adenauer, and I think he became slightly doubtful in some of his most dogmatic opinions; in any case he realized that he was up against a pretty tough customer, with whom his normal 'personality methods' (with which he rules – even tyrannizes his party) would be of no avail. It was a magnificent duel, fought with great skill and excellent manners from his side and, I think, from my side too. We parted most amicably. I hope the results will be as desired.

I met many other leading Germans – but none of the skill and power of Adenauer. Tomorrow, I hope to meet Heinemann, reputed to be the other main figure in the opposition.

Fritz's paper caused a few ripples but did not effect the fundamental changes in German industry that he had hoped for. Germany is now one of the most capitalistic of Western economies and it is generally assumed that the 'economic miracle' that took place in the 1950s was due to a policy of free enterprise and private ownership. Certainly the economy of Germany, stupendous as its achievements have been, did not delight Fritz in later years. He was disgusted, if that is not too strong a word to use for the feelings of a man who became loved for mildness and gentleness, by the 'fat cats' of German industry.

After stating his position in the 'Socialisation of German Industry', Fritz carried on working late each night studying every aspect of the economy and making countless recommendations. His memoranda, which he wrote with care and pleasure, covered many fields – prices and wages, employment, industrial organization, currency and specific industries. He dealt with some subjects with detachment but others took him over completely. While he was wrestling with a problem, he could not sleep properly at night and worked himself into a state of tension until his ideas had formulated themselves sufficiently to be transferred to paper. His tension was increased by his bachelor existence. Letters from Muschi were like manna from heaven but Muschi was not as conscientious a letter-writer as he was, feeling that her own domestic news was of no interest to a man making history. Her long periods of silence pushed him into a state of disequilibrium and despair.

He feared she might be being unfaithful to him. In fact, she was feeling inadequate and doubting her value to him. The sense of urgency and exhilaration, of total commitment to his work in his letters, seemed sometimes to leave no room in his life for a wife and three children, the last of whom he hardly knew, and inhibited her from writing about her daily life which she assumed must bore him in the excitement of his own life.

Fritz's letters were full of dramatic effect. After his 'Socialisation of German Industry' paper he turned his attention to a specific industry: coal. 'I am completely submerged in COAL,' he wrote to Muschi. 'We must get a coal policy. Or else we shall be murdered and rightly so. I shall start shouting at the top of my voice.'

Studying the structure of the economy as a whole for the first time he realized that coal was the lynchpin upon which the recovery of Germany depended. Without this source of energy nothing could be achieved. His interest in coal was in all respects a foretaste of what was to come. He had made a crucial discovery which affected all his future work. *Energy was the foundation stone of industrial recovery.* Germany's source of energy was coal. Without coal nothing could happen. The main coal-producing area lay in the Ruhr, part of the British Zone. All the Allies wanted coal and all shouted for more. Those at the centre of the disputes were the men actually in charge of coal production: Brigadier Marley, Harry Collins, Peter Spencer, Frank Wilkinson. Their instructions were: no coal for Germans. All coal must be distributed to the Allies. It was a totally unrealistic policy. The proper functioning of the mines depended on the reactivation of local industries to provide urgently needed supplies from bricks, pit props, and lift shafts to helmets. The reactivation of local industries depended on coal but as *German* managers were in charge they were not eligible for coal. So it was a vicious circle.

The British team at the Ruhr were sensible and independent men. They wanted to get on with the job of getting out the coal and to do so had to disregard the rules for coal distribution. Harry Collins was in charge of production and he worked closely with the German managers to make sure that their needs were adequately supplied. There was no secret about it and soon a furore hit the coal production team. The Americans sent down a dozen men to complain. It was at this point that Fritz stepped in and began to push for a proper coal allocation policy. Naturally it raised the whole question of reparations. Fritz's view was that European and German interests were one and that to hound and harass the Germans was an act of European suicide. The fate of the German economy was the fate of the European economy.

It was not a view shared by all the Allied personnel, some of whom appeared to regard the Germans as some sort of sub-race. These, although in the minority, nevertheless succeeded in souring the atmosphere. Fritz felt extremely hurt when his ideas were criticized for being 'typically Germanic'. He tried to rise above nation and race so that he could work for the alleviation of suffering, for the rebuilding of a better and more stable society. He was not 'sticking up for the Germans', he was working for Europe. A terrible tragedy had befallen Germany and it was the task of men of good will and ability to do their utmost to restore order and sanity.

Fritz's interest in coal was more fundamental than merely achieving a proper coal allocation policy. His task was to get decision-makers at the highest level to understand that without coal nothing could be achieved in the task of reconstruction, and that miners must consequently be treated as a priority. It was clear the importance of coal had not been understood by the decision-makers, and when food shortages began to hit the population it was not long before miners' rations were also to be cut. The announcement was followed by an immediate twenty-five per cent fall of output. The miners made Fritz's point for him. Heavy work makes hungry men. Without coal the wheels of industry stop. The miners' rations were restored at once.

Fritz was often distressed by the pettiness and small-mindedness that he experienced and made his friends amongst the generous and compassionate. Harry Collins was such a man. When the Americans complained that the German population did not appear grateful enough for the grain and bread provided by the United States, it was suggested at the highest level that each loaf of bread should bear a sticker saying 'this loaf comes to you by courtesy of the U.S.A.'. Harry Collins happened to be present at the meeting at which this was discussed and suggested that instead of a sticker, the German Bishops should be summoned and instructed to alter the Lord's Prayer to say 'Give us this day our American Bread'. After this, no more was heard of the American stickers – and this story no doubt cemented a life-long friendship between Fritz and Harry Collins.

Lighter moments between the serious demands of his situation were welcome, for sometimes Fritz felt that he was getting too serious. On the few weekends he would allow himself off from the stresses of the week he would seek distraction in the occasional film, concert or play, he would walk in the Grunewald or even sail.

There were plenty of clubs with pleasant facilities for the Allied personnel. There were also dances to which he would escort a member of the female staff, taking care this time to reassure Muschi that there was no danger and that she was always uppermost in his thoughts.

Not all time taken off work was given entirely to relaxation. He had many other demands on his time. His strong sense of duty towards his family added to his burdens, although he never seemed to shoulder his filial responsibilities with resentment or unwillingness. He had exemplary compassion, concern and love for his parents and for his sisters and brother and was unhappy that they, in their turn, did not appear to understand the pressures that were upon him. All the time he sensed that they felt that he neglected them. In June he wrote to Muschi, 'My parents and Edith have no conception of the life I am leading here ... They think I am neglecting them. But many things just can't be done. I can't travel about freely – over such distances when every day counts. We are here dealing with the life and death of millions.'

Nevertheless, he took off what time he could to try and reduce the hardships his family were enduring. He was very concerned for his brother Hermann, who was unwell in a prisoner-of-war camp, and tried to pull what strings he could to get him released. Sonny Wax, then on the legal side of the Control Commission, was largely responsible for hurrying along Hermann's release. Fritz then took time off to drive him home to their parents. He returned disillusioned. His brother seemed to be in better physical shape than himself and he felt that his family were not showing the courage and determination to work for a better future that he expected. Even Edith, so often a soulmate, wrote to him that God had ordained all the present misery and that the masses must suffer it so that they should find their way back to God, 'meanwhile', she added, 'all efforts to help are quite useless and superfluous'. Professor Schumacher's comments, though well meant, were equally damning. He thought it was time Fritz settled down and achieved something of greater permanence in his life. While he was glad to see his son among those who served humanity, he still felt it was time Fritz looked after his own interests. 'Encouraging, isn't it?' Fritz unburdened himself to Muschi. 'Both letters are extremely well meaning but they show a complete lack of understanding for the desperate struggle we are fighting here. Instead of advising the selfish people and the defeatists to "go to it", they are advising *me* to be selfish and defeatist. *"Herr, vergib ihnen, denn sie wissen nicht was sie tun!"* ' [Lord, forgive them for they know not what they do.]

Even Uncle Fritz, who had always been an ally, appeared not to understand the full horror of what had happened to Germany and the true meaning of Fritz's work of reconstruction. His death in 1947 saddened Fritz but his Will confirmed the fact that the divisions brought about by the war were too deep for even time and good will to heal. Fritz, as second son, was to have inherited his uncle's signet ring. Now he heard that it had been left to the Bremen Museum. Uncle Fritz had broken with tradition because he felt Fritz had broken his links with Germany. He did not want the ring to leave Germany. Another thread with the past had been severed and another indication given to Fritz that nothing could ever be the same again, even if Germany was thoroughly cleansed of all the influences of Nazism. The two concepts of being a German patriot were as divisive after the war as they had been before. Genuine opposition to Hitler and love for Germany were not as strong as the suspicions that the shadow of the war put between those who left Germany and those who stayed. Fritz's mother, sensing the disappointment that Fritz felt at Uncle Fritz's gesture over his ring, had a copy made and Fritz wore it together with his wedding ring for the rest of his life. It was a distinctive ring, a dark blue crest engraved in a pale blue stone, which drew attention to his gentle and well manicured hands. It also symbolized the deep attachment Fritz had for his country and his family. He was proud to be a Schumacher but he was a new Schumacher, making a new beginning as he gradually realized that the past could never be restored.

It is difficult to assess the real impact that these divisions within his family had on Fritz. He refused to discuss unpleasant emotions and the indications are that he did not even allow himself to think about them. He saw his duty to his family to build bridges over the gulf that separated them. Nevertheless, the tensions, however unacknowledged, remained. It was more difficult later to reconcile other differences of opinion when a lack of understanding existed on an issue which was of such importance to both sides.

These small but significant signs of the irrevocable divisions that the war had caused were even more noticeable in his daily work, and Fritz could find little evidence of good will to heal the breach. Later, in 1950, he wrote to Muschi of how he had continually been subjected to 'the most monstrous opinions – whether British opinions about "the Germans" or German opinions about "*der Engländer*" '. People came to tell him 'that all the Allies want is to ruin Germany or all the Germans want is to start another war ... ' He was in the lonely position of seeming to belong to neither side but being identified with both. It made him long all the more for Muschi and the children to comfort and encourage him.

It was a problem from which neither Fritz nor Muschi could escape. For Fritz it was a personal and a professional reality. His origins and his nationality caused a constant conflict. There were Germans for whom he was a traitor who had left the sinking ship and had now come back to lord it over them, and there were the English who regarded him as a German whose interests were bound up with Germany and who could not trust him as an Englishman. Fortunately not all felt like this and there were many who, although admitting to a realization at the back of their minds that Fritz was originally German, did not regard it as a factor against him. But it all added to the stresses and strains which eventually wore him down.

For Muschi, surprisingly, the decision to return to Germany, to join Fritz, was very difficult. She was tired of their wandering life and wanted to put her roots down. The boys were both thoroughly English and she felt that it might be better not to disrupt them once again. More than that, she wondered whether their presence in Berlin might not be a distraction to Fritz in his important work. Much as she longed to return to her beloved Germany, she was also afraid of what might await her there. Despite her new nationality she was still a German at heart. How could she take being on the side of the victors and yet identifying with the vanquished? She feared that there would be no place for her.

From this time on she was torn in two. As soon as she returned to Berlin she felt happier than ever before. She had come home. Soon she was able to visit her parents, see her brothers and sister in Reinbek. The family had been extra-ordinarily fortunate during the war and had escaped un-scathed. No life had been lost, no damage done to their property. Not even the fact that Rudolf Petersen had had a Jewish mother had affected them. He had kept a sufficiently low profile throughout the war to survive and be elected as Lord Mayor of Hamburg when it was all over. Muschi's mother had found it less easy to adapt herself to the régime. There were certain issues on which she refused to compromise even if they were only symbolic. She refused to allow the Nazi flag to be raised on her house on the many occasions that the population were forced to show their loyalty. No amount of persuasion, nor the threat that they might be doubly endan-gered by disobeying the rules because of the Jewish blood in the family, would move her. She would not stand by and see that detested flag raised. Eventually a solution was found. On all flag days Mrs Petersen would be seen striding out of her house not to return till nightfall. If the flag was there, she was not.

Rudolf Petersen's position was not so clear-cut. He had had no sympathy with Fritz's position when Fritz and Muschi had left Germany in 1937 and events did not entirely remove his anger and disapproval. When the war was over he let it be known that he had forgiven Fritz and acknowledged that Fritz had some right on his side although his own position had also been a correct one. In his position as Lord Mayor of Hamburg after the war he very much hoped that Fritz would be able to come to Hamburg to help him in his difficult task. It is probably fortunate that Fritz was needed elsewhere.

For Muschi these tensions beneath the surface meant that her loyalties were torn in two. Soon she wished she could also tear her body in two. Shortly after her arrival in Berlin it became clear that her sister Olga, married to a businessman, Werner Traber, and with three small children, was suffering from cancer. Her husband was in a sanatorium in Switzerland with T.B., the children were with Muschi's mother in Reinbek and Olga was dying in hospital. Whenever she could Muschi travelled to Reinbek to support her mother and in November 1947 Olga died. Their sharing of this loss brought Muschi and her mother even closer together. Muschi was now torn between her own children and husband and a strong feeling of duty towards her mother and the children of her sister. She could only hope that her return to Germany could be a permanent one and that she would be able to fulfil these two duties properly.

If she ever really believed that this hope would be realized, then her own children soon showed her that the pull between England and Germany, the effects of the hatred generated by the war, which they had tried to avoid in their own family life, had affected the next generation. She was unhappy at the lack of ability that the boys showed in German and soon after their arrival proposed to Christian that they spoke only German during the holidays. Christian, a burly lad of ten, to all appearances tough, strong-willed and forceful, burst into tears and begged her not to make him do such a thing. Muschi wrote about the incident to her mother-in-law with great sadness. 'He does not want to be reminded that we are German. Often I find that hard, because of course, I feel more at home in everything German.'

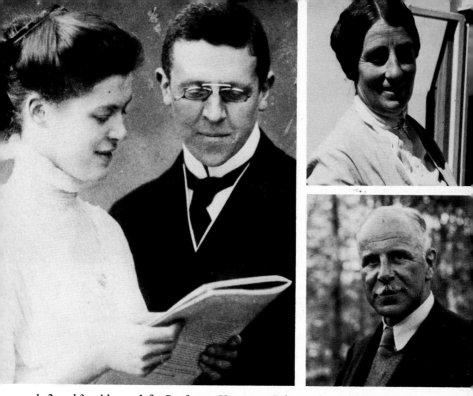

1, 2 and 3   Above: left, *Professor Hermann Schumacher and his wife Edith;* top right, *Olga Petersen, Muschi's mother;* below right, *Rudolf Petersen, Muschi's father*

4 and 5   Below: left, *Fritz's childhood home in Berlin;* right, *the Petersens' house in Reinbek, near Hamburg*

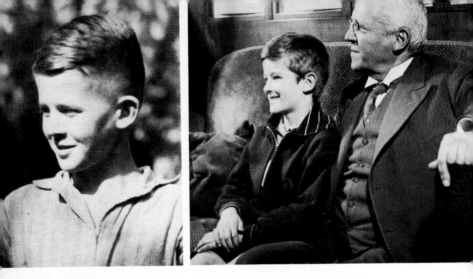

6 and 7   Above: left, *Fritz at about ten years old;* right, *Professor Schumacher with Fritz's younger brother Ernst*
8   Below, *Fritz as a student, talking to Edith*

9 and 10   Above: left, *Fritz's engagement to Muschi Petersen,
August 1936;* right, *the wedding, October 1936*
11   Below, *Muschi, Fritz and Edith on holiday in the Alps in the late
1930s*

12 Above, *Holcombe, the Schumachers' house in Caterham*
13 Below, *the Schumacher family in the early 1950s: from left to right, Christian, Muschi, Virginia, Barbara, John and Fritz*

14 and 15   Above: left, *Werner von Simson;* right, *David Astor with Adam von Trott, 1939*
16 and 17   Below: left, *Fritz with Muschi, 1960;* right, *Fritz, early 1960s*

18 and 19   Above: left, *Alfred Robens (left), Chairman of the National Coal Board, with Fritz in Japan, 1963;* right, *Fritz in Java, 1977*
20   Below, *Fritz with Vreni and Bishop Michael Bowen in 1976, at his confirmation*

21 and 22 Above: left, *Fritz with his younger sister Elisabeth, 1970;*
right, *Edith Kuby, Fritz's older sister, 1976*
23 Below, *Fritz with President Carter, 1977*

24   Above, *Fritz a few hours before his death in Switzerland*
25   Below, *Fritz and Vreni Schumacher's children in 1983: from left to right, Robert, Nicola, Karen and James*

14

---∞∞∞---

The Final Break

On January 1st, 1947 the American and British Military Governments announced that their two zones had been merged to make one integrated economic unit. The statement went on:

> The agreement contemplates an economic programme designed to make the area self-sustaining in three years. This programme will not only result in decreasing the costs of occupation for the area but will also make possible the gradual restoration of a healthy non-aggressive German economy which will contribute materially to the economic stability of Europe.[1]

Naturally economic union with the American zone somewhat changed Fritz's position. The Americans too had their economic advisers. There were more committees to attend; more people to win round to his ideas. When the Marshall Plan went into effect in April 1948 meetings at the newly formed Organization for European Economic Co-operation (O.E.E.C.) also took up more and more of his time. But the growing bureaucratic structure with which he had to battle did not diminish his efforts. There were so many fronts on which he had to keep up a sustained and persistent attack. Coal has already been mentioned and in that area he had some measure of success. Other campaigns were less fruitful, the opposition greater. From the start he had persistently called for financial reform in Germany as a prerequisite for economic recovery. Almost every memorandum had somewhere a plea for swift action to sort out the financial chaos and the useless currency. He backed up his pleas with plans, schemes which he believed could be quickly and effectively implemented. His unsolicited outbursts did not enhance his popularity with the financial division who considered them an invasion of their brief, but Fritz and the financial adviser had a mutually low opinion of each other, and Fritz pressed on undeterred. He had been thinking about currency reform since 1945 when he and Walter Fliess had written a pamphlet together. In 1946 he drew up another comprehensive scheme which he put forward at every opportunity. He strongly condemned the British plan for reform by stages and believed it imperative that if confidence was to be restored in the currency, any action that was taken should be swift and complete.

There were other implications in his scheme. Currency reform was an ideal opportunity to make sweeping changes in the distribution of wealth. He did not want the rich to get richer at the expense of the poor, and when currency reform finally came in June 1948 he criticized it on precisely those grounds. He acknowledged that it had an immediate beneficial effect on the consumer economy but he believed that its social consequences would be disastrous and its economic effect dubious.

Currency reform and various other developments in the recent past have produced an exceptionally great concentration of wealth and income in the hands of a small minority of the German population. This minority is not yet spending its current income on consumption and taxes, and yet, it is also refusing to make its unspent balances available for investment. The basic explanation for this abnormal behaviour lies in the fact that most of these 'unspent balances' consist of what might be called tainted money; they arise from tax evasion, the liquidation of undisclosed hoards of goods, or transactions which it is desired to keep secret because they yielded an extortionate rate of profit ... The vast majority of the population, on the other hand, has been deprived of its savings by currency reform and commands a current income that is barely sufficient to cover its requirements for food, rents, and low value essential consumer goods.[2]

He concluded that if drastic action was not taken to increase investments then unemployment, already growing, would again get out of hand and a slump would follow. He was very critical of the German government and their apparent lack of proper concern and activity and concluded, in his final report with the Control Commission:

> Western Germany is not richly endowed with natural resources. Her principal asset is the industriousness and skill of her population. There is no evidence that the Federal Government has any plans to mobilize this asset to the utmost. Mass unemployment is accepted as 'structural', although it is admitted that investment could substantially reduce it. There is a fear of increasing employment (and thus purchasing power) because a man who works spends more than a man on the dole. Federal Government is thus content to offer a programme which promises no recovery or consolidation during the remainder of the ERP period; which tackles none of the burning problems of Western Germany – such as housing and the absorption of the expellees: – which holds out no promise of viability for many years to come; and which threatens to leave Germany, poisoned by mass-unemployment, as a 'serious danger for the whole of Western Europe'.[3]

Looking at the German 'economic miracle' of the 1950s and 1960s one might wonder at Fritz's despondency and totally wrong prediction. Currency reform, of which he was so critical, has been pointed to as the source of the so called 'miracle'; Dr Erhard has taken the credit and his name has gone down as a sort of Moses taking the children of Germany into the land flowing with milk and honey. Fritz, however, always denied that he had been wrong in his critique of the currency reform or that it had been the real cause of Germany's economic 'take-off'. He maintained that his predictions would have been proved correct if it had not been for the outbreak of the war in Korea. The effect of the Korean war, he claimed, changed the economic situation in Europe and came to the rescue of Germany.

Whatever the economic effects of the German currency reform, it cannot be denied that the following day, as queues of people waited outside post offices to claim their allocation of Deutsche Marks, the shelves of shops were suddenly full of goods. Sanity had been restored. Politically too, there were significant consequences. The discussions had been long and protracted between the four occupying powers, the Russians and the French obstructing all the plans the Anglo-American delegation put forward. Eventually the Americans and the British decided to go it alone. The French were pacified by various bargains (among them a higher coal allocation in which Fritz had a hand), but the Russians' fury could not be contained and they retaliated viciously by sealing off the borders of their zone, cutting Berlin off from the rest of Germany.

The Russian blockade was countered by a stupendous Allied effort to 'carry on as normal'. The most ambitious airlift programme imaginable was organized and non-stop aeroplanes droned over the Russian zone to Berlin day and night carrying essential supplies. Even coal was flown in by air. It was a time of great uncertainty and great stringency. Berliners were only allowed two hours of electric power a day and if these happened to occur at three in the morning housewives just had to get up and do their cooking in the middle of the night.

Among those affected by the siege of Berlin were Fritz and Muschi. At least Fritz could escape to normality from time to time on his trips to Paris but he was concerned whether Muschi could bear this new tension and uncertainty. From Paris he wrote on June 29th, 1948:

I am deeply unhappy about leaving you alone just now. Can you still bear it? The situation is very uncomfortable. I have a vague hope that perhaps one doesn't get quite as nervous about it in Berlin as one gets when being so far away and having only the newspapers to go by. But I doubt it.

There is of course only one consideration: yours and the children's safety. Never mind about our things. I would even write off my books – and the grand piano. It is even not necessary to 'write them off' yet. Either there is an evacuation or there is not. In the former case I just can't believe that the three Western Powers would tolerate being robbed of the private possessions of their people. But all this is quite secondary. If you feel unsafe or if you would feel happier in Hamburg: go to Reinbek for a holiday.

For some months before the siege of Berlin there had been talk of Muschi and Fritz transferring to Frankfurt where the bizonal economic headquarters were situated and from where Fritz could more easily travel to Paris to increasingly frequent O.E.E.C. meetings. The political uncertainties of Berlin now made such a move even more desirable and a month later the family – Fritz, Muschi, Christian, John and I (it was my birth in London Fritz had narrowly missed when he left for Germany in May 1946) – moved to Hoechst in Frankfurt.

The move to Frankfurt was the turning point for Fritz. Possibly the atmosphere in Berlin, the city of his youth, had had something to do with his hopeful dedication, possibly the elation of being in on things right from the beginning had kept him going. But in Frankfurt he began to feel less and less optimistic about the work he was doing and its achievements. This was also partly because he had felt near to a significant victory as he moved to Frankfurt. He had a new scheme up his sleeve which he was pushing for all he was worth. In 1948, the year of the Marshall Plan and the O.E.E.C., Fritz became very involved in the discussions which eventually led up to the European Payments Union. The plan Fritz put forward was not dissimilar to his multilateral clearing plan but he had developed and expanded it to meet the particular circumstances of Europe. At first he was confident that the sixteen member countries would view it favourably. In his letter of June 29th he wrote to Muschi from Paris:

I would have returned long ago if my presence here were not absolutely essential. The fact is that I *am* setting the pace here; that my thoughts and proposals *are* dominating the present work of the Conference. I have now worked out a complete and almost foolproof scheme for European Co-operation, – the only complete scheme so far in existence. It had been circulated to all Delegations and, very likely sixteen governments are considering it at present. Never before have

I been so near to achievement. If I can push it through now I shall have done something for Europe.

Success was not to be. The plan was not accepted and Fritz put his failure down to the fact that he could not spend enough time in Paris and so 'the infant that came into the world so joyfully has fallen into bad hands,' he wrote to his parents in September. 'These have ruined him to such an extent that I doubt whether he can survive.'

An American lawyer, Kingman Brewster (later U.S. Ambassador to London), who was present at the discussions believed it failed for other reasons. He thought that the scheme was too original for the assembled governments. Fritz was aware too that the stumbling block was Whitehall. He was very depressed and wrote in October to Sir Cecil Weir, 'In conclusion I should like to say that the present tendency in Paris fills me with apprehension and gloom.'

In the middle of the following year, when the battles had finally been lost, Fritz was relieved that it was all over. Even defeat was better than the endless wranglings. But it had not been entirely fruitless for him. Thinking afresh about trade and its efficient organization had given him new insights. He still thought in terms of large comprehensive schemes to solve the problem he had identified but he saw that changes had taken place in the elements that made up the problem, which a new scheme would have to take into account. It was more complicated than he had realized because the quantitative changes in trading arrangements had had qualitative effects. The bilateralism which he had condemned had originally functioned when trade had taken place between many small traders ('the atomistic system of private traders'). A qualitative difference had taken place as small private traders became integrated into national groupings, protected by all sorts of price mechanisms and price support systems. 'The atoms have become lumps of matter (or energy) of very much differing size-weight-shape-chemical quality.' Multilateralism had applied to these new rules and laws – the law of the big number. Now Fritz believed things had changed again: 'The units have grown from the free enterprising atoms – John Smith and Jack Jones – to the size of an integrated rock (I won't say: Atom bomb) e.g. the U.S.A. In other places, however, only the size of a brick – U.K. or a little marble – Ireland. How could the law of the big number – The principle of Indeterminacy—work as between rocks and little marbles?'[4]

This led him to look more closely at the reasons for the new situation which he concluded was due to the change in industrial and agricultural techniques. Industrial equipment had developed from being small-scale, short-lived and highly versatile, to being large-scale, long-lived and highly specific. A new 'law of mechanics' had to be worked out to explain and regulate the new economic machine.

With the failure of his European Payments Scheme Fritz shelved this line of thought for the time being. He had experienced repeatedly how his grand schemes, which were designed to solve major problems, had not received recognition. Again and again he was driven to conclude that the 'experts', particularly in his field of economics, did not have the powers of understanding that he had. They failed to find the right solutions because they were incapable of penetrating the real core of the problems, and therefore they were unable to understand the proper solution when it was offered to them.

In Germany, where he had the strong conviction that he was responsible for the fate of millions, even 'the life and death of millions', such a failure to get his 'solutions' across and accepted was the cause of tremendous tension and nervous strain. All around him people were thronging with demands and questions and he became acutely aware of the need to judge between the essential and the inessential, not only in his job but in life in general. What was it that prevented most people from distinguishing between what was really important and what was not? And how was he to develop this ability which he had always assumed he had?

Such questions had already occurred to him when, inundated with more work than he could handle on his arrival in Berlin, he had to distinguish between the many pressing demands that landed on his desk from dawn to dusk. Immersed as he was in the economic problems of Germany, he realized that to do his job properly he had to give some time to more general questions. As soon as Muschi had joined him and relieved him of the daily domestic pressures he began to search for answers in books by Epictetus the Stoic, August Bier and Ortega y Gasset. It was a new departure and one he felt needed explanation. In March 1947 he wrote to his parents:

> My main endeavour is to discover what is important and what is unimportant in this world. Most of us waste our time with all sorts of side issues. But we will never find our way out of the current disorder if we do not find our way back to a sense of the essential. In this sense these seemingly remote areas of learning do have a lot to do with my work. They give me an orientation in the big things and the strength to carry out thousands of details with utter commitment, but without losing my soul to my work.

As the demands of this new path of enquiry became more time-consuming Fritz had to pack more and more into his already overfilled day. He began to rise earlier, starting his studies at six in the morning. He felt much better for the peace of the early morning, he told his parents.

> The main thing is that once again I have a bit of time for myself during which I can work at my own questions in peace. This has an extremely healing influence on my whole frame of mind and so on my health. I just don't feel like letting myself be completely consumed by my work and living out the definition of an expert 'who knows more and more about less and less'.

He got more peace than he bargained for because his demanding schedule proved too much and in the spring of 1948 he went down with pneumonia. The six weeks off work were a gift to him. He read constantly, Schopenhauer and the complete works of Maxim Gorky. Schopenhauer particularly gave him tremendous pleasure: 'I can think of nothing better to read – perhaps even no better way to spend my time than to "think with the mind of Schopenhauer",' he wrote enthusiastically to his parents.

Away from the battles to get his ideas through he was able to think carefully about the failure of the 'experts' to understand the real issues of the problems they tackled. The expression 'An expert is someone who knows more and more about less and less until he knows everything about nothing' was to him an amusing but profound truism. It led him to think more deeply about the failure of the intellectuals and academics to recognize the real danger of Hitler and by upholding the truth of their discipline to resist his rise to power. He said in a lecture in March 1948:

> Our crisis – much wider than just Germany, did not come to pass because of a failure of doctors, engineers or lawyers as doctors, engineers or lawyers. They did not fail as experts but as people.
>
> Man does not wander alone through the world but with others, so one can say that our task is a double one:
> 1. to fully develop oneself
> 2. to form one's relationship to other people – family, groups, one's countrymen, mankind, – sensibly, ethically, or expressed quite simply, with joy. I do not need to emphasize particularly that this division is artificial. One without the other is impossible.[5]

It posed again those questions which he had pondered in the war years in Eydon. What is the purpose of man's existence? Are there moral values? Is there any other useful tool beyond scientific fact and logic? His conclusions in 1943 had satisfied him. Logic and scientific fact were the only methods by which an intelligent person could make sense of the world. But since then his experience had failed to confirm this belief. As he travelled around Germany he had come to the conclusion that the unintellectual peasants had more understanding and more rounded personalities than the most clever expert, who had had the benefit of a proper education. If one could succeed in being an expert but fail as a person something was wrong in the aims of education. By failing to understand man's task in life, education failed to provide people with the proper tools. The answer, Fritz suggested, was not returning to the unintellectual state of the peasant but to restore education to its proper function of teaching people how to think. Facts and the scientific method alone could not produce ideas.

Ortega y Gasset, the author who had so inspired him when

as a student he had set off for America, was his inspiration once more and Fritz quoted from *The Mission of the Universities* to illustrate his point:

> The medieval university does no research. It is very little concerned with professions. All is '*general culture*' – theology, philosophy, 'arts' – ... It was not an ornament for the mind or the training of the character. It was, on the contrary, the system of ideas, concerning the world and humanity, which the man of that time possessed. It was consequently, the repertory of convictions which became the effective guide of his existence.[6]

There was an important message here for someone who regarded himself as an exceptionally clear thinker. Was the 'system of ideas', the 'repertory of convictions' which Fritz had worked out effectively guiding his existence? He was beginning to discover that his creed of the early 1940s was no longer satisfying him. In examining how to think effectively, facts and logic had failed to help. And as Ortega y Gasset forcefully pointed out there was a difference between facts and knowledge. 'The man of science can no longer afford to be what he is now with lamentable frequency – a barbarian knowing much of one thing ... From all quarters the need presses upon us for a new integration of knowledge, which today lies in pieces scattered around the world. But the labour of this undertaking is enormous.'

The message was so clear to Fritz that he felt that the answers he had been searching for were within his reach and must be offered to others. He began at once to write a book to show people how to think clearly. It was now obvious to him that clear thinking required one to ask the right questions and to be well informed politically. This was the task of the universities and the educational system: to open people's eyes to the political and ethical realities about them and teach them how to relate one to the other. But his 'book' did little more than stimulate him to further reading. As he wrote, he discovered that he was uncovering more questions than he was answering and his own ideas needed more substance.

They were not destined to come to fruition in Germany. By the middle of 1949 Fritz's heart was no longer really in his work and he was looking for a change. The defeat in the battle over the European Payments Union symbolized the waning of his influence and that of the Allied powers generally. Germany would now go its own way and as Fritz was not happy about the way German politicians were choosing, it did not make sense for him to stay. In October 1949 Sir Cecil Weir left Germany. Fritz had regarded him as an ally and as his 'battering ram' but they had disagreed over the European Payments question and Fritz was finding himself out on a limb.

The future took care of itself. Since the days at the Oxford Institute, Fritz's reputation had been growing. His self-confidence was not based on false pride. People did take note of him. Soon after his arrival in Germany in the summer of 1946 he had been offered a highly lucrative and 'safe' job as Director of the United Nations Economic and Social Council in New York. His sense of mission to Germany was so great at that time that he had no doubts about turning the offer down at once. There were other less significant but flattering incidents. He reported one which took place in July to Muschi, much amused.

On Saturday, there were lots of people, mostly from 'Public Relations', the journalistic type. I asked a French lady to dance with me and the following conversation ensued: –

She: You are the bearer of a very famous name.

I: Possibly. What does the name convey to you?

She: Isn't your name Schumacher – well, that's the leader of the S.P.D. And there is also a famous economist of that name.

I: An economist? Where?

She: At Oxford.

I: There is no economist of that name at Oxford.

She: Oh yes there is. I have read everything he has written.

I: Then you must have read everything *I* have written.

She: Don't be silly. You are not from Oxford are you? You can't be the Oxford Schumacher. You are only a little boy.

I: Maybe I am. That is a failing only time can mend. At any rate, the only economist of that name at Oxford is me.

> She: But this is incredible. – And I have been reading
> your writing with such *veneration* (All this in a
> French accent).
>
> I: That will now cease, I hope.
>
> She: I don't know what to say. I can't get over it. I must
> have a drink ...

This sort of thing happens quite frequently. Sometimes I
am asked whether I am a relation of the Schumacher who is
Economic Adviser to the Control Commission. It is really
very amusing.

Inconsequential as such conversations were, except to amuse
and boost Fritz's ego, they served to assure him that the future
would look after itself. In November 1949, this view was confirmed when three offers came Fritz's way. The first was another U.N. post, this time in Geneva. Fritz turned it down, it
was not what he wanted. The second was an invitation from
the President of Burma asking Fritz to become his economic
adviser. Again, Fritz turned it down. It was not what his family
wanted.

The third job fitted his hopes and aspirations exactly. It was
from the British Government. Fritz was asked to return to
England as Economic Adviser to the National Coal Board. It
was the ideal opportunity. He wanted to return to England.
The experiment to live in Germany again had not worked. His
own status as an Englishman had been fraught with tension
and difficulty. The lack of sympathy with his stand over Hitler's
Germany disillusioned and saddened him, and his decreasing
influence, and particularly the fact that Germany was set on
a course directly opposite to the one he recommended and
had worked for, convinced him that his task in Germany was
over.

The job at the National Coal Board on the other hand
seemed to offer everything he felt he lacked. It would give him
status in the community to which he wanted to return. The
suggestion that he should be appointed had come from the
highest level. At one of his weekly meetings with Lord
Hyndley, Chairman of the N.C.B. since nationalization, the
Minister of Power, Hugh Gaitskell, had suggested that the
Board might find it useful to employ an economist. Hyndley

asked whether the Minister had anyone in mind and Gaitskell had replied 'Fritz Schumacher'.

Also present at the meeting were the Permanent Secretary, Sir Donald Ferguson, a junior minister, Alf Robens, and Hyndley's deputy, Sir Arthur Street, who had known Fritz since his appointment to the Control Commission. He heartily endorsed Gaitskell's suggestion.

Such knowledge helped Fritz's self-confidence as did the announcement of his appointment in the *Financial Times*: 'Mr Schumacher, who had an outstanding career as an economist at Oxford before the war, joined Sir Cecil Weir's staff in the early days of allied occupation. He was later mainly concerned with the analysis of German economic trends and is regarded as one of the most able men on the staff of the British Control Commission.'[7] More important was the significance he felt the job itself had. It contained all the elements of his thinking on industrial development, peace and socialism. It was an opportunity to match his skills as an economist, businessman and creative thinker, in an industry which he knew was unrivalled in its importance for the economy. While fighting for a proper coal policy in Germany he had learnt that energy was fundamental to all industrial activity, that the recovery of Germany depended on coal output. He had realized that energy was the foundation stone of industry, and coal, being indigenous to Europe, was the foundation stone of the European economy. In putting the coal industry on a firm footing he was working at the very centre of the economic life of the country. The British industry, although nationalized since 1946, consisted of a host of different scattered mines whose owners had for years jealously guarded their independence and which now had to be welded into a cohesive whole. He realized too that a strong indigenous coal industry was in the interests of peace. If an industrial nation could avoid depending on imported energy it would be avoiding the dangers to peace that international trade in such a sensitive commodity would bring.

Politically, too, the offer appealed to him. He had been a member of the Labour Party since 1946 and a supporter of nationalization and centralization of certain industries, and as a socialist he had every interest in making this new great experiment of nationalization work. He was committing himself to an exciting experiment dreamt of for years by socialist writers and thinkers. The socialist revolution he had antici- pated as he studied Marx in the cottage in Eydon had not come about in Germany, nor had he been more successful in his own attempted revolution to get his paper on 'The Socialisation of German Industry' accepted in the first years after the war. But all the while the revolution had been taking place in England and Fritz was eager to play his part.

For Fritz the decision seemed straightforward. The only complication was Muschi. For her, his decision was terrible. Her loyalty to her mother had always been immense and now that her sister Olga's children were in the care of her parents, it was even stronger. She felt it her duty to be a mother to her sister's children as well as being a wife to Fritz and a mother to her own children. For her the obvious solution was to stay in Germany where she knew a man of Fritz's ability could easily find work. Once again the conflict between head and heart arose: Fritz's intellectual needs against Muschi's emotional ones. Once again the power of the intellect was the stronger. Fritz was determined to return to England and felt moreover that he needed it for his whole being. He wanted to breathe the air of England, and live in that very different atmosphere. He tried hard to convey this feeling to Muschi. After a week in England, the first in April and his first at the Coal Board (during which he caught such a heavy cold that he had to take two days in bed), he wrote to Muschi: 'This last week I felt more cheerful than I can remember for at least eleven years. You will discover the same when you come. It has been an enormous load and burden living in Germany (in our parti- cular position). You have *every reason* to look forward to your return. It will be grand.'

Anxiously he asked the next day: 'Do you now feel reconciled to all the changes I am imposing on you? I am doing my best to lighten your burdens. You have a lot to look forward to here. So don't get too much attached to Reinbek, please.' Reinbek, he knew, was the real threat to their happiness. Muschi could not let go of her home. Her attachment to her family grew stronger with every year that passed.

When at last she joined Fritz in London at the beginning of May 1950, it was a difficult time for them both. Fritz was grieved by Muschi's unhappiness at the prospect of her future away from her family; Muschi was unable to control her feelings, sad and homesick and yet feeling disloyal to her husband. For a while she wavered, unable to accept that there was really no choice in the matter for her. And when he saw her, Fritz, who had always been confident in her strength and loyalty to withstand the difficulties they encountered in their life together, recognized that their marriage had reached a crisis point. Even after they had found the house they wanted and Muschi had returned to Germany in June to finalize the move, there was still a question mark in the air whether she would return and Fritz wrote to her once more about the crisis.

> The thing that got me worried is the problem Germany/ England or Reinbek/Caterham. Because there I am completely powerless to make an adjustment on my side: there is no choice for me. I could not possibly return to Germany – it would finish me. I think that even you do not really have a choice – if only because of Christian. But if you think you have, it is difficult for you and may become dangerous. What worried me no end was that you would choose England and Caterham so reluctantly that everything here would become a frightful burden for all of us.

Muschi chose England and Caterham, but it was with difficulty. Her home always remained in Reinbek and the heartache she felt each time she left it never abated.

15

Caterham

The move to Caterham in 1950 was a public statement of permanence. For twenty years Fritz had been shifted around by the tides of history. In 1950 when he bought the house he was to live in until his death, he put down his anchor. The house was called Holcombe. It was cold, not particularly comfortable, but spacious with a four-acre garden set in beautiful green belt Surrey countryside. Fritz loved it. There was space for him to have his own study, there was more than enough space for a vegetable plot, there were outbuildings where he could set up a work bench. The children loved it. Even when Virginia was born in 1951, we were still able to have our own rooms, the garden was ideal for adventures and wild games, there was space for a succession of rabbits, guinea pigs, canaries, goldfish, chickens and a dog, all of which lived and died under our care. Muschi did not love it – except for the happiness it gave her husband and children. For her it was uncomfortable, cold, and hard work, particularly in the garden which she found a great burden. Most of all, Holcombe was too isolated for her. She found it hard enough to make friends with the reserved English, but even more so when she spent so much of her time scrubbing, washing and weeding. The interlude in Germany with its unreal living conditions for the members of the Allied Control Commissions had reminded her that life could be easier than it had been and now was again. Her hands grew red and in the winter became covered in painful chilblains. Their bedroom, painted a cold blue when they moved in, chilled her from the moment she woke in the morning and yet she could not find the energy to redecorate it: it stayed that way for ten years.

Fritz on the other hand was filled with energy now that he was master of his own home again. He became a passionate gardener and for some years he spent his annual holidays making compost, sowing comfrey to feed a cow which never came, growing quantities of Swiss chard that none of the children liked eating, and also providing the family with other vegetables, soft fruit and salads. He took the garden very seriously and at once joined the Coal Board gardening club and the Soil Association. His eyes were opened to a whole new way of thinking. The Soil Association claimed that modern farming was going up a blind alley, was actually harmful to the long-term interests of the soil. Its philosophy was far broader than mere gardening. It was concerned with 'wholeness' and health in the broadest sense, believing that the base line from which to work begins in the soil itself. Their message was quite simple: look after the soil and your plants will look after themselves. Then, not only will you have healthy and nourishing plants, vegetables, fruits, salads and grains, but you will also have healthier animals and people. Fritz discovered that there had been small groups promoting these concepts since the early part of the century, who had broken away from the ideas dominating scientific thinking. Perhaps the earliest was Rudolf Steiner in the nineteenth century but following him came many others: Sir Robert McCarrison, Dr Francis Pottinger Jnr, and Dr Weston Price in the medical field; Sir Albert Howard, Dr William Albrecht and Dr E. Pfeiffer in agriculture; followed by a new group of men and women such as Dr George Scott-Williamson, Dr Lionel Bicton, Dr Dendy, Professor Barry Commoner, Rachel Carson and Lady Eve Balfour. Lady Eve Balfour was one of the pioneers of the Soil Association itself. She began organic farming in the early 1930s and in 1939 began experimental research on her farm to promote the ideals of organic husbandry. In 1947, the newly formed Soil Association took over her work. Fritz was so impressed by the Soil Association that he at once began to implement organic methods in his own back garden. He made enormous compost heaps, offending the neighbours by the cartloads of manure he imported from a nearby pig farm to improve the quality of the chalky soil. He also tried to conduct experiments. Somehow he had acquired some wheat that had been found in the tombs of the pharaohs, grains thousands of years old grown in the once fertile Sahara desert. The ancient wheat grew but it was sterile. Fritz was astonished that after thousands of years there should still be life in the grain.

The garden became Fritz's passion. He got up at 6 a.m. to work outside before he went to the office, he worked at his compost when he returned from the office at seven in the evening; at weekends he would be found again in the garden slowly transforming it into a workable patch. The soil was not very good but he had confidence that it would be transformed within a few months so that the family would be self-sufficient in food in a year. The work made his elegant, beautifully manicured hands lose some of their softness. A new style of entertaining also developed at Holcombe. It could hardly have been a more striking contrast to the round of cocktail parties and dinners of the Control Commission days. Guests were most heartily welcome, but if they wanted to see Fritz they had to make sure they came in their gardening clothes. Two of the closest friends of the family at the time, Vera and Henry Morley, were counted on to keep the strawberry patch going. A thankless task as the harvest was usually gathered prematurely by the children.

Fritz's natural inclination to weld his ideas and actions into a unified whole made his gardening interests a complementary part of his work at the Coal Board as he explained to his parents, somewhat tongue in cheek:

Last week the Coal Board Gardening Club had invited an Expert from the Soil Association to show a film and give a talk on 'Organic Farming'. I was asked to take the chair, not as a garden expert but as a senior member of the Coal Board. In my introductory talk I said that in my opinion there were two primary factors in the economy – Food and Fuel – everything else was secondary. To listen to a lecture on food production in the Headquarters of fuel production was therefore the most significant concentration on the essential that I could imagine.

Slowly a new way of living evolved and Fritz was well pleased. He explained his new attitudes to his sister Edith in November 1951:

> I have rarely felt better in my life. We are 'building' – our house, our garden, our friends – let alone the family. For this reason I have hardly any time for anything else, besides this 'circle' of mine. All my free time goes into the garden and into directing the children into productive activities. In many ways our house is an oasis in the desert of today's civilization. Of course we participate and make as much use as possible of the useful accoutrements, but we try not to let ourselves be pulled into all the useless hokus pokus. This at any rate is my great aim – to prevent the children becoming mere consumers without having a creative attitude to their lives. For that reason I have started all sorts of new things, for example, baking bread for the family. Once one has started it one wonders why one hasn't always done it. (The bread made from whole wheat, stone ground flour is of course infinitely more tasty and healthier than any bread from the baker.) Home produce from the garden has the same purpose: only in this way can the children of the modern world get some idea of what life and work really is.
>
> But I express myself badly. I am the anti-intellectual intellectual. That means that the 'pure' intellectual is for me a horror of our time – much more fatal than the non-intellectual. I have had a week's holiday and have done so much manual labour that I can hardly hold my fountain pen any more. Actually I should have used my holiday to work out a new 'energy policy'. I have finished it in my head but I cannot get down to putting it on paper. It is terribly important but at the moment, compared to my compost, seems quite unimportant.

Fritz's creative interests were not confined to gardening and bread baking. He very much wanted the children to learn through creative work. Schooling until then had not been all that successful. After the Burgess Hill experiment the boys had had a succession of tutors who had generally given up the struggle to maintain discipline after a few weeks of chaos. Once in Frankfurt, Christian had gone to boarding school and in England it was decided that he should continue to board in an English school, Westbury House, until eventually he decided to go to the independent boys' school, Caterham School, conveniently situated opposite Holcombe, where John also went. Fritz, however, wanted to foster more creative learning than school provided and with his father's and Uncle Fritz's education in America in mind bought the boys a small printing press for Christmas. He tried to inspire them with stories of their ancestors, how the original Schumacher Brothers had had their own business, printing little books for a variety of clients in New York. But although the boys enjoyed listening to stories of how their grandfather and great-uncle had clambered about the smouldering buildings of a German newspaper to salvage print for their own use, and how they had rewritten the poems of a client because they had not had enough 'e's in their supply of letters, they were never inspired beyond printing a few Christmas cards, letterheads and visiting cards. A business did not materialize. Fritz's efforts tended to have a similar fate. For a while he tried to mend the family's shoes, but found it too difficult to get supplies, and there still exists a box of broken watches and clock bits which Fritz had tried to mend without great success. But he undertook his practical activities with the greatest enthusiasm and encouraged the children to try all sorts of things from carpentry (for which John was provided with a proper carpenter's bench) to the sewing and weaving by which we made a motley collection of unfinished Christmas presents for our German relations for many years.

The pleasure Fritz derived from the new activities helped him to avoid getting 'eaten up' by his work at the Coal Board in the way his work had taken over in the past. Holcombe, the garden, and his new way of life removed the temptation to bring work home and the forty-minute train journey to London and back provided him with time to read. He wrote to his parents, 'I can only hope that I can now stay here for many years so that I can work in peace.'

His success in avoiding getting taken over by his Coal Board work speaks for his tremendous enjoyment of his home life for he began his work at the N.C.B. bubbling with enthusiasm. Not even the problems with Muschi had been able to cloud his optimism. 'Things are starting well here at the N.C.B.,' he had written to Muschi on his first day. 'I am glad to be in this purely British outfit, where the first two chaps I was introduced to were Mr Gottlieb and Mr Picciotto ... Everybody is frightfully nice to me, – expecting great things. I am telling them that I shall take a long time before I can say anything and that I don't know nothing.'

Of course, the coal industry as such was not new to him but he began his investigations at an even more basic level than the ins and outs of the workings of the British Board. His starting point was to look at all sources of power, both existing and potential, and put coal in a wider context. He lost no time. Within three days of joining the N.C.B. he attended a top-level meeting of experts, which included Charles Ellis, one of the members of the team who had split the atom. The implications of nuclear energy were discussed, and Fritz offered to summarize the issues afterwards; it was the best method of learning quickly. All the information he gleaned went straight into his notebook of basic facts – a method of information gathering and storage he had developed in the Control Commission. The next day he reported to Muschi, 'I am working through a lot of "basic" stuff on coal and all the other sources and forms of power, working out all the most important information relevant to Coal Board economics – things for most of which other people have to dig in files and reports or which they have to get someone else to work out for them.'

After a fortnight he knew enough to draft some chapters of the Annual Report. It was an ideal way to learn what had been going on and led Fritz quickly to the conclusion that not very much progress had been made since nationalization in 1946. There was a great deal for him to do and he realized that his success would depend on the use the members of the Board made of him. The 'big chiefs', whose servant and adviser he would be, made an instant impression: 'Every one of them could have been my father,' he wrote to Muschi.

There was one exception: E.H. Browne. Fritz was full of hope that this would be a fruitful relationship, reporting to Muschi: 'The most interesting man here seems to be the Director-General of Production, Mr E.H. Browne, aged thirty-nine. He has been described to me as a "genius". I met him yesterday and was most intrigued. You will hear more about him during the next few years. If he is really a "genius" – you know I am going to fall in love with him. I wished he were.'

The other Board member who Fritz knew might be crucial to his work as Economic Adviser, was the Deputy Chairman, Sir Arthur Street. Unlike the Chairman, Lord Hyndley, Sir Arthur knew exactly how to use Fritz and what his value to the industry could be. He encouraged Fritz and listened to him so that Fritz felt confident that he would be able to achieve great things. This confidence was to be short-lived. On February 24th, 1951 Sir Arthur Street, aged only fifty-eight, died quite unexpectedly. It was a tremendous blow to Fritz who knew that he would feel the loss personally and professionally. He wrote to his parents the following day:

> He was the most significant person that I have got to know in my professional life. It was he who sent me to Germany five years ago, and he appointed me to the Coal Board just over a year ago. I have worked in the closest co-operation with him for the last (almost) eleven months. He *was* the Coal Board, and the gap which he leaves behind is just unimaginably big. I have no reason to worry about my own position. But I will always miss Sir Arthur, I will always mourn him. He was goodness and wisdom personified, and his larger than life presence was at the centre of every constructive effort at the Coal Board and beyond.

The loss of Sir Arthur Street had a significant effect. He died before Fritz's role had been properly established, and Fritz was left without an ear on the Board. He found himself in a lonely and isolated position in which he produced ideas, made suggestions and made himself available for advice and consultation at all times, but felt continually that he was being seriously underutilized. The papers he put in front of the Board were often unsolicited, and the very nature of the job meant he was always in danger of treading on people's toes. As he asked questions about the industry, his rigorous investigations took him into many areas that were not strictly economic; technical processes, financial policy, personnel management, safety, industrial relations, every aspect came under his scrutiny. Not surprisingly, some specialists resented Fritz's questions and disputed his competence and right to enter their field, regardless of whether his suggestions had value. Fritz found hostility both at the pits and at the Board.

There was another blow in 1951. In the general election the Labour Government lost power. The attitude of the new Conservative Government towards nationalization was another element of uncertainty in the progress of the coal industry.

These factors did not deter Fritz from doing a tremendous amount of work for the Coal Board. He saw his function primarily as the one person in the industry who was paid to think. He was paid to sit back and take time to reflect on the industry as a whole and provide guidelines to the areas in which the specialists should direct their expertise.

16

Learning How to Think

The art in his job lay in knowing how to think. In Germany he had adapted his day to include an early morning period to study this question but in Caterham that time was filled by his new responsibilities as a householder and the demands of the garden. Fortunately another time was available: the forty minutes' train journey between Caterham and Victoria where Hobart House, the N.C.B. headquarters, was situated.

For Fritz this was a welcome gift of time when he could pursue his private studies. He knew the reserve of the English would guarantee his peace and in fact travelled uninterrupted in the same compartment with the same people for twenty years during which time he did a large proportion of his intensive studies! After a look at the papers – at that time the *News Chronicle* and *The Times* – he would take his book out of the brown leather N.C.B. briefcase. At first he read about South America – Prescott's *Conquest of Peru* and *Conquest of Mexico* – which took him back to his own family and their adventures in nineteenth-century Colombia, then his attention turned Eastwards to more ancient civilizations. He became caught up in the cradle of the Indus and then China and found that he could not study their civilizations without paying close attention to their religions and philosophy. It was an absorbing and challenging new study which was as disturbing as it was exciting. He was confronted with teaching which contradicted everything he had held valuable and had cultivated in himself. His whole life had been based on the assumption that his

228

intellect, powerful and penetrating, was the tool that would lead him to knowledge and understanding. His intellect had guided him through his life. His intellect had helped him to discern the real core of the problems the world was facing, and had enabled him to work out new and comprehensive solutions. His intellect had shown him why so many of his contemporaries, supposedly experts in their field, had failed to recognize not only the truths he put forward, but also a deeper level of truth which had been betrayed by Germany and the Nazis, namely the failure of the educational system to teach people how to think because of an obsession with facts and expertise. He believed he could think more clearly than most, that he knew how to concentrate on essentials and that the tools required for such thought were rationalism, logic and reason.

In his new reading he discovered that the Eastern mystics and philosophers not only had something to say about their own way of life, they also offered an answer to the questions that had preoccupied him increasingly after the war. What had caused men to fail as people despite their high level of expertise? Everywhere he read, the answer seemed to be the same.

The present crisis in human affairs is due to a profound crisis in human consciousness, a lapse from the organic wholeness of life. There is a tendency to overlook the spiritual and exalt the intellectual ... The business of the intellectual is to dispel the mystery, put an end to dreams, strip life of its illusions, and reduce the great play of human life to a dull show, comic on occasions but tragic more frequently. The primitive cults which helped their adherents to live healthily and happily on their own plane are dismissed as crude superstitions. Everything is stripped of soul, of inner life. This world is all and we must rest content with it.[1]

Words such as these were a profound shock. The very values he had held up to be the way towards wisdom and truth were here dismissed. He had always held that 'the business of the intellectual is to dispel the mystery, put an end to dreams, strip life of its illusions' but regarded this as their strength and virtue, making progress possible, and this new teaching told him he was reducing life to a meaningless show. The challenge was so fundamental that he either had to dismiss it out of hand or take it seriously, and study further. But honesty prevented him from abandoning the study for there were aspects that accorded with his own observations of life in the last few years such as the 'wholeness' or, as he put it, 'rounded personalities' of many simple unintellectual people. He wrote to his parents:

Through this contact with Indian and Chinese philosophy and religion, my whole way of thinking has come into motion. New possibilities of knowledge (and experience) have been opened to me of whose existence I had no inkling. I feel as men during the Renaissance must have felt. All the conclusions I had come to have to be thought through again. And it is not only thinking that is influenced. But it is not easy to describe all this. I have the feeling that I will look back to my forty-first year as a turning point for the rest of my life.

The admission that his whole way of thinking had perhaps been wrong had an immediate and dramatic effect. Once he admitted the possibility that there were forces in the world which defied rational analysis, which could not be explained scientifically, it opened the floodgates of a new kind of knowledge which he had previously refused to give any recognition whatsoever. In his efforts to correct the imbalance that his insistence on facts and rational thought had produced, the pendulum swung with increasing force in the opposite direction. He joined the Society of Psychical Research and examined every non-rational, non-factual belief he came across. From saying that no intelligent man should believe anything that could not be proved, he now took the opposite view that nothing should be dismissed because it could not be proved.

It was not only the possibility of higher spiritual forces that claimed his attention but all sorts of other unexplained phenomena. This change in his perception of the possible coincided with the publication of several books on flying saucers. Fritz not only took them seriously but was thrilled to meet several people who claimed to have seen them. His friends and acquaintances were incredulous at this transformation, Nicki

Kaldor among them. A weekend of Fritz enthusing about flying saucers could not convince him of Fritz's sincerity. It was so out of character that Kaldor could only assume it was all a big joke.

The bombshell that had been dropped into Fritz's life was not only that there was the possibility of a non-factual and non-rational side to life, a world which the writers he now studied called 'the spiritual', but also that they claimed that this could not be understood or reached by means of the intellect. This was the biggest leap of all. The intellect which Fritz had regarded as the most precious and powerful weapon he had, by which he had measured himself against other great men, was not only useless in this new teaching but actually regarded as a hindrance.

He was not left to ponder this paradox for long before a new discovery gave him the first clues to its meaning. Extraordinarily the contact came through the National Coal Board. The British Coal Utilization Research Association (BICURA) was run by a man named John G. Bennett who was also a disciple of the spiritual master named G.I. Gurdjieff. At weekends the BICURA laboratories at Coombe Springs were transformed into a centre for a band of spiritual seekers who met to explore the meanings and implications of Gurdjieff's teachings. Gurdjieff's teachings immediately appealed to Fritz. They explained the paradox of the uselessness of knowledge, including spiritual knowledge. Gurdjieff taught that such knowledge was just so much 'intellectual baggage' if the seeker had not 'woken up', 'become conscious'. He taught that man was a clever machine which reacted to stimuli but that was not the true destiny of mankind. A truly complete person was one who had such awareness and control that he could learn to act rather than react to the stimuli of daily life. Bennett, who had known Gurdjieff, taught consciousness-developing exercises, types of meditation which the adherents of the Gurdjieff movement called 'work'.

It was no mean task to let go of that part of him which he had always prized, to try and empty himself and begin to let his heart work. It was a totally new experience. In February 1952 he confided in his mother that, 'I fear that it will be more difficult for me than for many others, because I have depended on the intellect to such an extent that it now tries to push itself into the forefront at every opportunity.'

But he persisted, and as he practised the 'work' he believed that he felt his understanding increasing. He shared all his experience with his mother and after six months' daily struggle and intense reading, wrote to her in April 1953: 'The crux of the matter – and that of all other "schools of wisdom" is the method of allowing a deep inner stillness and calmness to enter, – a stillness not only of the body, but also of thoughts and feelings. Through this one gains an extraordinary strength and happiness.'

This made him want more than ever to share his new experience with Muschi. Time at Holcombe did not heal the unhappiness she felt about leaving her parents and Germany. Her frequent trips home only served to intensify her unhappiness and restlessness. Fritz's own new discoveries convinced him that Muschi would only overcome her inner conflicts by treading the path he was now following. But he had spent fifteen years trying to do the very opposite. He had used all his intellectual power to demolish her religious faith because he said it was superstitious, irrational and could not stand up to intelligent scrutiny. Now he was suddenly talking about 'intellectual baggage' and flying saucers and Muschi felt very confused. Her unhappiness made her want to withdraw from his world and find comfort in her children and the visits to Reinbek.

Few other people were aware of the extent of the changes going on within Fritz besides Muschi and his mother, particularly not within the Coal Board circle. But there was one exception, a colleague, Sam Essame, who, like all Fritz's early Coal Board associates, knew Fritz as 'James'. He had met Fritz three days after Fritz had joined the N.C.B. Essame ran training courses for Coal Board employees, out of which the N.C.B. Staff College later developed. From the outset Fritz had been invited to lecture at the courses which were held at a hotel in Hastings. Generally he was scheduled to address the group in the morning and would arrive the night before for dinner at 6.30. After dinner he might give a talk or he and Essame would spend the evening discussing the next day's talk over a drink. One evening in 1953 the relaxed evening developed in a different way. For some reason Fritz decided to tell Essame of his new line of inquiry. Essame was fascinated and the next thing the two men knew was that it was a quarter to five in the morning. The morning's lecture had been forgotten. They had spent the whole night talking about Bennett and Gurdjieff. In the grey of dawn they walked along the sea-front hastily discussing Fritz's lecture. It was delivered a few hours later with Fritz's usual polish, giving no hint that he had prepared it in the hour before breakfast.

Their long conversation had an unexpected benefit. Sam Essame and his wife decided to accompany Fritz to a course of lectures on Gurdjieff given by Bennett. For the first time Muschi agreed to come too. It was a breakthrough. At this time Fritz had also begun to combine Gurdjieff's 'work' with yoga and Muschi now joined him faithfully every morning. While it did not diminish her unhappiness, she began to see that her task in life was to accept her situation. In her letters to her mother she acknowledged the difficulties without complaining and marvelled at Fritz's patience with her low spirits and lack of energy.

The difficulties with Muschi and the death of his father in 1952 drew Fritz closer than ever to his mother. He had been comforted when his father had suddenly opened his eyes on his death bed and, taking Fritz's hand, had smiled and said, 'Life is indeed rich'. It was a reassuring end to the years of hardship and obscurity into which the once eminent professor had had to sink, but more than that, it was a father's last words to his son. Fritz was only beginning to realize that life held more riches than he had dreamt of, and partly because of his natural inclination to share his new discoveries with those close to him and partly because he saw how his mother's life had collapsed without his father, confided in her some of his most inward feelings and experiences which he was sure would give her new strength and purpose.

In the summer of 1953 he had become very interested in another of Gurdjieff's disciples, Maurice Nicoll, who had linked Gurdjieff's teachings with Christianity. Nicoll impressed Fritz even more than Bennett and after reading one of his books, *The New Man*,[2] suggested to his mother that they should translate it together. It was exactly what she needed.

Her personality had been smothered by a lifetime of devoted service to her husband. She found it hard to come to terms with herself as an independent person after his death. The material in *The New Man*, with which she occupied herself, as well as the task itself, gave her new understanding and confidence. Her relationship with Fritz entered a new depth which enabled her to understand him more fully and also gave her a unique understanding of the other work he was doing 'in the world'. This link with Fritz helped her too to perform a role not many mothers-in-law would succeed in accomplishing. She supported Muschi and gave her strength by her understanding, both of Muschi's unhappiness (for she too would have preferred Fritz to return to Germany to be nearer to her) and by her joint work with Fritz on a book whose Christian links made Fritz's new interests more acceptable to Muschi.

While the paths of Gurdjieff, yoga and in particular Maurice Nicoll, were ones Muschi was slowly prepared to tread with Fritz, his next phase was much more problematic for her. Despite his enthusiasms for Nicoll's work, with its Christian basis, Fritz was really drawn to the East. In 1953 he met another of the men who were to influence his life: Edward Conze. Conze was an extraordinary character who had been a Buddhist for many years. He regarded himself as the reincarnation of a Tibetan Buddhist sent to enlighten the West in his new life as a sort of exile missionary. Fritz's relationship with Conze was on the one hand that of pupil and on the other a modest benefactor. Conze often lived on the brink of poverty and it was not difficult to give him material help. In the autumn of 1953 Conze gave a course of lectures on comparative religion in Sanderstead, a small suburb of Croydon. The course lasted for four years and Fritz attended enthusiastically, taking Muschi with him. On the evening of the lectures Conze would often come to Holcombe for a meal. He hated children and at Holcombe the feeling was certainly reciprocated. We ridiculed his unsympathetic and shabby appearance. Conze was a passionate smoker and smoked throughout his lectures. Fritz frequently gave him cigarettes – it was a kindness he was glad to show. If he did not have a packet of cigarettes to give, he emptied the box of cigarettes kept for visitors into Conze's own empty carton. One afternoon, unfortunately, Christian and John had filled some of the ends of the cigarettes with small explosives. As usual that evening Conze lit up a cigarette soon after he had begun his lecture. As soon as it was finished he got out another. As he drew on it it exploded in his face. It was harmless enough but Fritz was frightfully embarrassed as he realized what had happened. The children were triumphant.

Muschi, too, had mixed feelings about Conze. His lectures on comparative religion were superb. He had profound understanding and was a gifted teacher. But his influence on Fritz worried her in some respects. Conze was a Buddhist and there was no doubt that Fritz was greatly drawn to Buddhist teachings. She could recognize that there was much to be learnt from the East but a wholehearted embrace of an alien religion was quite another matter. Then Conze introduced Fritz to astrology.

Fritz was immediately fascinated and impressed by Conze's remarkable knowledge and intuitive gifts. He appeared able to pinpoint people's sunsigns after only a cursory glance, as Fritz experienced on more than one occasion. Two struck him particularly. Conze appeared to avoid Fritz one lunch-time at the Vega. Later he came to Fritz saying, 'Who was that disgusting Virgo you were with?' On checking the birthday of his companion Fritz found out that he was indeed a Virgo. On another occasion when he introduced Conze to a friend, Conze said, 'What, another Taurus?' Again he was right. Fritz found his own case even more convincing. Shortly after meeting Conze he wrote to his mother asking the exact details of his birth. Born on August 16, 1911 Fritz knew he was under the sun sign of Leo and the moon at that time was in Taurus, but he needed to know the exact time of birth for Conze to plot the rest of his horoscope, particularly the planet in ascendant at his birth.

Unfortunately his mother no longer remembered the exact time of his birth and Fritz's complete horoscope remained a mystery. Conze, however, had no doubts, knowing Fritz and his close ties to his family life, and was convinced that Fritz's ascendant lay in Cancer. Many years later Fritz's mother unearthed the record of his birth and all Conze's convictions were confirmed. Fritz found his horoscope very interesting. He referred to himself as a 'frustrated Lion'. Leos tend to be outgoing, jovial, generous people who are eager to be in the limelight and in positions of leadership. This can certainly be said of Fritz, but in his horoscope lay a number of obstacles to his Leo nature represented in his astrological chart by planets which lay in what is called a square to his Sun sign. Most prominent was his moon in earthbound Taurus, but also significant were the positions of Mars and Saturn. These signs suggested that Fritz's life would not be plain sailing, that he would have to overcome a number of difficulties before he would find the right course. The strong concentration in Fritz's horoscope of earthbound signs were an indication of a stable and practical nature, but their position within the twelve houses of the heavens were concentrated in the air houses, signifying a strong empirical intellect.

Fritz found all this fascinating. He worked out all his children's horoscopes and those of other members of his family. He believed that astrology did work and that used correctly and wisely it could be a useful instrument in understanding one's fellow men and their apparent defects or difficulties. When one understood their horoscope, it was easier to exercise patience and compassion. He believed that learning from 'what is written in the stars' could in fact be a tremendous opportunity for growth and full living, helping people to discover their own weaknesses and how to overcome them.

How was it possible that Fritz could take these sorts of things seriously when not long before he had been adamantly against everything that was not scientific, not based on fact? What allowed the clarity of fact to be clouded by the voice in himself, like Hamlet to Horatio, that 'There are more things in heaven and earth Horatio than are dreamt of in your philosophy'? There is no doubt that the distressing years in Germany had something to do with it. The emotional shocks had begun to awaken the world of his heart and of feelings, and thereby introduce questions in his mind about the condition of man which fact, science and reason did not seem to be able to answer satisfactorily. Yet many people experience such uncomfortable nigglings without paying them any attention. Why did Fritz?

Fritz himself had quite a simple answer to this question. He repeated it again and again. He said it was his work in the garden, working with the soil. Yet, his days at the farm in Eydon had been spent outside doing intense physical work and had coincided with his most vehemently rational and anti-spiritual stage, a stage which he was later to describe to his sister Elisabeth as his 'anti-Christian trauma'. The crucial factor he felt lay in the methods which he was now employing. Occupation with organic husbandry had opened his mind to the possibility of new vistas. His acceptance of the organic approach rather than the conventional chemical approach was, in a sense, an act of faith. It had opened the door to other acts of faith. There was little scientific evidence at that stage to convince the doubter of the 'muck and mystery' way of thinking. But to Fritz 'it made sense'. 'Of course, I don't myself understand anything about it all,' he had written to his parents right at the beginning of his gardening discoveries, 'But I have read a lot and it makes sense that nature is an unbelievably complicated, self-balancing system in which the unconsidered use of partial knowledge can do more harm than good. As far as I can see, chemical agriculture has over-reached itself. It is working against nature instead of with her.'

The Soil Association was, in a sense, a source both of stimulation and of answers to these questions, and was the practical arm of Fritz's new approach to life and his newly discovered philosophy. As the Soil Association researched into better methods of organic farming he avidly read their journal *Mother Earth*, implemented their advice and conducted his own experiments. He attended the Open Days at Haughley in Suffolk with as much enthusiasm as he attended Bennett's or Conze's lectures. A framework had developed in which his own 'wholeness' could begin to grow. Week by week he baked his bread, day by day he did yoga and his spiritual 'work', and those parts of the day not filled by the garden or the office were taken up by lectures and books. He was beginning to see that there might be the possibility of a new understanding and a new peace.

But it brought with it its own form of restlessness. The more he immersed himself in Eastern teaching, the more he longed to experience the East for himself, to find a teacher there to initiate him into the deeper mysteries of Eastern forms of meditation. To Muschi these deepening inner stirrings represented a growing threat. Her attempts to take an interest, such as participating in his yoga, did not reduce the tension between them. At the beginning of 1954, when she accompanied her parents on a cruise to Egypt, even their correspondence was marred by the gulf between them. She wrote sadly that she felt a lack of contact with Fritz in his letters and he admitted that his inner changes might well be responsible. 'As you know, ever since 1950 a big change has been in progress inside me, – a reorientation in the entire attitude to life. This, of course, creates certain problems and a certain restlessness, and on many things one doesn't know what to think or say. Perhaps that is the reason why you don't "feel me in my letters".' He added that 'the explanation may also be much simpler, namely, that these letters are written without any real knowledge where you are and what you are doing... can you imagine what it means to me that you you have actually been there, that is: in the East, outside Western civilization, have actually seen it with your own eyes.'

In fact he was sharing a significant part of his life with his mother, whose work with him on *The New Man* had brought them very close. In the freedom without Muschi's anxiety about his spiritual adventures, he had had an experience which confirmed to him that this new path was that of truth and enlightenment, and wrote to his mother:

On Monday, February 1st during my daily quarter of an hour, I came into contact with 'X'. As one can read in all the books, this cannot be described in words. But suddenly all sorts of things that I had not understood became completely clear – and in the most simple manner. Not that anything dramatic happened – no light, sound, vision or experience; but merely an indescribable detachment from all that which usually tries to distract one during this quarter of an hour, and then, or with that, a new understanding. Sentences and scripture that had been a mystery to me up to now and which I have since re-read suddenly became completely un-ambiguous and true. It became clear what Buddhists and Taoists understand by 'emptiness', 'nothingness', 'Nirvana' or 'Tao', and how it is possible that 'Plenum', 'abundance', 'All' or 'Life' can be used just as well. Since the 1st February

I have not had any more doubts about the 'truth' of 'work' – that is; that it really shows the right path.

Since then, not surprisingly, I have not been able to re-establish this contact. On the contrary, the 'quarter of an hour' has become more difficult than before. But an infinitely enlightened understanding has stayed and will, hopefully, remain. I write about this like one who seeks after gold, who shares with his fellow seekers that he has actually seen gold in the place where they are all looking. As I have in no way earned this rich strike, I can't expect recurrence just like that. But that there is something to be discovered has now moved from the region of doubt (with good will) into certainty.

The tragedy was that he could not share this new insight with Muschi. In the summer of 1954 their relationship reached a new low. During his holidays, while Muschi was in Reinbek, he attended a course of talks on 'Christianity and Yoga' with his sister Edith in Germany. He confided in Edith at length about his difficulties, Muschi's fears about the direction of his studies, her persistent homesickness and the apparent insolubility of these problems. The further his understanding and confidence in the path he was following progressed the more strain there seemed to be on their marriage. The way of enlightenment was a lonely business.

17

———∞∞∞———

The Breakthrough

The loneliness Fritz felt in his spiritual endeavour was matched by a similar isolation in his work in the material world of the office. His little notebook of facts, in which countless apparently diverse and unrelated statistics were painstakingly recorded, began to throw up some startling conclusions.

His aim had been to have a compendium of facts and statistics readily accessible so that as Economic Adviser to the N.C.B., he could instantly lay his hands on the facts and figures relevant to any question he was asked. The primary concern of the industry was how to speed up the extraction process because the demand for coal far exceeded the supply, a situation that was to last until 1957. The more specific conclusions Fritz reached on the industry's performance, his recommendations, and the reactions of the Board will be dealt with in a later chapter. He was, however, working on another line of thought at the same time as he was making recommendations on how to improve efficiency and increase the output of coal. In his little book of statistics he had noted down all the facts and figures he came across about world energy supply and the trends in demand. He looked not only at current production figures and current demand, but also at the projected figures for the future and, very significantly, at the figures for demand in the past.

As he studied reports on the growth of energy consumption and production, particularly in America, he saw that since the war the statistics had taken a dramatic turn upwards. As he examined the various means of obtaining energy, he saw that the supply, particularly in the West, came from predominantly non-renewable sources of energy. Western industrial society had based its industrial production on fuel that could not be replaced. Coal that was taken out of the ground was gone for ever. The same applied to oil and to natural gas. These sources of energy were finite and elementary arithmetic showed that there would come a time when the ever-increasing demand for energy could no longer be satisfied. Industrial society was clearly based on very shaky foundations. In the autumn of 1954 Fritz made his startling conclusions public for the first time at a conference in Germany.

> We forget that we are living off capital in the most fundamental meaning of the word. Mankind has existed for many thousands of years and has always lived off income. Only in the last hundred years has man forcibly broken into nature's larder and is now emptying it out at a breathtaking speed which increases from year to year. Only few people realize how brief this forceful entry into the larder is, how quickly the rate of emptying out is rising year after year, and how large the percentage of that already taken is. Every now and then there is an outcry about sulphur and zinc, but that subsides again because it turns out that modern industry is extraordinarily flexible and something new is invented. But if one looks more closely, one has to come to the conclusion that all this adaptation and invention continually demands the expansion of one product, namely energy. The whole problem of nature's larder, that is the exhaustion of non-renewable resources, can probably be reduced to this one point – Energy. If one asks about the future of the economy, ultimately one is asking about the future of an energy economy.[1]

What Fritz's figures had shown was that if the world demand for energy continued to expand the way it had done in the last hundred years, then modern society, based as it was on industrial activity and the assumed existence of limitless fuel, was in for a nasty shock. The bottleneck to progress was not merely the speed at which coal could be extracted, in the long term it was the fact that Western civilization lived on capital instead of income. And the end of such a mode of living, as all individuals who have tried it know, is bankruptcy.

They were prophetic words. But they fell on deaf ears. It was a period of industrial expansion, there was a vision of the future when technology would ensure that there was plenty for all. No one was interested in listening to an economist who told them that the future was built on dreams.

His vision of industrial society containing the seeds of its own destruction in its dependence on finite resources had repercussions on another area to which he had been giving some thought. In 1951 he had been invited to join discussions on the development of industry in the 'underdeveloped nations of the world' by the 'Wilson Committee on World Organisation', a small committee of M.P.s, economists and other experts, set up by the Association of World Peace under the chairmanship of Harold Wilson. The committee's brief was to study the problems of the 'war on poverty'. It was becoming evident that the increasing discrepancy between the world's poor nations and the world's rich nations might become a new source for instability in the world.

In 1942 Fritz had worked on a theory of industrialization and produced a rather theoretical paper in which he questioned current theories. 'Every constructive programme of development gets into conflict with the traditional theory of comparative costs,' he had written. 'It must do so, because the theory is based on assumptions which are not in accordance with the most striking facts of our age.'[2]

But although he had maintained that social, political and cultural decisions must be taken into consideration as well as the economic factor, he did not develop these ideas, so that his contribution to the Wilson Committee was very much coloured by more conventional thinking. As far as he was concerned, the dangers to world peace lay in the imbalance in the trading positions of the rich and poor nations. 'There are no *moral* issues involved,' he wrote in his notes.

We should go for a *reasonable* international division of labour. Instead of further disturbing the balance between primary (food and raw material) and secondary (manufacturing) production, development can be so directed as to restore that balance. This would require a blend of egotism and altruism on the part of the developed country which is far more difficult to achieve than either single-minded self-ishness or an altruistic crusade. It requires a policy with a freely acknowledged dual purpose, which could be put into the words:

> We will help you to raise the level of production, of productivity, and of welfare in your country – but we shall give preference to the development of such types of pro-duction as will restore the 'balance of stages' and thus benefit not only yourselves but ourselves as well.[3]

Since writing those words he had begun his study of the East. This included the writings and speeches of Gandhi, a man whom Fritz admired and whose assassination had greatly shocked him while in Berlin after the war. Gandhi had a very different view of economic development which needed to be examined carefully.

Gandhi, Buddhism, energy supplies of the future, industrial development, the 'war on poverty' – all these separate strands of thought occupied Fritz's mind and – as the different elements in the soil come together to produce a beautiful flower after the seed has been planted – were waiting to come together to nourish a new, more complete idea.

The 'seed' which was to draw all these elements together was an invitation from the government of the Union of Burma to come to Burma as an Economic Adviser. The job was for a high-level economist, with considerable experience in the plan-ning and execution of economic development plans, and a specialized knowledge of modern fiscal theory and practice. It was well paid, and funded by the United Nations. Fritz wanted very much to accept and the pressure from Burma was steady, with a constant stream of telegrams and letters. But an agree-ment by the N.C.B. to release Fritz for a few months was necessary. Eventually U Nu, the Burmese Prime Minister, approached the British Minister of Power, Hugh Gaitskell, directly. Fritz was given unpaid leave from the National Coal Board for three months at the beginning of 1955. Fritz was very excited. He wrote to his mother: 'As you can imagine, I am full of expectations. I cannot describe how much it interests me to get to know the Orient. Is that which we have found in books alive there – or has it also been destroyed? Is it possible to build a bridge between the East and the West? Can one really help the Burmese without harming them? So many questions!'

On January 2nd, 1955 Fritz left on his Oriental adventure, accentuating the change of lifestyles he was about to experience by stopping off first in New York. 'This American madhouse,' he wrote to Muschi. There in the cold he was prepared by the U.N. for his work in the heat of Burma. He had already prepared himself as much as possible. Spiritually he felt that the last four years had been preparation for this pilgrimage. As an economist he had also tried to do his homework, although his conclusions about the Western industrial economy gave substance to his doubtful question, 'Can one really help the Burmese without harming them?'

The impact of Burma was far greater than he had expected. After a few days in Rangoon he tried to convey something of what he felt to Muschi:

I am in excellent spirits and excellent health. Gradually I am finding my feet. But there are too many impressions, there is too much to absorb and to sort out. That's why it is difficult to write about it. What a marvellous experience it all is.

Well, how can I begin at the beginning? The people really are delightful. Everything I had heard about their charms and cheerfulness proves to be true. They move about in a very strange way. There is an innocence here which I have never seen before, – the exact contrary of what disquieted me in New York. In their gay dances and with their dignified and composed manners, they are lovable; and one really wants to help them, if one but knew how. Even some of the Americans here say: 'How can we help them, when they are much happier and much nicer than we are ourselves?'

... I think there really is some work for me to do here, but it may be negative rather than positive, persuading them not to do various things rather than telling them what to do. Because of the positive side they need no advice: as long as they don't fall for this or that piece of nonsense from the West, they will be quite alright following their own better nature.

Fritz was overwhelmed by the colour and gaiety of Burmese life. Notwithstanding a certain degree of dirt and chaos in Rangoon itself, he found the Burmese people clean, beautiful and distinguished-looking. The jarring notes were not sounded by poverty and degradation but by the garish incursions of the West into this otherwise picturesque way of life. He had never experienced such wholesale pleasure in living, such joy, such lack of concern about the trappings of life as he found in the Burmese people. Every event he attended rang with the sounds of happy laughter. He did not see the desperate poverty reflected by the national income statistics and the income *per capita* figures he had read. The first lesson to be learnt was that income statistics could not be relied upon as a measure of poverty. He saw very clearly how poverty and wealth went beyond material possessions. The Burmese lived simply. They had few wants and they were happy. It was wants that made a man poor and this made the role of the West very dangerous. 'The whole Orient is coming out in Western spots,' Fritz wrote to Muschi.

There is no doubt that the West, even though its days of power in Asia are done, has won all along the line and is winning more every day. Mr Copnall is going to introduce 'modern art'; horror comics are already available in Burmese, ghastly American films are shouting at you from advertisements all over the place, and 'industrialization' is doing the rest. The only stronghold is in the monasteries, but for how much longer?

Fritz's specific task was to evaluate the work of an American team of economic experts, and to make suggestions about the fiscal and trading position of Burma. The longer he stayed in Burma, the lower his opinion of the American economists fell. After one month he wrote to Muschi, 'My opinion is that they have given a lot of sound advice and have also done a lot of damage (because they are all American Materialists without any understanding of the precious heritage of a Buddhist country), and my problem is how to get my views across without making enemies. So far, I have succeeded.'

Three weeks later his remarks were less charitable: 'I am writing my final report ... It is a difficult report to write, because I really want to tell the Burmese Government a few truths about the quality of the advice they are getting ... But how to put it?'

The Burmese Government was not prepared for the advice it got. Indeed Fritz himself was treading new ground. It had quickly become obvious to him that Burma was not post-war Germany. In Germany the problems of poverty, of non-existent economic activity, had been so acute that many people believed that it would not be possible for Germany to take its place alongside the industrialized nations of the West for many generations. Yet by 1955 such expectations had already been proved wrong. Germany had risen from the ashes. But the unexpected lessons of Germany's recovery were not applicable to Burmese conditions. Germany had been 'developed' in the past and therefore had the skills and expertise to draw on, Germany was a Western country with Western ideals and aspirations, and a Western approach to economics. Burma was quite different, a country with aspirations and ideals traditionally opposed to those of Western civilization, deeply rooted in the spiritual traditions of Buddhism. Fritz saw that the effect of economic contact between East and West had not been to transfer Western economic philosophy, which had made the economic development of the West possible, but had merely transferred Western demands. He realized that economic development in Burma was not a question of matters such as trading arrangements, as he had advocated in the days of the Wilson Committee, it was far more fundamental, it required a different kind of economics altogether, a 'Buddhist economics'. Fritz discussed this approach in a paper entitled 'Economics in a Buddhist Country'.

'Economics means a certain ordering of life according to the philosophy inherent and implicit in economics,' he wrote in a paper to those who might have ears to hear. 'The science of economics does not stand on its own feet: it is derived from a view of the meaning and purpose of life – whether the economist himself knows this or not. And ... the only fully developed system of economic thought that exists at present is derived from a purely materialistic view of life.' Materialistic economics was not compatible with spirituality, Fritz argued, not with Christianity, Hinduism or Buddhism. Yet, while no system of economics existed that was compatible with spirituality, there existed an economist whose economics was based on such criteria. This was Mahatma Gandhi. 'He had laid the foundation for a system of Economics that would be compatible with Hinduism and, I believe, with Buddhism too.' Gandhi's economics were derived from the concepts of *Swadeshi* and *Khaddar*, and he had said that the poverty in India was largely due not to the adherence to these concepts but the departure from them. *Swadeshi*, economically speaking, could be summed up by saying: if you cannot get what you want in India then, never mind the deprivation, you must do without it. *Khaddar* meant to spin with one's hands and wear nothing but homespun garments. Fritz applied these concepts to modern economic problems, to the sort of questions he was supposed to be considering. He gave as an example the question of freight rates. An economic expert

may be inclined to advise that the rates per ton/mile should 'taper-off', so that they are the lower the longer the haul. He may suggest that this is simply the 'right' system, because it encourages long distance transport, promotes large scale, specialised production, and thus leads to an 'optimum use of resources'. He may point to the experience of the United States, the United Kingdom, Germany, etc. - all 'advanced' countries employing just this 'tapering' device. Do you see that in doing so he would be recommending *one particular way of life*, - the way of materialism? An 'economic expert' steeped in Gandhian economics would undoubtedly give very different advice; he might say: 'Local, short-distance transportation should receive every encouragement but long hauls should be discouraged because they would promote urbanisation, specialisation beyond the point of human integrity, the growth of a rootless proletariat, - in short, a most undesirable and uneconomic way of life.' Do you see that economics does not stand on its own feet?

A Buddhist approach to economics would be a 'middleway', Fritz suggested, based on two principles. The first was a definition of limits. A Buddhist approach would distinguish between misery, sufficiency and surfeit. 'Economic "progress" is good only to the point of sufficiency, beyond that, it is evil, destructive, uneconomic.' His second principle struck at the very basis of Western industrial development, and followed on directly from the first. He wrote:

A Buddhist economy would make 'the distinction between "renewable" and "non-renewable" resources'. A civilisation built on renewable resources, such as the products of forestry and agriculture, is by this fact alone superior to one built on non-renewable resources, such as oil, coal, metal, etc. This is because the former can last, while the latter cannot last. The former co-operates with nature, while the latter robs nature. The former bears the sign of life, while the latter bears the sign of death. It is already certain beyond the possibility of doubt that the 'oil-coal-metal-economies' cannot be anything else but a short abnormality in the history of mankind – because they are based on non-renewable resources and because, being purely materialistic, they recognise no limits ... The New Economics would be a veritable 'Statute of Limitation' – and that means a Statute of 'Liberation'.[4]

These two principles, inseparably linked, were an astonishing statement for a Western economist to make in 1955 when the emphasis everywhere was on growth, increasing exploitation of seemingly unlimited supplies of natural resources, when the only bottleneck that was recognized was that much needed resources could not be got out of the ground fast enough. It was some fifteen years later before *Limits to Growth* shocked the world by announcing that non-renewable resources were not only limited but were fast running out.[5]

The Economic and Social Council of Burma was not impressed. Fritz had to circulate his paper privately for it to see the light of day. His subsequent reports were couched more in the language which economists found acceptable and comprehensible, but he did not change his message. He recommended that the Burmese Government should reverse all its development policies and reduce its dependency on Western advisers. No Western adviser should be without a Burmese counterpart and steps should be taken at once to train young economists. The rural development programme, rightly emphasized by the Burmese, must not be neglected because of an overemphasis on urban projects and massive projects to develop the infrastructure of the economy. The development programme recommended by Burma's American advisers had, for example, become obsessed with the problem of transporting rice at the expense of producing it. At the end of the day, Fritz maintained, Burma would have a system of transport and no goods to use it. As far as trade was concerned, Fritz emphasized the need to concentrate first on a degree of self-sufficiency. 'As far as I can see,' he wrote, 'there is no country in the world that has ever achieved substantial economic development without protection against the competition of more advanced producers abroad. Nor is there any case known to me of successful development that did not at first look like a policy of "economic self-sufficiency".'[6]

Between his paper on 'Economics in a Buddhist Country' and his final report, Fritz had written four papers for the Government. None received any response. Just as in the Control Commission and at the Coal Board, he was dependent on others to implement his ideas and they did not appear equal to understanding them. In Burma there was the added problem of administrative disorder. The Executive Secretary to the Economic and Social Board, U Thant, later Secretary General of the United Nations, with whom Fritz was supposed to work, had only taken up his post the day Fritz arrived in Rangoon. Fritz wrote later (in August) to the United Nations organizer of his trip, Habib Ahmed:

U Thant, in spite of his exceptional qualities in many other directions, had neither the time nor the inclination, nor indeed the ability and background knowledge, to fill the post effectively. He was himself fully aware of all this; as it happened he held the post only for three months, but these were precisely the three months of my stay in Rangoon. It was a period during which, as one might say, 'Hamlet' was played without the Prince of Denmark. The centre piece of the economic planning machine had been removed and had not been effectively replaced. This, of course, gravely prejudiced my own work; without exaggeration I might say that I was accredited to someone who did not exist.

But he was not despondent, and wrote to Muschi: 'The Burma Government is a pretty chaotic affair ... They are surrounded by American advisers, and they may never hear my "small still voice". But even if Burma does not learn from me, I am learning a lot from Burma.'

He had learnt more from Burma than he had dared imagine. His quest for the meaning of life led him to ever new and deeper discoveries.

He was not merely referring to what Burma had taught him about economics. Muschi was worried about the other aspects of Burma's influence on him. She had written to him that his interest in Buddhism was imposing a new strain on her and begged him not to forget Western traditions and replace them with new beliefs and culture. He had tried to allay her fears:

> Please, Muschilein, there is no conceivable cause of strain in this, my sole motive and interest in Buddhism is in getting rid of all sorts of weaknesses and defilements in my character – of all the things that really could impose strain upon you and others. Even the Threepenny Opera contains the lines: 'Ein guter Mensch, wer wär's nicht gern!?' [A good person, who wouldn't want that?] Apart from this I am pursuing my livelihood, doing my duty as best I can – much the same as I would do in London or Berlin or anywhere else. There is no question of taking the new and not leaving any room for the old: I just carry on as anybody else, with many demands on my time and being unable to do all the things I mean to do.

After this he took care in what he shared with Muschi and it was his mother in whom he confided what was to be the highlight and real purpose of his visit to Burma. He had come to learn Buddhist meditation or 'Sattipatthana'. The Burmese yellow-robed monks were a presence in Burma that no one could get away from, a daily reminder of the Buddhist faith on which the country's culture rested. They were never a nuisance, although they were beggars, for they never accosted anyone but wandered quietly from door to door for their alms. Buddhists were all around him and yet it was difficult at first to make the contacts that would lead him to a 'master', to gain him entrance into inner or higher circles. Strangely it was two Germans who opened the doors for him. The first was a sixty-year-old German by the name of Georg Krauskopf. He had been a Buddhist for forty years and was the German representative of a World Buddhist Congress that had just been held in Burma. He had stayed on to study meditation and as soon as Fritz heard about his presence in Burma he looked him up. He described what happened to Muschi:

> I went to search for him and managed to find him in a very lonely place, looking very strained and somewhat exhausted. He had just finished his course and not knowing any English felt utterly lost and lonely. The astonishment and delight on his face as I approached him cannot be described. One could see his thoughts: What, a white man. Where do you come from then? He is not coming to me is he? My goodness, yes! A German here in this isolation!
>
> Well, then Herr Krauskopf, a man of sixty but looking fifty, was nearly beyond himself and I have literally spent all my free time with him all last week.... a more delightful man you have never met ... In Germany he is nothing, just a penniless refugee from East Prussia ... Here in Burma he is treated with great respect and affection and provided with everything he needs. During this week I have learned many things from him which it would have taken me months to discover otherwise ...

Krauskopf remembered Fritz ever afterwards with gratitude too. Fritz had appeared on the scene like an angel of mercy and rescued him and the fact was mentioned in every letter he wrote to Fritz for many years after this happy meeting.

The other German was a Buddhist scholar, Frau Dr Kell. Fritz described her to Muschi as his 'best contact here (my "girl friend") ... she has real knowledge, has been here for a year, and works with some of the greatest Buddhist scholars. I have met more Burmese through her than through the job.'

Through her eventually it was arranged that he should spend every weekend in the most highly respected monastery of Burma. It was the most difficult and most rewarding task he had ever undertaken. Slowly he was taken through the steps of meditation. At first, sitting in his monk's cell, he was allowed only to watch the rising and falling of his abdomen, mentally repeating, 'rising falling, rising falling', as he breathed. His intellect, which was normally never still, had to be pushed to one side. His mental effort had to be directed towards a concentration on what seemed essentially to be nothing. His quarter of an hour's 'work' had already shown him how difficult this could be. His intellect, which he had thought was a tool he could direct wherever he pleased, showed itself to be a completely untrained, undisciplined intruder into the silence, roaming around introducing distractions. The monks taught him how to cope with the distractions, how to still his restless mind. He was taught not to worry; merely to note the distractions but not to follow them or fix on them, and then to return to his task of attending to the movement of his abdomen.

After some time the monks allowed Fritz to progress to the next stage. He left his cell to pace up and down the monastery garden, concentrating on each movement of his body as he walked, noting his distractions and returning his attention to his body.

At last he was deemed ready to be initiated into the deeper secrets of meditation and instead of fixing his mind on his body he was given a prayer, or mantra, to repeat. As he persisted in these exercises he found that their effect was quite unexpected. Not only did he feel a profound peace and stillness afterwards, much greater than he had experienced with his daily 'work', but he found he had a new clarity of thought which made him realize that what he had regarded as clear thinking before was in fact nothing of the kind. It was only when he had stilled his ever-restless intellect that he began to feel true understanding. He realized he had found the gold he was seeking. With words paraphrased from scripture he described the experience: 'I came to Burma as a thirsty wanderer, and there I found living water.'

18

-----∞∞∞-----

'I am a Buddhist'

Fritz's return from Burma was scheduled for April 1st, the same date as his departure from America nineteen years earlier and the date he began work at the Coal Board in 1950. But on April 1st, 1955, instead of flying towards Europe, he was in bed in Rangoon's clinic with a high fever. The nurses at the clinic greeted him joyfully as he was admitted. He had been a regular visitor to a fifteen-year-old German boy in the clinic who had lost both legs in an accident on his ship while docking in Rangoon. The boy spoke no English, had no mother, and his father in Germany had never shown much interest in him. Now he lay alone in Rangoon, dreading being shipped back to Germany where the future seemed very bleak. He was well cared for by various American and English expatriates, but few could speak German so that Fritz's visits were of great psychological importance. Eventually the boy's father came to Rangoon to fetch him and for some time afterwards Fritz received very positive letters from him as he overcame his handicap with great courage and fortitude.

Fritz remained in the Rangoon Clinic for a week and then, with his temperature still at 103°F., flew home to England and hospital in London. His illness was never satisfactorily diagnosed and it was another month before he was fit enough to return to the National Coal Board. He had been on unpaid leave from the National Coal Board and it was a month without pay. Fritz wrote to the United Nations in New York claiming his lost salary and medical expenses. It was the one

253

sour note of his Burmese experience. The United Nations quibbled over his claim and it took a year before he was reimbursed.

Fritz's enthusiasm for Burma made an immediate impact on all who knew him. His return from the East is the first vivid memory I have of him. His dedication to his work and his interests had made him far less of a central figure in my life than my mother. But it was not just the presents – the wonderful paper umbrellas, the bags and the colourful material – which impressed me. It was the appearance of the little Buddha in his study and three ivory monkeys with their hands clasped over their ears, eyes and mouth, that shrouded his reappearance in mystery. Such objects spoke to me of his 'other life' of spiritual exploration. To adults he was more explicit, overcoming some of his former reserve on these matters by his bubbling enthusiasm. Soon after his recovery he went to lunch at the Vega restaurant where he had always been a regular customer. He came over to the Vega's owner, Walter Fliess, exclaiming, 'Walter I am a Buddhist'. Some friends and acquaintances found his enthusiasm rather embarrassing. Shortly after his return to England he was invited to talk to the Romney Street Group, a luncheon club which he had addressed before on economics topics. The members were mostly civil servants, M.P.s, academics and journalists, attracting many eminent speakers whose talks were followed by lively discussions. This had also been the case after Fritz's previous talks, but his unexpected lecture on Buddhism stunned them into silence. Many were moved by his sincerity and depth of feeling, but they were embarrassed by the topic.

Fritz was not put off by such a reception. He continued to enthuse. Buddhism had opened his eyes. It had enabled him to pass another milestone. Through Buddhism and Buddhist meditation he had experienced a spiritual peace and fulfilment that he found more real than all the facts and logical arguments he had expounded ten years earlier. Buddhism had finally removed the barrier to accepting not only the validity of religion but the necessity of religion. He had found that once he embraced this way of thinking wholeheartedly, it had led him to understand things of the world more clearly. His thinking about his own subject, economics, had been revolutionized by his recognition of the importance of spiritual values.

For all his enthusiasm, however, Fritz did not make the mistake of assuming that he had now reached the goal of life and found all the answers to his questions. He realized that the enlightenment he had experienced in Burma was a beginning, a stepping-stone, a new orientation, an initiation into a new path in his life. The rethinking of his entire philosophy of life which had begun in 1951 could now proceed with a new certainty and confidence. Having understood something profound about Buddhism and its extreme relevance to the way of life in the East, he accepted that, as a Westerner, he must look into Western traditions which must contain the same kinds of truths. Having made the leap of faith in Buddhism he could now be confident that the writings of Christian mystics, saints and theologians were based on truth too.

This conception of the unity of the great religions was very difficult for many of Fritz's friends to understand. For those who knew him well in his youth and during the war, he had been a man whose intellectual extremism and violent atheism had seemed unshakeable. The changes that had been going on within him since 1951 had not been obvious, only their outward manifestation – such as Fritz's sudden enthusiasm for such things as astrology and Unidentified Flying Objects. These had seemed laughable and not to be taken too seriously. It seemed as though Burma had been his light on the road to Damascus, his conversion. To all intents and purposes Fritz was now assumed to be a Buddhist. A few people realized that this was not the case, that Buddhism had been the means of opening the door to other things. Edward Conze, himself a Buddhist, was one of these. He recognized that Buddhism was a great influence on Fritz's life but in his peculiar way of looking at people through the eyes of an astrologer believed that to push Fritz into fully-fledged Buddhism would be a grave mistake. Conze believed that if he had wanted to, he could have led Fritz into becoming a Buddhist but he restrained himself. Fritz's horoscope told him that Fritz would be temperamentally unsuited to the Eastern way. His ascendant in Cancer meant he was a home-loving, family man who would do violence to his personality if he took up the detachment and inner homelessness essential to a Buddhist's spiritual journey.

Whether Conze was right in assuming that he could have influenced Fritz to take up Buddhism fully is impossible to judge although the independence with which Fritz made the rest of his decisions would suggest that it would have been more difficult than Conze thought. Possibly too, Conze's real influence had been earlier when, teaching Fritz about comparative religion, he had sown the seeds for Fritz's understanding about the inner unity of the great religions.

Fritz's return home to England was not marked by an intensification of his study of Eastern religions, nor by the strain on his relationship with Muschi that might have been expected. On the contrary, his studies were directed into Christian thinkers, St Thomas Aquinas, the mystics, writers such as Guenon, Jacques Maritain and the lives of the saints, and he and Muschi found a new understanding and a path which they could genuinely travel together. There were still difficulties because Fritz's questioning intellect could leave no stone unturned in his search. There were some forms of spiritual life that Muschi found hard to take and into which she could not follow him with ease. But she was now free to follow her own path with his support and although he did not yet accompany the family to church, finding what he learnt in Burma and from Gurdjieff more helpful, he did not oppose their going any longer. He found that he could follow Gandhi who had said, 'In matters of religion I must confine myself to my ancestral religion; that is, the use of my immediate surroundings in religion. If I find my religion defective, I should serve it by purifying its defects.' His eyes opened in Burma, Fritz realized that he knew very little about his 'ancestral' religion. By concentrating on its defects he had missed the point completely.

For four more years he immersed himself in study. Each week he and Muschi eagerly attended Conze's lectures. As they came to an end in 1958 Fritz, as part of the course, delivered a talk on Gurdjieff and the 'work', and his fellow pupils were so impressed that they asked Fritz to lead them in a group meeting after the lectures had finished. For about a year a group of people met weekly in Fritz's study at Holcombe and under his leadership explored new areas of enlightenment together. Some of the group went on to follow the teachings and practices of Pak Subud, a twentieth-century Muslim religious leader. Muschi was unhappy about the Subud development and Fritz, although he attended some meetings and went into the movement in some detail, eventually decided it was not for him either.

By the beginning of 1959 Fritz felt that his studies had taken him to a point where he could usefully help others who were searching for some meaning in their lives. He had first publicly stated his new orientation in May 1957 when he had broadcast a talk responding to a much acclaimed book by Charles Frankel, *The Case for Modern Man*.[1] Fritz's talk, called 'The Insufficiency of Liberalism', took this book to task and provoked a large bag of correspondence. His talk was a statement of the progress of his own life in describing what he called the 'three stages of development'. The first great leap, he said, was made when man moved from stage I of primitive religiosity to stage II of scientific realism. This was the stage modern man tended to be at – and the stage he himself had so vigorously defended in his correspondence with Werner von Simson during the war. Then, he said, some people become dissatisfied with scientific realism and they realize that there is something beyond fact and science. Such people progress to a higher plane of development which he called stage III. However, to those in stage II, stage I and stage III look exactly the same. Those who have progressed to stage III are seen as having had some sort of brainstorm, a relapse into childish nonsense. Only those who have been through stage II can understand the difference between stage I and stage III.

Only someone who believed himself to be on this higher plane of consciousness could make such a statement, but Fritz was not yet ready to identify himself with any creed or system of beliefs. He was indignant when one correspondent, a humanist, published in the press, criticized his talk as typical for a 'Catholic economist', quoting another critic who had said 'For sheer wooziness [his talk] would be difficult to better.' Fritz's reply was icy:

In your letter to the *New Statesman and Nation* you refer to

257

me as a 'Catholic Economist'. I am not, and never have been, a Catholic, nor do I wear any other label.

Years ago, when I called myself a 'humanist' it was not considered compatible with the principles of humanism

(a) to use arguments 'ad personam',
(b) to attack people without reasoned argument, particularly by quoting insulting language used by others against them, or
(c) to publish falsehoods about them.

Is this no longer so?

In 1959 he was given the opportunity to spell out his new structure of belief and its ramifications on all aspects of life. Through Conze he had for some time been back on the W.E.A./London University lecture circuit as a lecturer on economics and in 1959 he decided to submit a curriculum for a radically different course of lectures. He called it 'Crucial Problems of Modern Living'. In this course, which was to be twenty-four lectures lasting one academic year 1959-60, Fritz proposed to examine the answers he had found to his own questions of 'what is the meaning of my life?' and 'what am I to do?' The organizer of the lectures promptly turned down his proposal. Fritz was an economist and not a philosopher and therefore not eligible for such a course. But Fritz was determined to fight to get his course accepted and after some fairly acrimonious correspondence finally succeeded.

His lectures were received well by his students and Fritz was pleased with the material he had put together. It was a tremendous strain preparing each week's talk and involved him in much more work than he had anticipated, but it was a rewarding and enlightening task in which his own thinking developed and was consolidated to such an extent that he felt ready to put it together in book form when the course had been completed.

His employers, however, were less enthusiastic. The tutorial board was more concerned with organizational aspects of its courses than with their content and Fritz blatantly disregarded the rules set by the Department of Extramural Studies. He did not maintain a proper register, he did not set the students written work, and when asked to fill in the end-of-course report he airily said the standard had been 'astonishingly high', but only produced evidence of two pieces of written work from a class of twenty students. He was not asked to repeat the course the following year.

However, in 1961 and 1965 Imperial College invited him to give shorter courses on the same theme. Again the students appreciated the lectures and his audiences grew each week. From the first lecture Fritz was controversial and challenging. No one in the audience was able to listen without being forced to reconsider a lifetime of cosily held views. He warned them that the answer to his first and fundamental question 'What is man?' 'penetrates everything, colours everything, determines everything.'

The students had to decide what they believed. Was man an accidental collocation of atoms, here on earth by chance, or was he a created being on a journey to something higher? This difference, the difference between *homo sapiens* and *homo viator*, he maintained was crucial to every question that followed. It was only half a joke when he said, 'Everyone should declare himself on his visiting card: John Smith (creature) or John Brown (accident).'

There was no doubt what Fritz would have put on his visiting card. It was not so much that he totally rejected the idea that man may have evolved slowly but he utterly rejected the proposition that there was no purpose, no creator behind the progressions. He was fond of illustrating what he considered to be the absurdity of the theory of accidental and mindless evolution by saying that it was like a man some time in the future excavating an old car dump. Right at the bottom he would find the oldest, most primitive models, then the model T Ford, then nearer the surface the old wrecks would become more and more sophisticated. Some would have rather extravagant wings or other features which did not seem to contribute to the efficiency of the car and such features would be seen to have disappeared later. How absurd for the archaeologist to assume that these models had developed on their own, to devise a theory which excluded the most important factor, that behind the evidence of the evolving car lay the inventor, the brains, who directed the development.

But in the case of human life Fritz maintained that there

were profound implications to the belief that man evolved without a deliberate act of creation by a creator. Without a creator, *homo sapiens* was a purposeless accidental happening, in a purposeless world. As such, he was part of a mechanistic, deterministic system and had no freedom, no responsibility for his actions. There was nothing to live for, nothing to strive for, because if man was the highest form of life one could not strive for anything higher.

Homo viator, created man, on the other hand, was a man on a journey. He had been created with a purpose, with a task to develop within himself higher powers of consciousness. In this way he was distinguished from animals, and he was free. He could, of course, use his freedom to reject his humanity but his freedom gave him responsibility for what he did with his life. Fritz also criticized the 'blind evolutionists' on scientific grounds.

> Instead of asserting that many – even most human actions are 'determined' or mechanical, it is asserted that all of them are. Instead of saying that some forms are the products of 'blind forces plus natural selection' (which may be verifiable), it is asserted that all forms are such products.
>
> Assume that determination accounts for 99.99% of all phenomena. If science says 99.99%, it is not in conflict with religion; on the contrary, it confirms it; it remains, moreover, in its proper place and territory and true to its own principles [of verifiability or falsifiability]. But if science says 100% instead of 99.99% it steps outside its proper knowledge and is in total conflict with religion.[2]

There was no need for science to be in conflict with religion, Fritz pointed out, if science did not step outside its sphere of concern. He did not think that science and religion were on the same level. They inhabited different planes: one higher, concerned with spiritual matters and one lower concerned with material matters. The two did not touch and there was no reason to try and reconcile them. Such attempts did disservice to both. For this reason he deplored the conclusions of Pierre Teilhard de Chardin, the Jesuit Palaeontologist so highly thought of in many Catholic (and other) circles. Fritz disapproved of Teilhard, both for what he had said and for the way in which he had agreed to have his work published posthumously after being forbidden to do so by his superiors. No good could come out of such dishonesty, Fritz said. For some time he considered writing a book showing why Teilhard's ideas were not of God, but eventually he decided it was not worth spending any effort on such a negative project and expressed his opinion by omission. Teilhard is not mentioned at all in *A Guide for the Perplexed*, but in his lectures at Imperial College Fritz spoke out against him. He quoted from Teilhard's book *The Phenomenon of Man*: 'The dream which human research obscurely fosters is fundamentally that of mastering ... the ultimate energy ... and thus, by grasping the mainspring of evolution, seizing the tiller of the world. I salute those who have the courage to admit their hopes extend that far; they are the pinnacle of mankind.'[3] 'This,' Fritz said, 'is the extreme formulation of the Hubris of *Homo Sapiens*, who wants to become god. As the serpent said, "And ye shall be as gods".'[4]

In his copy of Teilhard's book Fritz is even more forthright in his opinions. All over the margins are scribbled exclamations like 'rubbish', 'typical rubbish', 'concentrated rubbish' and 'dreadful'. More seriously, Fritz made a connection with the type of thinking that Teilhard was advocating and the rise of Hitler. It was not just that Hitler had had aspirations to 'seize the tiller of the world'. Since the rise of the Nazis in 1933 Fritz had felt that the academics and intelligentsia of Germany were ultimately responsible for not standing up for the truth and thus rejecting Hitler from the very beginning. Then he was concerned with scientific truth. Now he came to a very different conclusion. He saw that the very preoccupation with science to the exclusion of any higher spiritual values had left a vacuum in the hearts of the people. The preoccupation with material things, materially provable truths, excluded the possibility of inner aspirations and spiritual yearnings, and left a vacuum which had to be filled and into which flooded the concept of the Führer, the superman, the Aryan ideal. It was *homo sapiens* who, in the absence of any higher purpose for his life, could only aspire to raise himself to power. *Homo sapiens* looked upon knowledge as a means to manipulate the world to obtain that power, to seize the tiller of the world, to become God.

Had man acknowledged that he was in fact *homo viator*, he would have recognized a purpose outside himself, and searched for a different kind of knowledge, the knowledge to lead him to God. Fundamental to the life and progress of *homo viator* was the recognition of responsibility. For Fritz there were three people who should bear the blame for modern man's refusal to accept or recognize individual responsibility. He called them a 'devilish trio'. These were Freud, Marx and Einstein, who had all been corrosive agents in a world where man no longer believed in a need for personal perfection. By blaming everything on unfulfilled sexual frustrations, Freud had removed personal responsibility for man's actions and had opened the door to an attitude in human relations which was concerned only with self-fulfilment without regard for others. Marx, by blaming everything on the bourgeois, had driven personal concern and responsibility into a hatred for others, and Einstein had removed the need for any absolute standards for good and evil by saying that everything was relative. This again provided the perfect excuse for avoiding personal responsibility, or upholding or striving for the good and the beautiful.

In his lectures at London University in 1959–60 Fritz examined the implications of the belief that man was *homo viator* (created man with a purpose) for politics, economics and art, all servants helping man reach a higher plane of existence. For *homo sapiens* the only purpose of politics, economics and art was to further his greed, animal lusts and desire for power. Fritz's high-principled approach to the arts made most of it seem to him to be a waste of time or worse, but it must be said that his appreciation was extremely limited and, as he grew older and busier, had in practice less and less place in his life. He might acknowledge the sublime beauty of Mozart but he generally listened to Italian opera – Verdi, Bellini and Donizetti – and, towards the end of his life, a mish-mash from 'One Hundred Best Tunes'.

Literature was subjected to the most stringent tests. 'High art used unworthily is corruption,' he had said in a talk a year earlier. 'The test is a perfectly simple one: in reading the book, am I merely held in the thraldom of a daydream, or am I obtaining a new insight into the meaning and purpose of man's life on earth? Dissipation by reading is certainly not immoral and equally certainly corrupt.'[5] His knowledge of novels stemmed from reading he had done as a younger man. If he read a novel after middle age it was because it was of particular significance in understanding a contemporary controversy, such as D.H. Lawrence's *Lady Chatterley's Lover*, which he read after the trial and then hid carefully behind the biggest, most boring-looking book in his study to avoid the children finding it. His judgment of other works never took literary merit into consideration either. Manzoni's *I Promessi Sposi* was a favourite because of its high moral tone, whereas Tolstoy's *Anna Karenina* he held to be a corrupting influence because the central characters were made attractive in their decadence.

Shakespeare and Shaw were the only playwrights he thought worthwhile and for his lectures at Imperial College he used Beryl Podgson's esoteric interpretation of Shakespeare extensively to illustrate his point of the purpose of art. Taking him to the theatre was a risky business but one thing was always certain: however much he had apparently enjoyed a play, he would always leave, often still chuckling, saying, 'What a lot of nonsense.' Occasionally there would be unexpected exceptions. In the early sixties he read something about Marilyn Monroe and overnight his attitude to films, which he generally avoided, changed. Suddenly, to our great surprise, Fritz insisted on taking the family to see one of her films. But he was disappointed and could barely sit through to the end. His attraction to Marilyn Monroe vanished in an instant.

Great painters, too, failed to win his approval if they were born after the Middle Ages, which he considered the greatest period of art. The great cathedrals built at that time symbolized for him the true purpose of art: both a product of man's striving towards heavenly perfection and an example to those of later generations. Twentieth-century art on the other hand symbolized the meaningless existence of *homo sapiens* and he assumed that most modern painters were laughing at the world for its absurd adulation of canvases full of meaningless marks.

When it came to politics and economics his views were as extreme but based on a deeper knowledge of the subject. He was particularly struck by the fact that life consisted in solving problems.

> It is when we come to politics that we can no longer postpone or avoid the question regarding man's ultimate aim and purpose. For politics regulate man's common or social life, and man is in fact unthinkable without such a social life ... Human life ... is composed of divergent problems ... life is therefore a strain-and-stretch-mechanism. Its problems can never be finally solved – except in death.

> It follows that the problems of politics are equally 'insoluble', a fact clearly recognized in 'dialectics'. I say therefore; *either* you believe in God, then you will pursue politics 'mindful of the eternal destiny of man and of the truths of the Gospel'; or you believe that there are no higher obligations, then you cannot resist the appeal of Machiavellianism – politics as the art of gaining and maintaining power so that you and your friends can order the world as *they like it*. There is no supportable middle position. Those who want the Good Society, without believing in God, cannot face the temptations of Machiavellianism; they become either disheartened or muddleheaded, fabulating about the goodness of human nature and the vileness of one or another adversary. (Everything is the fault of Khrushchev, Nasser or Gaitskell.) Optimistic 'Humanism' by 'concentrating sin on a few people' instead of admitting its universal presence throughout the human race, leads to the utmost cruelty.[6]

Politics, Fritz went on, deals with hope. Hope has nothing to do with science and therefore politics cannot be scientific. This brought him on to Marxism to which he devoted an entire lecture. Despite the profound changes in his inner life Fritz had not lost his respect for Karl Marx, but the new dimension of his learning had changed his evaluation. 'Lenin once said that Marx synthesized German philosophy, French socialism and British classical economics. This is the strength of Marx. In this he has no rival in the nineteenth century, apart from the Thomist synthesis which Leo XIII brought back into the centre of Roman Catholic thought around 1850.' Fritz believed that the Marxist system was brilliant and compared with other ideas had an element of grandeur, even nobility. Its truths were in the Christian tradition but they were to a large extent rendered ineffective by four evils. And evil could not be overcome by evil. Marxism was a realistic system but its realism was made negative by its exclusively materialistic analysis. Dialectics Fritz described as 'one of the finest flowers of the human mind ... These principles, of course, are simply an insistence on not being stupid. But it is their merit to formulate what is required for being intelligent.' However, dialectics without a higher level led inevitably to atheism and a petty bourgeois hatred of what one could not understand.

He also believed that Marx's insistence on the dignity of man and of work was enormously important, but again the insistence on violence which accompanied this negated the nobility of the concept and could lead only to Machiavellianism. Lastly Fritz pointed out that Marx had said that out of the evil of the bourgeoisie had come the material foundations for socialism. This was like the Christian belief that human nature, although burdened with sin, is nevertheless capable of good. But attached to Marx's analysis was the invention of a new hatred – class hatred. This hatred and the materialistic interpretation of history introduced into the positive and useful contribution of Marxist analysis

a hateful and mean kind of depth analysis ... similar to Freudian psychology. Everything has a sinister 'deeper' meaning. This is the final degradation of the intellect. 'Double talk', Utopia of a classless society which forgets all about sin, is thus burdened with the previous undermining of all standards of decency ... The necessary critique of capitalism and bourgeois degradation proceeded through means that were themselves degraded ... Yet [Marxism's] great truths could win the day – if it can shed its parasitical materialism and atheism and thus reconnect with the sources of its truth, the great Graeco-Christian tradition of the West.[7]

If the root evil of Marxism is hate, then, Fritz argued, the root evil of capitalism is greed. This brought him on to what he called the 'religion of economics', a creed which with its roots in materialism and false belief that it was a science, led to a

265

degradation of everything higher in life, to a contempt of the person and to a misuse of nature. 'Economics is typically the product of the bourgeois spirit which, recognizing nothing beyond the visible world, is solely interested in *manipulating the world* "for gain".' Such an approach, Fritz insisted, cannot 'lead to anything real because man is *not homo oeconomicus* and if he is treated as if he were he will go to pieces. But to the extent that he becomes *homo oeconomicus*, economics becomes true and scientific and man ceases to be man.'

In his final lecture Fritz gave his great rallying cry which he ultimately expressed so well in his two books, *Small is Beautiful* and *A Guide for the Perplexed*, over ten years later.

> Our Age [is] one of the maximum opportunity for 'development' and the maximum temptation not to use the opportunity, indeed absolutely to abuse it ... It seems quite clear to me that in the School of life we have moved up into the sixth form where entirely new tasks are having to be tackled, namely two:
>
> (a) we must now live without war,
> (b) we must now learn to live on income rather than capital (exhaustion of fossil fuels, etc.).
>
> Both these tasks require the attainment of a higher level of consciousness, called AHIMSA or non-violence ... If we want to preserve human civilisation we must learn 'non-violence' in *all* activities – not only politics but also economics, medicine, agriculture, horticulture, industry, etc. This really *needs to be worked out* ... Pacifism is *not possible* if you persist in any kind of violence against all parts of creation except man.[8]

Fritz called for an inner development, or raising of consciousness, so that the urgent requirements to ensure the world's survival could be worked out and put into practice. The weakness of the Christian church, he suggested, was an apparent lack of precise instruction on how to 'have the faith'. For instruction on how to do this, he directed his audience towards the oriental creeds whose strength he saw in their precise instruction for those on a serious spiritual search, which he had not discovered in the Christian church. They boiled down to something very simple but very difficult, namely: take yourself in hand, control your mind by recognizing the aimless drifting of your life and thoughts, control your body through posture, relaxation and breath control for 'a slack body is a slack mind'. And control your morality for morality means order and immorality disorder. The techniques for achieving control in these three areas of mind, body and actions were to be found in all religions. Fritz named a few – yoga and meditation from the East, the traditions of Greek and Russian Orthodox mysticism, St Ignatius Loyola's three types of prayer, Gurdjieff's 'work', and the techniques of F.M. Alexander in the West. Any of these would lead to self-control and self-awareness and beyond.

When these lectures were over Fritz intended to stop and write his book there and then. Events, however, overtook him. The next ten years were to be an explosion of activity, reaching a climax when his books were published, in which he pursued the implications of his words into all human activity.

19

The National Coal Board

Much of the work Fritz did in the 1950s, which led up to his lecture course in 1959–1960, was a direct consequence of his job at the National Coal Board. The death of Sir Arthur Street in 1951, removing Fritz's most important line of influence in the Board, heralded a decade of frustration and under-utilization in which he was eventually forced to conclude that he could be doing more useful work elsewhere.

The positive side to this unsatisfactory situation, and one which Fritz freely acknowledged, was that he had a degree of freedom to follow his other interests. He had time to read and think deeply about the many questions stimulated by his reading. This did not mean that he sat around with his feet on his desk reading uplifting works to while away the time. He worked a full day and by normal standards his work was prodigious. But his capacity was greater and his mind was never still.

The pressing problem facing the coal industry when Fritz joined in 1950 was how to supply enough coal to fill the huge and growing demand brought about by post-war reconstruction, and Fritz set out at once to discover ways of increasing efficiency and preventing waste. There were about nine hundred different mines to be considered and five tiers of management structure, and Fritz saw that it was impossible to weld such an enormous industry into a cohesive unit without having some means of acquiring a clear and concise picture of what was going on. This was not available. Although masses of statistics were being collected all the time and sent to the statisticians in Hobart House for analysis, few were really useful pointers to the state of the mines or indicators of the problems that were hampering the efficient supply of coal. For this reason, in Fritz's view, the Board was not able to formulate the sort of policies that could really get to grips with creating an efficient and dynamic framework for the industry. Fritz's suggestion, however, that a new approach should be made to the whole area of statistics and statistical analysis was ignored and it was to be twelve years before he was allowed to put this vital proposition into practice.

The other fundamental problem that Fritz immediately identified in the industry was that of human relations. He believed that this had a far more significant effect on efficiency than technology. 'Here, as everywhere,' he wrote to his parents in November 1950, 'it is human relations, that is the relationship between worker and management, that need improving far more than technology. The mine managers are experts in machines but not in leadership. The wonderful machines are of no use at all if the workers don't feel like working. One needs to start on this human element.'

It was a theme he was to pursue relentlessly, which he had already faced in Germany after the war and towards which he had tried to contribute a solution in his plea for the socialization of German industry in 1946. Then it had seemed to him that doing away with private profit by putting the means of production into public hands was a crucial factor, both in changing attitudes in industry and in removing the danger of concentrating economic power in the hands of a few private individuals at the expense of the nation as a whole. 'Yet within six months he had seen that three years of nationalization had failed to make any impact on attitudes in industry, and the following year, 1951, when the Conservatives were returned to power, it became even clearer that public attitudes had not been touched either. The success of the new government's campaign against the nationalized industries, reflected in the hostility of the press, highlighted the extent to which the nationalized industries were lonely 'socialist islands in a sea of capitalism'.

The change in the public atmosphere under the Conservatives caused Fritz to think much more deeply about public ownership and its importance in changing society. The crux of the matter was the question of profit. To a socialist the evils of private enterprise were rooted in the fact that its sole justification was private profit and private gain. Nationalization, by placing ownership in the hands of the nation, removed the danger of exploitation and other excesses perpetrated by private greed and meant that the workers were contributing not to an individual's wealth but towards the nation as a whole of which they were part. Yet Fritz was faced with the fact that this beneficial aspect not only failed to impress or positively motivate the miners but also caused considerable confusion among socialists. It led him to two inescapable conclusions: firstly that generations of 'capitalistic working for profit' had moulded attitudes which would take time and patience to change, and secondly, that ownership, although vitally important, was only an element in a framework within which new aims and ideals had to be set.

He tried to clarify these points both within and outside the industry. The problem of profit had many implications. In articles and lectures he pointed out that the profit motive, with its simple appeal of reducing every decision to the one question of how it would affect profits, had led people to believe that efficiency and profit were synonymous. Now they were faced with a new scenario. Nationalized industries had been set up to serve the nation as a whole and the removal of profit-making from the centre of the stage had confused even the best minds as to the lines on which the industry should be run. If there was no profit there was public outcry that the industry concerned was inefficient, yet if there was a profit it was accused of overcharging the public. He wrote:

> The first thing I should like to emphasise is that, while the word profit, with some people, may have a bad sound, this sound attaches only to *private* profit and cannot possibly attach to any profit of public enterprise. That is, because what is often considered objectionable is the *private appropriation of wealth* through profit-making; but in the case of *public* enterprise there is no private appropriation of wealth at all ... As a general rule and within certain reasonable

limits, nationalised enterprise should strive to maximise profits, so as to make the greatest possible contribution to public revenue and capital formation.[1]

In other words, over a wide area of decisions the Board must indeed act 'commercially', in the interests of the N.C.B., just like a private firm acting in its own interest. But all the time the Board must consider 'the public interest', whatever that may be, and in case of conflict must give precedence to the public interest over the interest of the N.C.B. . . .

It can easily be seen, therefore, that efficiency for the Coal Board does not always mean the same thing as it would mean for private enterprise. Nor can it be measured in the same way. Yet, when we have recognized these – and other – differences, we shall do well to remember the identities. Nationalized industry is every bit as much concerned with the attainment of maximum efficiency as is private industry. Once the public interest has been recognized by the Board's adoption of certain specific points to that end, then – within the framework thus given – the criterion of efficiency must rule supreme.[2]

These similarities between the operation of private and public industries were the source of much confusion, particularly as there were a number of large private firms which had an enlightened policy towards their workers, a fact exploited by the Conservative government in their campaign against the nationalized industries. Such private firms, it was argued, performed both functions more efficiently than their public counterparts. But Fritz insisted that these suggestions merely clouded the fact that there was an essential difference between the two types of ownership:

It is necessary to recognize that private ownership of the means of production is severely limited in its freedom of choice of objectives, because it is compelled to be profit-seeking, and tends to take a narrow and selfish view of things. Public ownership gives complete freedom in the choice of objectives and can therefore be used for any purpose that may be chosen. While private ownership is an instrument that by itself largely determines the ends for which it can be employed, public ownership is an instrument, the ends of which are completely undetermined.[3]

By 1959 the importance of this essential difference was beginning to show itself as the coal industry was put to the test by the sudden change in the market, felt since 1957. In that year, demand had suddenly fallen and the coal industry entered into a prolonged period of crisis. Although the seriousness of the crisis at first remained unrecognized by most of the policy-makers at the Board, the adverse effects of the cutback in demand on the employees in the industry were minimized. Fritz had a different view of the crisis from most of his colleagues – an issue which will be dealt with later in this chapter – but he believed that the way it was being handled by the Board was a vindication of the ideals of nationalization. They followed a policy which put men before money, despite the fact that this caused a tremendous amount of criticism outside the industry.

It is a sad reflection on the confusion of thought prevailing in our society that the Board has come in for the most violent criticism on precisely those policies which are its finest achievements – policies with which it not only lived up to its highest obligations as a nationalised industry but also recognised the fundamental truth – which should be completely obvious in an affluent society – that it is wrong to chase after a trivial and temporary economic advantage at the cost of grave hurt to a considerable number of honest and guiltless fellow-citizens.[4]

It was hardly surprising that with such confusion over the true value of nationalization in the top levels of the industry and in government attitudes, the high ideals of the socialist pioneers should fail to penetrate to the workers. But Fritz saw a more sinister influence at work in the failure of these ideals to spread. 'The nationalized industries are founded on a higher ideal than personal greed: on the idea of service. But this idea cannot penetrate down to its workers when the ideological currents of society as a whole are flowing in the opposite direction.'[5]

What Fritz meant was that the effect of capitalism, whose

motive force was the satisfaction of greed, had replaced the concept of just pay for an honest day's work with an ideology which praised those whose gain was in inverse proportion to the amount of work they had done. It was symbolized for Fritz by the prominent attention given to the football pools, where the aim was to make money without doing any work at all. In a society where such attitudes were praised, the virtues of hard work and honesty were seriously undermined regardless of whether the ordinary worker was employed by a public or a private enterprise. 'The people inside . . .', explained Fritz, 'are as much in the grip of the "profit ideology" as the people outside. They get confused.'

Fritz's understanding of the subtle influences of generations of capitalism, private ownership and private profit on attitudes in society strengthened his belief that new forms of industrial organization must be found. The first step was to change ownership, but nationalization had shown clearly that this was not enough, a completely new structure must follow. He realized, too, that one could hardly expect the workers to respond to the ideals of the intellectual socialists when their work was soul-destroying in its tedium. This was also an area where the nationalized industries could spearhead the way to change.

> Here, I believe, lies the greatest contribution which nationalized industry could make – and ought to be given a chance to make – to a new industrial outlook. We must *invest* in the reduction of boredom. Stupid work produces stupid or desperate people. Mere Welfare and Education, Consultation and Conciliation cannot offset the effects of shovelling, shovelling, shovelling all day and every day. All these worthy efforts will come to naught if we fail to reduce soul-destroying boredom.[6]

Turning to the question of the framework of industry, a part of which was the change of ownership from private individuals to the public, Fritz drew on ideas on which he had been working since the war. As early as 1941, when his mind was still very much occupied with matters of international trade, he had at the centre of his analysis the concept that a proper structure must incorporate the opposing elements of freedom and planning, or control. Nations had to be free to determine their own policies and yet, within the framework of their co-operation over trade, there needed to be definite controls so that their behaviour did not endanger other nations. In his multilateral clearing plan Fritz tried to build in the controls in subtle ways, using moral pressures and persuasion rather than rules imposed from above.

His studies, in quite a different field after 1950, namely Eastern wisdom and religions, had reinforced these ideas. He had realized that life itself is a process of constantly reconciling opposites. His favourite example was from the French Revolution where, he pointed out, the opposing concepts of liberty and equality were reconciled by a third and what he would call 'higher' concept of fraternity. His visit to Burma had shed more light on the reconciliation of extremes as Fritz studied the Buddhist concept of the Middle Way, but had also added to his thinking in other ways. He had come across the Buddhist concept of work, of the value of work as a good in itself for the development of man's whole-being, and this had strengthened his concern about the destructive effect of many jobs on the personalities of those subjected to boring, repetitive tasks.

More obviously linked to the whole question of the structure of nationalized industries had also been his work on the socialization of German industry. In these proposals he had put forward suggestions for many different kinds of socialized enterprises, each appropriate to the type of business being put in public hands. As he came across different kinds of socialized enterprises in Britain he took careful note of their structures and the effects they seemed to have on their employees.

All these different strands of thought formed the background to his thinking about the structure of the nationalized coal industry. Right in the centre was the question: how, in such a vast industrial set-up, is it possible to allow enough freedom to enable people to use their initiative and be given the responsibility necessary for them to achieve satisfaction from their work while at the same time enabling the Board to keep a firm control over the workings of the industry? As usual he tried to devise a specific plan to solve these problems. In 1958 he submitted to the Board a paper which he thought would satisfy the criteria he had set himself. It was called

'Financial Control', and proposed that while the Board should retain overall control of policy for the industry as a whole and concern itself with planning, prices, research and development, and such top management questions, the day-to-day running of the industry should be put into the hands of those who actually produced the coal, namely the area managers. He proposed that they should be left to manage their own affairs and be given their own banking systems. These would quickly reflect anything that was going wrong, and would force the area to go to the Board for assistance or to justify the deficit they had acquired. 'It is the Board, not the Area, that ought to be able to sit still until something happens. It is the Area, not the Board, that ought to have to take the initiative if the Area's accounts go into the red.'[7]

The scheme was too revolutionary for the Board, preoccupied by 1958 with the problems of overproduction after years of coal shortages. Once more Fritz's ideas were ignored. The Board, then under the Chairmanship of James Bowman, were not men of vision and daring, Fritz thought, but men who allowed themselves to be discouraged by the unsympathetic political atmosphere and public criticism, and whose concern rarely went beyond the immediate calling of their expertise. Their narrow view prevented them from making use of their economic adviser and left him in the frustrating position of feeling that he had many of the answers to the industry's problems up his sleeve but no audience eager to watch him produce them and act upon his suggestions.

It was, in a sense, a continuation of Fritz's position since the outbreak of war. He was as powerless as ever. His experience at Prees Heath was still relevant: persuasion, explanation, kindness, clarity and justice had to remain substitutes for getting his way through the power of his position or by force. He did not despair at the failure of the men at the top to understand what he considered were the real problems of industrial society: he went directly to the men, to the managers in the areas, to the staff trained by Sam Essame; and everywhere his skills as a public speaker, his clarity of thought and his ability to tailor his message to the audience he was addressing endeared him to his public and increased their understanding of the industry they were serving. On a personal level too, Fritz kept his door open to all. He maintained his motto 'I never met a man I didn't like,' and only admitted to one real failure. He detested the Board's scientific adviser, Jacob Bronowski, and confessed: 'I couldn't find it in my heart to like the man.' When Bronowski finally left the Board for America, Fritz commented, 'America's loss is the Coal Board's gain.' There are some, including David Astor, who believe that Fritz's intense dislike of Bronowski was largely because they were very similar men, both brilliant and very arrogant. Be that as it may, Bronowski was to Fritz the epitome of *homo sapiens*, a man who believed that he had evolved in a purposeless world and to whom Fritz could only say, 'Well, speak for yourself.'

The many others who came to Fritz's little room which for years overlooked the inner courtyard of Hobart House, were received with courtesy and friendliness. His relaxed manner gave his visitors the impression that he had all the time in the world to listen to their problems and over the years his advice was sought on a wide variety of questions, many of them personal and unrelated to Coal Board business. Colleagues would drop in for a chat and many would feel that they came away having learnt something new and useful. There were occasions when this rule of friendly courtesy was broken. If anyone came to Fritz for advice and then started disputing what he said, he could become extremely annoyed and impatient, eventually sending them out with an icy reminder that he was a busy man who could not afford to spend his time with people whose only intention was to waste it.

Despite his openness to all who sought his advice, and their evident respect and appreciation of his willingness to listen, Fritz remained a lonely figure. His penetrating, questioning mind made many of his colleagues uncomfortable, if not sometimes resentful, and he had few allies on the Board itself or in top levels of management. There were notable exceptions, although not all were based at Hobart House, among them Harry Collins, Sam Essame and Geoffrey Kirk. They were all men with whom Fritz could discuss many aspects of his interests. Until 1956 he lacked someone with whom he could work closely. Then he recruited a young Scottish economist who became more than just a support in the office, and who was to play an important part in Fritz's life. George McRobie was an economics graduate from the London School of Economics. He had worked for some years for Political and Economic Planning (P.E.P.), where Fritz had first come across him. Fritz was giving some help on a P.E.P. study on energy and liked George at once. He was a man who listened and understood what Fritz had to say, a perfect sounding-board who was able to make the right comments and ask the right questions. He was an idealistic young socialist too and, above all, had a sense of humour and enjoyed the good things of life. When Fritz and George were together the chances were that a bottle of whisky would be near by and there would be a good deal of hilarity and ribald humour which reflected little of Fritz's high ideals and morality. With George Fritz could join the ranks of ordinary mortals for an evening.

Possibly this is the reason that, despite an otherwise close relationship, Fritz did not share much of his inner spiritual life with George. In 1956, when their partnership began, he naturally told George a great deal about Buddhism and Burma but it was more in relation to 'Buddhist economics', than its implications for personal development. He discussed with George at length the whole question of world energy consumption and the conclusions he had come to about the future of industrial society, conclusions which had been reinforced by his Burmese experience, and used him to try out the many lectures he gave in England and in Europe on the subject.

In every lecture he made the same basic plea backed up always with the latest statistics from every publication of good repute that he could find. He was particularly careful to scour the publications of the major fuel industries and to use their figures to make his points. The statistics he quoted about projected fuel consumption and estimated reserves always came from the industries themselves. He merely put the two figures together and by making what he called exploratory calculations came to his startling conclusions. For example, in 1956:

It is hard to comprehend the changes the world has experienced during the last *fifty* years ... It is even harder to comprehend the changes of the last *ten* years – the changes since the end of the second world war. It is easy enough to describe them; but it is very difficult to understand their meaning ... During the last twelve years or so the world has burned more oil than in its entire previous history. During the last twenty years, it has used more steel than in its entire previous history. And if we take all 'non-renewable' resources together – all metals and fossil fuels – we find that during the last thirty-five to forty years man has used up more of these irreplaceable assets than the whole of mankind has used in its entire previous history. What are forty years in relation to the history of man? How long can we go on like this? ... At present, about four-fifths of the world's fuel supplies come from 'non-renewable' resources, from coal, oil and natural gas ... Four-fifths, in other words, is capital; only one-fifth is income. Eighty percent of the world economy is based on fuels which cannot last forever. If we double, and double again, the speed with which we remove these resources, are we not removing the foundations upon which we have built our house?[8]

In October 1958 in a general talk about fuel he said:

All modern industries, and large sectors of modern agriculture too, depend on fuel and power ... The first important fact about fuel, therefore, is the universal, inescapable need for it. The second important fact is that the overwhelming proportion of the fuel and power used in the world today stems from *non-renewable* sources ... The third important fact about FUEL is the unevenness of its distribution over the face of the earth ... Economic expansion is the common ideology of all mankind today. Technological progress supports this ideology ... two facts stand out, first, that the question of fuel supplies under conditions of sustained world economic expansion is the greatest unsolved question in the economic field which mankind has to face, and, second, that it is Western Europe more than any other part of the world, which is most directly involved.[9]

In another talk that same year he went further: 'Instead of concentrating on long-term forecasts of requirements, they might make long-term studies of availabilities; they might open people's eyes to the fact that the problem of resources is in no way solved and that the way we are carrying on exposes our own children to totally insoluble problems.'[10]

Apart from George McRobie and Harry Collins, Fritz's ideas met little support. It was assumed that oil and nuclear energy, neither of which had been properly exploited, would fill the so-called energy gap. Nuclear energy Fritz dismissed as being unimportant in the equations. He did not believe that it would make a serious impact on energy supplies in the foreseeable future. At first he was also somewhat dismissive about oil as a serious source of fuel in the West – both because he thought it unlikely that Europe would be able to pay for it but also because it would be a politically unwise act to depend on the Middle East for such an important product. As early as 1952, arguing for a strong coal policy, he had said (my italics):

During the next two decades it is most unlikely that the supply of oil and natural gas will keep pace with requirements ... In other words, the world will have to look to coal to take the load of the additional requirements for heat and energy. When you turn to Europe the picture is clearer still. At present more than eighty per cent of Europe's heat and energy requirements are being met by coal. Now that the United States, in spite of producing more than half the world's oil, has become by far the largest oil importer, the chances of Europe's being able to buy (and pay for) greatly increased quantities of oil – which would have to be obtained almost exclusively from the Middle East, *politically not the most stable part of the world* – are very small.[11]

Fritz was soon proved wrong in his assumptions about oil, which in less than one decade was to become a major source of energy in Western Europe, but his point that the Middle East as a major source of oil for the West was politically undesirable because of the area's instability, was a vitally important one. Fritz seemed to think that this was self-evident and did not bother to spell out the implications, until some years later he realized that even experienced politicians seemed to be blind to the political realities of oil dependence.

These first warnings were uttered in a period of acute energy shortage but in 1957 the picture suddenly and dramatically changed. By the end of the year the N.C.B. found a stock of coal on their hands. Demand had fallen significantly. At first this was explained by a warmer winter than usual and a downturn in the economy, but as coal stocks continued to rise it became clear that something more serious was happening than a mere hiccup in the economy. What had changed was the supply of oil. Cheap oil from the Middle East had begun to flow to Britain in significant quantities.

Fritz regarded the situation with the greatest possible disquiet. It was clear that politicians in general did not share his view that it was inadvisable to allow the British economy to become dependent on imported fuel, in particular from an unstable part of the world. He suggested at a conference to the Federation of British Industry in 1958:

> Quite apart from the balance of payments problems created thereby a development of this kind ... would mean the end of Western European independence. The whole Western European economy would become so vitally dependent on Middle Eastern oil that anyone in a position to withhold, or even only to disturb, these supplies would be Europe's master. If present plans are carried through, the position will be irretrievable within twenty years from now. Western Europe will then have attained a position of maximum dependence on the oil of the Middle East precisely at the moment when the first signs of a world oil famine become visible. The political implications of such a situation are too obvious to require discussion.[12]

These views were received with ridicule and disbelief. Those who had not immersed themselves in world fuel questions like Fritz, but whose blinkered view looked only at Britain, or possibly Europe, could see only that the demand for coal had fallen because cheap oil had taken its place. Their conclusion was obvious: the days of coal were over. From a period of frantic expansion the coal industry was now faced with an apparent need to contract. Fritz had praised the way this contraction had begun in his vindication of nationalization quoted earlier. Only those mines that were almost worked out were closed and the men were absorbed in other parts of the industry; cuts were made in strip mining that used mainly machinery; voluntary Saturday working was stopped and import contracts were terminated as soon as was possible. Such adjustments, although costly, were gentle and safeguarded the long-term interests of the industry, so that while output objectives were scaled down from 250 million tons per annum to 200 million tons per annum, the ability of the industry to respond to an upturn in demand in the future was not harmed.

By 1960 the general consensus of opinion was that the age of coal was over. Even members of the N.C.B. believed this and felt the Board should now bow to the inevitable. An O.E.E.C. report by Professor Austin Robinson, and many other reports that followed, argued the same point over and over again: Western Europe's coal was no longer needed. Fritz did not agree. His calculations based on the figures produced by the energy industries themselves still convinced him of the fragility of an economy utterly dependent on the stocks in nature's energy larder. The fact that he had been wrong in assuming that the West would not substantially increase its imports of oil did not change the fundamental point he was making: at the current rate of increase of demand for energy there would come a time when the larder would be found to be empty. The advent of oil merely gave a little more time to make the adjustments that would be necessary to survive this threatening crisis. But he could not get this view across. His opposition to contracting the coal industry was interpreted as a vested interest. By 1960 the cry outside the coal industry was to contract the industry substantially, a prospect greeted with joy by the Government and the press: it was a sign of progress that the days of the unpleasant and dangerous job of the coal miner was nearing an end. It was clear that the coal industry would have to fight for its life.

After ten years in the coal industry Fritz was utterly convinced that the days of coal were not only not over but that never before had it been so important to keep a healthy, vigorous industry going. While he recognized the fact that coal could not hope to compete with cheap oil, which was virtually being dumped on the British market, he emphatically repeated his view that in the longer term it was essential to keep the coal industry going at a stable level for the economic future of Britain. To reduce the size of the industry drastically in the short term was in fact to kill the industry for all time – mines could not be closed temporarily. They required constant maintenance. Nor could manpower in the industry be treated in such a cavalier fashion. The families and communities that had grown up around mining activities had taken generations to establish; once broken they would take many years to build up again, notwithstanding the devastating social consequences of mass unemployment.

After years of preaching the dangers of the limited nature of the energy supply, the very foundation of Western economic life, Fritz knew it would be the height of folly to shut down such a major source of energy. Yet his colleagues at the Board seemed unable to grasp the point. There were those, including E. H. Browne, who believed that nuclear energy would fill the gap if and when it came and wished that Fritz would concentrate his mind on the vital issue of closing down the industry with the least harm to the mining communities. Others did not believe in an 'energy gap' at all. Fritz was very depressed. He wondered whether the time had not come for him to leave the Coal Board and follow up some of his other interests. He did not regret his ten years at the Board but the fact was that for ten years he had been talking about very serious issues and his employers in the Board had taken little or no notice. His feelings were reflected in a dream which he often had at that time. He would see the Board members sitting around the Board table talking earnestly and making big decisions. After every decision a member would get up and go over to a large switchboard into which he would insert a plug or move a lever which apparently implemented the decision. After a while Fritz became curious and went over to the switchboard to see how it worked. He would look behind it and discover that it was not connected to anything. It was a totally useless bit of equipment, as useless as the gestures and decisions of the Board.

Taking this as a sign that perhaps he should move on, Fritz looked at the various options that were open to him. His lectures at London University were proving to be a great success and he wanted to put his thoughts together in book form. After his ten years in nationalized industry and his thoughts about the structure of industry, he wanted to spend some time on a detailed study of socialism and its significance in British industry – another possible book. Since Burma he had also become involved in the growing concern about the underdeveloped nations and in early 1960 had received two invitations to work in India, one from Rosenstein Rodan, at Chatham House during the war, and one from the leading Indian socialist and Gandhian, J. P. Narayan. Surely it would now be right to turn his back on Hobart House and take up one or more of these threads.

The issues at stake were too important: it was a waste of time producing ideas for people who were not prepared to take them up. A year earlier, in his article for *Socialist Commentary*, he had expressed the enormity of what he considered the implications of modern industrial life:

> What is at stake is not economics but culture; not the standard of living but the quality of life. Economics and the standard of living can just as well be looked after by a capitalist system, moderated by a bit of Keynesian planning and re-distributive taxation. But culture and, generally, the quality of life, can only be debased by such a system. Socialists should insist on using the nationalised industries not simply to outcapitalise the capitalists – an attempt in which they may or may not succeed, but to evolve a more democratic and dignified system of industrial administration, a more humane employment of machinery, and a more intelligent utilisation of the fruits of human ingenuity and effort. If they can do that, they have the future in their hands. If they cannot, they have nothing to offer worthy of the sweat of free man.[13]

20

―――∞∞∞――――

Year of Crisis

Throughout his married life Fritz had too strong a sense of purpose to allow anyone else – even his wife – to affect his decisions about his career or employment. Although he always discussed his plans with Muschi, she knew that her role in his decision-making was to be a sounding-post, allowing him to think aloud in her presence. This time, however, Muschi's role in Fritz's future was vital. To give up the Coal Board and settle down to writing books, with four children, a wife and a mortgage, was a decision which could not be made alone. On the other hand, a period in India did not particularly appeal to Muschi.

Then, at Christmas in 1959, Muschi developed jaundice and the after-effects lingered on well into the spring of 1960. Muschi had never before experienced a day's illness and had it not been for the Swiss *au pair*, Vreni Rosenberger, the household would have collapsed. Fritz was not very domesticated. His contribution was to the necessities of life – bread and garden products – not to such mundane things as clean shirts and shoes. Vreni was only eighteen and very shy. She had to be coaxed to enter into family life and was somewhat overawed by her tall, good-looking employer, so idolized by his wife. She was quite relieved that every evening after returning home from the office he would go straight up to Muschi's room, and spend the evening sitting there at the end of Muschi's bed talking and reading, only leaving to prepare his weekly lectures for London University and deal with his correspondence.

It was clear no plans could be made until Muschi was better and Fritz wrote accordingly to J.P. Narayan, expressing his interest in a spell in India but deferring his decision.

Muschi's recovery was only temporary. In early May 1960 she collapsed again in great pain. After a five-hour operation at Guy's Hospital in London, the surgeon told Fritz that there was little hope. Muschi had cancer of the intestines with secondaries in her liver. That night Fritz returned home exhausted. The only emotion he betrayed was a deep anger against the medical profession. He believed the initial tumour, which was the size of a tennis ball, should have been spotted far earlier. Otherwise, his one aim was to keep life going as normally as possible. He tried to cling on to some hope that a cure could still be found, and told very few people, apart from his mother, the truth about Muschi's illness. Even Muschi's parents were not told. After their experience with Olga's death of the same cancer, Fritz wanted to spare them for as long as possible. But everywhere he turned, whether to 'orthodox' or 'alternative' medicine, the answer was the same: it was too late to help Muschi.

Once again Vreni took over the household. This time it was without direction from upstairs. As soon as Muschi was well enough, she wrote to Vreni from hospital saying that she was not to worry about the house as long as the children were happy. But there was an enormous amount of work to be done, work formerly shared by the two of them: the fires to make for hot water, the clothes to be seen to, the cooking and the shopping, and Fritz's clean white shirts and stiff collars. Vreni had lived alongside Muschi long enough to know the pride she took in her husband's elegant appearance. Fritz began to appreciate Vreni's care more than ever. There was pressing work at the office, pressure from India, and the unthinkable future without Muschi ahead. To be protected from household duties at this stage was at least something for which he could be grateful. Nevertheless, he tried to step up his contribution: on Sundays he would help with the washing-up. It became a family event with Fritz at the sink and Vreni, Virginia and me drying the dishes and putting them away.

In the next months some hard decisions had to be made. Fritz's own future was put to one side as he considered how

Muschi was to be cared for as her illness progressed. The summer holidays were approaching and it was clear that the usual six weeks in Reinbek for Muschi, Virginia and me would not be possible. Fritz suggested that we, now aged fourteen and nine, might accompany him to Switzerland for a change while Muschi went to 'convalesce' in Reinbek. Muschi welcomed this solution. Although no one had told her what was wrong with her, it seems she sensed the truth. Before she left, she said to Mrs Richmond, the wife of the Minister at Caterham Congregational Church where she had been a faithful member, 'I am going to Germany. I don't want the children to see me decline.'

Virginia and I were delighted to be going to Switzerland for a change, although I shared my mother's regret for every missed opportunity to visit Reinbek. As we said goodbye to her I lingered in the cold blue bedroom. I could not bear to leave the small, frail figure whose warm personality had been the centre of my life. Then I hurried to the waiting green Volkswagen, crammed with luggage, where the others were waiting and we drove away without looking back.

The summer passed. As the last hope for Muschi faded, Fritz prepared Christian and John, both away from home, for the truth. Virginia and I were in complete ignorance, aware only that Muschi's illness was serious but not that it was fatal. Then Fritz began to spend more and more time in Reinbek, first with Muschi at her parents' house and then in the Bethesda Hospital in the nearby town of Bergedorf. He spent hours at her bedside reading to her and talking to her of the things of the spirit which for so long had torn them apart and now brought them together in the most extraordinary way. They were closer than ever before, their attentions focused in the same direction. Fritz wondered at Muschi's strength and courage. Determined not to waste her time in hospital she had set herself the task of learning the Gospel of St Matthew by heart. As her body wasted away and she suffered the indignities that cancer of the liver brings, her spirit seemed to grow before his eyes. An intensity burnt fiercely in her blue eyes as they sank deeper into her face.

Only one thing still held them apart. Muschi had not been told the truth about her illness. Fritz would not talk to her about dying or death. Then one day, after Fritz had returned to the Petersen house from a long spell with Muschi, knowing that it was now only a matter of days, the telephone suddenly rang. It was the hospital. 'Please come at once,' he was told. 'Mrs Schumacher is very upset about something.' Fritz found Muschi in a state of great agitation. With more emotion than she had shown for weeks she cried, 'Why won't anyone tell me the truth? What is the matter with me?' Fritz still shrank from uttering the fatal words. Finally, exasperated, she asked, 'Is it the same as Olga?' As Fritz nodded affirmation, relief and great peace came into her face.

For three more days Muschi radiated joy and peace. On the morning of October 26th Fritz sat with her as usual. His sister Edith, who had joined him in Reinbek, waited outside the room. As she sat there she had a strange experience, as if a huge flock of white birds were flying from Muschi's room up, up, up into the sky. A moment later Fritz opened the door. It was all over.

It was not until after the funeral, at which only Christian represented the children, that Fritz returned home. He now had the ordeal of breaking the news to his two daughters. He had done all he could to protect us from the pain of Muschi's illness and under Vreni's care and the undisturbed routine of term-time, life had passed without too much anxiety. Temporary losses can be accommodated easily enough. He knew that when the telephone rang at Holcombe and the news came that 'Papa is on his way home', there would be joy at the prospect of seeing him again. But he did not have to say anything as he walked through the front door in the early evening, accompanied by Christian. Vreni, Virginia and I stood waiting in the hall. As he came in, the first thing I saw was Muschi's little white plastic overnight bag in his hand. It had always gone everywhere with her. Now it had returned alone. I knew immediately she would never come back.

Fritz, outwardly strong to the children, was completely devastated by his loss. Often Vreni, looking in at the study to say goodnight, would find him weeping uncontrollably. At lunchtime he would frequently leave the office and visit Vera Morley in her little mews flat behind Selfridges. Vera had been one of Muschi's closest English friends and in her company Fritz talked and wept freely. He longed to make contact with Muschi's spirit in some way and attended a few meetings of the Subud group where, he had been told, bereaved people sometimes felt the presence of those who had died. But always he experienced nothing at all. He felt utterly alone and deserted like a dog without a master, and wrote to Muschi's mother in November:

> I notice myself, that for twenty-four years I have, so to speak, carried everything that I have done to Muschi like a dog. What does the dog who must go carrying do now? To whose feet can he bring the things that he has hunted? Just at the end, a few hours before her death, Muschi said her full name a few times, very clearly and distinctly, as though she had drawn a line through her life and now named that which she was taking over with her. So perhaps the 'carrying' can go on, though not to the living but to the heavenly Beatrice who will probably have much higher demands.

But Fritz saw clearly that Muschi's death had in itself been an experience after which he could never be the same as he was before. He added in the same letter: 'It is an extraordinary blessing for me, and reason for gratitude that I was able to be present at her death – a death in which the great spiritual strength that flowed through her became ever clearer.'

In his despair Fritz clung on to one hope: that Muschi's death had not been without meaning in his life. It had happened at a moment when he had been considering change. These decisions could not now be taken. He wrote to his mother: 'My main desire is to wait quietly until perhaps it may become clear to me what Muschi's death "means" for the development of my life. Only when this becomes clear can I take new decisions.'

Meanwhile it was important to carry on as near to normal as possible, and throw himself once more into his job at the Coal Board. This required the solution of an essentially practical problem: how to keep the household going. Vreni agreed to stay on another year while Fritz made alternative arrangements. He tried to make life as simple as possible for her. During Muschi's illness the solid fuel boiler had been replaced by an automatic gas central-heating system. He replaced his shirts and stiff collars with drip-dry nylon shirts. Vreni, unwilling to see the deterioration in Fritz's appearance, kept on with the ironing until one of his new shirts melted under the iron. But Fritz was realistic enough to recognize that as a normal full-blooded man he would need more than a housekeeper and from the beginning held the desirability of remarriage in his mind. There were plenty of willing candidates: old secretaries, widowed and divorced friends, ladies young and old who had long fallen for his charms. As far as he was concerned only one or two were serious contenders, but a brief and discreet trial prevented what would have probably turned out to be a ghastly mistake. Unaware of this method of elimination Virginia and I instinctively recognized one of these as a real threat. She had been (and remained) a close family friend and I later learned that Muschi had recommended her to Fritz on her deathbed. We merely felt that she was too clever for us and we called her 'the snake'. The others were all known as 'the bogies'. It was quite obvious what their intentions were – even we could see what an attractive proposition Fritz was. We loathed most the ones who tried to get at him through us. One had an enormous bosom and embraced us constantly. We thought the sensation of enveloping darkness must be like drowning. Eventually Virginia, aged nine, said, 'If she does that again I'll punch her in the stomach.' She went straight to the drawing-room and stood affectionately near to her prey. I watched with glee, wishing I had the courage to do the same.

While 1960 was such a disastrous year domestically, it was fortunately very busy at the Coal Board. The National Union of Mineworkers had begun to take action to fight for the life of the coal industry. They were more receptive to Fritz's arguments for maintaining stable coal production and the dangers of severely reducing the industry than some of the Board, and his commitment to the ideals of nationalization made him a natural person to turn to at this moment of crisis. With the active assistance of the National Coal Board, the N.U.M. undertook a massive and unprecedented educational campaign in the form of a study conference to examine and to inform top-level decision-makers about the implications of the new energy situation and its effect on the coal industry. Fritz lent his unqualified support to the venture, releasing George McRobie for three months specifically to help with the organization and planning.

The study conference was attended at the highest level: politicians, captains of industry, responsible journalists, and international trade unionists. Harold Wilson and George Brown attended as leaders of the Labour Opposition. Their presence was one of the hopeful notes of the conference for they assured different members of the assembled company, including Fritz and George McRobie in a number of private conversations, that they were completely behind the coal industry's cause, that any future Labour Government would take this cause very seriously, and, in particular, that they understood the need to maintain a stable industry. They agreed that the current annual output figure of 200 million tons would be a level of output they would support as the desirable size of the industry.

The conference was one of the more positive highlights of the year. The other was the announcement of the appointment of Alf Robens as Deputy Chairman of the Board, to succeed James Bowman as Chairman in early 1961. Under Alf Robens, the atmosphere at the N.C.B. changed almost overnight. Robens, a charismatic and energetic figure, knew that he had a battle on his hands and was determined to make the most of it. He had the gift of recognizing those who would be useful to him and immediately took Fritz into his confidence. At last, after ten years in the wilderness, Fritz was to come into his own. Rather than being regarded merely as someone whose role was to stimulate discussion and provoke arguments around the Board table, he now became more or less an adviser to the Chairman, and a strong partnership was formed which was to last for nearly ten years. Fritz became utterly devoted to Robens and had nothing but praise for his new boss. Robens gave Fritz new confidence and in the dark days following Muschi's death and his adjustment to life without her, Robens kept Fritz's head above water. By the end of Robens's first year in office, just after Christmas, Fritz wrote to his mother: 'Since Wednesday I have been back at the office where all my ideas and suggestions are being taken up by everyone. The work of many years now actually seems to be about to become reality. That, of course, is fun. I get on very well with the Chairman.'

At home his devotion to Robens was ridiculed as was the newly found confidence that Robens gave him. Virginia was furious when one day she discovered that in her little notebook listing the top twenty records each week, Fritz had gone through each list carefully altering the title of one popular record at the time called 'Charmain' to 'Chairman'.

Even more annoying was his sudden habit of name-dropping. At every mention of a name in the headlines he would casually remark, 'Oh, look at this, he used to be a friend of mine,' or 'I knew him well during the war.' At other times there would be a few more details. 'Oh look at this picture of Harold Wilson: I remember when I met him at New College in the Senior Common Room where he was a don. Just a young fellow. He came to me and said he was going to give it up and go into politics. I must say I was amazed at his courage to give up such a safe and respectable career for the uncertainties of politics.' As Fritz and Muschi had rarely entertained while at Holcombe, these claims seemed very far-fetched to us. We eventually cured him by pointing to every eminent and unlikely name we saw, saying, 'A friend of yours in the paper again I see, Pop.'

It was not only his rising star at the Coal Board that kept Fritz going that first year after Muschi's death. His other interests (which will be dealt with more fully in subsequent chapters) were also beginning to take up more of his time. Since 1955 he had thought deeply about the links between economics and war, once more in the light of his concept of Buddhist and Gandhian economics. He had been appalled while in Burma to learn that both Britain and France had the atom bomb and had written to Muschi: 'I think that India, Burma and the other countries of South-East Asia are the only hope for the world. If they can keep independent of either the two great power blocs, Nehru and U Nu might introduce something new into the deadlock, a spiritual force that could "overcome the opposites". The fact that Britain and France are now also producing H Bombs is a clear demonstration to me that they cannot do it.'

Linking the problems of international affairs and international violence now that man had the atom bomb, to the problem of 'how to conduct economic affairs in a manner that is compatible with both permanence and peace', he came to the conclusion that, following Gandhi, 'it is also a problem of "non-violence", but a much more subtle one than the first.' These conclusions, published in an article called 'Non-Violent Economics' in August 1960 in the *Observer* brought together a number of threads he had been following since 1955.

A way of life that ever more rapidly depletes the power of earth to sustain it and piles up ever more insoluble problems for each succeeding generation can only be called 'violent'. It is not a way of life that one would like to see exported to countries not yet committed to it. Of course, it has its attractions. But this is not an argument in its favour any more than an individual's enjoyment of lavish living justifies him in squandering his own and other people's capital.

In short, man's urgent task is to discover a non-violent way in his economic as well as in his political life. It is obvious that the two are closely related. Both represent very real challenges to human goodwill, patience, and rationality. The real pessimists are those who declare it impossible even to make a start ...

Non-violence must permeate the whole of man's activities, if mankind is to be secure against a war of annihilation. Economics, like politics, must be led back to an acceptable philosophical base. Present day economics, while claiming to be ethically neutral, in fact propagates a philosophy of unlimited expansionism without any regard to the true and genuine needs of man which are limited.[1]

The article, which provoked quite a large post-bag, was Fritz's manifesto for the next stage of his life: not only to develop a non-violent economics but also to develop a non-violent way of life. The best teacher he knew was Gandhi, whose way of non-violence, *satyagraha,* he later described: 'It is a very, very tough one. To the cowards and so on he [Gandhi] would say, "Oh no you cannot be non-violent. You are not there yet. This is a higher state, not a lower state."' 'We are not here to be passive,' Fritz explained. 'We have to stand up. The Christian words "Do not resist evil," are not to be interpreted in this [passive] way.'[2]

Fritz understood this distinction although he was not a pacifist. 'I am perfectly willing to defend myself and my family,' he said. But he was an ardent peaceworker and fully supported the efforts of the C.N.D. campaigners, writing to his mother at the launch of the campaign in 1961: 'The sudden outbreak of sense under the otherwise not very estimable Bertrand Russell has pleased me. Best of all I would like to march with them to Trafalgar Square.'

In early 1961 he visited Poona for a week to address a seminar on 'Paths to Economic Growth' and was stimulated into thinking more and more about India's economic problems in the light of non-violence. At the same time he was engaged in writing a major paper on 'Socialisation in Britain'. This was the next step in his thinking about organizational structures and was a study of various forms of socialized industry in Britain, but it also contained Fritz's views of what he saw as authentic socialism, a view which did not conflict with his plea for a non-violent economics. Tracing the development of socialism from Robert Owen and Patrick Colquhoun he came to the conclusion that English socialism had a unique quality:

The great line of outstanding writers and artists who exercised a decisive influence upon the socialist movement is in itself sufficient indication that 'socialism' was by no means primarily concerned with economic matters. It was man's entire personality, his humanity, that was at stake; indeed, one might even say that this was a religious issue, a battle for the soul of man....

British socialism began, and is only to be understood, as a movement of protest and rejection. It set its face against the exploitation and pauperisation of the masses - an economic critique; against the degradation of the individual and deprivation of his rights - a political critique; against the uprooting and debasement of people and their standards - a social and cultural critique; and against the entire system of values of capitalist society - a predominantly religious and ethical critique. The purely technical economic motive, namely the desire to increase efficiency through nationalisation, which at the present time stands so much in the foreground, was originally and until quite recently of negligible significance.'[3]

Much of this paper bore the mark of a thorough acquaintance of the work of R.H. Tawney, whom Fritz greatly admired and who had, with Gandhi, greater influence than any other writer on his economic thinking.

With so much work on his hands Fritz began to get up at 6 a.m. again every morning so that he could give some time to Virginia and myself in the evening. Then in May he received another setback. He had decided that it would lighten Vreni's burdens if she could drive the car. The nearest shops were a mile away. On the third driving lesson, driving through the isolated country lanes, Vreni suddenly panicked and crashed full speed into a telegraph pole which collapsed under the impact of the accelerating car. She was unhurt but Fritz was in agony. He had broken two ribs and, to make matters worse, the ambulance could not be reached because the nearest telephone had been put out of order by the fall of the telegraph pole.

The accident had unforeseen reverberations which passed unnoticed by all but the principal players. Fritz, forcibly kept at home for a few days, was nursed tenderly by Vreni. Slowly his vulnerability and her care began to change their relationship. Autumn came. The question of Vreni's successor arose again. A lot of teasing went on over the supper table. 'Vreni will just have to marry one of the boys.' It seemed unthinkable that she should leave in the new year. Yet no alternative arrangements were made. Fritz just smiled.

On the last Sunday in January Fritz and I went to church together. Since my mother's death he had taken her place in the local Congregational church. It was a beautiful sunny winter morning and we walked the mile to church. On the way back we had almost reached home when he suddenly turned to me and said, 'Barbara, I have something very important to tell you.'

I am not given to second sight, nor had anything happened to give me cause to know at once what he was going to say. But before he had uttered another word I knew with horror that he was going to tell me that he was going to marry Vreni. I heard the words as an echo and could only ask, 'When?'

'Tomorrow,' came the unbelievable reply.

Until that moment I had thought of Vreni as a close friend and confidante. I could not believe that she would allow my father to betray my mother by letting him *really* love her. Anxiously I asked, 'Are you going to sleep with her?'

It was the only time my father ever turned on me in a sudden rage. 'Why don't you leave that to me,' he shouted. He had no understanding of what lay behind the question.

Consequently he was unprepared for the hostility that followed. He showed no psychological insight into the situation into which he had plunged the family. Out of loyalty to Vreni he gave no reassurance, particularly to me as I had been very close to my mother, that his remarriage did not eradicate his love for Muschi. He interpreted my hostility as jealousy. To make matters worse he rarely mentioned Muschi again, referring to her when he did as 'your mother'.

He was more careful and understanding with others. He tried to play down the normal feelings which he had for Vreni, preferring to let people think that the match was just a good solution to his difficulties. He was, after all, thirty years older than his new wife and was slightly embarrassed by the new life welling up inside him. He hid the truth from his mother, writing to her carefully:

Dearest little mother.

Do not fall off your chair when you read this letter. I have made Vreni Rosenberger my wife. It was an extremely difficult decision. The boys were very much in favour; Barbara greatly opposed, which tried me very much. Such a decision at my age, with open eyes without the tailwind of passion, with so much for and against, under pressure of time, against opposition from inside – oh dear, how strenuous, how exhausting! Now the agony of decision is over and I hope that my nearest and dearest will not let us both down in giving us their good wishes.

Last week, by the way, Vreni and I went to her parents in Switzerland. We were well received there. Vreni does me a remarkable amount of good; my worry was whether I would be able to be worthy of her honour in the time I have left. Who knows?

With heartfelt love, Fritz.

The force of passion was dulled only in so far as other considerations had been taken into account when making his decision. There was the difference in their ages. Fritz was aware that the chances of leaving a young widow behind him were high. More important were the differences in their interests and experience. Fritz was a man of the world, moving in circles to which Vreni had never had access and was not particularly anxious to experience. But he also had behind him inner struggles which had finally resolved themselves into a certainty about the purpose and direction of his life. Vreni had no such experience. She was still at the beginning of the journey. She looked to him as her guide and the director of her life. At first she was not aware how far he filled her inner space, how he became the meaning and purpose of her life. As she realized that she was only alive when he was at home, and ceased to exist the minute he left the house, she turned to him for advice and guidance on how to improve her character and develop inner strength. He offered her no help. He would merely smile benignly and say, 'To me you are a banquet.'

He no longer felt the need to include those around him on his spiritual journey. Muschi's death had given him the certainty to proceed alone. The 1950s had been a time of preparation both in his inner, and in his outer, public life. Muschi's death had been the final trial of his period of preparation. His marriage to Vreni coincided with a new, more outward-looking phase. Meditation, prayer and spiritual reading was something he could now do alone. For Vreni this was a great hardship. Not only did she genuinely want him to help her put her inner house in order, but she felt that by closing the door of his inner life he was denying her access to the most important part of his being.

There might have been several reasons for Fritz's reserve. He did not deny the anguish his turbulent quest had caused Muschi. He had tried to force his beliefs on her and in the end had seen her make her journey alone. He was also watching his children growing up. He saw how it was necessary to allow them to think for themselves and make their own discoveries and mistakes. In this sense Vreni was no different from John or Christian, all three were in their early twenties. Fritz may have seen that she must be allowed to develop and flower in her own way without his active guidance or interference. Perhaps too, his attitude reflected the change in himself at which he had been working so hard, that of a transition from a mind-centred life to a heart-centred life. Fritz's mind was a public place, his heart private. As the years wore on and he became a public figure, his mind fed him with information but his heart interpreted it so that all who heard him experienced a direct appeal to their hearts' understanding, not their cold intellectual assent.

So it became at home. While there was still tension after his marriage, he did not talk about what was going on in his heart; what he said, the way he talked, the emotion he began to convey, the warmth of his affection which he slowly allowed to the surface – all reflected the fruits of a new orientation. What he lacked in psychological understanding he made up for with patience and good-humoured affection, avoiding at all times situations where arguments could arise and, by his own example of gentle kindliness, gradually defused the tensions. It was an exercise in non-violence as harmony was restored and he attributed none of it to himself but always insisted that it was Vreni who was the 'good spirit in the house', 'a real treasure'.

After the first teething troubles of Fritz's marriage were over, life at Holcombe settled down to normal. John and Christian had left home, Virginia and I were still at school and a new arrival, Robert, was filling the house with the contented gurgles of a plump, happy baby. Fritz was thrilled with this new son, who was a sensitive and deep child, and reminded him of his brother Ernst. As Fritz became an increasingly public figure and spent less time at home with the family he appreciated the harmonious life at Holcombe more than ever before. 'Coming home is for me the best part of travelling,' he said. Although he was always under tremendous pressure from work the study door would be open for all to come and talk, or, as happened on many a winter evening, to play cards with him, listening to Donizetti's *La Sonambula*. In his wrought-iron lampstand was stuck a tiny bunch of plastic roses which he would ceremoniously present to the winner. The parchment shade of the lamp had a carefully folded piece of carbon paper stapled on to it to shade his eyes when reading, and on his head, keeping his hair out of his eyes, would be a white cloth cap which he also wore when making the bread every week. It was the most disgusting object, greasy inside and dusty yellow outside from the bouts of smoking that interspersed his frequent attempts at being a non-smoker.

Despite his new domestic responsibilities (there were to be three more children after Robert), Fritz worked harder in the 1960s than he had ever done before but he never lost the air of being relaxed and having time for all. As Christian and John left home and married, followed by Virginia and myself, we were replaced first by Robert and then Karen, a bundle of energy whose interest in everything around her contrasted with Robert's more sensitive and inward approach. Karen's birth coincided with that of Fritz's first grandchild, Vanessa, born to John and his wife Jill. It caused a sensation in Caterham when father and son came together to the Congregational Church some months later to have their daughters christened at the same service.

Robert was the only boy for some years. Vreni had another daughter in 1969, Nicola, by which time there were three more granddaughters. Fritz wrote to his mother: 'How this will all look in seventeen years' time is hard to imagine: six Schumacher girls aged between seventeen and twenty! One more than the five Dionesians!'

The only sign that Fritz was busier than ever was the change in his letters to his mother. They were no longer long and detailed accounts of his inner life, but short accounts of the children. As each baby came along he felt he had discovered anew the mystery of life and birth. He was struck each time with wonder at the new personality emerging, describing it to his mother as if he was experiencing it for the first time. For those old enough to observe his infatuations with his youngest child it was an amusing and endearing spectacle. For the child who had been replaced by the baby it was sometimes painful and bewildering. But Fritz did not possess that kind of sensitivity although he might have learned by the time the eighth child, James, made his appearance in 1974.

This full domestic life was kept very much apart from Fritz's professional life although he greatly enjoyed taking Vreni with him to some public functions. He was very proud of her youth and would point to his colleagues, gleefully saying, 'Look at old so-and-so. How can he bear to be stuck with that old creature.' Or, if the wife was attractive despite her thirty or so years' advantage of Vreni, he would say, 'How can she stand being stuck with that senile old fellow.' This was generally after a few glasses of wine when less charitable traits in his character began to emerge. Vreni was so modest she could never understand his pride and assumed that her only value to him was in keeping him comfortable. She suffered from feelings of inadequacy because she was unable to stimulate him mentally and asked him why he had not married someone more intellectual, as his colleagues had done. He was horrified. 'I would never have got any peace,' was his reply. Vreni gave him peace. Not that life is peaceful with four young children, but that was not the kind of peace Fritz meant. He meant freedom from the constant challenge of his professional life, from the high tension of intellectual exchange. Vreni's acceptance of his way of life, her care, and generous understanding that she had to share him with a wide public enabled him to be the relaxed and warm person he became as their relationship matured. She left him free to do the work he knew he must, although the cost to her was high.

21

A Fruitful Partnership

Muschi's death, Robens's arrival at the National Coal Board and Fritz's marriage to Vreni all combined to show Fritz that there were no longer any decisions to be made about his future. With the prospects of a new family on his hands he could not start taking risks and leave his job, nor did he want to, as Robens gave him justified hope that he was going to be taken seriously at last. With his domestic life settled, he could give himself up to his work again. As before, it took precedence over everything else. Not even a new young wife, suffering the first discomforts of pregnancy as well as the hostility of a teenage stepdaughter, kept him at home when work dictated otherwise. Before Vreni had time to accustom herself to her status as a mother, Fritz, utterly confident in her ability to cope, departed in November 1962 for a six-week visit to India. He counted on her support just as he had confidence that Robens, who was using him to the full, would nevertheless allow him leave of absence. Neither let him down.

Under Robens Fritz at last filled the role he had hoped to fill since his first job as Economic Adviser in 1946. This time he had the ear of someone who wanted and respected his advice. Fritz did not mind one bit that some of his colleagues resented his sudden move from the periphery to the centre of N.C.B. decision-making. His only concern was that everything he had worked on should at last see the light of day. That some Board members, particularly those who had been close to Bowman, felt Robens was creating a court atmosphere and that Fritz was known as the 'court jester' (a name originating from Bronowski) did not deter him. Robens was going to use him and that alone made it worth staying at the N.C.B.

The problems Robens inherited needed decisive and strong leadership. He became Chairman of the Board when Europe was preparing to shut down its coal industry for ever. But Robens was not the sort of man to preside over a declining industry. He understood at once that it was important to keep the coal industry going and used Fritz to feed him with all the arguments he needed in the battle to keep the industry not only alive but also thriving. Robens did the fighting, Fritz supplied the ammunition. Battles were fought on many fronts but throughout the decade under Robens the battle-cry was the same, '200 million tons output per annum.' The most important task was to try and convince the Government and public opinion that the coal industry was worth saving. The feeling throughout the industry was that this would be very hard under the Conservatives and that the only real hope was to get Labour back into office. Labour was traditionally the friend of the miner, Robens was a former leading Labour politician and Wilson and George Brown had pledged themselves to the 200 million tons target at the 1960 N.U.M. Study Conference, professing to have understood all the arguments put forward to maintain a strong coal industry.

When Labour won the general election in 1964 Fritz was therefore jubilant, particularly when, soon after taking office, George Brown issued a White Paper in which he upheld his pledges at the Study Conference of 1960, saying that the Government believed in a strong coal industry. But it soon became apparent that this assurance was not worth the paper it was written on. The Labour Government believed in cheap oil and in high technology nuclear energy. Bitterness between Wilson and Robens was increased by the frequent changes of the Minister of Power so that it was impossible for a proper working relationship with the Government to be established, let alone to achieve an understanding of the real issues. Wilson's Government, blinded by the benefits of short-term, cheap energy, turned their back on the people; blinded by the seductions of high technology they put their money into nuclear-powered stations and forced the pace of pit closures to accelerate. Life under Labour was far worse for the industry than under the Tories. Fritz felt disgusted and betrayed. He never trusted Wilson again and although he maintained his support for the Labour movement, declaring that his hand would wither if he ever voted Conservative, he no longer believed that the socialists in power were following the true path of socialism. The only advantage they had over the Tories was a greater concern for the fate and future of the redundant miners. Here the principles of socialism were allowed to play their part and money was available to ease the suffering of the unemployed and their families. Fritz, grieved by the social effects of the closures, travelled endlessly around the country trying to keep up the morale of the men and tried to liaise with the M.P.s of the worst-hit areas in preparation for the closures. But not even questions in the House from M.P.s such as Judith Hart, in whose Lanarkshire constituency all the pits were closed within a space of three years, could persuade the Government to think again.

The arguments with which Fritz furnished Robens, and which he himself put forward endlessly in lectures and articles, were basically the same as those he had put forward in the 1950s, only stronger. He pointed out the finite nature of the non-renewable energy resources and the foolishness of abandoning one major source just because another happened to be cheaper in the short term. With the formation of OPEC in 1960 Fritz had hoped that politicians would recognize that the Middle East would not supply the West with cheap oil for ever. Yet to his astonishment OPEC was not taken seriously at all by politicians or economists. 'They are beginning to recognize their strength,' Fritz insisted. 'When they see that their oil isn't going to last for ever, you can be sure that they will take action. They have no alternative. They won't want to go back to sand and camels.' Ridicule was the only response to this suggestion. Nor did politicians accept the political argument that it was dangerous to depend on the unstable Middle East. Not even the 1967 war seemed to bring this home. Fritz could not get across the fact that coal's inability to compete with oil was a short-term phenomenon, that as the oil sheiks saw that their oil supplies were limited, prices would rise and coal would once again become a viable alternative source of energy. And very few people understood the even longer-term factor – that as non-renewable sources of energy became increasingly depleted it would be vital to have every option at one's disposal. This long-term view was particularly important in the case of the coal industry. Of course, it would be extremely costly to keep the coal industry going until coal was competitive again but, in Fritz's view, this was precisely the sort of situation for which nationalization had been created. It was in the best interests of the nation to have a coal industry, even though it was not economic in the short term.

While everyone on the Board understood the effect that closure would have on the industry's ability to produce coal in the future, not all of them understood the reasons why this should cause the gravest concern to the nation. Some were not convinced by Fritz's predictions that oil prices would rise and that by the 1980s energy shortages would begin to be felt. Others believed in the power of science to find a solution. They held the view that world energy needs of the future would be met by nuclear energy. Only the social arguments for keeping the industry going united the Board.

To Fritz the failure of some Board members to understand the issues was cause for despair. The arguments were so obvious to him, the writing on the wall for industrial Europe so clear if the importance of coal was not understood, that he could only assume his colleagues lacked some essential mental equipment. Their faith in nuclear energy horrified him more than anything. He had been collecting statistics about nuclear energy since his first meeting on the subject three days after joining the coal industry and had watched its progress closely. There was no question in his mind that the impact it would have on the supply of energy in the 1960s, 1970s and 1980s would be negligible. Not only was it the wrong kind of energy, contributing only to base load electricity needs, but in percentage terms of total energy needs, its contribution was insignificant and would continue to remain so beyond the energy gap. To replace coal by nuclear energy just did not make economic sense. All the figures spoke against it.

I go and look at these vast buildings ... I reflect that they are as big as the Cathedral of Cologne which has taken many centuries to build. Well, this was built in as many years. A little human being looking at it is overpowered by the impression, but through the jaundiced eyes of an economist one wants to go a bit beyond this visual impression and work out how much it's worth in terms of fuel. Well, a station ... is likely to have a twenty-five year life, it's reckoned to have an annual output of about 1,000,000 tons of coal equivalent, so it's worth about 25 million tons of coal over its entire life. Well, of course, on these statistics we can forget it. If we shut a pit with 25 million tons of reserves it doesn't even get into the papers. Certainly not into the national papers.[1]

In fighting to keep a role for coal it was Coal Board policy to attack the nuclear option furiously with the economic arguments. But Fritz had deeper reservations about nuclear energy than the economic and practical objections he put forward. He had voiced these as early as 1955 in 'Economics in a Buddhist Country'.

It is already certain beyond any possibility of doubt that the 'Oil-Coal-Metal-Economies' cannot be anything else but a short abnormality in the history of mankind – because they are based on non-renewable resources and because being purely materialist, they recognize no limits. The frantic development of atomic energy shows that they know their fate and are now trying, through the application of ever increasing violence against nature, to escape it. Atomic energy for 'peaceful purposes' on a scale calculated to replace coal and oil, is a prospect even more appalling than the Atomic or Hydrogen bomb. For here unregenerate man is entering a territory which, to all those who have eyes to see, bears the warning sign 'Keep Out'.

A decade later none of these arguments had penetrated and as he watched the coal industry run down and the government contracts being given to the inexperienced atomic energy industry, he decided that the time had come to put the full story to the public. The opportunity came when he received an invitation to speak to the Clean Air Society, a society dedicated to fighting pollution. It was not pollution from coal that threatened the world, he told his audience. There was now an ultimate pollutant that threatened the whole world: from the nuclear energy industry. Backing his argument with more statistics and authoritative references than usual to give his argument credibility, he drew a grim picture of the dangers inherent in the production of nuclear energy, proclaiming that it was the ultimate expression of the violence of the materialistic rule of the religion of economics.

The furore that erupted the day after he had delivered his lecture took him completely by surprise. He was violently attacked in the House of Commons and his lecture condemned as irresponsible, chiefly by the Liberal M.P. for Orpington, Eric Lubbock, and the Minister of Power, Richard Marsh. I was at Holcombe that evening. As he came into the kitchen where we awaited him for supper, he wore the same expression of suppressed pain and suffering on his face as he had done some years earlier when he broke his ribs in the car accident with Vreni. He was bewildered and hurt. It seemed to him extraordinary that he should be so ferociously condemned for saying that the production of nuclear energy carried some terrifying potential dangers to mankind, especially as he knew – as he pointed out in a letter published in *The Times* a week later on October 25th, 1967 – that he was 'not alone in taking the view that – in the absence of necessity – even a small amount of genetic damage cannot be justified or excused by economic considerations.'

More expressions of support followed from many unexpected quarters. The most revealing was from a member of Harold Wilson's staff at 10 Downing Street who, having had access to many papers in possession of the Prime Minister that were utterly in agreement with the views Fritz had been expressing, was disgusted at the sheer hypocrisy of the Government's reaction to Fritz's lecture. The incident left Fritz with a hidden hostility towards his major critics and he was not sorry when Eric Lubbock lost his seat at Orpington in the next general election.

Without governmental support during the 1960s or public recognition of the importance of a strong coal industry, and with oil prices at levels tantamount to dumping, it became more important than ever to make the industry as efficient as possible and go all out for a massive sales drive. It was the opportunity for which Fritz had waited for over ten years and one by one his schemes and suggestions were put before Robens. In 1963 the suggestion he had made twelve years earlier, that there should be a completely new statistical approach, was taken up, and Fritz was appointed Director of Statistics in addition to his role as Economic Adviser.

Fritz was delighted with his appointment as Director of Statistics. He said to his new staff, 'I must have done something very good in my last life to have deserved this.' The work seemed to him to be pure joy. He lost no time in making changes so that statistics were no longer collected for their own sake but could give a clear picture of the state of the industry at a glance and could lead to action. He instituted a system of 'green papers' on which the key figures of the industry were circulated to all Board members and managers. He took great care not only with giving the maximum information with the minimum of figures, but also with the presentation of the statistics. He sent his statisticians out to comb the stationery shops of Victoria and further afield to find exactly the right green folders and paper he had in mind. Such was their admiration for their new Director that no one resented being used as errand boy. The whole department was behind him and worked willingly and hard. Fritz's method of handling them was still based on personal qualities rather than power. One member of the department, Brian Simpson, commented, 'He had one terrible, ghastly weakness ... he had rosy coloured spectacles. He could not believe people could be so stupid, particularly senior people.' But this was in fact his method of getting the best out of people. By giving the department the impression that he thought they were all great and far more capable than they thought they really were, Fritz gave them the feeling that they had something to live up to. Brian Simpson, however, learned from experience that Fritz did see the reality of people's faults. After Fritz took over the Statistics Department Simpson left for a year because of a personal conflict with another staff member. When the staff member in question left, Simpson reapplied to join the Statistics Department. At the interview Fritz smiled at him in his most charming way and said, 'I am glad to see that you have recovered from your illness.'

Fritz's main preoccupation in the Statistics Department was with devising methods of obtaining and presenting figures to show which areas in the Coal Board's activities needed attention. He distinguished between 'information for information', which showed what had happened but had no further interest, and 'information for action', which gave a picture of the movement in the industry and highlighted the areas where attention needed to be given. It needed skill and discernment to single out those figures which could 'sing' and to avoid obscuring their message with other figures. In the year of his appointment Fritz dramatically demonstrated his ability to make this discernment.

That year Fritz and several Board members accompanied Robens on a trip to Japan. Fritz enjoyed the trip hugely. He was very impressed with the cleanliness and industry of the Japanese and was charmed by the Geisha girls and tea ceremonies. When it came to going down a Japanese pit, however, he graciously declined, preferring to sit and enjoy a Japanese Garden while the rest of the party went underground. Later Robens asked Fritz why he had not wanted to view the Japanese pit. 'Well,' Fritz explained, 'I had a look at the safety statistics and it was clear that one in seven was injured every so many days so I came to the conclusion that it was not a risk I ought to take. And', he added, 'one man came up with his head bandaged.' This story would have been amusing had it not been for the fact that two weeks later an explosion in that very mine caused the death of 450 miners.

The task of the statistician, Fritz believed, was to produce figures that led to action. This required a certain change of image for the statistician. Their status should correspond to the key role they played in every part of the industry. With clear and useful statistics, Fritz could enter into the whole spectrum of coal extraction, transportation and sale and see where the problems lay. With this tool he could point to areas which previously had been the domain of men with particular expertise and experience such as mining engineers, geologists, and colliery managers, and alert them to problems they had not recognized.

This resulted in a number of battles. Mining engineers were not too keen on being told what to do by a remote figure in Hobart House. Fritz understood this and tried to let the figures do the talking. It was as clear to him in 1963 as in 1951, when he had written to his parents that, 'The most wonderful machines are of no use at all if the workers don't feel like working', that the maximization of output depended on the full utilization of the available cutting machines. It did not matter if the industry had the finest cutting machines in the world. If they were not cutting, then money was not coming into the till. The problem was pinpointing the most significant obstacles to continuous cutting.

Fritz was sure that factors other than the organizational and engineering difficulties were causing stoppages. The output statistics, which had been based on output per pit, covered too large and too diverse units to be useful indicators of where the bottlenecks were. Fritz's hunch was that the crucial statistic would be the coal faces themselves – tons per face per day: he homed in on details to verify his hunch – use of machinery, distribution of pit props, methods of working, shift patterns, shaft capacity, transport in the mines. The figures built up a picture which showed him that output was related to the length of the coal face. As soon as the length of a coal face dropped below a certain level, output per day fell considerably. The reason turned out to be simple. In a short coal face the miners had to spend more time cutting into the rock face at either end of the coal seam to allow space to turn their machines than they were able to spend actually moving along the face cutting the coal. He had quite a battle persuading the mine managers that faces under a critical length should not be opened up.

He did not even have the full support of the Board, some of whom disputed the significance of his tons per face per day statistic. Eventually he achieved his aims by subtle methods. He insisted only that a record should be kept of all working coal faces where output was less than about 200 tons a day. This record should be open at all times for visiting officials from Headquarters who could ask the Pit Managers to justify continuing to work on an unproductive face. The point was made without a public showdown. Short faces were soon eliminated. In 1966 forty-three per cent of coal faces produced less than 200 tons a day and together accounted for less than ten per cent of total output. Between 1966 and 1968-9, the number of faces worked fell from 2,000 to 649, whereas output fell only from 174 million tons to 109 million tons. Colleagues in the Statistics Department marvelled and commented that when Fritz wanted his way, 'Machiavelli wouldn't have stood an earthly.'

He came up with other astonishing conclusions in the area of safety. Accidents at the pits were generally put down to geological factors. This would have suggested a certain randomness in the figures for accidents above and below ground but Fritz found that far from randomness there was a perfect correlation between accidents at the pit head and in the pit itself. Pits with high accident levels below ground also had high accident levels above ground. Good records below ground were similarly good above ground and the same correlation could be found all along the spectrum from the good pits to the bad pits. This pointed inescapably to the conclusion that accidents were not largely a factor of geology but a function of management, high standards and care. Accidents above the ground were caused by sloppy, messy conditions, in other words, bad management. The fact that such pits also had high below-ground accident levels suggested that standards might be similarly low in the pit itself. The Board, however, did not at the time take much notice of this discovery.

The close contact Fritz had with the actual workings of the industry after 1963 deepened his understanding of the needs that had to be recognized in restructuring the organization. When, in 1965, a committee was set up under the chairmanship of Harry Collins to make recommendations for streamlining the industry Fritz was very glad to serve on it and again put before the committee ideas which he had worked on in the 1950s. The principles of large-scale organization, which had developed out of his thinking on ownership, the function of work, and the necessity for freedom and control in industry, played an important part in the reshaping of the coal industry. His reorganization of the Statistics Department was already a major contribution towards unobtrusive control. The committee then went further in removing some of the bureaucracy that had developed over the years, reducing the management tiers from five to three and so shortening the lines of command throughout the industry. This helped create what Fritz felt to be of fundamental importance in large-scale organization, namely the possibility of greater freedom for initiative at lower levels in the industry. 'If they can do the job within their own freedom and responsibility,' he wrote, 'let them do it; take the risk. This is the only way to safeguard human dignity, but also, in the end, to get the best performance out of people.'[2]

Although his Area Bank Accounts idea of 1958 was not resurrected, the areas were organized into quasi-firms, including not only the deep mining function of the Board but also its subsidiary industries. Each quasi-firm had its own balance sheet which was carried forward each year so that it was very clear whether or not it was performing satisfactorily, and it was left alone unless its performance was not up to scratch. Those who performed well were given greater responsibility, those who did not perform adequately had to have a valid reason for not doing so if they were to be allowed to continue holding the responsibilities which they had been given.

These changes combined both tighter control, by shortening the lines of command, and greater freedom at the day-to-day level of operations. For this to work satisfactorily Fritz said there was a further principle which the industry would have to follow. He called it the principle of the Middle Axiom. It was not something which could be written into the instructions on how to reorganize the Board, for it meant wisdom and understanding the Buddhist Middle Way. It was the art of transmitting instructions and orders without appearing to diminish the freedom of those under command. In other words, the art of reconciling the irreconcilable opposites of the need for freedom in the organization and the need for control. Fritz thought the answer, in so far as it could be laid down, lay in the sort of action he had taken to implement his recommendations about coal face length. Another example occurred when Fritz wanted to improve the safety measures at the collieries. Left to themselves, some Area Managers would let things slip, yet direct orders from the Board would lead to all sorts of problems. Fritz's solution was to ask the Area Managers to submit statistics about their safety standards. With sufficient time to submit their figures, they would be able to tighten up on those aspects which they had neglected before completing the survey. Thus action was achieved without exhortation or orders from above. With his statisticians he called the method 'Impact Statistics'. To his family he said, 'You must be as cunning as a serpent and as innocent as a dove.'

22

---∞∞∞---

Small Talk

As an economist Fritz had one great handicap, for which Beveridge bears not a little responsibility: he was concerned more about people than efficiency. 'Never forget that your first responsibility is to the men,' he told George McRobie when he joined him at Hobart House in 1956, and his own feelings of responsibility drove him on to think about organizational structure, nationalization and work with the needs of working men firmly in the forefront of his schemes.

Beveridge, and then Buddhism and Burma. Beveridge taught him how to identify with the needy and the working people, Buddhism taught him that the purpose of work was more than fulfilling material needs, that its function was also the development of human potential and man's relationship with his fellow beings and towards God, and Burma showed him that the assumptions he had made as an economist did not accommodate this new understanding.

Shortly after his return from Burma in 1955 he described the impact of Burma on his economic thinking to his sister Elisabeth.

Now I have been back in my office for two months and see the world through slightly Burmese tinted spectacles. In any event it has been a great gain for me to have been 'out there' and to have seen that there is another way. But there arise weighty problems for an economist and business man. In Burma the people are so happy because they have no wants:

they have so much time because they have no labour saving machinery and methods; their heads and hearts are kept free for inner matters because they are not obsessed with outer things. What can an economist do when his job is to double the 'social product', the so-called standard of living every twenty-five years? Oh dear, oh dear, the Burmese think we are all completely mad – and they would like to acquire as many of the Western 'achievements' for themselves as quickly as possible.

He had already shown what he thought the task of a Burmese economist should be with his paper 'Economics in a Buddhist Country', but his advice to the Burmese to promote their cottage industries and develop as much self-sufficiency as possible before Western economics ruined both their inner and outer way of life had not been received with much enthusiasm. It did not deter him from continuing to work on this idea on his return to England, using every opportunity to lecture about his Burmese experience and its implications on Western aid to the 'underdeveloped' countries. His ideas never failed to have a dramatic impact. They were not only a critique of the way in which the West was trying to help the poor of the world, but also of Western economic life itself. Those who believed they were doing good works did not take kindly to being told that they would do better to leave well alone. Some of his audience were shocked at his message, as the Secretary to the National Peace Council, Eric Baker, wrote to Fritz after a talk in October 1955:

Quite obviously the criticisms which you had to make of technical assistance as you have seen it at work in Burma were quite new to most of the people there, and it was a rude shock to their energetic sympathy for the Burmans to be made to stop and think out whether they were in fact taking the best way of helping them. That it was a shock to them was quite clear from the fact that almost all the questioners patently misunderstood what you were trying to say. Quite clearly they would go home and worry over it for some time yet.

313

Through such thought-provoking talks Fritz's name became known among circles concerned with the developing countries, and in July 1958 he was introduced to a leading Indian disciple of Gandhi's, Jayaprakash Narayan, who was on a visit to London. It was the beginning of a long friendship. J.P., as he was known, recognized in Fritz a kindred spirit, and a man who could help India.

In the spring of 1959 Arthur Koestler wrote three articles about Indian poverty and the Bhoodan movement for the *Observer*. The Bhoodan movement was trying to create spiritual and economic regeneration amongst the Indian people and was organized by leading Indian Gandhians, amongst whom were Jayaprakash Narayan and a mystic, Vinoba Bhave, whom Koestler described as 'the last of the Saints'. Vinoba had undertaken to walk from village to village all over India persuading rich landowners to give up a proportion of their land to the poor, a campaign which seemed to be achieving remarkable success as a result of his sincerity and evident holiness. The response provoked by the articles persuaded David Astor, then Editor of the *Observer*, to call a meeting of some of those who had expressed interest in helping the Bhoodan movement and in June 1959, under the guidance of a friend and writer on South African affairs, Mary Benson, 'British Bhoodan' was founded.

Among those invited to meet with David Astor in his office were Ernest Bader of the Scott Bader Commonwealth, who had been in India a year or so earlier and had seen Vinoba at work, Donald Groom, a Quaker who had worked with Vinoba for three years, Lady Isobel Cripps, Mary Benson, John Kane, and Fritz. Fritz was invited because of his experience in Burma and his challenging views on economic aid to the poor countries of the East. The Bhoodan movement interested him very much and he explained to the assembled company how the conventional approach to overseas aid – the raising of national income – did not necessarily help people in a country like India but could indeed make them poorer by giving them Western tastes. He thought a movement like Bhoodan could cut through conventional thinking which held that help could only be given through the banking system to large projects. It could show that simple assistance like providing a village with a

314

pump could make a significant impact on a village development scheme.

The meeting ended without any specific agreement on action but unanimous agreement that their support for Indian Bhoodan should be directed by those at the grass roots of the movement, namely the Indian leaders themselves, and a letter pledging support and asking for guidance was drafted to J.P. Narayan.

Nothing very much was achieved by British Bhoodan but its existence was of great significance for Fritz's life. First of all it brought him together with Ernest Bader. Bader was a Swiss industrialist who had emigrated to England as a young man before the First World War. He had been determined not to become a wage slave but to be responsible for his own life and by the end of the Second World War had become a very successful and wealthy businessman. It then occurred to him that his success was dependent on the very slavery that he had vowed to avoid for himself and, unable to live with this contradiction, decided to take a courageous and revolutionary step: he handed his company over to his employees. Scott Bader and Co. Ltd became the Scott Bader Commonwealth, a pioneering common ownership firm.

Ernest Bader was of great interest to Fritz for two reasons, apart from the fact that Fritz liked the dynamic old man whose fiery nature was full of contradictions. (Fritz described him as very militant pacifist, a very dictatorial democrat, a very intelligent ass and an assinine genius.)[1] He felt that Ernest Bader's story was a great one, not because of his business success but 'because when someone wakes up "Nel mezzo del cammin di nostra vita" ... [it] is always a great story. This is what human life is about, and that he is prepared to be generous and not clinging, abandoning his ownership: that is a great story.' For this reason alone he would have been glad to meet Bader, but it was also an important encounter because of his interest in the implications of ownership and the structure of socialized industries. The Scott Bader Commonwealth added a new dimension to the concept of non-private ownership. In this model the workers themselves were the owners, they benefited directly from the profits which, after a proportion had been taken for further development of the firm, were divided equally between the owner-workers and charity. In the Scott Bader Commonwealth welfare was not a handout from above, it was administered by the workers themselves. It seemed an ideal answer to the problem of private industry and the all-pervading profit motive.

Bader recognized that Fritz was a man of integrity and, in his impulsive way, immediately tried to snap him up for Scott Bader. Fritz was a little more cautious but he kept in close touch with Bader, studied the Commonwealth for his paper on 'Socialisation in Great Britain' and eventually, in 1963, joined the Trustees of the Company after forging a more permanent link with Ernest Bader by asking him to become Robert's godfather.

Friendship with Ernest Bader was an important consequence of the meeting in David Astor's office, but more significant still was the connection with India. In November 1959 J.P. Narayan came to England again. A month earlier he had arranged the publication in India of 'Economics in a Buddhist Country' under the title *Towards a Statute of Liberation* and reported to Fritz that it had been favourably received by many Indians. It was the beginning of a process in which Fritz found himself explaining to Indians, including Gandhians, the real meaning of Gandhi's economics, the concepts of *Swadeshi* and *Khaddar* and their practical application. In this process Fritz was himself led towards a completely new understanding of economic development and for this reason would have accepted Narayan's invitation to go to India in 1960 had it not been for Muschi's illness and eventual death.

Even without the immediate possibility of a visit to India on the horizon, Fritz continued to keep in touch with J.P. The Bhoodan movement was encountering a number of problems and much of the land that had been redistributed had remained unused and undeveloped by the villagers. The urban Bhoodan movement had even greater problems and J.P. appealed to Fritz again to come and help them to interpret the words of Gandhi in a practical and dynamic way for the poor of India.

Fritz's domestic situation did not allow him to contemplate a prolonged visit but in January 1961, leaving the children in Vreni's capable hands, he eventually paid a flying visit to Poona to speak at an International Seminar on 'Paths to

Economic Growth'. It was his first experience of real, devastating poverty, quite different from his trip to Burma where the simplicity, cheerfulness and rich inner life of the people had belied the poverty indicated in the statistics. In India he saw despair, a complete collapse of spirit, of the soul of India. He spoke passionately and urgently, developing all the themes on which he had worked in the past five or more years. He attacked the Western concept of economic growth, pointing out that for reasons of energy consumption alone it would not be possible for the whole world to achieve the level of prosperity and consumption of the West. He attacked economists such as W.W. Rostow and his 'take-off into self sustained growth' as irrelevant to the realities of the developing countries; he spoke out against the commonly held view that economic development could only be valid when it was synonymous with Westernization. Again and again he returned to the people of India themselves, asking:

> Why is it that the people are not helping themselves? What has come over them? On the whole, throughout history, all healthy societies have managed to solve their problem of existence and always with something to spare for culture. Grinding poverty with malnutrition and degradation, with apathy and despair, as a permanent condition of millions of people, not as a result of war or natural catastrophe – this is the most abnormal and, historically speaking, an unheard-of phenomenon. All peoples – with exceptions that merely prove the rule – have always known how to help themselves, they have always *discovered a pattern of living which fitted their peculiar* natural surrounding . . .[2]

In searching for an answer to this question Fritz looked back ten years to his daily train journey to London when he had first begun his enormous re-education programme. He recalled one of the first books he had read then: Prescott's *Conquest of Mexico*. There perhaps lay an answer: 'Now I shall venture to suggest the reply that the cause lies in the impact of the modern West upon these societies and populations. The paralysis or apathy . . . is similar to the paralysis of the Aztecs when they met Cortes and his men sitting on the backs of horses and equipped with firearms. It was not the power of the Spaniards that destroyed the Aztec Empire but the disbelief of the Aztecs in themselves.'

The impact of the West, Fritz continued, was not merely fatal in its destruction of India's belief in itself but compounded itself in the completely misguided attempt at aid. The transfer of Western methods, modern transport systems, and high technology merely served to make the problems all the more devastating by creating a dual economy of a small Westernized sector within an ever-deteriorating morass of traditional society. The answer was not to speed up the expansion of the Western sector, which in itself caused the sickness of the traditional sector, but to go to the aid of the vast traditional sector. 'Help those who need it most,' and 'Find out what the people are doing and help them to do it better,' were the two slogans Fritz offered those concerned with the development of their country. The traditional body had to be protected from the Westernized sector. Modern factories, even if located in areas of poverty and unemployment, did not help if they depended on materials and machinery from another district. The effect of a modern factory was not to create incomes for the mass of the people but to put out of work small local craftsmen who could not compete with cheap mass produced goods. Ultimately the effect was greater poverty because by destroying the modest income of local craftsmen, the factory's output thereby destroyed its own markets.

It was only after his return from India that Fritz, still very much preoccupied by the tremendous problems he had glimpsed, began to grope towards ideas that eventually were to contain, to his mind, the solution to the problem of poverty. He tried to penetrate to the very roots of the problem. India seemed to be a dying society, not an emerging one, dying not only economically but also culturally. The two were clearly not unconnected. Fritz realized that culture and intellectual activity could only flourish in a society that was more than purely agricultural. Development was not a question of material wealth so much as intellectual or cultural achievement which stimulated and fertilized economic achievement. He put these ideas clearly in a letter to Shri Shankarrao Deo, an Indian working at the Gandhian Institute of Studies at Varanasi:

What I had in mind when talking of intellectual starvation was first of all the dying away of non-agricultural production in rural areas and the resulting impoverishment of the whole local community both materially and in terms of job opportunities. It seems to me significant that in the Christian tradition we talk of the 'City of God', never of the village of God. Human life, it would seem, can come to a full flowering only when it ceases to be *purely* agricultural, that is when cities are founded in which an intense intellectual life can develop. These cities offer both opportunity (as symbolised by Jerusalem) and temptation (as symbolised by Babylon). Both the best that human nature is capable of and the worst comes from the city, never from purely agricultural population. Village life, therefore, it seems to me, must be closely connected with town life, and by 'town' I do not mean vast conurbations of the modern type.

The question, therefore, was how to upgrade village life, how to inject culture, in its broadest definitions of non-agricultural activity, into rural India. With this structural concept in mind, Fritz began to think more deeply about the question of technology and technology transfer, and its implications for job creation. 'What', he asked 'is the chance of providing modern factory employment for all or most of these people who are hanging around the factory gates, hoping against hope?' The answer hinged on the cost of creating each work place, which depended on the technology used. He saw at once that the cost was too high for the poverty-stricken Indians to create mass employment if it was to rely on modern technology. Fritz suggested that a formula which would determine the level of technology, and therefore the cost of each job affordable by a given society, was related to the average income per head of the working population. In England, for example, in the early 1960s, one could roughly say that the average (national) income per head was about £1,000 per annum. So was the average capital cost per work place. In India, on the other hand, an investment of £1,000 represented perhaps twenty or thirty years' income of one (average) man. Therefore the cost per work place in India should be one twentieth or one thirtieth of that of an English work place.

Fritz concluded:

> The upshot of this analysis can be stated quite simply and is in line with actual historical experience. Economic development is obviously impossible without the introduction of 'better methods', 'higher technology', 'improved equipment' – call it what you like. But the degree of 'betterment' or 'improvement' must be such that the great mass of producers upon whom the survival of the country depends, can – so to speak – keep in touch with it. The steps must be small, so that they produce stimulation and not discouragement. In terms of capital expenditure, the improved method, the higher technology, must be *accessible* to the majority of existing producers, even if only a minority will actually have the drive to reach out for it. Intellectually, the better method must equally be *accessible* to the average man without a college education. All development, like all learning, is a process of stretching. If you attempt to stretch too much, you get a rupture instead of a stretch, or you lose contact and nothing happens at all.

With the consideration of the cost per work place and its implications for the level of technology employed, Fritz had moved a long way from the protection of cottage industries which he had advocated in Burma. He still insisted that it was essential to protect indigenous production from Western mass-produced goods but he had not yet solved the problem of how to achieve, in Gandhi's words, 'Production by the masses rather than mass production'. For this he needed to return to India for a slightly longer spell. In early 1962, no longer burdened by the worry of domestic arrangements after his marriage to Vreni, Fritz at last felt free to contemplate a return to India. It was arranged for November of that year.

It was a strenuous trip but proved to be another turning point in Fritz's life. He travelled the continent of India day in and day out, seeing sights which filled him with sadness and wonder. He was struck by the aristocratic appearance of so many Indians and found it hard to understand how they could have fallen to such depths. But his contact with administrators and government officials soon gave him an answer to why everything seemed so hopelessly chaotic. He was taken from one village to another. He spent some days talking with Vinoba Bhave, but the two men must have had opposing signs in their horoscopes for Fritz, though respecting Vinoba's work, was not drawn to his personality. He was shown humble rural industries and high technology aid projects so starkly in contrast with each other that suddenly it was as if a light went on in his mind. He looked at the simple potter, or weaver toiling with incredible patience at his craft with the most humble and often quite inadequate tools, and then he watched the sophisticated factory machinery rolling out the same products. At one such ceramics factory he began to talk to a young Indian minding a machine. He had come from a nearby village to train in the new factory. 'What will you do when you have finished training?' Fritz asked him. 'Start your own business?' The young man stared at him. 'How could I possibly do that?' he replied. 'I shall go to the town and look for a job.' And Fritz thought of the thousands of pavement dwellers all over Indian towns and cities, all on the same search. Some might be trained as this young man was, but none of them would ever have the capital to make use of such skills. Then it all clicked into place, the need for masses of jobs, the ratio of income to cost per work place, the destructive effect of modern technology on the stagnating hinterland of India where the traditional way of life was no longer a living healthy fabric but was rotting, dying, and hopeless. He had almost reached this point the year before when he had written that technology and skills must be accessible to those who needed it, but the real evidence came then. What was needed was a level of technology better than the simple methods used in the rural hinterland, more productive than the traditional tools, but far simpler and less capital intensive than the modern technology imported from the West. What was needed was an intermediate level of technology.

Fritz lost no time in discussing this new concept with the Indian planners whom he had come primarily to advise on that 1962 trip. The Gandhians among them recognized at once the sense in what he was saying. Great plans were made to start development projects all over India, concentrating on an upgraded level of technology that could help uneducated villagers to improve their productivity by steps. Fritz was acclaimed as the man who could interpret Gandhi to the Indians. He had taken Gandhi's ideas and formulated them in a practical, comprehensive way that seemed utterly relevant to India's needs, which gave hope and new energy to a gigantic task.

On his return to England Fritz discussed his ideas with friends and colleagues. At the Coal Board George McRobie was one of the first to act as a sounding board for the concept of intermediate technology. In 1960 when Fritz had discussed leaving the Board for a post in India he had suggested that George go with him. Both men were very much involved in the problems of India. There were others too. Since the days of British Bhoodan, Fritz had become more involved with a group called the African Development Trust and had become one of their trustees together with Mary Benson, Arthur Gaitskell, Mr and Mrs Raven, Christopher Cadbury, Michael Scott and Charles Brook-Smith, all very experienced in the problems of developing countries. The A.D.T. were primarily engaged in supporting the efforts of Guy Clutton-Brock in building up a multi-racial community project around an Anglican Mission Farm in Rhodesia and other similar initiatives in Malawi, Botswana, Tanzania and Zambia. Fritz's ideas were relevant to their work too, and provided Fritz with the opportunity to work out and polish his new concept for its public launching. In late 1963 the Secretary of A.D.T., Peter Kuenstler, left suddenly for a post with the United Nations and a new Secretary, Julia Canning Cook, was appointed. She was the sort of woman to whom Fritz felt instantly attracted; dynamic, intelligent, experienced and instinctively able to understand what he was saying. It was the beginning of a very fruitful partnership and close friendship.

As yet there had been no opportunity to do something really practical about the idea of 'intermediate technology' and anyway Fritz's life at the National Coal Board had taken on a new and busy turn with the exciting new partnership he had formed with Robens. 1963 was the year in which his responsibilities were increased with his appointment as Director of Statistics. He was also travelling all over Europe defending the coal industry from the general attack on coal, which was not confined to Britain but was common to other European coal producers. On one such trip he received an encouraging sign of public recognition from the Technical University of Clausthal in Germany, which awarded him the Honorary Degree of Doctor of Science. Thenceforth he was known as Dr Schumacher, one of the few academic doctors who have never obtained a degree. With this new burst of activity Fritz could no longer contemplate taking on the sort of advisory role in India that had attracted him a few years earlier. He was delighted therefore when George McRobie decided to go to India for six months in 1964 to inject a bit of dynamism into the introduction of intermediate levels of technology in India and generally assess how things were progressing since the resolutions taken at the Planning Conference Fritz had attended in 1962. The reports coming back had not been too promising.

Fritz stood once more on the sort of threshold he had had to cross on several occasions before in his life. He had conceived another of his world improvement plans and the time had come to see that it was implemented. The Indians' recognition and acknowledgment of the importance of his idea had proved its applicability. It was time to go to the highest level to sell the idea to policy makers throughout the world.

The opportunity arose in September 1964 at a conference in Cambridge attended by some of the world's top economists, among them Fritz's old colleagues of Oxford days, Tommy Balogh and Nicki Kaldor. Fritz prepared his paper very carefully, giving the economic argument for an intermediate level of technology in language to which his august colleagues could relate. He named the concept simply 'Intermediate Technology'. When he had delivered his address there was uproar. Fritz's ideas were so far from the conventional economic theories of the day that they were rejected out of hand. For two days Fritz's paper dominated the conference. Most vociferous amongst its critics was Nicki Kaldor. Fritz left with little doubt that his colleagues amongst the economists were not going to help him change the world.

The vehemence of the attack he received in Cambridge did not discourage him from his efforts. Rather, it reaffirmed his severe criticism of economists and economics as it was practised in the West. More discouraging was George McRobie's report on his return from India. There was little actual work going on in India, he told Fritz. One of the reasons was that they had no real concept of what intermediate technology was. They did not know where to obtain it and could think only in terms of crudifying existing sophisticated processes, which had led to the widespread belief that intermediate technology was something inferior, something second best.

About this time Vreni, beginning to become aware of her dependence on Fritz, realized that she must put her life on more solid foundations if she was to survive the increasingly frequent lonely evenings and periods when Fritz was travelling, lecturing on Coal Board business or on economic development. One evening, as soon as he was home, she settled herself in her usual position down at his feet in the study. The gas fire was on and he sat in his armchair next to his laden bookshelves. His hair was beginning to grey now at the temples, and his suit jacket, hanging on a peg on the door, had been replaced by a comfortable woollen cardigan. Vreni, black curls bobbing in her anxiety, put her problem to him and asked whether she could undertake some form of training so that she could have her own life and career to occupy her. She suggested nursing. Fritz listened seriously and thoughtfully. 'Of course you must if you feel that is what you want,' he said finally. 'We will make all the necessary arrangements.' Then he added, 'But, please wait a bit until I have established "intermediate technology".' It was the nearest he ever got to admitting that his whole success depended on the undemanding care of his wife at home. Vreni abandoned her idea of a career.

After the Cambridge furore and ensuing publicity, Fritz and George decided to pay a call on Barbara Castle, Minister of the recently created Ministry of Overseas Development. She received them warmly and her sharp mind had no difficulty in understanding the gist and the validity of Fritz's argument. She said that if the Ministry could be shown the demand for such an intermediate level of technology they would fill it. But, in fact, this reply was as much of a rejection as the Cambridge economists' fury. The millions of peasants throughout the world who needed help had never heard of intermediate technology. They could not possibly begin to demand it without a massive education and publicity campaign, and for this Fritz needed money.

Having failed to convert or convince the academics or the

politicians, Fritz turned next to the people. Once again it was David Astor who had a hand in the breakthrough. He asked Fritz to write an article for the *Observer* on intermediate technology. Fritz called it 'How to Help them Help themselves'. Week after week passed and the article did not appear. Eventually Fritz lost patience. He wrote a letter to the *Observer* saying, 'My usual fee for an article written on request and not published within six months is one hundred guineas.' Within a week the hundred guineas arrived in the post and no article appeared.

Now Fritz began to feel action was urgent. One fine but freezing spring morning he rang Julia Canning Cook. After lunch he took her by the arm and, propelling her up and down St James's Park, talked at her for several hours. Julia felt that for most of the time she need not have been there. He was not interested in her, merely in a listening post. At last he came to the point. 'I want to leave the Coal Board,' he said. 'I want to concentrate my efforts on Intermediate Technology which I believe is crucial for the future.' Addressing Julia directly at last he asked her, 'How can you guarantee to create an organization that will support me and my two small children and household?' Julia's answer was as blunt as his question, 'No way. You have to do an act of faith the same as the rest of us.'

Fritz was not yet ready for that act of faith, although Julia felt that he had made up his mind to leave the Coal Board as soon as he found a cushion to soften the financial responsibilities he still had. In the event he was not called upon to make the act of faith at that point. For another five years Robens agreed to supply the cushion, provided that Fritz stayed at the Coal Board. He allowed Fritz as much time as he needed for intermediate technology matters, knowing that even on short time Fritz would serve him with diligence and commitment.

There was still a problem of money, to give publicity to the concept of intermediate technology. Then, one Sunday morning in August 1965, Fritz opened his *Observer* and found his article on Intermediate Technology on the front page of the review section. The response that followed was tremendous. The letters pouring in showed Fritz that he had struck a chord in the hearts of many people who were concerned about the problem of world poverty. It struck him that if those with power and influence were not prepared to come to the aid of the poor, then perhaps ordinary people would. George McRobie agreed with him and suggested that some of those who had expressed interest should be called together to discuss practical action. It was George's last task before returning to India to convene the meeting at the offices of the Overseas Development Institute in Piccadilly. His suggestion proved successful. After two meetings, attended by people from a number of different disciplines, it was decided to form a group with a secretary and each person present handed over five pounds towards the cost. Julia Canning Cook, who attended those first meetings, agreed to act as midwife to the infant and the Intermediate Technology Development Group was born and housed in the offices of the A.D.T. at Hop Gardens.

The terms of reference of the new group were summed up in the slogan Fritz had coined in 1961: 'Find out what the people are doing and help them to do it better.' A worldwide network of individuals and projects was soon established which showed very clearly both the need for and the existence of a technology more appropriate to the needs of the poor. Fritz's hundred guineas from the *Observer* article helped to fund a publication bringing together information about the equipment that was available for the small-scale farmer and craftsman. The demand for this modest guide led to a more ambitious publication: a buyers' guide for small-scale equipment. It was called *Tools for Progress*. By this time the group was beginning to grow. It had moved to King Street in Covent Garden and had half a dozen members of staff, some paid, some more or less voluntary workers.

The history of the Intermediate Technology Development Group is one of tremendous response to a good idea, of how, when the seed of the idea fell on good ground, it grew and yielded fruit a hundredfold. From the buyers' guide, grew the attempt to fill the gaps in technology that obviously existed. Fritz's idea was not to dredge up nineteenth-century technology but to use the best of twentieth-century knowledge and techniques and apply them to creating new and simple methods. Advisory groups were set up to work on building methods and materials, agriculture, water provision, small industry, medicine, education – the list went on growing as

more specialists became interested in applying the concept of
intermediate technology in their field of interest. Fritz's idea
was to use the skills of students and the resources of university
departments, particularly in the engineering faculties, to develop new technologies. He saw it growing as a source of Ph.D.
subjects for students and practical help for the group.

Once it had got going, the Intermediate Technology Development Group took off on a life of its own, so that today its
problem has become its unwieldy size. It is not the place of this
book to trace this development in detail. It is, however, relevant to trace Fritz's involvement. His role very soon became
largely twofold, to raise money and to sort out personal problems. As the group's activities expanded, the need for funds
naturally grew and Fritz spent a great deal of time cap in hand.
It was not a task he enjoyed nor one that became less pressing
as the group's annual financial needs reached a quarter of a
million pounds. He wanted to make as many of its operations
as self-financing as possible, selling publications, setting up
independent groups throughout the world with I.T.D.G. acting only as the centre of the great net, putting people in touch
with each other but letting them do their own work. As the
group expanded, so did the number of independent-minded
and creative staff, and the group was rarely without tensions.
Fritz was called in frequently to sort out crises caused by rows
in the office. Although he was not involved with the day-to-
day running of the group he was a father-figure to all those
involved, there to listen to their problems, give advice, guide
their thinking and smooth over clashes of personality. Fritz
was very good at being the peacemaker. He was less accomplished at hiring and firing. Personnel often tended to select
him rather than the other way round. If he was approached by
someone with enthusiasm and a bit of know-how Fritz instantly recognized the positive qualities in his would-be employee and as often as not a niche was found. Fritz's positive
personality, always seeing the best in everyone he worked with,
generally produced the best out of these employees, but away
from his direct influence their less positive attributes soon
became apparent, and it was not obvious to all why Fritz might
have chosen some of his colleagues. Occasionally it became
necessary to get rid of someone who proved to be a disaster

and whose faults the group, with its slender resources and ever empty bank balance, could no longer afford to accommodate. Such a problem occurred very early on in the group's life when it had only three employees. Fritz could not bring himself to act decisively and tried every way he could think of to get the unfortunate man to recognize his failings and resign. This gentle method failed to achieve the desired result and tempers began to get very frayed at the office until a member of the group's council took the matter into his own hands and for the first time an employee of I.T.D.G. was dismissed. Fritz was relieved but unhappy. He had wanted to avoid inflicting the humiliation of dismissal on a person of good will. Had it been at the Coal Board he could have just been 'moved sideways', but with a staff of three – well, what could one do?

The foundations of the Intermediate Technology Development Group at last enabled Fritz to implement one of his world improvement plans and eventually affect thinking on the tremendous problem of world poverty. Even Nicki Kaldor, one of his strongest critics, now goes so far as to say that there is value in the concept of intermediate technology. It represented a profound change in Fritz's personal development. He had spent many lonely years in which the solutions he had proposed for major problems in the world had remained unrecognized, or too controversial to be acceptable to those who had the power to implement them. Keynes, Stafford Cripps, Cecil Weir, the Coal Board, the Burmese Government, the Indian Government, the economists of the 1960s and the Ministry of Overseas Development, all of these ultimately had failed him and rendered him powerless.

The concept of intermediate technology was another such world improvement plan. Again he tried to go to the top to get it implemented, again those who had the power failed him. And then the ideas which developed from his 'Statute of Liberation' had their own liberating effect on him. He perceived that this plan was different. In the past his plans had depended on government action, on the changing of 'the system', on structural alterations. The concept of intermediate technology was free from this necessity. The earliest slogan he had coined held the answer: 'Find out what the people are doing and help them to do it better.' Action would result not from government intervention but from the people themselves. Here too lay the great power and appeal of intermediate technology. In it the most humble people could find hope that they could raise themselves above grinding poverty.

The response to intermediate technology came from all over the world from people who were actually spending their time trying to improve farming methods, or small businesses, or manufacturing. It gave hope to people at all levels, to the farmer who could improve his output by a better designed hand-plough, to the builder who could make more mud bricks with a more efficient hand-press, to the potter whose hand-made pots grew at twice the rate on a wheel powered by foot pedal or even a small engine rather than a wheel spun by hand.

Fritz had been right all along. It was possible to achieve results without power and force. But what he had not realized was that those whose humble daily actions seemed quite insignificant were those who had the power to change the world. It was this message of hope, that each individual had the power to effect change in his own humble, apparently insignificant life, that spread like wildfire and that led to the most dramatic change of all in Fritz's life.

23

Travel and Challenge

It was fortunate for Fritz that he was working for Alf Robens
when the idea of intermediate technology really began to take
off. Not long after the Group's registration and independent
establishment from the African Development Trust in 1966,
he began to receive invitations from presidents and policy-
makers throughout the world. They all wanted to know how
the concept of intermediate technology could be applied to
their particular problems of poverty. Fritz discussed each step
with Robens. They were good enough friends to talk about
wider issues than just coal business, and Robens realized that
Fritz took intermediate technology very seriously indeed, seriously enough to leave the Coal Board if it stood in the way of
progressing I.T.D.G.

So began a new phase of Fritz's life where half his time was
spent travelling to the peoples of the third world with the
purpose of upgrading their standard of living and means of
production, and the other half spent on the problems of what
he had come to believe was the 'overdeveloped world', where
the desire for surfeit was threatening the whole economic structure.

Extensive travelling was not in itself a new way of life for
Fritz. Much of his time had been spent in the air or on the train
between lectures and conferences all over England and Europe,
but such trips were generally never longer than a week, usually
a few days, so that although there was a great deal of coming
and going Fritz could count on spending at least some evenings

a week at home with the family. His frequent trips taught him the maximum economy in packing his luggage. He would leave the house for a week carrying only his briefcase and a small hold-all which was supposed to contain his ironed shirts and suit jacket as well as his night attire. It was sometimes a nightmare to Vreni wondering how he would look at an important lecture. One afternoon the secret came out. The family had a lazy hour in the garden while Fritz went upstairs to pack his things for a week on the Continent. I was to drive him to the airport. When it was time to leave I went upstairs to ask if he was ready. I found him in his shirtsleeves looking a little sheepish as if he had just escaped being caught out at something naughty. As we drove off I remarked on the economy of his luggage. He chuckled and confessed that I had almost caught him at his packing. He had been very worried that someone would come in and conclude that he was completely mad. 'You see,' he explained, 'I have developed a very clever way of packing things in a small space without getting them creased. First I put on my pyjama jacket, then on top of that my shirts, then my suit jacket and last of all my dressing-gown. Then I carefully take it all off together and roll the bundle up and put it into my hold-all.' His dread had been that someone should have come in while he was standing fully clothed in his entire week's wardrobe with his arms sticking out stiffly like a scarecrow.

With the advent of intermediate technology this type of travel changed. That is to say, the short hops to Europe and around England were interspersed with much longer absences of four or six weeks. It was an extraordinary process of history repeating itself. Once again, as in the 1940s, Fritz was engaged in work which he believed was vital for the future of mankind, and once again his family life was threatened with impoverishment as a result. Vreni, who lived for the moments when Fritz came home, for the evenings when she could sit by the gas fire in his study, surrounded by his books, and listen to him talking about his work, his life, his ideas, who felt that his words and his warmth nourished her soul and her spirit, was suddenly faced with the prospect of not seeing him for weeks on end. For six years she had lived with him at the centre of her life. It seemed as if the purpose of life itself was to be taken from her.

Yet if the opportunity presented itself to accompany him on his trips abroad she was generally reluctant to go. The small children seemed an insuperable obstacle. Fritz on his part valued a travelling companion. He hated to travel alone. He did not find that he could really enjoy himself alone, or appreciate the experience of a new land without someone to share everything with, to talk to and listen to his reactions and new ideas. Above all he knew that he needed the warmth of human companionship in the impersonal life of hotel existence. He had matured sufficiently since he was alone in Oxford in 1943 to recognize that what he thought then was the pursuit of freedom and openness in his marriage was in fact weakness, but he knew himself well enough to realize that he was still susceptible to his weakness, particularly as his charm reached nearly every woman he met. He was most susceptible when in the company of women who admired him for his ideas, with whom he already shared a lot mentally. Vreni, aware of this ever-present threat, withdrew more into her life at Holcombe.

At first, however, as intermediate technology took up more of Fritz's time Vreni had hoped that she might see more of him than before. Early in 1967 Fritz was beginning to find that the demands on his time were getting beyond his ability to do all his tasks justice. He had also become a Trustee of Ernest Bader's Scott Bader Commonwealth, a task which took him to Wellingborough in Northamptonshire for a day every month and it seemed sensible to try and reduce his commitment to the Coal Board. Robens agreed to let Fritz work a three-day week. The glorious prospect of a four-day weekend at Holcombe, writing, gardening and generally allowing himself time to think out the many new implications of the concept of intermediate technology never really materialized. Many Mondays were taken up with Scott Bader, Fridays generally disappeared in lectures, meetings, fund-raising efforts for I.T.D.G. Then came the first of the invitations to the Third World: from Peru. Fritz was glad to accept the invitation, not only because it was a sign that his message was reaching across the world but also because it was another contact with his roots. South America, the Andes, took him back to the adventures of his father and Uncle Fritz in the wilds of Colombia exactly a century ago. Recalling the primitive travelling conditions of his ancestors, Fritz felt that he must go well prepared on his travels, even if that only meant carrying a full wallet to cope with all eventualities. Unfortunately it was the autumn of 1967, a time of stringent currency restrictions when money was not allowed out of England. As I was travelling with him I was very anxious about our financial resources, but he seemed unperturbed. When he unpacked our bags in Lima I saw why. His socks were stuffed with five-pound notes.

The first person we met in Lima was a man by the name of Michael Lubbock. Fritz, still smarting from his encounter with Eric Lubbock, was horrified to discover that Michael was a cousin of his sworn opponent. He trod gingerly at first in establishing the views of a man who was to play a vital role in his trip and was relieved when he found him to be of 'sound' opinions. Peru confirmed all the conclusions Fritz had come to in India. Poverty had the same characteristics world wide: rural depopulation, mass migration into the capital city, in this case Lima, at a scale which made nightmare conditions. He was also impressed by the spectacular landscape of Peru and its contrasts: the moonscape of the coastal desert plain, the imposing Andes and the steamy jungle to which he was taken by presidential plane. When the invitation came from President Belaunde to visit the interior of the country Fritz was as pleased as a schoolboy with a treat. He flapped around searching for his least creased clothes as though he was going to a ball rather than a journey into the jungle. He had had his share of ridicule from the economists in Lima, who could only see the advantages of modern economies of scale in factory production and failed to grasp that the detrimental effects the cheap goods had on the rest of the primitive economy eventually destroyed their market. He was delighted that this time the man who really mattered was taking him seriously. Unfortunately a coup not long afterwards ended any immediate hope of intermediate technology in Peru, but Fritz retained a life-long affection for President Belaunde.

On returning from Peru, Fritz received an invitation from President Nyerere of Tanzania. This invitation also pleased Fritz as he had been encouraged and impressed by Nyerere's Arusha Declaration, published that summer, pledging Tanzania to self-reliance and a socialist form of development. Fritz, too, had long wanted the chance to see a bit of Africa, as he had found it difficult to identify with the people he was trying to help in the African Development Trust when he had no visual image of the type of society, traditions, or culture with which he was dealing. Again I accompanied him. This time his contraband was whisky rather than five-pound notes. As soon as we arrived at Heathrow Airport he bought four bottles, leaving his ticket at the Duty Free shop in his agitation. But even Fritz was unnerved when he discovered that the customs officials were as active in darkest Africa as in Western Europe. Before reaching Dar es Salaam the plane touched down in Nairobi, where an acquaintance was waiting for him to exchange a few words over the barrier. Fritz quickly offloaded a bottle and we both breathed a little easier.

A day or two after arriving in Dar es Salaam in June 1968, we were taken to the presidential residence to be received by Nyerere. Knowing that the President was a Roman Catholic, Fritz had brought him a gift of four volumes of *The Sunday Sermons of the Great Fathers*. Fritz was delighted with his choice of gift and showed more pleasure over his offering than his host. Then he asked Nyerere what he wanted him to do. Nyerere's answer was simple and direct: 'I want you to help me implement the Arusha Declaration,' he said, and added that a trip had been arranged to show Fritz the work that was already in progress in the key areas of the country. It was a fascinating tour: an unforgettable experience for me, and an eye-opener to Fritz. Although many of his conclusions about the problems of poverty were once again confirmed, there were significant differences from the other parts of the Third World with which he had become acquainted. India and parts of South America were places whose history stretched back to periods of high culture. India had decayed because it had gone through and beyond civilization into stagnation; Africa was still an infant society, pre-civilization, a traditional society that had not yet reached the heights of culture that so many other societies had reached. Nevertheless, the remedies for their poverty were similar, even culturally. One of the recommendations Fritz made to Nyerere was 'to bring culture into the rural areas'. 'The elements of culture are visual matter, music, reading matter, industrial skills . . . and body culture,' he wrote. 'In all these respects the rural areas are poverty stricken.' His argument was that culture was not the luxury of a rich society but a prerequisite of development, that agriculture itself was no basis out of which culture and development could grow, but that culture 'stimulates the mind and that is the starting point of everything ... it is too often overlooked that culture, and not money, is the primary motive power of development.' It was the same point he had made in India in the years before the idea of intermediate technology was born.

The second major difference that struck Fritz was the role of the non-indigenous population. In East Africa it was evident that the major entrepreneurial initiatives were coming not from the Africans but from the Asian population. It was also evident that feelings ran high in some areas because of Asian economic superiority. Fritz thought hard about this problem throughout the trip and eventually came to the conclusion that the Tanzanians had the choice of either 'using the Asians or losing them'. He believed that it was in Tanzania's interests to keep the Asians and use them as a sort of internal source of aid. They had the entrepreneurial talent, business flair, and skills lacking in the community. Fritz recommended that every established Asian firm should be encouraged to expand and diversify into African ventures, to which it should give technical and commercial assistance free of charge. In this way the Asian community would not only be able to continue its own business ventures but would also create good will and really useful assistance to the African community. In addition to this suggestion Fritz added some practical advice on how the state could become involved in successful business without over-centralization or bureaucratization.

Fritz's trip to Tanzania had a strange and unexpected spin-off. It was during this absence that Vreni fully realized the implications of his new crusade. She was deeply unhappy while he was in Africa, suddenly aware of how much she depended on him to fill her life and to provide her with strength, inner harmony and a purpose in life. She wrote to him of her loneliness, of her desolation, hoping for the vacuum to be filled by his letters. But Fritz no longer wrote the long, informative letters of his youth and early adulthood, through which his personality came so strongly to his correspondents. As his travelling became more hectic, never spending more than a few days in one place, his letters became correspondingly shorter and to the point. No heroic words of comfort but, 'Keep your chin up,' was all the response Vreni received. It made their separation complete and she was thrown entirely on to her own inner resources which she found to be inadequate. She knew that unless she developed some inner resources of her own she would remain desolate and unable to live a proper life in the many lonely weeks she knew the future held.

Vreni's inner dependence on Fritz had become apparent to her before his trip to Tanzania but in a less intense form. Then she thought the answer was a career: this time she felt more was needed than keeping busy. She needed help but Fritz had passed through his evangelizing days and no longer tried to shape his wife's inner life or her beliefs. Never did he try and force down her throat his diet of St Thomas Aquinas, St John of the Cross, Joseph Pieper, The Early Church Fathers, Jacques Maritain and Friedjof Schuon. He was content to see her reading Dickens and Jane Austen or the occasional biography of someone he admired such as Goethe. Perhaps the experience of Muschi's death had taught him humility. Anyway, Vreni's own inclinations had not been of a spiritual nature. Since coming to Holcombe she had reacted very strongly against a religious institution in which she had spent some of her youth, and Fritz had to some extent taken the place of God. When Fritz left for Tanzania, in desperation she turned to the local Catholic priest for strength and comfort.

Father Scarborough was an old and experienced priest, who received Vreni kindly but not with the open arms she had expected. Far from welcoming her into the fold of the Catholic Church as she had anticipated, he merely suggested that if she was interested she should try and come to Mass from time to time.

When Fritz returned from Tanzania he found his wife regularly attending Mass. The next time she went he accompanied her. Although he was so well acquainted with Catholic writers ancient and modern, he knew next to nothing about the actual form of worship in the rites of the church. He was fascinated, struck particularly by the reverence with which the priests handled the chalice and the paten after they had distributed communion, the care with which every vessel was carefully wiped and polished.

A few weeks later the Catholic Church hit the headlines. Pope Paul VI issued his famous Encyclical *Humanae Vitae*, in which he reaffirmed the Church's belief in the sanctity of marriage and marital love and its rejection of the uses of artificial methods of contraception. The day after it was published Harry Collins came into Fritz's office. Since they worked together on the Collins Committee, Harry had provided Fritz with a number of Encyclicals after discovering that Fritz had quoted from an Encyclical on work to make a point.

'I've got a spare copy of the latest Encyclical if you'd like it, Fritz,' he said.

'Is it *Humanae Vitae*?' Fritz asked.

'Yes it is.'

'I've not only got a copy, but I've read it,' Fritz replied.

'What do you think of it?' asked Harry.

The answer was surprising. 'If the Pope had written anything else I would have lost all faith in the papacy,' Fritz said.

Vreni too found great comfort in the Pope's controversial pronouncement. For her, the message it conveyed was an affirmation and support for marriage, for women such as herself who had given themselves entirely to their marriages and who felt acutely the pressure from the world outside that shouted ever louder that homebound, monogamous relationships were oppressive to women and prevented them from 'fulfilling themselves'. She returned to Father Scarborough and asked him to accept her for a course of instruction in the Catholic faith.

At the same time, but quite unbeknown to Fritz or Vreni, I had also been going through a period of soul-searching. It had come to a head in Africa when the whisky, the irritation at the incompetence surrounding our arrangements and, it seemed to me, the constant repetition of obvious truths (in other words the by now familiar practical application of the concept of intermediate technology) had changed my view of my father. Until then he had been superhuman, a god. In Africa he was revealed as having feet of clay. The discontent and restlessness this induced forced me to face issues I had striven to avoid for some years. One of these was a strong attraction to the Catholic

Church which I had felt since my schooldays but had always feared to explore.

Shortly after the publication of *Humanae Vitae* I went to Holcombe to inform my father of the step I was going to take. I was more nervous of Vreni's reaction than his. By this time she had become my closest friend and I dreaded jeopardizing our relationship. But the evening turned out very differently. To my astonishment it was Vreni who was sympathetic and my father who bombarded us with a barrage of aggressive questioning. We were both taken by surprise. We knew of his sympathy with the Catholic Church and his devotion to many Catholic writers. Some time later he explained that he had wanted to make sure that we knew what we were doing and had therefore taken up the position of Devil's advocate. At my reception into the Catholic Church some months later he presented me with the same gift as he had given Nyerere earlier that year, *The Sunday Sermons of the Great Fathers*, inscribed with the words: 'To Barbara, with love and good wishes, joy and fullest approval. Papa.'

After this, Fritz's support and approval was so unreserved of the step that wife and daughter had taken that it naturally prompted the question, 'If you agree with the teachings of the Church, why don't you become a Catholic too?' His answer was, 'I couldn't do it to my mother.' It seemed a strange answer from someone whose life had already consisted of a series of dramatic changes that had caused his parents anxiety or even sorrow. Generations of antagonisms and suspicion since the Reformation had left their mark and Fritz seemed to regard the step into the Catholic Church as more revolutionary than his involvement with Marxism or Buddhism.

Vreni was now better armed to cope with Fritz's frequent absences abroad. She had a source of new meaning in her life and was not left with the feeling that she had been put on ice every time he left. When Fritz confessed later that year to having succumbed briefly to female temptation, she had the strength to smile and say, 'I don't blame her', and developed a particular affection for the lady in question.

The most important trip in 1969 was to Zambia. He was delighted to be travelling together with Julia who was by this time married to Bob Porter, a senior official in the Ministry of

Overseas Development. Julia knew Zambia well and they were both welcomed warmly by Zambia's President, Kenneth Kaunda. Fritz found his host to be a man wholly understanding of his way of thinking and ideas. Their meeting lasted late into the night and Fritz was so excited at the real contact they had made that he felt compelled to wake Julia and give her a blow by blow account of their conversation until the early hours of the morning. There had been a complete exchange of trust and confidence with Kaunda which was to be proved in the following year when Fritz visited South Africa.

The invitation to South Africa came from the Christian Institute to look at the African homelands and advise on black development. Fritz had no hesitation in accepting, this time taking Virginia with him. He was not concerned about the political implications of the visit or its repercussions on other African nations. His only consideration was that desperate people had asked for help and that it was his duty to respond to such a cry. He did not accept the argument that to promote the development of the homelands was to assist the South African Government in justifying their policies of apartheid, nor did he in fact consider the *theory* of separate development iniquitous. As a concept he thought apartheid, or separate development, was a perfectly sound approach to balanced and healthy economic development, and completely in accordance with the views he had evolved since his first contact with the Third World in Burma. Then he had advised the Burmese to cut themselves off from Western influences and develop their own resources, replacing every Western adviser by a Burmese counterpart as soon as possible; in India he had witnessed the effect of the West creating havoc with the very deepest levels of self-confidence and self-esteem of a nation. In Africa he had seen that wherever the white man had appeared, the black man had been exploited. Again and again the story was the same. White men with their superior skills and technical know-how, built up over generations, trod the black man underfoot, stole his land and made him his slave. That was what Fritz found iniquitous, the fact that in a mixed society the white man always came out on top, whereas the bottom of the social, economic and political pyramid was always black, either trodden under or sinking under because of a lack of skills and

339

experience. The only way to give the blacks a fair deal, Fritz believed, was to allow them to develop without white domination, which meant separate development.

To this extent Fritz was a supporter of the concept of separate development. This was not the same, however, as supporting the South African Government's practice of apartheid. He abhorred what he called petty apartheid, the discrimination against the blacks within the white areas. He saw too that within the white areas separate development was not in fact practised, but precisely the type of social and industrial organization which he condemned: the whites using the blacks as their slaves, disrupting the stability of black family and community life. But this evil did not in his eyes make it wrong to help the blacks in their own areas. On the contrary, he believed, the stronger they became the less they would ultimately be forced into situations where they were exploited.

In the emotionally charged arena of South African politics an attitude quite free from political considerations, such as Fritz's, was unacceptable and incomprehensible. Again and again he was pressed into discussions and arguments about South African politics. When he said he was impressed by what he saw in the African homelands, someone in his party would immediately jump up and say that he might not be so impressed if he knew about the politics behind the appearances. This sort of thing soon began to irritate Fritz. If the conditions of the people were improving, then the political machinations behind the improvements did not concern him. What concerned him was that human beings who were suffering desperate poverty were beginning to get the chance to do something for themselves without white domination.

It was this emphasis on letting the people help themselves that eventually got him into trouble and made some people believe that he had carried his refusal to acknowledge political realities to a level of dangerous naivety.

Included in his tour of the South African homelands was a visit to Swaziland, Botswana and Lesotho. The presence of the secret police throughout the trip should have warned him of the dangers but he was merely amused that he should be regarded as a potentially subversive agent. He chuckled at the fact that the texts of his speeches were grabbed for scrutiny by the security forces as soon as they were delivered (it was a novel way of reaching an unlikely audience), and he was vain enough to assume that the red carpet laid out on the Botswana runway was for him (until his aircraft taxied by to make room for the country's President who had just landed).

As Fritz viewed the development projects in the British Protectorates he noticed that the white man was very much in evidence in these black countries. There were white shop-keepers, white administrators, white teachers, all along the line. It was the very opposite of what had impressed him in the homelands where these posts were all filled by blacks. As he observed this contrast he commented on it, and as his comments were made in public they threw him headlong into a huge row. Only the South African Government was delighted and claimed him as a champion of apartheid. A man like Schumacher, friend of the very countries so bitterly opposed to South Africa's policies, was a coup indeed.

When Fritz returned to London he found himself in an even more furious hornets' nest, the principal hornet being one of his closest friends, Julia Porter. Fritz's remarks had put her in an embarrassing position. Her connection with Fritz at I.T.D.G. naturally identified her with his views, but these views had been interpreted as an attack on British Government policy in the Southern African Protectorates, the very policies represented by her husband in his capacity as a senior member of the Ministry of Overseas Development. There was a bitter scene from which Fritz retreated hurt and bewildered. He could not understand why he had elicited such fury.

He soon learned too, on his return to London, that his incautious remarks had caused offence further afield. President Nyerere was reported as being very annoyed and this rumour was lent credence on a subsequent visit to London by the Tanzanian President when Fritz, although invited to a reception for Nyerere at 10 Downing Street, was not asked to meet him privately to discuss the aftermath of his Tanzanian report. Fortunately the ripples caused by this incident did not appear to extend any further. Kenneth Kaunda at least continued to support Fritz and showed that he understood the purity of Fritz's motives by not taking offence at his political blunder.

Fritz's refusal to take account of the political implications of his visit to South Africa was reflected in a general refusal to be drawn into a discussion of the political implications of the concept of intermediate technology. For him intermediate technology was the way in which it was genuinely possible to help the poor. He said from his German experience that it was easy for the rich to help the rich; it was just a question of money. He further added that it was possible for the poor to help the poor. But for the rich to help the poor was very hard indeed. Intermediate technology was the great vehicle of breakthrough, the means by which the poor could be helped without the handouts and welfare inherent in Western thinking. In fact intermediate technology had tremendous political implications and was closely connected with Fritz's thinking on socialism. It is the ideal way of attaining the sort of socialism that Fritz advocated, a socialism which did away with the concentrations of economic power, a socialism which gave people work that allowed them to be fully human, fully conscious members of the body politic instead of automatons serving machines that served rich or powerful masters as remote as the state. Small-scale technology, small-scale enterprise, workshops and small factories serving a community and served by a community; that was real socialism in action, where no one need be exploited for another's gain. Fritz had argued for smaller organizational units. Intermediate technology was the technology to go with such units.

It is not surprising that Fritz was intensely interested in what was going on in China at the time. There, it seemed, was a living example of intermediate technology with its widest implications in action. He subscribed to a magazine, *China Reconstructs*, and glowed over the examples of intermediate technology, even though they were often sandwiched between pictures of uniformed ladies with guns. The good struck him more forcibly than the bad he could do nothing about. He read Mao's little red book with as much interest as he had read Tawney and Gandhi before that. Mao was another great man who had understood some basic truths, truths about never forgetting one's responsibility to the people. Mao also knew how to communicate with the people and there was a lot to be learnt in his direct and straightforward method. Fritz was, after all, rather partial to inventing slogans himself.

There was another line of argument about intermediate technology into which Fritz refused to get drawn. It was generally voiced by students of philosophy and went roughly as follows: 'Well, what happens after intermediate technology? Isn't it just a way of getting to where we are now in the West? On the one hand you criticize the West and on the other you are trying to get the Third World on the same road.' Such talk would annoy Fritz intensely. He would become extremely impatient and show less than polite respect for the sincerity of the questioner. He regarded such a question as completely invalid – a non-question. First of all it showed a complete lack of understanding for the realities of poverty, which it is man's duty to try and alleviate at whatever cost. But secondly, it showed a total lack of understanding of the philosophical thinking behind intermediate technology. It was so much part of Fritz's thinking, so much the foundations on which all his thinking had come to be based, that perhaps he took it too much for granted and eventually omitted to explain to people that it was not a contradiction to describe his philosophy as a statute of *liberation* at the same time as calling it a statute of *limitation*.

It was a paradox which was explained by a true understanding of the nature of work. 'The Buddhist point of view takes the functions of work to be at least three-fold: to give a man a chance to utilize and develop his faculties; to enable him to overcome his egocentredness by joining with other people in a common task; and to bring forth the goods and services needed for a becoming existence.'[1]

The West concentrated on the third of these functions and had become trapped in materialism. Recognizing that work was necessary to one's personal development and one's relations with others introduced limitations of a material nature but liberated the real essence of the human being. Intermediate technology was the technical means by which this balance could be achieved. It made possible the step from misery to sufficiency essential for man to be fully human. It was not merely the means to an end of material surfeit.

343

24

'Retirement'

As the 1960s drew to a close the pressure on Fritz became greater still. Intermediate technology was taking up more and more time, both because of the demand for Fritz to travel abroad and because of the needs of I.T.D.G. for funds and general guidance. Responsibilities at the National Coal Board had increased since 1967 when Robens made Fritz Director of Planning in addition to his role as Economic Adviser and Director of Statistics, and Fritz's other interests at the Scott Bader Commonwealth and the Soil Association, whose council he had joined, also made their demands on his time.

By 1970 Fritz reached a moment of decision. He felt he had done all he could in the battle for coal. He was fond of saying, 'The chickens are about to come home to roost.' The first oil crisis was not far away, and on February 4th, 1971 the *Guardian* newspaper was to report: 'It is already clear that the coal industry has been run down too quickly and up to one hundred pits could have been saved if the Government had not been so cocksure about the short term prospects for nuclear electricity, natural gas and the continued availability of cheap crude oil.'

With his warning unheeded for so long there was a great deal of work to be done in sowing seeds for a new way of life. Fritz believed that changes would eventually be forced on the world in a much more dramatic way than would have been the case if he had been able to reach the hearts of men fifteen years earlier. He wanted at last to write the books that had been on his mind for years.

Nevertheless, it was not easy to decide to leave the Coal Board where he had been for twenty years. Apart from the practical consideration of earning a living with a wife and three children to support, the youngest of whom, Nicola, was not yet a year old, he still felt a strong loyalty to Robens. Fritz was unsure whether Robens would in fact leave or be offered another term of office at the beginning of 1971 when his current term was due to end. At first, while discussing the matter with friends and colleagues, he put off making a decision, waiting to see what Robens was going to do, but the weeks passed and there was no hint of his feelings on the matter. In fact, Robens was just as much in the dark as Fritz, as he had not been approached by the Government. Fritz did not know this and, feeling he could wait no longer, went to see Robens. He had decided to take the risk and retire early – 'After all,' he kept telling everyone who marvelled at his decision, 'Adenauer and Churchill both started new and successful lives at the age of sixty so why shouldn't I?' He was ready to make his act of faith.

He did not leave his financial affairs entirely to Divine Providence however. His discussions with Robens included a new appointment as part-time Adviser to the Statistics Department and Robens let Fritz go with great generosity. Fritz also formalized his relationship with the Scott Bader Commonwealth who employed him as a consultant to the firm. But to all intents and purposes he was now on his own and ready to face what was to become perhaps the most astonishing and dramatic part of his eventful life. The time had come to draw everything together.

The impact of Fritz's 'retirement' took a while to make itself felt. His trip to South Africa followed closely on its heels and it was not really until late summer that he sat down at his desk to begin writing his book. He found, now that he should have had more time, that it was far more difficult than he had imagined to sit down and write. There seemed to be so many other distractions. He liked to stay in bed longer for a start, pampered by Vreni who brought him up breakfast with his post in the morning. There were many books he wanted to read again, and he wanted to pay more attention to the garden which had been sadly neglected for the last ten years.

The garden, which had been the source of inspiration for his first turning point, drew him as much as ever. Although he was twenty years older and no longer as fit to do the heavy work, he was still full of ideas and experiments. He tried a variety of methods to eliminate the heavy work: first covering the garden with newspapers, which blew everywhere at the first breath of wind; then changing to long sheets of black polythene which were supposed to eliminate weeding as well as digging. He came to the conclusion that as there was no substitute for compost, which was heavy and needed shifting from compost heap to bed, that the real problem for the gardener was to devise a way of lifting and shifting heavy weights. As his sixtieth birthday was approaching the family decided to buy him a mini-tractor. Fritz's mother had great doubts about this idea. She did not think that Fritz would want such a sophisticated piece of equipment. She turned out to be quite right. He declined the suggestion immediately saying that it was too high a technology for the purpose it was to serve. After careful consideration he eventually bought himself a battery-operated wheelbarrow which he found a simple and effective solution to the problem of moving compost. A year or two later a mini-tractor mowing-machine was, however, added to the considerable stock of garden equipment that had accumulated in the garage at Holcombe. Despite all his ideals Fritz never mastered grass-cutting technology and one mower after another was tried and found wanting until the most sophisticated of all proved the answer to the extensive lawns. The shortest-lived mower was an electric one which on its first day of use had its electric cable chopped in half by Robert who was racing around with a little hand mower. The cable was never replaced.

The garden, gradually taking shape again out of the wilderness that had grown around the house since Muschi's death, gave Fritz great joy. It also made him feel easier about accepting the invitation to become President of the Soil Association in 1970. His commitment to the Soil Association ideal was as strong as ever. He had enormous admiration for Lady Eve Balfour, its founder, and was devoted to one of the leading lights of the organization, Joy Griffiths Jones. He always referred to her as 'Joy of my life', and was deeply grieved when she was found to have cancer.

The Soil Association was a cause to which Fritz gave a great deal of thought. He had a debt towards those who had helped him in his first steps towards changing his life and he discharged it conscientiously, leading the Association from an organization concerned exclusively with research to an outward-looking concern publishing its conclusions more widely and offering practical advice on a hitherto unheard of scale. Always ready to forge links between different interests he was very pleased when a project developed between the N.C.B. and the Soil Association over the reclaiming of slag heaps in South Wales. No avenue was ever too insignificant to demonstrate the use of sound and healthy methods.

Not all his contributions could remain voluntary however. He had to take a more realistic look at his activities when he began to face the unpleasant task of demanding payment for his work. Sometimes he felt angry at what seemed to him to be a failure to appreciate his work in the offer of poor remuneration. The B.B.C. were the target of one indignant outburst. As no figure had been mentioned in the contract he had signed for a broadcast, he was disappointed and angry when, after giving his talk, he was sent only a small token fee. As he received the cheque for about twenty pounds the window cleaner was busy outside his study windows. He wrote angrily to the B.B.C. detailing his train fare to London, the number of hours he had had to travel and wait at the B.B.C. and so on, and pointing out that it amounted to a wage of under two pounds an hour, less than the rate of pay for the window cleaner. 'It is my ambition,' he wrote, 'to earn at least as much as a window cleaner.'

There were other tasks he tried to avoid by naming an absurd fee. It did not always work. When he wrote to the United Nations in Geneva that his fee for an article they wanted (and which he did not feel like writing) would be £200, he assumed they would be put off. He was horrified when the money was sent by return and he was forced to write the article.

Between gardening, lecturing, travelling to Northamptonshire to the Scott Bader Commonwealth or to East Anglia for the Soil Association, let alone his frequent trips to London to the N.C.B. and to I.T.D.G., Fritz's main task was still supposed to be writing his book. There were in fact two books he

347

wanted to write. The first was a kind of spiritual map – he already had the title: 'A Guide for the Perplexed' – in which he wanted to draw together the threads of his spiritual quest for the benefit of others who were confused at the conflicting goals of the world and could no longer find the signposts to the road they yearned to travel.

The second book was the practical side of the road, drawing together the threads of his conclusions about how to live life in the world, the kind of outer life that was compatible with a healthy inner life. He was as yet uncertain as to the title of his book and toyed with 'The Homecomers' because he believed that the things he was advocating represented a turning around towards sense, a turning away from the 'forward stampede' that characterized modern life. The subtitle he chose held the explanation: 'Economics – as if people mattered'.

Although he felt that the first book was more important, Fritz began with the second. With calculating realism he had decided that the book on economics would sell better than the spiritual book and that he might therefore reach a wider readership if he published the more popular book first. He was convinced that 'The Homecomers' would be a bestseller. He referred to it as his 'Goldregen', the German for Laburnum, but literally translated meaning 'golden rain'. The family looked on sympathetically. 'Poor fellow. What a disappointment he is going to have,' was in more than one mind. 'Fancy thinking such a book could shower him with money.'

Imposing his own discipline was more difficult than Fritz had anticipated. Countless people seemed to want to see him and it took him some time to tumble to the important conclusion that, as he put it, 'It is as far from Caterham to London as it is from London to Caterham.' This discovery enabled him to tell all those who wished to see him to come to Caterham. He began to rely heavily on his past articles and lectures to form the body of the book, adding a little here, updating a little there, and adding linking passages. A few chapters were quite new, but some came from articles he had already published in magazines for which he had been writing regularly. These were principally two: *Manas*, an American publication edited by Henry Geiger, and *Resurgence*, a journal that described itself as the 'journal of the fourth world', started by

John Papworth and later taken over by Satish Kumar. *Resurgence* espoused the ideas of smallness and decentralization and provided a forum for radical alternative thinkers of the day, such as Leopold Kohr, an Austrian Welsh Nationalist, Ivan Illich, dynamic challenger of all things establishment, and John Seymour, leading light in the self-sufficiency movement.

As Fritz sat in his study, his typewriter before him, he began to feel the lack of stimulation that the constant company of his working life had provided. At Holcombe, apart from those who visited him, the atmosphere was quiet and domestic. His first four children had all left home, but he enjoyed his second family immensely and all three children were allowed to come and go into the study whenever they liked, often to play with a box of watch and clock bits left over from his early do-it-yourself days. Noisy games among his papers were discouraged, although he did not need silence to work. His taste in music, never very highbrow, now narrowed itself down to other people's choices. Strains of 'A Hundred Best Tunes' would float through the study door instead of the voices of Maria Callas and Tito Gobbi; and accompanying the music would be the waft of cigarette smoke. The creative state of tension that he required had to be induced with the aid of tobacco and a glass of whisky.

Some way through compiling his book it became clear that he had also had other thoughts on his mind. Suddenly, quite unexpectedly, in the spring of 1971 he asked Vreni to go to Father Scarborough and tell him he wanted to be received into the Catholic Church. It was strange that a man used to conversing with presidents should find it necessary to use an intermediary to arrange a talk with the local parish priest, and no doubt it was even stranger to Fritz to be told that Father Scarborough had taken a dim view of this indirect approach and had merely retorted, 'He'd better come himself if he is interested.'

For some months after this, Fritz went every Wednesday morning to receive instruction from Father Scarborough. He did not share the contents of his talks with Vreni nor did he complain that he already knew everything after years of study and reading, and it was obvious that his affection and respect for his local parish priest grew with each session.

On September 29th, 1971 Fritz was received by Father Scarborough into the Catholic Church. Vreni, my husband Don and I (all converts to Catholicism) were the only witnesses. He was very moved as he recited the Creed and took Communion. He had, at last, come to rest after a long and restless search. He had, as he put it, 'made legal a long-standing illicit love affair'. As for his mother, she was not shocked as he had feared. She merely smiled and said, 'Nothing can surprise me anymore with Fritz.' For Fritz the decision had come after long years of study and struggle. It was an acknowledgment that after examining every option and refusing to accept anything without taking it apart and putting it together again himself, that the time had come to stop searching and accept what was there. Several years later he put it this way:

It has taken me a long time to discover why religion has split up into so many different religions: it's so you can choose the one that is most practical for you. The most practical to me was the Roman Catholic version of Christianity, and now I am relieved of such totally offbeat questions as: How could something incredible, like the human being, have come about by an accidental combination of atoms? So I say, come off it, this is just stupid. I don't know how it is, but I believe that there is a Creator. The moment I believe in this higher level, it would be most improbable that the Creator could have put into life such loquacious beings as you and I and never say a word to us. He has actually communicated to us.

This is called by the simple word 'revelation'. We have the sacred books of mankind, and having spent many, many years studying them, not only in the Christian tradition, I find that it's the same spirit that is communicating to all of us. By various means, in a subtle way, an educative way. You always have to stretch yourself to understand; it is not meant to be automatic. This is the great education we can receive in life, and once we get hold of that, then suddenly we find that we are no longer worried, we have actually to act in this life, we can distinguish between the phony and the real questions, and we're happy.[1]

Before he had completed the manuscript of his book he had another crisis to face. At the beginning of 1972 cancer was diagnosed in Vreni. Fritz was desolate. This time he did not hide his tears even from the children. It seemed unbelievable that the same curse should strike a second time. Fortunately it was not to be fatal and Vreni was successfully operated on, but Fritz was left with the question, 'Why cancer twice?' There seemed no rational explanation so he turned to irrational theories. Eventually he heard about a water diviner in Germany to whom he sent a map of the house site and the surrounding countryside. It was returned with a simple, if to most people extraordinary, explanation. Two water courses ran some distance below the house. This, it was said, always had some malign effect. A strange looking object, not unlike a miner's lamp, was enclosed with instructions to keep it always in the house: it would counteract the malign influences of the water courses. There was no charge for this service. The magic lamp stands in Fritz's study to this day. No one dares to remove it or examine it closely for who knows ...

Other explanations have been offered which may be as far-fetched (or as true) as the water courses. One is that in both cases the cancer was a form of unconscious protest at a relationship which demanded, by and large, a complete surrender to Fritz's drive and goals in life. Selfless devotion to Fritz's cause ruled out any kind of more obvious self-fulfilment. Muschi and Vreni suffered, not because they were thwarted or frustrated in following a much desired career or goal of their own, but because Fritz's brilliance cast a shadow over their own self-esteem and self-confidence. Not only did they feel unworthy of his love and real devotion but they felt inadequate in a worldly sense too. In fact their illnesses should have made it quite clear to them that they were also Fritz's life force, but such sentiments were not something Fritz was good at expressing. He would try to tell them in a roundabout way, for example, by telling the following story – one of Fritz's favourites. An American lady had an old black servant who served her loyally. The mistress was mystified at the devotion of her servant to a husband who over the years beat her regularly, never got a job and was generally drunk. 'Tell me,' she asked her servant one day, 'why do you put up with that

351

husband of yours? He never lifts a finger for you after you have been out all day working, and he drinks away all the money you earn.' The old negress replied, 'Well you see, Mam, it's like this. I makes the livin' and he makes the livin'' worthwhile.'

After Vreni's operations were over and she was able to make his life 'worthwhile' again, Fritz put the finishing touches to his manuscript. Reading it before delivering it to his publisher, Blond and Briggs, he was spellbound. 'Brilliant,' he commented after each chapter. 'It comes as a complete surprise to me that I have written this marvellous stuff.' With that he delivered it to Blond and Briggs who immediately threw out his title 'The Homecomers'. With a flash of inspiration Anthony Blond suggested: 'Small is Beautiful.'

Small is Beautiful was published in 1973. The reviews, such as they were, did not suggest that a bestseller had been launched into the world. Fritz was not discouraged. He had learnt after a lifetime of world improvement plans that the only things that really work are those that start in a small way, for only they can grow healthily. *Small is Beautiful* began with modest sales, but every quarter the figures increased at a geometric rate until both the book and its title was suddenly everywhere. The title *Small is Beautiful* had the appeal of one of Mao's slogans and was used even in the most inappropriate contexts, such as advertisements for Japanese electronic equipment. But the Japanese also published a translation of the real thing as did countries all over the world from Iceland to Portugal. As each new edition appeared, Fritz's post-bag increased. By the end of the year he was receiving twenty to thirty letters a week asking him to address meetings and give lectures. He found himself in the position of a prima donna with two years' bookings in advance.

With public recognition came public honours. The following year, in 1974, when the Queen's birthday honours were announced Fritz's name was among those awarded the C.B.E. This honour and sign of official recognition meant more than the public prestige it conferred, as did subsequent invitations to Buckingham Palace for a private dinner with the Duke of Edinburgh and later luncheon with the Queen. It was a reassurance that his consciousness of his foreignness, still with him after forty years in England, did not form an unbridgeable barrier with his adopted compatriots.

With this lead, more honours followed: Honorary degrees from Concordia University in Canada and the Catholic University in Leuven came first, then English Universities: first Reading, and then the Open University. He was given an Honorary Fellowship by the University of Manchester Institute of Science and Technology and elected Fellow of the Royal Society of Arts. In Europe he was presented with a medal by the Italian President, Luigi Preti, and given the European Essay prize from the Charles Veillon Foundation for his collection of essays in *Small is Beautiful*. Awards in America and Canada excelled every other in their praise. In America he was presented with Carborundum's Award for Excellence and the Vanier Institute of the Family in Canada decided to bestow upon him the Wilder Penfield Award for 'wisdom and leadership in the evolution of human society'. This honour, however, was collected for Fritz posthumously by Robert.

This sudden recognition which had eluded him for so long surprised Fritz when it came. Meeting his friend from wartime Oxford, David Worswick, he said, 'When I was a young man I thought those chaps at the top were there because of the system. Then, as I was making my way to the top, I understood that you got there because of merit. Now that I've got to the top I realize that it's pure chance.' The arrogance of the young crusader and deviser of world improvement plans had mellowed. He had seen that his true cause grew of its own accord because of the truth and authenticity of its message. There was no longer room for anything else but preaching and pleading for action. There was no shortage of opportunity to preach. In the next three years he travelled to every continent from the United States to Australia, the West Indies, the Pacific Islands, and the East Indies. India had received him before this shower of recognition had burst upon him. He had travelled there in early 1973 with Virginia. Although he had been received by Mrs Gandhi and prominent government ministers, as well as visiting J. P. Narayan and his friends in action in the Indian Appropriate Technology Group, he was despondent about the trip. 'India is a sewer,' he said sadly as he returned, weary after the comparative physical hardships he had endured while travelling and depressed by the apathy and slow progress of the work.

The hectic programme he set himself began to age him rapidly. His hair, only streaked with silver at the temples when he left the N.C.B., turned suddenly white. It grew longer over his collar and, although he still tried to keep it sleek with hair cream, lost its elegance of former years. He grew sideburns of which he was very proud and fingered constantly as he spoke, stroking them downwards in a movement ending at his chin. He began to put on weight as he finally gave up smoking for the last time, and his dress became more casual still, his former trilby hat replaced by a wide brimmed hat which gave him an American air. He looked gentle and benign, blue eyes twinkling and kind under bushy white brows and surrounded by the most good-humoured wrinkles. He had entered the final stage of his life: that of a guru figure.

Fritz's emergence as a guru figure became apparent first in America. *Small is Beautiful* had appeared when many young Americans, shocked by the aftermath of the Vietnam war, were looking for new solutions. Thousands found answers in *Small is Beautiful*. Jerry Brown, the young Governor of California, used it in his election platform. Fritz had put into words ideas which made sense, which people could respond to with their hearts and minds. What was more important: his words were not just hot air, they were practical and down to earth, and they put the whole man back into the picture.

Fritz made two major trips to the United States in the 1970s, as well as several shorter ones. During the first, in 1974, it was clear that his message was beginning to strike home with the young. Everywhere he went he was received enthusiastically and his lectures had capacity audiences. It was a grass roots response to a grass roots philosophy. Jerry Brown, who in a mixture of personal conviction and political shrewdness caught the mood of his Californian electorate, was alone among politicians in America to respond. Fritz, while heartened by the response of the young, nevertheless returned home somewhat disheartened by the frantic pursuit of material satisfaction by those who refused to open their eyes to the realities of the economic, energy, environmental and human crisis around them. He saw highlighted in America the rejection of ancient virtues which he believed were still crucial to Western economic life, particularly the Cardinal Virtue of Prudence which he had described in *Small is Beautiful*: 'It signifies the opposite of a small, mean, calculating attitude to life, which refuses to see and value anything that fails to promise an immediate utilitarian advantage.'

He preached that the affluence of the West was not the norm but an abnormality which the 'signs of the times' clearly showed was coming to an end. One such sign was the inflation that had started to plague Western economies. Fritz saw inflation as the effect of a power struggle: 'People ask what causes inflation. A very easy question to answer ... prices are put up. Unfortunately the language of most people who talk economics is so sloppy that they prefer to say prices rise ... as if prices were balloons. No. Prices are *put* up and when you put it that way you can ask who put them up. Those who have the power to do so and can get away with it. The powerless cannot get away with it.'[2]

Another sign of change lay in the shift of those who held power. 'Various groups, who have hitherto counted for little, have discovered their essentiality and therewith their power.' This discovery led such groups to demand a greater reward for their labours so that, for example, garbage collectors could suddenly demand the same or more than University professors. 'The party is over ...' Fritz said, and asked:

Whose party was it anyhow? That of a small minority of countries and, inside those countries, that of a minority of people. And as the party became more and more swinging, an increasing number of people began to realize that the party was not for them but that, at the same time, *they were needed to keep the party going*. And that is why we have inflation now. It is these people who have done the most to wake up society, and you may say that they have done the most to set the inflationary spiral going ... Those whose power has grown want to change the status quo; and those whose power has waned want to defend it. The former normally collect a very great deal of abuse whilst those who defend the status quo feel extremely self-righteous.

In making this analysis Fritz did not exclude the additional pressures to put up prices, which came from the struggle over limited resources such as oil and phosphates, but he insisted that both sources of pressure could only be contained through 'justice', and 'justice' involved setting a limit, knowing when enough was enough. In practical terms Fritz suggested that meant a ceiling to salaries and had strong words to say to those who argued that limits to pay make it difficult to attract the 'best' people into the most important jobs. 'This argument misses the point. Those who cannot accept that enough is enough are *not* the best people; they are dangerous people who make our problems insoluble and we cannot have them as top civil servants, industrialists, judges, generals, etc.'[2]

It is hardly surprising that this kind of message appealed more to young radicals than to the 'establishment'. To those who dismissed him as a crank he replied with delight: 'A crank is a piece of simple technology that creates revolutions.' Meanwhile, he saw in the young the hope for the future, particularly in America where, although he saw much which he regarded as downright evil, he also saw many seeds for new healthy growth in a changing society. While in America an event occurred which increased his reputation as a crank. It was the birth of his last child, James. He had received the news of Vreni's pregnancy with slight misgivings. 'Now people really will think I am eccentric,' he had said. The news of James's birth in 1974 came while he was addressing a large audience of young people, and it endeared him to them – this elderly, white-haired man clearly still so young at heart and full of life. It had taken the person who had answered the transatlantic call some time to grasp the message and Virginia, who was phoning through the good news, had had to repeat several times, 'Yes, that's right, not a grandson, a son. Dr Schumacher has just had a son.' Fritz was delighted to have another son. It had always been his ambition to have six sons. Each daughter had been accompanied by an apology from her mother. However, with eight children he was now prepared to let that ambition remain unfulfilled.

Returning home after his American trip, Fritz tried to settle down to giving his second book, *A Guide for the Perplexed*, some attention. He was not altogether satisfied with his publisher and decided to offer the *Guide*, as it became known in the family, to someone else. He prepared a synopsis and sent it to Collins. It was returned with a rejection. He wrote back saying that he was sorry that they had been unable to recognize that his ugly duckling was in fact a swan, and sent the synopsis to Jonathan Cape. It was accepted at once.

The *Guide*, which was to begin where Fritz's 1959-60 lectures at London University had left off and which Fritz anticipated would run into several volumes, still remained unwritten. The demands on Fritz's time were so great that he hardly had time to change the contents of his suitcase or overnight bag before he was off again to another conference or lecture. There was a growing sense of urgency about him. He was unable to be ruthless and refuse the many invitations he received because he believed his message to be of such importance to the future that every opportunity to spread the word had to be utilized. His presence and the contents of his message were in the great tradition of the Old Testament prophets. He was travelling the world preaching the message, that unless mankind recognized the road that they were travelling and acted quickly, they would not get out of the mess for which they were heading at an alarming rate. His sombre message was always brought home with an amusing story, his version of a parable. What better way to illustrate the blind headlong rush into chaos than by telling the story of his visit to an iron curtain country where, he said, he was bombarded with the most severe criticism of Western economic life? 'The West,' he said he was told, 'is like an Express train hurtling with ever increasing speed towards an abyss. But,' added his iron curtain host, 'we shall overtake them.'

Fritz's final job was very clear. It was that of a prophet whose task is less to prophesy doom and destruction than to explain the signs of the times, to interpret to the world what is happening, what the consequences of mankind's actions are, and to offer hope that another way is possible. No prophet has ever offered hope for the future as an easy option, but the message throughout the centuries had always been the same: turn away from the road that you are treading, turn back to what is true and good and whole. This did not mean turning the clock back. Fritz did not condemn the twentieth century and advocate a return to medieval times. His message always contained words like, 'We must use our knowledge, use the best of what we have.' But at the centre of his message was the point that unless it is recognized that there exists something higher than man which gives a point to man's actions, then there can be no future worth contemplating. The recognition of a purpose and an existence beyond that of man was something which Fritz had learnt was more than a mental act: it required the action of the heart. 'Modern civilization can survive only if it begins again to educate the heart, which is the source of wisdom; for modern man is now far too clever to survive without wisdom.'[3]

The urgency of his message increased the urgency which he felt about getting to grips with *A Guide for the Perplexed*. He intended it to be a handbook for those who took his message seriously but did not know where to turn for guidance. In 1976 he worked more systematically than before. He knew that he must complete the book quickly. He believed that time was running out for the world. The sense of urgency within him concentrated his ideas to such an extent that the volumes that he had expected to write were distilled into a slim volume of less than 150 pages. It was a volume intended to answer more fully the challenge with which he had ended *Small is Beautiful*, where he had written: 'Everywhere people ask: "What can I actually do?" The answer is as simple as it is disconcerting: we can, each of us, work to put our own inner house in order. The guidance we need for this work cannot be found in science or technology, the value of which utterly depends on the ends they serve: but it can still be found in the traditional wisdom of mankind.'

It had taken Fritz many years to find his answers in traditional wisdom, to understand its meaning and importance. His task in *A Guide for the Perplexed* was to help those on a similar search to find their way through the confusing ideas of the modern world, to understand where they had taken a wrong turning or gone up a blind alley, and to point them back in the right direction. It was a book for the thousands who had asked him, 'What can I actually do?' and to whom his only reply could be, 'Begin with yourself.' In his Epilogue to the book he wrote: '*The modern experiment to live without religion has failed*, [his italics] and once we have understood this, we know what our "post-modern" tasks really are. Significantly, a large number of young people (of varying ages!) are looking in the right direction.' It was for them that he wrote the book, to share with them the happiness he had discovered in the pursuit of understanding. It was stated clearly in the title page: 'Man has no reason to philosophize except with a view to happiness,' a quotation he took from St Augustine. Fritz's choice of a quotation from St Augustine was no accident. St Augustine had been a man who had known the pleasures of life and had tasted them. He had had a brilliant mind. Yet it was only when he had 'turned around' towards higher aims that his true potential could be revealed. Or in Fritz's words:

The art of living is always to make a good thing out of a bad thing. Only if we *know* that we have actually descended into infernal regions where nothing awaits us but 'the cold death of society and the extinguishing of all civilised relations', can we summon the courage and imagination needed for a 'turning around', a *metanoia*. This then leads to seeing the world in a new light, namely a place where the things modern man continuously talks about and always fails to accomplish can actually be done.[4]

25

---∞∞∞---

Public Property

Fritz finished *A Guide for the Perplexed* on January 29th, 1977. It was his wedding anniversary. He and Vreni had been married fifteen years. Once again, reading his completed manuscript, he was pleased and astonished at his work. He could hardly believe that he himself was the author of words so elegantly put together and with a content of which he approved so wholeheartedly. He was also relieved to have the work completed; the year ahead was fuller than any other since his 'retirement'.

Vreni was not happy with the programme he had ahead. She felt that he was overdoing things, quite apart from the fact that she was getting a raw deal. In November 1976 she had accompanied him to America to receive his prize for excellence from Carborundum. They had returned to England as dawn was breaking over London. The airport was deserted apart from the passengers from their aircraft. At passport control they parted company, Vreni leaving Fritz at the British desk while she went through the section for foreign passports. She had kept her Swiss nationality. It took her a little longer than him to complete the formalities and she emerged expecting to see him waiting for her but he was not there. Looking across the space between the two sections she saw him. He was lying on the ground, a crumpled heap of clothing. As she rushed over all he said was, 'I can't move my legs.' There was no medical officer around so early in the morning and it took some time to find a wheelchair. Eventually, in considerable pain, Fritz was helped into a taxi and Vreni got him back to Holcombe and into bed. It took a week before the use of his legs returned. Extensive tests showed nothing wrong. Later that winter Fritz read in *Time* magazine that a mysterious illness had been sweeping through the United States. He convinced himself that the symptoms were the same as those of his attack. He did not regard it as a warning. Vreni disagreed. She suspected that exhaustion and whisky had not a little to do with it, and she knew that his planned programme for 1977 would be dangerous on both those counts. Travelling and duty-free goods went hand in hand. The more he preached non-violence, the more he seemed to do violence to his own person by pushing himself to the limits.

His crusade had taken on its own momentum. Fritz was carried along in its increasing velocity. His message seemed to reach the most unlikely bedfellows. No longer did he speak only to the young, the drop-outs, the followers of the 'alternative' movement. There was recognition in the very bastions of establishment, in some multinational corporations themselves. To name just two, both Shell in Britain and Migros in Switzerland approached Fritz for advice. The unity of his message was beginning to get through. If the basis of Western economic life, namely energy, was not unlimited, then alternatives must be found. Such companies as approached Fritz were far-sighted enough to see that the general assumption that nuclear energy would fill the gap was not good enough, that the problem was wider, requiring a completely different solution, encompassing the rethinking of production methods and organization. They recognized that the broadest application of the concept of intermediate technology as a key to a new, non-violent economics was also appropriate in the West. Fritz wrote:

> The key words of violent economics are urbanization, industrialization, centralization, efficiency, quantity, speed. The violence, however, arises only from the absence of restraint, not from the things themselves ... The problem of evolving a non-violent way of economic life (in the West) and that of developing the underdeveloped countries may well turn out to be largely identical. Wisdom and voluntary

self-restraint are likely to be more important elements in the new synthesis than the most conspicuous achievements of Western science and technology, although they, too, will find their proper place. The whole man will be needed, his moral qualities no less than his intellectual powers. All peoples and all races will have to make their own specific contribution.[1]

Fritz's advice to multinational and national corporations did not shirk these issues, even if they were couched in language more comprehensible to his audience. He was realistic enough, however, to know that with the best will in the world, changes could not occur overnight. Everything he had proposed in the last twenty years had been based on sure organic growth, starting from where one was, not trying to do everything at once. He had no longer laid complete blueprints before people advocating total change in one go. Rather he encouraged them to embark on what he called 'building lifeboats'. He explained this quite simply: 'The only safe recipe for survival is deliberate experimentation. We have to develop a technology as well as an ownership structure to fit the new *material* and *social* conditions. How can we find the right answers without experimentation? Every sizeable company or other organization should run one or several semi-independent units which I should call "lifeboats".'[2] In practical terms Fritz meant that about five per cent of a company's research and development budget should be earmarked 'for totally unorthodox studies in the direction of smallness, simplicity and capital saving'. In this way, if the boat sank, then lifeboats, properly equipped with new experience, could save the crew. Five per cent would not constitute a radical change, yet it would lay the foundations for change.

Individuals who asked Fritz how to live in a new world would get similar advice. No one needed to be discouraged, for even small steps were important, like home bread baking, growing one's own vegetables and generally trying to simplify one's life. And because he understood the difficulties of swimming against the tide, he always advised people to join other individuals and groups with similar interests. His gentle, understanding, yet radical approach, appealed both to the 'alternative' movements, the readers of *Resurgence* – students and self-sufficiency people who were trying to return to a life of simplicity – and those at the other end of the spectrum, in big business. There was something in his message for everyone, which, combined with his sympathetic and delightful manner, bridged the unbridgeable gap between the establishment and the anti-establishment.

Once again it was in America that the range of his appeal was shown most clearly. In February 1977 he returned there for a six-week coast-to-coast tour and had an overwhelming reception. Lecture halls were filled to overflowing. In Ann Arbor, Michigan, he talked to an audience of five thousand. In many places the biggest halls were not spacious enough for the waiting crowds and loudspeakers had to relay his words to adjacent rooms. Thousands of young enthusiastic Americans had adopted him as their guru. Yet their enthusiasm left him despondent. Fritz feared that it would evaporate as quickly as it had appeared and never become translated into the hard action necessary to transform the world. 'He saw a danger that his words could be inflated into gas balloons, which would carry people gently over the landscape of the world's problems at a considerable height, in the illusion that their trip was changing life below.'[3]

There were others, it seemed, who had the opposite worry: that Fritz's tour would be followed by radical action. Half way through, as his audiences grew daily, he was suddenly provided with a police escort. Threats had been made on his life which the police were taking very seriously. There were suggestions that Fritz's opponents came from the most powerful industrial and business interests in the United States, who recognized the danger to their existence if Fritz's message really caught on and became policy and practice. They did not like to be told that the idolatry of giantism was responsible for 'a system of production that ravishes nature and a type of society that mutilates man'.

Fritz was more hopeful about influencing policy than wide-scale practice in America for, unlike on his previous tour, by 1977 his message had penetrated into many other levels of American life. Jerry Brown was no longer alone among politicians in his support and the many State Governors, prominent academics and industrialists who wanted to meet Fritz gave the tour a nightmarish quality. There were no gaps in his schedule for rest, let alone to prepare his lectures. So many meetings, discussions and lectures had been arranged that even at breakfast Fritz was expected to give of himself. Those closest to him, who had organized his tour and who professed to understand fully his message, seemed unable to put it into practice on this tour, pushing Fritz beyond the limits of his endurance. Never before had Fritz felt so exhausted. The preacher of gentleness, non-violence, concern for people and their needs was driven with insufficient concern for his needs until eventually he felt at breaking point and thought he would have to cancel the rest of the tour. It was at that point that he received an invitation to meet Jimmy Carter at the White House. It gave him new strength to continue and ended the tour on a high note. With Carter's support, Fritz hoped that there might at last be some progress in the move to sanity. But the usual optimism could not dispel the fundamental weariness and he returned to England in the middle of March utterly exhausted.

His exhaustion was apparent in his lack of buoyancy. He had been exhilarated by his visit to the White House but his fatigue was deep and there was no time to rest. April was filled with numerous meetings and short trips to the Continent, and in May he returned to the United States. I.T.D.G.'s success and growth was accompanied all the time by worsening financial crises which fell on his shoulders, and he turned to the U.S.A. for assistance. The occasion for his visit was a conference. It summed up all that was wrong with the modern way of life. The entire visit was spent underground in a conference centre where everything from the light to the food was artificial, and all the while they talked. His despondency grew.

The pace continued. June passed in a haze of lectures and brief visits home for a change of clothes. The strain was beginning to tell. Fritz was less optimistic, sometimes irritable. A colleague, Jack Wood, who had known Fritz for twenty years, saw this change with anxiety. 'You are going to kill yourself if you go on working at this pace,' he warned Fritz. Fritz merely shrugged his shoulders and, with a whimsical smile, replied:

'Well, someone has to do the work.'

In July he set off again, breaking new ground, this time to Indonesia and Australia. In Indonesia he suffered from pains which he put down to indigestion. In Australia he was taken over by a small film company to take part in a film about deforestation. He was very enthusiastic about this for trees had become his latest passion. He had long agreed with Gandhi that India's problem would be solved if every person planted a tree every year for five years. For years he had belonged to a group calling themselves 'Men of the Trees', interested in reclaiming the Sahara, and he watched with dismay as the abuse of trees made the production of more Saharas more and more likely all over the world.

He thought of trees in terms wider than that of conservation, believing that they held the answer to the world's food problem. He admired their beauty as well as their function as the most wonderful three-dimensional food producers, which sheltered animals grazing under their branches while benefiting from their enriching deposits on the soil around. Trees could be grown on land less suitable for crops, and while producing food they would also add to the preservation and health of the countryside. When an old American conservationist, Richard B. Gregg, sent Fritz some books on trees Fritz learnt of the trees that produced high protein beans or nuts which could be milled into flour and his enthusiasm knew no bounds. Several dozen protein bearing trees were eventually acquired and planted in the garden at Holcombe and the Soil Association agreed to set up a project to work on the idea.

The Australian film, called 'On the Edge of the Forest', gave a horrifying picture of the violence of deforestation. It was a stark contrast to the gentle, elderly man who walked with great wonder through the forest, marvelling at its resemblance to a great cathedral, and at the same time not failing to notice the beauty of the miniature eco-system at his feet. As the film ended, Fritz was seen walking slowly into the distance and disappearing into the sunlight. It was to be prophetic.

On his return Fritz appeared to have made up his mind to start reducing his commitments in earnest. He informed the directors at I.T.D.G. that they must begin to think about a successor for him. 'After all,' he said lightly, 'who knows what will happen to me.' Jack Wood, present at the meeting, was sure that he would never see Fritz again.

On a domestic level Fritz spent the month of August, the lull before his next bout of travelling, tying up various administrative ends. It was also a family month. August 16th was Fritz's sixty-sixth birthday and the family celebrated it with him at Holcombe. We met again on August 27th for Christian's birthday. That second evening, surrounded by his family, Fritz was in a strange mood. The wine and whisky flowed freely and he seemed to indulge himself even more than usual. As well as Christian's birthday, he was celebrating a preview of the first copies of *A Guide for the Perplexed*, which he had just received. As he showed the copy to me he said, 'This is what my life has been leading up to.' A little later he and I talked about several marital problems in the family. As I had been happily married for seven years I asked him, 'Do all relationships have to have these crises?' He was silent for a moment and then, for the first time since my mother's death, began to talk to me about his relationship with Muschi. He told me of their very real problems, which, he said, were largely of a spiritual nature, and how, in the end they had resolved their difficulties, particularly through her illness and death. 'You have to decide that these things [marriages] are for keeps and find a way through the difficulties,' he concluded.

Later that evening Fritz decided to make a speech. It was long and emotional and he was visibly moved as he spoke. He spoke of the debt that the men of the family owed to their wives, particularly of his own to Vreni, and exhorted his sons not to forget to cherish the women they had married.

When we said goodbye, I asked my father if I could have a copy of *A Guide for the Perplexed* to take on holiday with me. A few days later, on Saturday September 3rd, the promised copy arrived, just as we were preparing to leave. The inscription moved me greatly. He had written: 'To Barbara Wood, whose existence fills me with admiration and delight, from E.F. Schumacher, alias Papa.'

I was unable to thank him for the day before, on September 2nd, he had left for a week's lecture tour of Switzerland. He was not as well prepared as usual for this trip. Only the first lecture was really thought out. It turned out to be one of his best and was received enthusiastically by an audience in Caux composed of Moral Re-armament followers. Ironically, he had accepted their invitation largely because the fee financed his fare for the rest of the tour. Afterwards, a young Indian journalist interviewed him and his delight in the company of such a charming young lady was captured by a photographer. The next morning, September 4th, he boarded a train bound for Zürich. What happened next is unclear. Some time between ten and eleven a commotion broke out on the train. 'Someone has been taken ill.' The train was stopped at a small town where a hospital was alerted to take the patient. Passengers looking out of the windows saw a large man being carried out to a waiting ambulance. Behind him came a railway official carrying a suitcase and a rather broad-brimmed hat. On arrival at the little hospital it was confirmed at once that the man was dead. Police coming in to identify the body found their job very easy. One officer remarked, 'He might have been prepared, everything is so orderly.' From the neat collection of documents, he identified: Dr E.F. Schumacher: Economist: Address: Holcombe, Wealdway, Caterham, Surrey, England. Telephone ... Next of kin ...

A few days later Vreni had a vivid dream. She was sitting in the drawing-room at Holcombe in front of the open fire when she suddenly became aware that Fritz was in the room with her. She looked up and saw him sitting in his chair. 'I just wanted to tell you what happened,' he said. 'On the train I suddenly felt ill and thought it was indigestion. I went to the toilets but it got worse. As I came out I saw a food vendor coming towards me. I asked her for help. Then I died.'

'Did you want to die?' Vreni asked.

'No,' he replied, 'but I was ready.'

September 4th had been a Sunday. At Holcombe a young mother's help called Tessa Midgely had gone into the kitchen sometime between ten and eleven while the rest of the family were at church to make herself a cup of coffee. As she put the kettle on she was startled by a crash on the kitchen floor. She turned to see a cup had inexplicably fallen out of the cupboard. It had broken into too many pieces to be repaired. She saw that it was Fritz's cup. Later that afternoon the police called with the news that Fritz had died.

I spent September 4th reading my new copy of *A Guide for the Perplexed*. I had never so much as glanced through *Small is Beautiful* having, I thought, heard its contents over and over again throughout my teens. But the new book, although also containing material about which he had talked a great deal, absorbed me from the minute I opened it at the first page. I forgot about children, unpacking and meals and some hours later my husband Don found me amongst the suitcases utterly oblivious of the chaos around me. That evening, unaware of what had happened in Switzerland that morning, I wrote an enthusiastic letter of congratulation to my father.

Early the following morning the news reached me. I returned to Holcombe immediately. That train journey was the only opportunity I had to mourn my father. The world had reached Holcombe before me. He had become public property.

Fritz Schumacher's death was followed by a mixture of emotions. Hundreds of letters expressed a sense of personal loss at the death of a man many had encountered, perhaps only once at a lecture, through an article or by reading *Small is Beautiful*. There was a feeling of floundering and again and again the question arose in a variety of forms, 'How shall we manage without him?' He had provided hope and inspiration to so many. Yet there was also a feeling of celebration, not for his death but for his life. His passing was not talked about in hushed tones but with positive energy: 'What shall we do now? We must not lose his momentum, we must build, carry on where he left off.'

On November 30th, 1977, not three months after his death, several thousand people came together in just such a celebration at Westminster Cathedral. Some came no doubt out of curiosity to hear Jerry Brown speak at the service, others came to hear Yehudi Menuhin and the gifted pupils of his school pay their tribute (for Fritz had been to talk to the pupils and been well received). But the crowds were there to celebrate Fritz: the atmosphere of joy told that. It was clear that Fritz's sudden death was not the removal of a vital prop. His unstinting work had ensured that throughout the world candles of hope had been lit. His personality, which had bridged the gaps between so many diverse groups, no longer provided that loose unity but he had sown seeds that had begun to grow. There was much talk about Schumacher Centres, organizations to carry on where he left off, societies, publications and buildings to be named after him. The discussions were not always conducted in the spirit of peace and reconciliation that he would have wished. Different groups had understood different parts of Fritz's message and few saw it as a whole. As one observer put it, 'It is a bit like the early churches. Everyone thinks they have got hold of the truth but each one has got a different part.' It seemed that a most important part of Fritz's message was sometimes forgotten: to start from where you are and grow from there, rather than build up a vast structure which ends as an empty shell or hot air balloon of words.

But these efforts, important and worthy in their way, were less important than the less dramatic and obvious effect of Fritz's life. Fritz was a man of hope. The doom and destruction that was in his warnings never overshadowed the optimism and hope that the worst could be avoided or mitigated. He knew that throughout the world there were people, small people, humble people, whose response to his message had resulted in action, in a reappraisal of their lives. That had been the great message of intermediate technology, that it was possible for action to begin in the here and now. Fritz had become a man of the people, his work was for the people and it was the people as individuals and small groups who, he knew, would ultimately turn the tide to sanity.

The emphasis of his final years was always on action. Again and again he said: 'First must come the word – intellectual effort. But then the word must become flesh.' His words were directed always at reality, at those who would translate them into a new life. They were directed always at individuals because they demanded a personal response, an awakening of the heart. He had always been a man of action himself, a fact which had given his words substance. He had put his ideas into practice at the Coal Board, at the founding of the Intermediate Technology Development Group, with his involvement at the Scott Bader Commonwealth, and numerous concerns not mentioned in this book. He had ideas which, because of his death, remained unfulfilled. He planned to begin a study of Islam to examine the implications of an Islam economics and he was working on setting up a study to examine the potential of trees for the future, work taken over by the Soil Association. Had he lived, he would no doubt have set many more ideas in motion. His role had been to awaken men's minds and inspire them into action. His last words to the world in *A Guide for the Perplexed*, published after his death, remain his memorial of hope and call for immediate response:

The generosity of the Earth allows us to feed all mankind; we know enough about ecology to keep the Earth a healthy place; there is enough room on the Earth and there are enough materials, so that everybody can have adequate shelter; we are quite competent enough to produce sufficient supplies of necessities so that no one need live in misery. Above all, we shall then see that the economic problem is a convergent problem that has been solved already: we know how to provide enough, and do not require any violent, inhuman, aggressive technologies to do so. There *is* no economic problem and, in a sense, there never has been. But there is a moral problem, and moral problems are not convergent, capable of being solved so that future generations can live without effort; no, they are divergent problems which have to be understood and transcended.

Can we rely on it that a 'turning around' will be accomplished by enough people quickly enough to save the modern world? This question is often asked, but whatever answer is given to it will mislead. The answer 'Yes' would lead to complacency; the answer 'No' to despair. It is desirable to leave these perplexities behind us and get down to work.

Notes

1 Grown in German Soil

1 This and further extracts from Professor Schumacher's memoirs are translated from H.A. Schumacher, *Lebenserinnerungen* (unpublished).
2 Quoted in William Guttmann and Patricia Meehan, *The Great Inflation* (Saxon House) 1975, p. 203.
3 E.F. Schumacher, *A Guide for the Perplexed* (Jonathan Cape) 1977, p. 1.

2 First Taste of England

1 Cameron Fraser and Michael Cresswell in conversation with the author.
2 *Cecil Rhodes and Rhodes House* (a pamphlet produced by O.U.P.) 1929.

3 Oxford

1 E.F.S., report to Herr Dr Remke, German Rhodes Scholar Committee, 8.12.1930 (translation).
2 Alan Bullock, *Hitler: A Study in Tyranny* (Odhams) 1952.
3 E.F.S., letter to Dr F. Jessen, 25.8.1937 (translation).

4 In New York One Walks on Air

1 Werner Brückmann, *Kansas 16/3200* (unpublished).
2 E.F.S., draft for chapter 'Inflation and the Structure of Production' for Professor H. Parker Willis and John M. Chapman, *The Economics of Inflation* (Columbia University Press) 1935.

5 Hitler

1 E.F.S., speech to Bryce Club annual dinner, Oxford, 1932.
2 Quoted in Alan Bullock, *Hitler: A Study in Tyranny* (Odhams) 1952.
3 E.F.S., draft for chapter 'Inflation and the Structure of Production', for Professor H. Parker Willis and John M. Chapman, *The Economics of Inflation* (Columbia University Press) 1935.
4 Sebastian Haffner, *The Meaning of Hitler* (Weidenfeld and Nicolson) 1979.

6 Muschi

1 The firms who formed the board of directors were: Gutehoffnungshütte, Oberhausen; Krupp, Essen; Otto Wolff, Köln, Berlin; A.E.G., Berlin; Felten & Guilleaume, Köln; H.A.P.A.G., Hamburg; R. Petersen & Co., Hamburg; Arndt & Cohn, Hamburg; Siemens, Berlin; M.M. Warburg, Hamburg.
2 Werner Brückmann, *Kansas 16/3200* (unpublished).

7 London

1 E.F.S., letter to the *Spectator* (unpublished), 8.11.1937.
2 E.F.S., letter to *The Times* (unpublished), 18.4.1940.

8 A Change in Lifestyles

1 Goethe, in a letter to H. Linden, 1829.

9 World Improvement Plans

1 E.F.S., talk on the 'Economic Basis of Peace and Reconstruction', 1943-4.
2 E.F.S., enquiry on 'The Conditions that Make Peace Possible' (early 1940s).
3 E.F.S., paper on 'The Economic Treatment of Post-war Germany' (early 1940s).

4 Ibid.
5 E.F.S., 'Free Access to Trade', February 2nd, 1942.
6 J.M. Keynes, 'Proposals for an International Clearing Union', April 1943.
7 E.F.S., lecture notes, 1947.
8 Quoted by E.F.S. in a letter to his parents, 16.4.1949.

10 Marx v. God

1 E.F.S., lecture notes on economic planning, 17.9.1942.
2 E.F.S., lecture notes for a course at Chipping Norton, October 1942.
3 E.F.S., lecture notes, 1942-5.

11 Oxford Again

1 Walter Fliess in conversation with the author.
2 E.F.S., draft for 'Full Employment', 1944.
3 E.F.S., lecture notes, 1944-5.
4 *Daily Express*, 3.2.1945.
5 *Oxford Mail*, 3.2.1945.
6 Glyn Thomas, *Leader*, April 1945.

13 An Englishman in Germany

1 The words should read, '*Ihr fährt ins Leben uns hinein.*' Goethe, *Wilhelm Meister*, Ch. 13.
2 E.F.S., 'Socialisation of German Industry', June 1946.

14 The Final Break

1 Joint Anglo-American press release, 4.12.1946.
2 E.F.S., paper for bi-zonal meeting, June 1948.
3 E.F.S., final report for the Control Commission, Berlin, 21.1.1950.
4 E.F.S., lecture notes, probably autumn 1949.

5 E.F.S., lecture, 'The Humanities and the Social Sciences', 17.3.1948.
6 Ortega y Gasset, *The Mission of the Universities* (Kegan Paul) 1946.
7 *Financial Times*, 7.2.1950.

16 Learning How to Think

1 S. Radhakrishnan, *Eastern Religions and Western Thought* (O.U.P.) 1939.
2 Maurice Nicoll, *The New Man* (Steward and Richards) 1950.

17 The Breakthrough

1 E.F.S., talk at the Hochschulwochen für Staatswissenschaftliche Fortbildung, autumn 1954, Bad Wildungen.
2 E.F.S., 'Towards a Theory of Industrialisation', 1942.
3 E.F.S., notes on chapter for Wilson Committee, 1951.
4 E.F.S., 'Economics in a Buddhist Country', February 1955, Rangoon.
5 D. H. Meadows, D. L. Meadows, J. Randen and W.W. Behrens III (Club of Rome), *Limits to Growth* (Potomac) 1972.
6 E.F.S., 'Final Report to Burma Government', end of March 1955.

18 'I am a Buddhist'

1 Charles Frankel, *The Case for Modern Man* (Macmillan) 1957.
2 E.F.S., Lecture 5, 28.10.1959 (London University).
3 Pierre Teilhard de Chardin, *The Phenomenon of Man* (English edn, Collins) 1959, p. 250.
4 E.F.S., lecture to Imperial College, 1965.
5 E.F.S., talk to organizing secretaries of the National Association of Mixed Clubs and Girls' Clubs, 'The Current Situation', 9.6.1958.
6 E.F.S., lecture notes, 1960.
7 E.F.S., Lecture 17, 1960 (London University).
8 E.F.S., final lecture, 1960 (London University).

19 The National Coal Board

1 E.F.S., 'Price Policy of Nationalised Industries', March 1955 (N.C.B.).
2 E.F.S., 'The Board's Economic and Social Problems', September 1958 (N.C.B.).
3 E.F.S., 'Is the Ownership Debate Closed?', *Socialist Commentary*, February 1959 (under the name of Ernest F. Sutor).
4 E.F.S., 'Prosperous Britain – Where does the Coal Industry Stand?', November 1960 (N.C.B.).
5 E.F.S., 'Reflections on a Theme. Does Nationalised Industry contribute to a new Industrial Outlook?', 1958 (N.C.B.).
6 Ibid.
7 E.F.S., 'Financial Control', November 1958 (N.C.B.).
8 E.F.S., untitled lecture, 1956.
9 E.F.S., 'Fuel', October 1958 (N.C.B.).
10 E.F.S., 'Long Term Demands for Fuel', 1958 (N.C.B.).
11 E.F.S., 'The Place of Coal in the National Economy', July 1952 (N.C.B. Summer School).
12 E.F.S., 'Nuclear Energy and the World's Fuel and Power Requirements', 10.4.1958 (Federation of British Industry Conference).
13 E.F.S., 'Is the Ownership Debate Closed?', *Socialist Commentary*, February 1959.

20 Year of Crisis

1 E.F.S., *Observer*, 21.8.1960.
2 E.F.S., interview with Susanna Hoe, 1976.
3 E.F.S., 'Socialisation in Great Britain', 1961.

21 A Fruitful Partnership

1 E.F.S., talk to members of the oil industry, 1965.
2 E.F.S., 'Freedom and Control in a Nationalised Industry', October 1964 (N.C.B.).

22 Small Talk

1 Susanna Hoe, interview with E.F.S., also quoted in her book *The Man Who Gave His Company Away* (Heinemann) 1978.
2 E.F.S., 'Roots of Economic Growth' (Gandhian Institute of Studies) 1962.

23 Travel and Challenge

1 E.F.S., 'Buddhist Economics' in *Small is Beautiful* and *Asia, a Handbook* (both published by Anthony Blond) 1973 and 1967 respectively.

24 'Retirement'

1 E.F.S., *Good Work* (Jonathan Cape) 1979, p. 139.
2 E.F.S., Address to A.G.M. of the Catholic Institute for International Relations, 13.6.1975.
3 E.F.S., 'The Roots of Violence', *The New Era*, January/February 1973.
4 E.F.S., *A Guide for the Perplexed* (Jonathan Cape) 1977, p. 153.

25 Public Property

1 E.F.S., notes, untitled and undated.
2 E.F.S., talk given in Ireland, 1975.
3 John Davy, obituary of E.F.S. in the *Observer*, September 1977.

Index